# RELIGIOUS RADICALISM IN THE GREATER MIDDLE EAST

# CASS SERIES ON POLITICAL VIOLENCE

Series Editors:
DAVID C. RAPOPORT, University of California, Los Angeles
PAUL WILKINSON, University of St Andrews, Scotland

1. *Terror from the Extreme Right*, edited by Tore Bjørgo
2. *Millennialism and Violence*, edited by Michael Barkun
3. *The Rise of Right-Wing Extremism in the Nineties*
   edited by Peter H. Merkl and Leonard Weinberg
4. *Religious Radicalism in the Greater Middle East*
   edited by Bruce Maddy-Weitzman and Efraim Inbar

**Forthcoming....**

*Violence in Southern Africa*, edited by J. E. Spence
*April 19 and Right-Wing Violence*, edited by David C. Rapoport

---

**The Begin-Sadat (BESA) Center for Strategic Studies** is dedicated to the study of Middle East peace and security, in particular the national security and foreign policy of Israel. A non-partisan and independent institute, the BESA Center is named in memory of Menahem Begin and Anwar Sadat, whose efforts in pursuing peace lay the cornerstone for future conflict resolution in the Middle East.

Since its founding in 1991 by Dr. Thomas O. Hecht of Montreal, the BESA Center has become one of the most dynamic Israeli research institutions. It has developed cooperative relationships with strategic study centers throughout the world, from Ankara to Washington and from London to Seoul. Among its research staff are some of Israel's best and brightest academic and military minds. BESA Center publications and policy recommendations are read by senior Israeli decision-makers in military and civilian life, by academicians, the press and the broader public.

The BESA Center makes its research available to the international community through three publication series: *BESA Security and Policy Studies*, *BESA Colloquia on Strategy and Diplomacy* and *BESA Studies in International Security*. The Center also sponsors conferences, symposia, workshops, lectures and briefings for international and local audiences.

Our current research foci are:

- Deterrence and Regional Security
- Israel Defense Forces of the Future
- Israeli Public Opinion on National Security
- Israeli-Turkish Strategic Ties
- Mideast Water Resources
- Middle East Arms Control
- Military Industries
- US-Israel Relations
- Palestinian Positions and Factions in the Peace Process
- Politicians and the Use of Force
- Proliferation and Weapons of Mass Destruction
- Regional Security Regimes
- Space-Based Weaponry
- Strategic Options in the Peace Process
- Terrorism and Low-Intensity Violence

# RELIGIOUS RADICALISM
## IN THE
# GREATER MIDDLE EAST

**Edited by**

**BRUCE MADDY-WEITZMAN**

**and**

**EFRAIM INBAR**

**FRANK CASS**
**LONDON • PORTLAND, OR.**

*First published in 1997 in Great Britain by*
FRANK CASS & CO. LTD.
900 Eastern Avenue, London
IG2 7HH, England

*and in the United States of America by*
FRANK CASS
c/o ISBS
5804 N.E. Hassalo Street, Portland, Oregon 97213-3644

British Library Cataloguing in Publication Data

Religious radicalism in the greater Middle East. - (Cass
series on political violence ; no. 4)
1. Religious fundamentalism - Middle East  2. Political
violence - Middle East  3. Middle East - Religion
I. Maddy-Weitzman, Bruce II. Inbar, Efraim, 1947–
303.6'25'0956

ISBN 0-7146-4769-1 (hardback)
ISBN 0-7146-4326-2 (paperback)

Library of Congress Cataloging in Publication Data

Religious radicalism in the Greater Middle East / edited by Bruce
Maddy-Wietzman and Efraim Inbar.
 p. cm. -- (Cass series on political violence ; 4) (A BESA
study in Mideast security)
 "This volume presents a selection of the papers delivered at [an
international conference in November 1994] "--CIP Introd.
 Includes index.
 ISBN 0-7146-4769-1. -- ISBN 0-7146-4326-2 (pbk.)
 I. Islam and politics--Middle East.  2. Middle East--Politics and
government--1979- I. Maddy-Weitzman, Bruce. II. Inbar, Efraim,
1947- . III. Series. IV. Series: A BESA study in Mideast
security.
BP63.A4M5372  1996
320.5'5'0956--dc20                                      96-42105

This group of studies first appeared in a Special Issue on 'Religious Radicalism in
the Greater Middle East' in *Terrorism and Political Violence* 8/2 (Summer 1996)
published by Frank Cass & Co. Ltd.

Printed in Great Britain by Antony Rowe Ltd, Chippenham, Wilts.

# Contents

# Preface

*Religious Radicalism in the Greater Middle East*, edited by Bruce Maddy-Weitzman and Efraim Inbar, is the fourth volume in the *Cass Series on Political Violence*, initiated in 1995. Most of the papers in this volume were originally delivered at a Begin-Sadat Center for Strategic Studies conference in 1994. They were re-written and supplemented by other papers for publication as a special issue of the journal *Terrorism and Political Violence* 8/2 (Summer 1996).

Religion has been a critical ingredient in every volume so far, a focus not foreseen initially. The Christian tradition is the preoccupation of the preceding volumes, and Islam inspires 13 of the 14 case studies here, with Judaism as the focus of the other one. The Christian groups studied earlier were all peripheral elements or marginal to the political mainstream; the instances examined here are all more central to the states in which they are found and more significant to the region and the international community as a whole.

The organization of this volume reflects that difference, for political importance is the dominating organizing theme here. The first category studied is that of 'Islamic Regimes', with Iran and the Sudan offered as examples. The second section, 'Islamic Opposition Movements', mirrors the fact that since radical Islamic movements have captured two states already, the first question when discussing other states (Egypt, Turkey, Saudi Arabia and Lebanon) is whether or not those states can also be captured. Indeed, the term the editors employ to characterize these instances – 'Islamic Opposition Movements' – suggests that they consider these groups to be alternative or shadow governments waiting for their turn to govern. (Since the volume has gone to press, Turkey has witnessed its first Islamist premier and the Taliban movement has captured Kabul and imposed *shari'a* law.) Three essays deal with Israel (no other state gets as much attention); the editors see Israel as being 'At the Core of the Region', a status with significant geographic and political meaning.

Although they were peripheral elements in their own states, the Christian groups studied in earlier volumes of the *Cass Series on Political Violence* sought to develop international ties and influences, but the results were insignificant when measured by the results here. Seizing states provides enormous international resources; and beyond that, Islam as a source of an international political identity seems unparalleled. The fourth section stresses international matters, largely in the 'Periphery Areas', i.e., North Africa and Central Asia. The fifth category explores the more general, international ramifications of radicalism, both in Israel and in Central Asia, while the final essay attempts to explain the differences between Islamic movements and their counterparts in other religious traditions.

*Religious Radicalism in the Greater Middle East* is a serious, thoughtful collection of essays written largely by prominent Israeli and Jewish academics, organized around questions of growing political importance. It is a valuable contribution both to the literature of the Middle East and to the more general relationships of religion, violence and politics wherever they intersect.

# Introduction

## BRUCE MADDY-WEITZMAN and EFRAIM INBAR

Contemporary calls for a return to Islam in order to solve endemic social and political problems in Muslim countries, while having gathered steam since the mid-1970s, are not new. They are rooted in previous historic experiences. Nevertheless, the current Islamic revival seems to have greater resonance, politically and socially, than in earlier periods, and over a wider geographic scope. The abilities of Islamist movements to depict the shortcomings, indeed the evils of the existing socio-political order have been more pronounced, and their organizational skills have often been impressive. As such, their prescription, the establishment of a true Islamic state based on the holy law, and the inculcation of religious values throughout society, have proved attractive to considerable portions of Muslim populations in the Greater Middle East.

The most dramatic expression of this complex phenomenon was the overthrow of the Shah and the establishment of the Islamic Republic of Iran in 1979. The events in Iran emboldened Islamist movements elsewhere, and combined with local circumstances to produce various outcomes: in some instances, violent, ongoing confrontations with the ruling authorities, as in Algeria and Egypt; episodic outbursts of violence in other places, as in the Gulf Arab monarchies; increased prominence among the Palestinians and Lebanon's Shi'i population with resulting impact in the Arab-Israeli sphere; redoubled efforts in the political arena, particularly in more pluralist environments such as Turkey and, to a lesser extent, Jordan and Yemen; the takeover of power in one additional country, Sudan; and the influence on political and social discourse everywhere. At the same time, Middle Eastern regimes have proved to be far more resilient than either western analysts or Islamist activists had anticipated, employing the considerable resources available to modern states to engage their Islamist opponents in complex, and often bitter struggles for power. The picture then is a varied one, differing from state to state, and movement to movement.

Recent events have also highlighted the fact that religious extremism in the Middle East is not the exclusive provenance of Muslim countries. Despite its vastly different socio-political environment, Israel has witnessed the emergence of Jewish religious-nationalist radicalism in recent years. Its most extreme expression was the assassination of Israel's prime minister, Yitzhak Rabin, in November 1995.

In any event, religious radicalism is both a phenomenon well grounded in Middle Eastern history and an authentic and significant response to contemporary conditions. It cannot, by any means, be downplayed as a passing fashion of disgruntled clerics confronted with the prospects of irrelevance in steadily modernizing, secularizing societies. Apart from its specific relevance in each country, religious radicalism also possesses wider potential implications, both politically and strategically.

The Begin-Sadat (BESA) Center for Strategic Studies at Bar-Ilan University convened an international conference in November 1994 to address these various issues. This volume presents a selection of the papers delivered at the conference, as well as additional solicited essays, on various aspects of contemporary religious radicalism, including their relevance to policy makers, in the Greater Middle East, covering the area from North Africa to Central Asia. The ideas and findings presented herein should prove useful to both scholars and the policy-making community.

The first two contributions deal with the Islamic regimes in Iran and Sudan. Haggay Ram looks at the tension, conflict and coexistence that characterize the relationship between the Islamic and the nationalist traditions in the Islamic Republic of Iran. According to Ram, a close examination of Iranian foreign policy shows that despite the apparent emphasis on the primacy of Muslim unity over the preservation of the Iranian nation-state, the Iranian *'ulama'* (clergy) have repeatedly acted to protect Iran's territorial and political integrity on the basis of *raison d'état*. In fact, the *'ulama'*'s millenarianism and commitment to an Islamic order is intertwined with nationalism in the political culture of revolutionary Iran.

The road to power of the Islamists in the Sudan is reviewed by Gabriel Warburg. Islam, he emphasizes, has always been an important part of the political landscape. Of special importance in recent years has been the infiltration of the army by Islamists, rendering the military an important arm of their power. He addresses several of the dilemmas faced by the regime in the area of political participation and the civil war with the non-Muslim South, which has been for years a problem for the Sudanese body politic. The desire to impose an Islamic order makes secession of the South more probable than in the past. The political problems at home, however, do not paralyze Sudan's foreign policy, which is revisionist, openly anti-western and supportive of Islamic opposition groups in the Arab world. On the whole, Warburg believes that the regime is in danger of collapse. He concludes by discussing the likely alternatives to the present regime.

The second part of the collection deals with Islamic opposition movements, which all deny the legitimacy of the secular state and/or the ruling elite. Elie Podeh reviews the struggle in Egypt, the most important

Arab country. He first maps the Islamic groups and analyzes systematically their modes of operation against the regime. These groups have demonstrated their ability to inflict serious damage, but according to Podeh, are unlikely to succeed in overthrowing the regime. Podeh presents the government's responses in the military, political and the socio-economic spheres, and concludes that as long as the regime maintains the loyalty of the state organs of coercion and control, and as long as it successfully denies legitimacy to the methods of the Islamic groups, these organizations cannot pose a viable alternative to the present regime.

Anat Lapidot dwells on the Islamic movement in Turkey, one of the regional powers in the Middle East. Lapidot argues that the deviation from secular Kemalism was the result of policies pursued by the military juntas and by subsequent conservative governments as a stopgap against left-wing ideologies. Ironically, this allowed the Islamic movement to flourish, particularly under the influence of the Iranian example. Interestingly, the growing appeal of transnational Pan-Turanism, following the emergence of independent Central Asian republics (of Turkish and Islamic origin) further eroded the nation-state framework. While the Islamic party, the largest in parliament following the 1995 elections, was initially excluded from the governing coalition, Lapidot argues that it is likely to have considerable influence on the legislative process and the political agenda in general. This is noteworthy particularly because full integration within the present political structure is not its proclaimed goal.

Joseph Kostiner points out that it was only in the 1990s that a more sustained, non-episodic, Islamic opposition emerged in Saudi Arabia, a country whose political system is, more than any other's, based upon Islam (the Wahhabi version). The development of Islamic opposition was due to the decline of what Kostiner terms the Faysal state order that prevailed since the early 1960s. Socio-economic fissures, a leadership crisis, the emergence of a well educated counter-elite and the growing sense of insecurity following the 1991 Gulf War enabled the crystallization of a mostly non-violent opposition which questioned the Islamic credentials of the present regime and offered a diffuse appeal based upon a blend of Wahhabi and western ideas. According to Kostiner, the challenge of the Islamic opposition is manageable, because it neither presents a clear ideology, nor possesses the means to take power.

In the last part of the second section, Eyal Zisser looks at the success of Hizballah in becoming a potent force within the Shi'i community in Lebanon and on the broader Lebanese political scene. He suggests that the process of rebuilding a Lebanese polity around the 1989 Ta'if agreement, and the ongoing peace process between Israel and the Arab world, threaten

Hizballah's *raison d'être*, and that these developments, coupled with the weakening of Iran, its patron, forced the organization to adapt somewhat to the confines of the Lebanese reality. Zisser also suggests that Hizballah's past policies and ideological inclinations reduce the possibility of further moderation as it struggles with the dilemma of integrating into a Lebanese political system which is not an Islamic republic.

Part three of the volume deals with religious radicalism within Israel, the West Bank and Gaza. Menachem Klein analyzes the ideological and political dilemmas faced by Hamas since its founding at the end of 1987. Klein shows how Hamas attempted to address the tensions between its universalist Islamic message and its particular goals as a Palestinian nationalist movement, while seeking to influence the evolving peace process. Klein focuses on the relationship between the nascent Palestinian Authority and Hamas, and argues that political exigencies have forced Hamas to widen the gap between its ideology and its political praxis.

Shmuel Sandler, writing about Jewish extremism, argues that while religious Zionism underwent far-reaching changes in the direction of ethno-nationalism after 1967, the religious-Zionist sector was not, on the whole, radicalized to the point of delegitimizing the state. Its two main ideological underpinnings, as well as the inclusionary type of politics generally characteristic of Israel's political system, have served to limit the potential for religious extremism. A more recent, dangerous trend, he contends, is the fusion of nationalism and ultra-orthodoxy, which does deny legitimacy to the current political order.

The Islamic Movement in Israel operates under two limitations: the fact that Muslims are a minority in the Israeli political system, rendering the traditional Islamist slogan, 'Islam Is the Solution', inapplicable without the destruction of the Jewish-dominated state; and the fact that the Israeli state is engaged in a complex peace process with the Arab-Muslim world. In the next selection, Muhammad Amara reviews the establishment of this movement in Israel and addresses its dilemmas resulting from these two limitations. While the movement has been almost completely non-violent and law-abiding, it remains ambiguous about whether to seek integration into Israeli society and about its preferred outcome of the Arab-Israeli conflict.

The fourth section of this volume moves the academic lens to the periphery of the Greater Middle East: Central Asia and North Africa. Jacob M. Landau argues that Islam in the six Central Asian republics, for many years suppressed and its institutions controlled by the communists, has become one of the ideologies competing to mould the identity of the new political bodies. Landau suggests that despite the widespread identification with Islam in the entire area, it is growing nationalist sentiments, chiefly in ethnic conflict situations, which have become the focal point of identity. Militant fundamentalist Islam is not yet an integral part of the political scene of the Central Asian republics and there is little cooperation among Islamist groups in different countries of the region.

Bruce Maddy-Weitzman assesses the depth of the Islamic radical challenge in the three North African countries of Algeria, Morocco and Tunisia. Following a review of the intellectual influence on the radical Islamists, Maddy-Weitzman analyzes the Islamic radical groups and their relations with the regime. In light of the different patterns in state-society/regime-opposition relations within the three states, Maddy-Weitzman cautions against adopting simplistic notions of an Islamic 'domino theory' for the area.

The fifth part of the collection looks at the international ramifications of the phenomenon of religious extremism. Efraim Inbar discusses the predispositions and goals of a variety of politically extreme Islamic movements toward Israel and the peace process. The obstruction of the peace process and the ultimate destruction of the Jewish state are their declared goals. Yet, an assessment of their actual politico-military capabilities shows that their short-run chances of achieving their aims are minimal. In the longer term, nuclear proliferation and possible instability of key Mideastern regimes is to be feared. The discussion ends with an evaluation of the mixed impact Islamic extremism has on the political debate in Israel over the peace process.

Robert O. Freedman reviews the new version of the 'Great Game' played out in Central Asia following the collapse of the Soviet Union and how radical Islam fits into it. Freedman argues that the initial fears in Moscow of a wave of Islamic radicalism in the region were unfounded, and that Russia was able to reassert a modicum of control over the region. In contrast, Turkey, which initially regarded the new Central Asian republics as its potential sphere of influence and obtained large financial and diplomatic support from the United States in exercising its influence, was not capable of successfully challenging Russia in the area. Freedman suggests that at the same time, Iran was more interested in good relations with Moscow (primarily to secure weapons) than in promoting Islamic radicalism in Central Asia, which in any case seemed not yet ripe for it. Freedman also analyzes the limited role of Israel in the attempt to combat religious radicalism in the region.

In the concluding selection, Gabriel Ben-Dor suggests that Islamic fundamentalism, while to some extent universal, should be understood in terms of a concrete society, theology and culture, and therefore focuses on religious fundamentalism in Middle Eastern Islam, while distinguishing it from fundamentalist tendencies in other religions. Ben-Dor argues that the Islamic tradition is all-encompassing, denying the separation of the political from other spheres of religious concern. Hence religious extremism in Islam has more and greater political implications than in other cases, amplified by the concept of *jihad*, which occupies an important place in the mind of Muslims. Furthermore, according to Ben-Dor, the motifs of afterlife and martyrdom are more pronounced in Islam than in other religions. This makes Islamic fundamentalism more immediate, more violent, more political and more popular than any kind of fundamentalism in any of the other religions.

Although the subjects analyzed in this volume are unique in many ways, several themes stand out as relevant to them all. These include the perceived illegitimacy of the state; the lack of responsiveness on the part of the regime; the involvement of well-educated cadres in the radical religious effort; the co-optation of western conceptualizations of human rights; the fight for justice against corruption; and above all a search for identity. It may be shown eventually that many other common experiences connect the religious radicals. Indeed, further research is needed on the importance of the Afghanistan War as a formative experience for many of the volunteers from Islamic countries, on their role in the crystallization of Islamic opposition groups and on their modes of operation in places as diverse as Tajikistan, Sudan, Egypt and Algeria.

The conference at BESA was co-sponsored by the Konrad Adenauer Foundation. The BESA Center is grateful to the Foundation for its support for the Center's activities. Special thanks are also in order to the Moshe Dayan Center for Middle Eastern and African Studies, Tel Aviv University. Three of its research associates have contributed to the volume, one of whom has also acted as co-editor; as such, it has served as a model of institutional cooperation and goodwill. Hava Koen, Michael Eichenwald and Avi Rembaum of the BESA Center indefatigably and cheerfully assisted on numerous administrative and editorial tasks. David C. Rapoport's comments served us well. Finally, we are deeply indebted to our authors, who patiently labored to revise and update their contributions in time to meet the publishing deadline. What is left is to pray for good times and balanced reviews.

# Exporting Iran's Islamic Revolution: Steering a Path between Pan-Islam and Nationalism

## HAGGAY RAM

This article focuses on the question of whether Iran's foreign policy over the period 1979–94 was a pure reflection of the clerical regime's millenarian crusade and its stated doctrine of exporting the Islamic revolution worldwide. Taking, *inter alia*, the controversy surrounding Iran's takeover of the island of Abu Musa in 1992, the article argues that Iran's actions were determined by a persistent sense of nationalism which was not less potent than its pan-Islamic vision. Iran's nationalist tradition has been able to survive as a major force in Iranian political culture, its sometimes 'Islamicized' form notwithstanding.

In his classic work *The Anatomy of Revolution*, Crane Brinton postulates that revolutions, 'as gospels, as forms of religion...are all universalist in aspiration'.[1] This proposition certainly holds true in the case of the Iranian revolution. Exporting (*sodur)* the Islamic revolution is one of the chief pillars of Iran's revolutionary ideology – and to many of Ayatollah Khomeini's disciples, the principal goal of Iranian foreign policy. Indeed, Iran's leaders hold that their country has a special duty to propagate its message throughout the 'oppressed' Muslim world. In carrying out this responsibility, Iran pursues two objectives. First, it seeks to mobilize the revolutionary fervor of Muslims everywhere to overthrow their respective governments and establish Islamic republics similar to that of Iran. Second, Iran works to restore the unity of the Islamic community – the *umma* – so as to enable Islam to play its ordained role in history.

However, a closer examination of Iranian policy calculations since Khomeini's February 1979 ascent to power reveals a more complex picture. Despite their apparent emphasis on the primacy of Muslim unity over the preservation of the Iranian nation state, the Iranian *'ulama'* (clergy) have repeatedly acted to protect Iran's territorial and political integrity on the basis of *raison d'état*. An example of this was Khomeini's acceptance of the 1988 cease-fire with Iraq, which he justified as being 'in the interests of Islam and the Muslims'.[2]

This apparent contradiction between dogma and praxis raises a number of questions, including: was Iran's foreign policy over the period 1979–94 a reflection of its Islamic universalist vision? Or, was the Islamic regime guided by genuine national interests relating, in the main, to *raison d'état*? In short, are the concepts of exporting the *Islamic* revolution and Iranian *nationalism* mutually exclusive, or can they exist concurrently? This article attempts to address these issues by examining the statements and policies of Iran's leaders since 1979. The takeover of the Persian Gulf island of Abu Musa in April 1992 by Iran will serve as a case study in this analysis.

Although this chapter excludes the 'voices from below', such voices do merit consideration. Indeed, I strongly believe that the official ideologies of states 'are *not* guides to what it is in the minds of even the most loyal citizens or supporters'.[3] Thus, Islam and nationalism in revolutionary Iran – to paraphrase Eric J. Hobsbawm – are 'dual phenomena, constructed essentially from above, but which cannot be understood unless also analyzed from below, that is in terms of the assumptions hopes, needs, longings and interests of ordinary people...'.[4] At any rate, I begin with an examination of the doctrinal foundations of Iran's Islamic vision, namely the Shi'i notion of *entezar*.

### *Entezar*: Dynamic Expectation of the Hidden Imam

The concept of exporting the revolution is deeply rooted in the evolution of the Shi'i doctrine of *entezar* (the messianic 'expectation' of the Hidden Imam). Even though we find both quietist and activist groups and doctrines among the early Shi'is, it is commonly held that the Imami or 'twelver' sect of Islam first shunned political activism in the mid-eighth century CE.[5] The failure of successive Shi'i efforts to regain the sect's 'usurped' and 'rightful' leadership of the Islamic community drove the early Shi'is to submit to the powers that be. As a result, there emerged the doctrine of the Occultation (*ghaybah*) of the Twelfth Imam, promulgated in 873–874 CE. This concept encouraged the faithful to wait for the return (*raj'ah*) of the Twelfth Shi'i Imam – the messiah (*mahdi*) who would appear at the End of Time – without actively altering their state of existence, as painful as it may have been. 'Such messianic expectations', Abdulaziz Sachedina notes, 'did not require the Shi'is to oppose the [political] establishment actively'.[6] It is therefore safe to conclude, as does Hamid Enayat, that the doctrine of *entezar* was 'one of the main causes of the notorious passivity of its adherents during the greater part of their history'.[7]

The revolutionary character of Shi'i Islam in the second half of the twentieth century inevitably rendered the passive implications of *entezar* null and void. In the late 1960s the celebrated ideologue of the Islamic revolution, 'Ali Shari'ati (d.1977), was the first to reject the passive interpretation of *entezar*.[8] Adapting his understanding of this notion to his overall conception of Shi'ism as an ideology of social and political revolution, Shari'ati held that 'true' *entezar* commands Muslims to take an active role in advancing the return of the Hidden Imam from occultation, and thus drawing nearer the Shi'ites' final redemption. He agreed that only the manifestation of the Imam would uproot oppression and bring justice to the earth, but in the interim, Shari'ati declared that the faithful 'must play a part' in bringing about the Imam's revolution, not with 'prayers . . . but with a banner and a sword, with true holy war involving all responsible believers'.[9] In short, he held that human beings are capable of hastening the coming of the *mahdi* by engaging in revolutionary action to eradicate oppression and tyranny and replace them with justice. According to Shari'ati's interpretation, the Hidden Imam will not reappear of his own accord; human intervention is required to pave the way for his return. People must strive for *universal* justice in order to occasion the *mahdi's* return.

The activist doctrine of *entezar* became the focal point of many official presentations and orations in post-Pahlavi Iran. Through the practice of *entezar*, it was claimed, the righteous make the environment favorable for the Imam's return. In June 1983, Hojjat al-Islam 'Ali Akbar Hashemi Rafsanjani explained, 'your child or spouse [went] away to the [war]front', and after a period of time he is expected to return home: 'You may consider these final moments as a state of *entezar*. Your ears are turned to the doorbell. You arrange the house for . . . the coming guest – in accordance with his desires, joy and opinion. Once you are in a state of *entezar*, you make conditions favorable [for the homecoming guest].'[10]

But what exactly is meant by making 'conditions favorable' for the return of the Hidden Imam? How does one arrange his 'house' (society) so as to make it habitable for the 'guest' (the Hidden Imam)? In June 1980, Hojjat al-Islam Sayyid 'Ali Khameneh'i clarified that society must approximate itself to the greatest possible extent to the conditions that will prevail upon the revolution of the *mahdi*. The Imam's society is built on the following foundations:

> First, on the elimination and eradication of the roots of injustice and overflowing tyranny (*toghyan*). I mean, in the society . . . [of] the *vali-ye 'asr* [the Lord of the Time; the Hidden Imam] there should be no oppression and injustice; not only in Iran . . . in the entire world. There should be no economic oppression, no political oppression, no cultural oppression, not any kind of oppression . . . [E]xploitation, inequality, unreasonable demands, and hooliganism . . . must be eradicated.[11]

Hence, making the environment favorable for the Hidden Imam means working to free the world from tyranny and oppression and creating a just social order, while 'Expectation' means taking concrete steps to implement at least part of the Imam's global justice.[12]

According to the Iranian ruling *'ulama'*, the Islamic revolution was in itself an act of dynamic *entezar*. It was, in the words of Rafsanjani, 'a drop of water in the vast ocean of the *mahdi*'.[13] And, according to Khameneh'i, it contained 'all the ingredients' of the *mahdi's* reappearance 'on a small scale' (*meqyas-e kuchak*).[14] For example, upon his return the Imam will 'confront all the great powers of the world'; likewise, the Islamic revolution 'has stood up against all great global powers'. Equally meaningful, insofar as the Imam is bound to introduce an eternal epoch of global justice, 'today . . . our revolution . . . is in the line of creating justice in the world arena'.[15] Lastly, the establishment by the Imam of a 'global Islamic government' (*hokumat-e jehan-e eslami*) was preceded by the revolution, which laid 'the ground for the global government of the *mahdi*'.[16] In short, inasmuch as the revolution was a manifestation of dynamic *entezar*, it was advancing the Imam's return from occultation:

> We, the nation of Iran, have . . . made a revolution. Our revolution was the necessary prelude and a great step in the path of that goal which the Imam of the Age (*emam-e zaman*; the Hidden Imam) was sent . . . to accomplish. If we had not taken this great step, surely the appearance of the *vali-ye 'asr* would be postponed. You, the people of Iran . . . [are] the cause of the advancement of the great human movement toward [its] destination in history, and the cause of hastening (*tasri'*) the appearance of the *vali-ye 'asr*.[17]

It was at this juncture that the Iranian *'ulama'* went a step further, claiming that the Islamic revolution was capable of 'drawing the return of the Imam . . . [even] nearer'.[18] By waging a victorious revolution, the Iranian people had 'drawn themselves one step closer' to the Hidden Imam; they 'are able, once again, to take a step, and another step, and another step, in bringing themselves closer to the Imam of the Age'.[19] That is to say, just as they had practiced *entezar* to rid their country of tyranny, they should free the entire world from oppression and injustice, because to do so will draw nearer the return of the Hidden Imam: 'Whichever of the perimeters of this Islamic zone [i.e., Iran] you are able . . . to expand and propagate in other locations, you have helped and have drawn near to the same extent the appearance of the [Hidden Imam]'.[20]

To sum up, through the practice of active *entezar*, the Iranian nation moved substantially closer to the promised revolution of the *mahdi*. However, Iran was also qualified to advance the return of the Imam further by extending its practice of *entezar* to other regions, eradicating oppression and tyranny from the entire world. Indeed, such was Iran's exclusive obligation. According to this view, Iran was the only country to have fully implemented the all-inclusive Islamic concept of justice and established the government of the *mahdi*, even if 'on a small scale'. These were 'the special leadership qualifications that Iran alone enjoys as compared to all nations of the world'.[21]

Accordingly, Rouhollah K. Ramazani referred to Iran as a 'Redeemer Nation'.[22] Consider the following words of Khameneh'i:

> We must . . . strive to export our revolution throughout the world . . . . The Qur'an is not confined to the town of Mecca, it is not limited to the Quraysh infidels. [The Qur'an] is not satisfied with . . . guiding the people of one town or one country to happiness and salvation. It is for the inhabitants of the world (*'alamin*), for [all] people and for mankind . . . . [T]he message of Islam must hasten to deliver the people wherever there is poverty, wherever there is discrimination, wherever there is oppression.[23]

This universal 'redeeming' role of the Islamic revolution was heralded by the Iranian leadership time and again. In June 1985, one ayatollah stated that 'the grain of the universal Islamic government started from here, and we still have to strive hard until it reaches its lofty summit'.[24] Likewise, Prime Minister Mir-Husayn Musavi asserted in February 1987, 'the movement of the revolution is part of the universal movement of the oppressed, and it is indivisible from the destiny of the rest of the Muslims'.[25] Also in April 1988 Khameneh'i assured the assembly of the Tehran Friday prayers that 'exporting the revolution is like a glitter of the sun of which rays . . . brighten the entire world'.[26] Finally, in the wake of Khomeini's death in June 1989, Ayatollah 'Abdul-Karim Musavi Ardebili declared, 'we are continuing the way of the Imam [Khomeini]'—and so, Iran will persist in the endeavor to 'deliver the deprived people and Muslims throughout the world'.[27]

It may be said, consequently, that the chief instrument for the realization of this objective was the exporting of the revolution, thereby propelling Muslim and other deprived nations to carry out analogous revolutions on their own respective soils. Indeed, a host of scholarly studies of the Islamic Republic and its ideology have illustrated convincingly the practical subordination of Iranian foreign policy to this millenarian vision.[28] Mention should be made of Iran's long-standing logistic and moral support for the Shi'i Hizballah in Lebanon, for the *mujahidin* rebels in Afghanistan and for the Islamic government in the Sudan, as well as its active involvement in subversive activities in most of the Persian Gulf states. Still, the question remains, was Iran's pursuit of its national interests invariably overshadowed by this universal vision? Was the foreign policy of the Iranian regime truly a monolithic reflection of the millenarian Islamic crusade?

**Nationalism and Islam: Mutually Exclusive or Intertwined?**

A society with a common religion will likely be characterized by over-all cohesion and collective self-consciousness. Religion is capable of reinforcing the attachment of a people to its territory, or in modern times, to its nation state. Conversely, as two opposing – sacred and secular – value systems (or as competing collective identities), religion can also undermine the legitimacy of the modern nation, thereby eroding the allegiance of a people to the territory in which they dwell.[29]

In Iran, Shi'i Islam has been, on the whole, a pillar of modern territorial nationalism. Indeed, Iranian national identity has been affected profoundly by Shi'ism ever since the Safavid dynasty (1501–1722) made Shi'ism the state religion. 'Shi'ism emphasized the uniqueness of Iranians as it formally separated them from the vast majority of Sunni Muslims, especially those in the surrounding Arabic and Turkish speaking lands'.[30] Edward G. Browne was therefore correct in observing that, prior to the twentieth century, no one suspected that loyalty to the state of Iran and loyalty to Islam were two different loyalties.[31]

The Iranian revolution of 1978–79, however, *ostensibly* marked the end of this often troubled, but nonetheless enduring, co-existence between religion and nationalism in Iran. 'In part', Hamid Dabashi observes, 'the Islamic revolution ... can be seen as a direct (Shi'ite) Islamic reaction against the artificial over-Persianization of Iranian political culture at the expense of its Islamic component'.[32] The Islamic revolution thus seemed to corroborate Richard W. Cottam's estimation in the mid-1960s that 'if a conflict of the two sets of values is likely anywhere it should occur in Iran'.[33]

Ayatollah Khomeini's outlook serves as an expression of the seeming defeat of Iranian nationalism. Although Khomeini's stance in the beginning of his political career was clearly more nationalistic than Islamic or universalist,[34] by the end of the 1960s his views had undergone a radical transformation. Marked by pan-Islamic motifs, Khomeini's vision appeared to have extended far beyond the borders of Iran. He called for the realization of Islamic unity that would obliterate prior national, 'artificial' divisions among contemporary Islamic states.

Khomeini's supra-nationalist tendency was most conspicuous in his 1971 programmatic work, *Velayet-e Faqih* ('The Governorship of the Jurisprudent'; or as it is entitled in the Arabic version, *Al-Hukumah al-Islamiyah*, 'Islamic Government'). Here Khomeini renounced nationalism as an imperialist conspiracy designed to sow discord among Muslims, in order to facilitate the advances of the 'infidel' West in the Islamic lands. He claimed that in the wake of World War I, the imperialist powers divided the 'Islamic homeland' (i.e., the Ottoman Empire) into 'peoples' (*shu'ub*) and 'petty states' (*duwailat*), placing in each an 'agent of their own' to safeguard their economic and political interests.[35] Khomeini called on all Muslims to unite under the banner of Islam to repel the imperialist onslaught: Islamic unity, he argued, would enable the believers 'to crush the human and tyrannical gods and icons that have plundered the world'.[36]

This universal Islamic vision was formally adopted by the *'ulama'* upon their seizure of power in 1979. Indeed, the Khomeini regime's self-styled obligation to spearhead Muslim unity was enshrined in article 10 of the Islamic Republic's Constitution, which reads as follows:

> All Muslims form a single nation, and the government of the Islamic Republic has the duty of formulating its general policies with a view to merging and union of all Muslim peoples, and it must constantly strive to bring about the political, economic and cultural unity of the Islamic world.[37]

Yet it would be wrong to conclude from here that the ruling *'ulama'* forfeited Iran's nationalist tradition in favor of their pan-Islamic vision. For, as we shall see, nationalism has indeed survived – albeit in modified form – under clerical rule and has continued to be a major force in Iranian culture.

Most observers contend that the revival of Iranian nationalist sentiment in post-Pahlavi Iran was especially noticeable *after* the outbreak of the Iranian-Iraqi War in September 1980.[38] Yet, the sources at hand clearly show that the nationalist tradition was an integral part of the *'ulama'*'s discourse before the war, although introduced under the guise of Islamic universalism. Consider, for example, this August 1979 statement by Ayatollah Sayyid Mahmud Taleqani (d.1979) on the Iranian nation's obligation to export the revolution worldwide:

> You must be the torch-bearers of *tawhid* [monotheism] and Islam in the world of heresy, idolatry, and matter-worship, in order to deliver the world. Just as after the first century of Islam the Iranians were able to make Islam flourish (all these *'ulama'*, all these jurists [*fuqaha'*], all these transmitters of Tradition [*akhbariun*], all these philosophers, all these painters – most of them were . . . Iranians). . . for this reason, we must be attentive. We have a heavy responsibility, not just a social responsibility toward ourselves, but the responsibility of the world's leadership. 'And thus we have made you [Iran!!!] a medium nation that you may be the bearers of witness to the people and that the Apostle may be a bearer of witness to you' (the Qur'an, 2:143).[39]

We see, then, that there emerged out of Taleqani's universal vision a genuine sense of national pride in the Iranian people's service to Islam. Taleqani is speaking here as a true Iranian nationalist – proud of his nation's cultural contribution to and preeminence in Islamic civilization.

Other Iranian officials expressed their patriotism under the veil of universal Islam. Ayatollah Husayn 'Ali Montazeri observed in December 1979, 'from the advent of Islam to this day, Iran has rendered [much] service to Islam. Although the cradle of Islam is Arabia . . . the services of the nation of Iran to Islam have been numerous'. Montazeri also recalled that all six books of *hadith* (Tradition) that the Sunnah regards as the most reliable (the *sitt al-sihah*) were compiled by individuals of 'Iranian' origin; 'none of them was an Arab'.[40] One may therefore agree with Shireen Hunter's conclusion that 'even the present [Iranian] regime, despite its anti-nationalist feelings, at times exhibits ethnic pride and refers to Iran's role in the development of Islamic civilization'.[41]

When the Islamic revolution entered its eighth year, Khameneh'i explicitly proclaimed the Islamic Republic's allegiance to Iranian nationalism. On the occasion of 'Unity Week' in November 1987, Khameneh'i discussed the issue of bringing Iranian Sunnis and Shi'is closer together. Within this context, he distinguished between 'positive' and 'negative' nationalism. The latter, he said, is 'condemned', because it brings about a 'schism among Muslim brothers', the Persian-Shi'i majority and those Iranian ethnic groups that adhere to Sunni Islam. The former, however, is 'good', as it denotes the unity of all 'citizens' for the 'protection of the country's borders against foreigners'.[42] In short, the unification of Iranian Sunnis and Shi'is has little to do with the universalist Islamic vision. Instead, it stems from the narrower, more immediate (and nonetheless legitimate) issue of fortifying the pillars of the Iranian nation state.

As mentioned, the eight-year Iranian-Iraqi War offers ample evidence of Iran's genuine adherence to its nationalist tradition at the expense of the proclaimed universal vision. To be sure, the *'ulama'* repeatedly attempted to broaden (or 'Islamicize') the national confines of the conflict, portraying it as a war between Islam and disbelief, a sacred *jihad* that Iran had undertaken on behalf of *all* Muslims – Shi'is and Sunnis, Persians and Arabs.[43] Nevertheless, soon after Iraq launched its invasion of Iran in September 1980, the Islamic Republic of Iran found it expedient to draw on Iranian nationalist sentiment, couched in Islamic terms, in order to enlist mass support for the war effort.

In September 1981, seeking to bestow an Islamic aura on the ongoing Iran-Iraq conflict, Ardebili cited an excerpt from a sermon delivered by 'Ali ibn Abi Talib (the First Shi'i Imam and Fourth Muslim Caliph) to his subjects on the eve of the Battle of Siffin (657 CE): 'Do you not see . . . that the boundaries of your state are getting shorter and shorter daily and parts of your country are being snatched and usurped . . . and your cities are being invaded?'[44] Interestingly, although the citation reflects the tones of universalist Islam, Ardebili's conclusions from the passage clearly support the view that the national tradition remains strong in the culture of the Islamic Republic of Iran:

> Do you not see Abadan? Do you not see Qasr-e Shireen? Do you not see other towns? . . . Do you not see [how the Iraqis] shed the blood of your youth on the soil of your country? You must resist the aggression committed by global oppression and imperialism against your independence and territorial integrity.[45]

Similarly, Hojjat al-Islam Hasan Ruhani disguised nationalist sentiment under the veil of Islamic universalism, asserting in July 1984 that Islam enjoins on all Muslims 'defense and *jihad*, so that they would be able to carry on their daily lives and observe their religion'. He then referred to Iran as the 'motherland' (*meyhan*), a term often used by the last Pahlavi shah. However, Ruhani (and others like him) was careful to add the term 'Islamic', turning Iran into the 'Islamic motherland'.[46] A year later Ruhani acknowledged that 'if defense in war is intended to preserve a piece of land or the life of a people, this defense is sacred'. Nevertheless, he continued, 'if defense takes the form of preserving religion, that defense is more sacred than everything'.[47]

If the Islamic Republic of Iran accepted the legitimacy of the separate Iranian entity, it also accepted, in principle, the existing international system based on congeries of territorial states. In other words, it appears that Iran actually recognized what James P. Piscatori calls the '*non*-universality of the Islamic community'.[48] Such a contention is further exemplified by the *'ulama'*'s explanation of the exact meaning of Islamic unity. They repeatedly argued that unity among Muslims did not necessarily mean the obliteration of the national divisions of contemporary states, nor their respective customs and religious and cultural heritage. Rather, Islamic unity is a 'unity of goals' or 'unity of purpose'. Unity, Khameneh'i declared in September 1984, 'means not that the Shi'is renounce their beliefs. . . . Our Sunni brothers have their own beliefs, we, the Shi'is, our own beliefs'. He added the following:

> We have no intention of bringing the Sunni brothers to Shi'ism or the Shi'i brothers to Sunnism. Rather, the unity . . . of Muslim brothers should evolve around a common axis and common bases. . . . Experience has shown . . . that diversity of beliefs never prevented two brothers from praying [together], from launching Holy War, from performing the annual pilgrimage to Mecca (*hajj*), or from issuing collective declarations on Islamic issues. What is important is unity of purpose and unity of principles, and this exists between the Shi'i and

Sunni brothers in all the Muslim lands. The best axis for the unity of the Islamic community is the [Prophet Muhammad]. . . . [A]ll the Muslim countries should lay aside their [petty] differences and strive to establish unity among all Muslim societies by creating one popular movement against the oppressors (*mostakbarin*).[49]

Islamic unity is thus defined as focusing on what all Muslims have in common – the Prophet of Islam, the Qur'an and the struggle against common enemies – *not* the merging of separate political entities or the nullification of all distinctions among Muslims. 'All Muslims', declared an Iranian official, 'should form one community with their different beliefs and with their different sects; a community governed by friendship, cordiality and cooperation, defending and supporting each other'.[50] In sum, the unity envisaged by the Islamic Republic of Iran was something of an alliance among the different Muslim states which safeguarded their territorial integrity and their national distinctive marks, rather than their actual political integration.

We see, then, that despite the *'ulama'*'s millenarianism and commitment to an Islamic world order, nationalism has remained active in revolutionary Iran and continues as a major force in Iranian culture – its accommodation to religious teachings, notwithstanding. As Allesandro Bausani rightly observed, Iran and Islam were never antithetical to one another.[51]

### The Abu Musa Affair: Iranian Nationalism and 'Reasons of State' at their Height

Iran's April 1992 takeover of Abu Musa – a strategic Persian Gulf island situated at the mouth of the Strait of Hormuz – is evidence to the continued centrality of nationalism in Iranian culture. Abu Musa and the Greater and Lesser Tunb islands were first occupied by Muhammad Reza Shah Pahlavi's forces in October 1971, immediately following the British withdrawal from the Trucial Coast principalities. Since then, the island of Abu Musa has been subject to a power sharing agreement between Iran and Sharjah, one of the seven constituent shaykhdoms of the United Arab Emirates (UAE).[52] The accord, however, 'did not resolve the issue of sovereignty, which remained a subject of [dormant] dispute between Iran and the UAE . . . with nationals of both states coexisting uneasily on Abu Musa'.[53]

As we will see, Iran's 1992 landing on Abu Musa and its assertiveness on the issue since have had little to do with exporting the Islamic revolution or with the *'ulama'*'s supra-nationalist vision. Rather, Iran's behavior and actions derived directly from its national-strategic interests. In fact, they were almost a carbon copy of the Shah's policy toward the island in 1971–72, which was motivated in the main by national considerations and the Shah's concern for the security of the Persian Gulf region.

Indeed, the policy of the Islamic Republic of Iran – as that of the late Shah – seems to fall in line with a number of salient patterns that have determined Iran's role in the Persian Gulf since at least the sixteenth century. The first of these is steadfast nationalism, guided by the perception that the Gulf has been an Iranian possession, a 'Persian sea', since Cyrus the Great and the first Persian empire. (Repeated Iranian claims to Bahrain during both the Pahlavi and Khomeini eras attest to that as well.[54]) And, although 'the mists of history afford little gratifying evidence to support any [Iranian] claimants ... [t]he national memory is far more important and deeply rooted than any reality or legal brief ever could be'.[55]

It is thus not surprising that immediately after landing its Iranian forces on Abu Musa, the Islamic regime – like the Shah's government in 1971–72 – repeatedly spoke of Iran's 'historic' claims to the island. Later, Iran used the same 'historic' claim in negotiating with the UAE over the sovereignty of the Tunb islands. Iran's self-styled obligation to propagate its brand of Islam on foreign soil did not figure in at all.

Indeed, the resemblance between Pahlavi and revolutionary Iran's (nationally-motivated) rationalizations of their actions in the Persian Gulf is striking. In a statement issued in October 1992, following the collapse of the Iranian-UAE negotiations over the disputed islands, the Iranian National Council categorically affirmed that Abu Musa and the Greater and Lesser Tunb islands were 'part of the Islamic Republic's territories'. 'These islands', the statement maintained, 'were occupied during the expansionist era of the aging British colonialism. In 1971, these islands were restored to Iranian sovereignty after nearly three years of talks.'[56] Likewise, responding in September 1992 to the Gulf Cooperation Council's (GCC) statement in favor of the UAE's claim, the Islamic Republic of Iran explained that 'based on firm, legal and historic documents and evidence, the Abu Musa and Greater and Lesser Tunbs belong to Iran'.[57]

Consider now the terminology with which the Shah's government rationalized Iran's initial occupation of the islands in 1971:

> For more than 80 years colonialism prevented us from restoring our sovereignty over the islands of Abu Musa and the T[u]nbs despite our incontestable historical rights. These islands are now under Iranian control again.[58]

Or in the words of the Shah (January 1972), 'historic facts and documents prove that these islands belong to us'.[59] Both Pahlavi and post-Pahlavi Iran thus justified their actions by drawing on Iran's national memory – a dominion where the discrepancy between the image and the reality of Iran's historic role in the Gulf is rendered irrelevant.

The Islamic Republic used its national memory to discredit the UAE's counter-claims to the disputed islands. 'If geographical demarcation was due to be decided by historical claims', the daily *Jomhuri-ye Eslami* cautioned the Gulf states, 'Arabs in the region would be the main losers'.[60] Responding to a statement allegedly distributed by the UAE in October 1992, according to which the UAE has 'exercised for long its sovereignty' over the islands, the daily *Kayhan* mocked: 'One may ask, how long has the UAE existed that it can say "for a long time". . . . Where were the boundaries of this country "a long time ago?"'[61] In sum, by articulating its own version of the region's political history, Iran sought to drive home the point that, with the sole exception of Iran, all the countries of the Gulf littoral, and the UAE in particular, 'have no historical continuity or depth'.[62] In doing so, it was relying upon historical, rather than religious, claims. Thus, Muhammad Javad Larijani explained, 'Seventy years ago, when many of these countries did not exist geographically, Iran maintained its sovereignty'.[63]

Iranian national sentiment was in full swing when the Islamic government called on all Iranians to unite in the defense of the *vatan* (motherland) against the UAE's and its Arab allies' designs to 'snatch' the islands. It warned its Arab neighbors not to 'violate' Iran's 'national sovereignty and territorial integrity',[64] or else Iran would 'retaliate' with all its might.[65] Iran, Rafsanjani warned the UAE in September 1992, is 'seriously adhering to the policy of resistance and defending our land and will not give in to humiliation'.[66] Lastly, the daily *Salam* let it be known that all Iranians, young and old, were 'ready to defend [their] legal borders'. He who seeks to test the Iranian people 'will be responsible for the consequences of [his] insanity'.[67] In this context of safeguarding Iranian national sovereignty, Rafsanjani dared those challenging Iran's claims 'to cross a sea of blood (*darya-ye khun*)' if they wished to retake the islands.[68] Once again, revolutionary Iran's staunch nationalist sentiment conforms to Pahlavi Iran's 1971–72 discourse on the island dispute: 'Millions of Iranians of every class and age . . . are expressing their complete support for the government and their readiness for any type of sacrifice to preserve the nation's independence, integrity and legitimate rights'.[69]

An analysis of the Islamic Republic's steps to enforce its control over Abu Musa and the Tunbs clearly shows that its prime intention was to 'Persianize' the islands, rather than 'Islamicize' them. In August 1992 Iranian authorities on Abu Musa denied port entry to a ferry from Sharjah. This incident brought the UAE-Iranian dispute to a boiling point. The boat reportedly carried teachers, along with their dependents, to the island for the start of the school year; some 200 Arab pupils remained on the island.[70]

With this, the Persianization of Abu Musa became a vivid reality, with 'Iran reportedly extending control over all aspects of the UAE islanders' life'.[71]

Sharjah's nationals in Abu Musa were henceforth treated as temporary 'guests'[72] and were urged to accept Iranian nationality or leave the island.[73] (Reports about Iran's intention to expel the Arab residents of Abu Musa altogether were subsequently denied by Iranian officials.[74]) Beginning in September 1992 the Iranian media referred to Abu Musa as part of Iran's Hormuzgan Province, pledging that it 'will become one of the most beautiful islands of the Islamic Republic of Iran in the near future'.[75] The Islamic Republic also celebrated the beginning of the new academic year in Abu Musa, where 'Iran's national anthem was played during the ceremony'.[76] Finally, the Iranian parliament passed a law in April 1993 extending Iranian territorial waters to include the disputed islands,[77] in effect annexing them to Iran.

From 1988 and the conclusion of the Iran-Iraq War, social and economic reconstruction became high priorities of the Iranian administration. To this end, Iran sought to enhance cooperation with the GCC states. However, Iran's actions in the Gulf strained Irano-GCC relations. The Iranian leadership therefore took pains to play down the islands dispute, claiming time and again that 'no [new] development had occurred on the island[s]'.[78] This 'business-as-usual' posture is worthy of a brief examination, for it too bears striking resemblance to Pahlavi Iran's handling of the islands affair, twenty years earlier.

In an obvious attempt to pacify the Gulf states, Iran's first deputy foreign minister 'Ali Muhammad Besharati explained in April 1992 that, by its actions, Iran was merely trying 'to infuse new life into the islands of the Persian Gulf', through a program of 'comprehensive construction' that had been under way 'for the last few years'. 'We abide', he concluded, 'by what Iran agreed with the UAE shortly after its creation in 1971'.[79] This statement represented an Iranian effort to allay the Gulf states' fears of a looming Iranian menace in the Persian Gulf. Iranian officials repeatedly explained that Iran's stance on the islands had not been altered, and that the islands' 'status [has] not changed'.[80] 'Nothing new has taken place', they pledged, and 'the islands' affairs are proceeding as before'. In short, 'the 1971 agreement . . . remains in force'; Sharjah nationals living on the island can continue their 'honorable life', as before, next to their 'Iranian brothers and sisters'.[81]

The 1971–72 islands imbroglio found the Shah in a similar circumstance. At that time he was seeking to accommodate the Middle Eastern Arab states with a view to winning their support for his ambitions in the Persian Gulf after British withdrawal.[82] Like the Rafsanjani administration in 1992, the Shah played down the depth of Arab resentment.

Consequently, his government hastened to explain that the shaykhdoms of Sharjah and Ras al-Khaimah (which claimed Abu Musa and the two Tunbs, respectively) were aware, in advance, of the landing of Iranian forces. The Iranian foreign ministry even went as far as to state that the 'landing of Iranian forces was in keeping with [Iran's] well-known intention to land forces there before the British withdrawal'.[83]

Iranian nationalism was among the guiding principles behind the Islamic Republic's assertiveness in the Gulf, although more concrete geopolitical considerations, quite similar to those of the Shah, were also at play. Writing in 1972, Ramazani finds that Iran's rulers have always 'aspired to playing a leading role in the Persian Gulf'.[84] He adds that external circumstances dictated whether or not Iran could in fact play a major role in the region. 'Most often adverse external circumstances limited Iran's freedom of action. . . . Conversely, when [a] favorable external environment coincided with the rise of powerful [Iranian] rulers, Iran played a more effective part in the Gulf'.[85] Certainly, the 1991 Gulf War (resulting in the severe weakening of Iraq), the end of the Cold War and the disintegration of the Soviet Union were all favorable for Iran. They afforded it a golden opportunity to achieve its long-standing goal of playing a major role in the Gulf. Indeed, Iran's most recent actions in the Persian Gulf can (and should) be seen as the continuation of old themes in Iranian political history, with no relationship whatsoever to its millenarian ideological crusade.

Finally, strategic interests relating to reasons of state were also among the motivating factors behind Iran's 1992 Persian Gulf adventure, just as they had been behind the Shah's actions of twenty years earlier. The Shah and Iran's Islamic government recognized the strategic importance of the islands, located as they are at the mouth of the Strait of Hormuz – through which the backbone of Iran's economy, oil, is transported. In the words of two specialists, 'The islands . . . are situated at a critical "choke point" near the strategic and easily blocked straits [sic.] of Hormoz'.[86] Their 'geographic position', the Shah explained in 1971, 'can make them issues of tremendous military value'.[87] On another occasion, in January 1972, the Shah offered the following scenario: 'if these islands are in the hands of irresponsible people, a small ship or even a motorboat armed with a bazooka . . . can cause trouble'.[88] The Shah's apparent lack of faith in the ability of the emerging Gulf Arab Federation to preserve the security of the Strait of Hormuz can in itself explain his decision to embark upon the islands adventure. It was perhaps because of a similar lack of faith that Iran's Supreme National Security Council stated in September 1992 that the 'security at Abu Musa is part of the undeniable responsibility of Iran'.[89]

Thus, Iran's long-term goal, both in the Pahlavi and post-Pahlavi eras, has been to shape decisively a security regime for the Gulf area, and it was for this reason, among others, that they set out to 'regain' or 'occupy' (according to the varying interpretations) the islands. The Islamic Republic of Iran may have also sought to signal to its neighbors that no joint security apparatus in the region could be effective without Iran's participation. Indeed, Iran has been critical of plans by the GCC states to enlist Syria and Egypt into Gulf security arrangements, as envisaged by the yet-to-be-activated 'Damascus Declaration' alliance of 1991. Moreover, Iran has also opposed the Gulf states' new, more explicit willingness to conclude defense pacts with the West, insisting in both cases that regional security was the responsibility *solely* of the Gulf littoral states.[90] At any rate, whatever reasons may be cited for Iran's assertive policy in the Gulf, its pan-Islamic vision was certainly not one of them.

## Conclusion

Revolutionary Iran has genuinely adhered to two visions – the nationalist and the pan-Islamic – which are not necessarily mutually exclusive. A potent cultural asset in Iranian modern history, the nationalist vision has been able to survive as a major force in Iranian political culture, its sometimes 'Islamicized' form notwithstanding.

Tension, conflict, coexistence and reconciliation have frequently played important roles in the relationship between the Islamic and nationalist traditions in Iran. Indeed, in post-Pahlavi Iran, neither tradition has been pure or based completely on one element. Rather, elements from the other have contributed to the forces which have made one tradition dominant at a particular time; the ascendancy of one does not mean that the other has permanently disappeared from Iranian culture.[91] Thus, that the leadership of the Islamic Republic has, at times, given precedence to reasons of state over those of the millenarian ideological crusade, should not by any means be taken as an indication that Iranian foreign policy has taken on an outlook of 'new realism'.[92] Instead, such considerations should stand as clear indications that nationalism has retained its viability as a legitimate cultural and political force in Iran.

Governments come and go, but political cultures endure. Indeed, there is a high degree of continuity in Iranian culture. Revolutions obviously occur within a specific set of pre-existing cultural patterns and many of these are carried over from the old regime. In Iran, as in other countries, 'revolutionary crises are *not* total breakpoints in history that suddenly make anything at all possible if only it is envisaged by willful revolutionaries'.[93]

## NOTES

1. Crane Brinton, *The Anatomy of Revolution* (NY: Vintage Books 1965) p.196.
2. Cited in P. Chelkowski, 'In Ritual and Revolution: The Image in the Transformation of Iranian Culture', *Views: The Journal of Photography of New England* 10 (Spring 1989) p.11.
3. Eric J. Hobsbawm, *Nations and Nationalism Since 1780: Programme, Myth, Reality* (Cambridge: CUP 1991) p.11.
4. Ibid., p.10.
5. See M. Bayat, 'The Iranian Revolution of 1978–79: Fundamentalist or Modern?' *Middle East Journal* 37/3 (Winter 1983) pp.30–42.
6. Abdulaziz A. Sachedina, *Islamic Messianism: The Idea of the Mahdi in Twelver Shi'ism* (Albany, NY: SUNY Press 1981) p.79.
7. Hamid Enayat, 'Khumayni's Concept of the "Guardianship of the Jurisconsult"', in James P. Piscatori (ed.), *Islam in the Political Process* (NY: Cambridge UP 1982) p.174.
8. For an analysis of Shari'ati's notion of *entezar*, see Mongol Bayat-Philipp, 'Shi'ism in Contemporary Iranian Politics: The Case of 'Ali Shari'ati', in Eli Kedourie and Sylvia G. Haim (eds.), *Towards a Modern Iran* (London: Frank Cass 1980) pp.161–2.
9. 'Ali Shari'ati, 'Entezar, the Religion of Protest', trans. by Mongol Bayat, in John J. Donohue and John L. Esposito (eds.), *Islam in Transition: Muslim Perspectives* (NY: Oxford UP 1982) p.303.
10. *Ettala'at* (Tehran, daily), 4 June 1983.
11. *Dar Maktab-e Jom'eh: Majmu'ah-ye Khotbeh-ye Nemaz-e Jom'eh-ye Tehran* 2 (In the Ideology of Friday: A Collection of the Sermons of the Friday Prayers of Tehran) (Tehran: Entesharat-e Chapkhaneh-ye Vezarat-e Ershad-e Eslami, 1364 Sh.) June 1980, p.200 (hereafter, *Khotbeh*).
12. Emami-Kashani stated in this regard: '*entezar* cannot serve as a pretext for the lack of holy war (*jihad*) ...against oppression and tyranny'. See *Ettala'at*, 18 March 1989.
13. *Ettala'at*, 19 May 1984.
14. *Khotbeh* 3 (1365 Sh.) 19 June 1981, p.200.
15. Khameneh'i in ibid., p.200.
16. Emami-Kashani in *Ettala'at*, 21 June 1986.
17. *Khotbeh* 2, 27 June 1980, p.201.
18. Rafsanjani in *Ettala'at*, 19 May 1984.
19. Khameneh'i in *Khotbeh* 2, 27 June 1980, p.202. See also Mahdavi-Kani in *Ettala'at*, 23 July 1983.
20. Khameneh'i in *Khotbeh* 2, 27 June 1980, p.202. See also Rafsanjani in *Kayhan* (Tehran daily), 10 July 1982.
21. Rouhollah K. Ramazani, 'Khomeini's Islam in Iran's Foreign Policy', in Adeed Dawisha (ed.), *Islam in Foreign Policy* (Cambridge: CUP 1983) p.18.
22. Rouhollah K. Ramazani, 'Shi'ism in the Persian Gulf', in Juan R.I. Cole and Nikkie R. Keddie (eds.), *Shi'ism and Social Protest* (New Haven, CT: Yale UP 1986) p.34.
23. *Khotbeh* 2, 28 March 1980. Also see Ayatollah Husayn 'Ali Montazeri in *Khotbeh* 1, 14 Sept. 1979, pp.54–5; Rafsanjani in *Khotbeh* 4 (1367 Sh.), 8 Jan. 1982, pp.186–8; and Khameneh'i in *Kayhan*, 4 Dec. 1982.
24. Ayatollah Jannati in *Ettala'at*, 22 June 1985.
25. *Ettala'at*, 7 Feb. 1987.
26. *Ettala'at*, 9 April 1988.
27. *Ettala'at*, 4 June 1989.
28. See John L. Esposito (ed.), *The Iranian Revolution: Its Global Impact* (Miami: Florida International UP 1990); David Menashri (ed.), *The Iranian Revolution and the Muslim World* (Boulder, CO: Westview Press 1990); and Ramazani (notes 21, 22). Also see Haggay Ram, *Myth and Mobilization in Revolutionary Iran* (Washington, DC: American UP 1994), especially chs. 6 and 7.
29. For a valuable discussion of this issue see Anthony D. Smith, *The Ethnic Origins of Nations* (Cambridge, MA: Blackwell 1986) pp.34–7.
30. Farhad Kazemi, *Politics and Culture in Iran* (Ann Arbor, MI: Center for Political Studies,

Institute for Social Research, U. of Michigan 1988) p.3.
31. Edward G. Browne, *A Literary History of Persia* 4 (London: Cambridge UP 1930) p.14.
32. Hamid Dabashi, *Theology of Discontent: The Ideological Foundations of the Islamic Revolution in Iran* (NY: NYUP 1993) p.10.
33. Richard W. Cottam, *Nationalism in Iran*, updated through 1978 (Pittsburgh, PA: Pittsburgh UP 1979) p.9.
34. See Ram (note 28) pp.196–7.
35. Ruhallah M. al-Khumayni, *Al-Hukumah al-Islamiyah* (Beirut: Dar al-Tali'ah 1979) pp.34–35.
36. Ibid.
37. Cited in Roger M. Savory, 'Ex Oriente Nebula: An Inquiry into the Nature of Khomeini's Ideology', in Peter J. Chelkowski and Robert J. Pranger (eds.*), Ideology and Power in the Middle East: Studies in Honor of George Lenczowski* (Durham, NC: Duke UP 1988) p.352.
38. Fred Halliday contended, for example, that 'Khomeini did talk, prior to Sept. 1980, of "the nation of Iran", but since the outbreak of war official propaganda...increased its stress upon this national element in appealing for support against the Iraqis'. See his 'Iranian Foreign Policy since 1979: Internationalism and Nationalism in the Islamic Revolution', in Cole and Keddie (note 22) p.106.
39. *Khotbeh* 1, 10 Aug. 1979, p.21.
40. Ibid., 7 Dec. 1979, pp.168–9. Also see Emami-Kashani in *Khotbeh* 4, 4 Dec. 1981, p.128.
41. Shireen T. Hunter, *Iran and the World: Continuity in a Revolutionary Decade* (Bloomington: Indiana UP 1990) p.12.
42. *Ettala'at*, 7 Nov. 1987. For similar expressions see Khameneh'i in *Ettala'at*, 15 April 1989.
43. On the Iranian campaign of Islamicizing/universalizing its war with Iraq, see H. Ram, 'Islamic "Newspeak": Language and Change in Revolutionary Iran', *Middle Eastern Studies* 29/2 (April 1993) pp.208–16.
44. *Khotbeh* 3, 18 Sept. 1981, p.413.
45. Ibid., p.414. For similar expressions see Hojjat al-Islam Shaykh Muhammad Yazdi in *Khotbeh* 4, 9 Oct. 1981, pp.30–1.
46. *Ettala'at*, 14 July 1984.
47. *Ettala'at*, 18 May 1985. Also see Khameneh'i in *Ettala'at*, 15 March 1986.
48. James P. Piscatori, *Islam in a World of Nation-States* (Cambridge: CUP 1986) p.46.
49. *Ettala'at*, 15 Sept. 1984.
50. Hojjat al-Islam Motaqadi in *Ettala'at*, 14 Oct. 1989.
51. Allesandro Bausani, 'Muhammad or Darius? The Elements and Bases of Iranian Culture', in S. Vryonis, Jr. (ed.), *Islam and Cultural Change in the Middle Ages* (Wiesbaden: Otto Harrassowithz 1975) p.47.
52. Under the terms of the 1971 agreement, Iranian forces were stationed on part of Abu Musa and the island's oil revenues were split in half, in exchange for an annual subsidy and continued control by Sharjah of the remainder of the island.
53. U. Rabi, 'United Arab Emirates', in Ami Ayalon (ed.), *Middle East Contemporary Survey* 16 (1992) (Boulder, CO: Westview Press 1994) p.778. For details on the origin of the Abu Musa dispute in 1971 and related documents, see Rouhollah K. Ramazani, *The Persian Gulf: Iran's Role* (Charlottesville: UP of Virginia) pp.56–68; and Shahram Chubin and Salih Zabih, *The Foreign Relations of Iran: A Developing State in a Zone of Great-Power Conflict* (Berkeley: U. of California Press 1974) pp.217–30.
54. On Iran's claims to Bahrain during the Pahlavi era, see H. Ram, 'UAR-Iranian Propaganda War in the 1960s: Ethno-Cultural Antipathies and Geo-Political Strife', *Asian and African Studies* 26 (1992) pp.223–48.
55. Graham E. Fuller, *The 'Center of the Universe': The Geopolitics of Iran* (Boulder, CO: Westview Press 1991) p.58.
56. *Voice of the Islamic Republic of Iran* (*VIRI*), 4 Oct. – *FBIS-NES* (*DR*), 8 Oct. 1992. Also see *Tehran Times*, 26 Aug. – *DR*, 9 Sept. 1992.
57. *VIRI*, 10 Sept. – *DR*, 10 Sept. 1992. For similar expressions, see *VIRI*, 11 Sept. – *DR*, 11 Sept. 1992.
58. *Radio Tehran*, 13 Dec. – *DR*, 14 Dec. 1971.

59. *Ettala'at*, 22 Jan. 1972.
60. *Jomhuri-ye Eslami* (Tehran, daily), 17 Sept. 1992.
61. *Kayhan,* 30 Sept. 1992.
62. *VIRI,* 30 Sept. – *DR,* 1 Oct. 1992.
63. *Iran News Agency*, 2 Oct. – *DR*, 5 Oct. 1992.
64. *VIRI,* 10 Sept. – *DR,* 10 Sept. 1992.
65. *VIRI,* 16 Sept. – *DR,* 16 Sept. 1992.
66. *Ettala'at*, 19 Sept. 1992.
67. *Salam* (Tehran, daily), 1 Oct. 1992.
68. *Ettala'at*, 26 Dec. 1992.
69. *Radio Tehran*, 2 Dec. – *DR*, 6 Dec. 1971. Also see *Radio Tehran*, 1 Dec. – *DR,* 3 Dec. 1971.
70. Rabi (note 53) p.779.
71. Ibid.
72. *VIRI,* 9 Sept. – *DR,* 10 Sept. 1992.
73. *Sawt al-Kuwait al-Duwali*, 6 Sept. – *DR*, 10 Sept. 1992; *AFP*, 10 Sept. – *DR*, 11 Sept. 1992.
74. See, e.g., Iranian Foreign Minister 'Ali Akbar Velayati's statement, *Iranian Television*, 22 April – *DR,* 23 April 1992.
75. *Iran News Agency*, 29 Sept. [*sic*] – *DR*, 21 Sept. 1992.
76. Ibid.
77. *VIRI,* 20 April – *DR,* 22 April 1993.
78. *Tehran Times* (Tehran, daily), 22 April 1992.
79. *Iran News Agency*, 21 April – *DR,* 22 April 1992. See also foreign minister 'Ali Akbar Velayati's statement, *Iranian Television,* 22 April – *DR,* 23 April 1992.
80. Rafsanjani in *Ettala'at*, 19 Sept. 1992.
81. See, e.g., *Tehran Times*, 26 Aug. 1992; foreign ministry statement in *VIRI,* 10 Sept. – *DR,* 10 Sept. 1992; Hojjat al-Islam Nateq Nuri in *Iran News Agency*, 13 Sept. – *DR*, 16 Sept. 1992; and Rafsanjani in *Ettala'at*, 19 Sept. 1992.
82. Rouhollah K. Ramazani, *Iran's Foreign Policy, 1941–1973: A Study of Foreign Policy in Modernizing Nations* (Charlottesville: UP of Virginia 1975) pp.421–2.
83. Ramazani (note 53) p.61. Also see Chubin and Zabih (note 53) p.222.
84. Ramazani (note 53) p.26.
85. Ibid., p.27.
86. Chubin and Zabih (note 53) p.222.
87. Ibid., p.57.
88. *Ettala'at*, 22 Jan. 1972.
89. *Iran News Agency*, 12 Sept. – *DR*, 14 Sept. 1992. See also statement by Iran's envoy to the United Nations, Kamal Kharazi, in *Iran News Agency*, 3 Sept. – *DR*, 4 Sept. 1992.
90. For treatments of Bahrain, Qatar, Oman and the UAE, see respective chapters by Haggay Ram, in Ami Ayalon (ed.), *Middle East Contemporary Survey* 17 (1993) (Boulder, CO: Westview Press 1995) pp.274–81, 556–7, 566–74, 697–707.
91. Kazemi (note 30) p.6.
92. Rouhollah K. Ramazani, 'Iran's Foreign Policy: Both North and South', *Middle East Journal* 46/13 (Summer 1992) p.395.
93. Theda Skocpol, *States and Social Revolutions* (Cambridge: CUP 1979) p.171.

# The Sudan under Islamist Rule

## GABRIEL R. WARBURG

On 30 June 1989 a group of army officers seized power in Sudan and overthrew the democratically elected government headed by al-Mahdi. The coup was engineered by the NIF, founded in 1985 by the Muslim Brothers. This article examines how the Muslim Brothers succeeded in penetrating the army and gaining a foothold within the officer corps, and attempts to explain why a political-religious movement opted for a military takeover. The political and ideological basis of the NIF are examined, including its adamant insistence on an Islamic state. The Sudan presents a unique case study: its three major political parties are led by leaders of Muslim movements who all support the promulgation of an Islamic constitution leading to an Islamic state. Why could Sudan not agree on an Islamic agenda without resorting to a military coup?

On 30 June 1989, a group of army officers headed by Lt. Col. 'Umar Hasan al-Bashir overthrew the democratically elected government of al-Sadiq al-Mahdi and assumed power in Sudan. It was the third military coup since the Sudan became independent in January 1956 and the second time that the military had seized power with the blessing of a political party. However, President Bashir's dictatorship marks the first time that a military junta assumed power in order to enforce a radical Islamist regime.

The first time the military intervened, in November 1958, they did so under the authority of the army's high command and were led by the chief of staff, General Ibrahim 'Abbud. The move was prompted by the Prime Minister, 'Abdallah Khalil. Khalil was the leader of the Umma Party, the political organization of the Ansar. His initiative had the tacit approval of Sayyid 'Abd al-Rahman al-Mahdi and Sayyid 'Ali al-Mirghani, the respective leaders of the Ansar and the Khatmiyya, the two major Islamic religious-political blocs in the Sudan. Bashir's coup, 31 years later, was inspired by the National Islamic Front (NIF), the largest opposition party at the time. The NIF feared that the government would rescind the Islamic Laws, implemented by the Numayri regime in September 1983 with the active support of the Muslim Brothers, in order to achieve a compromise with the Sudan Peoples Liberation Army (SPLA), which was leading the civil war.

A second similarity between 'Abbud and Bashir is that both of them denied the link between a political party and their respective coups. In 'Abbud's case, the truth came to light in 1965 when, following the regime's downfall, both the military and several of the civilians who had been involved admitted their complicity in the 1958 plot. In Bashir's case, the collusion of the NIF and its leader, Dr. Hasan 'Abdallah al-Turabi, can be assumed despite the denials of both Bashir and Turabi. Bashir's denial, in an interview with the London *Observer,* even went so far as to claim: 'We have no relations with the NIF, before, during or after the coup. We have no intention of co-operating with them'.[1] Irrespective of Bashir's rhetoric, it was not long before an alliance between the NIF and the new military junta was firmly established.

The second military coup occurred in May 1969 and was led by Col. Muhammad Ja'far al-Numayri. It started out as a secular-leftist regime following in the footsteps of President Nasir and the Egyptian Free Officers. However, after 1977 it changed course and gradually became identified with the Islamist movement. The shift culminated in the implementation of the so-called 'Shari'a Laws' in September 1983 and with the attempt to establish an Islamic state. In fact Hasan al-Turabi, who was then leader of the Muslim Brothers and had opposed Numayri in the early stages of his regime, became one of his closest collaborators after 1977.[2]

An additional peculiarity of the Sudan relevant to this study is the fact that its Islamist movements have dominated the political scene since the state achieved its independence in January 1956. The oldest and largest of these movements is the Mahdist Umma Party, led by al-Sadiq al-Mahdi. Al-Sadiq al-Mahdi is the great grandson of Muhammad Ahmad, the 19th century Mahdi of the Sudan. The Mahdist movement was started in June 1881 and succeeded in overthrowing the Turco-Egyptian rulers which had dominated the Sudan since 1821. It established an Islamic autocracy that was subsequently destroyed by the Anglo-Egyptian invaders in 1898. A second religious-political force is the Khatmiyya Sufi order. Surfacing in the 19th century as well, it stood in alliance with the Turco-Egyptian regime in opposition to the Mahdiyya. The Khatmiyya Sufi order continued to play an important political role during the Anglo-Egyptian Condominium and since Sudan achieved independence in 1956 has remained a prominent component of the Democratic Unionist Party. The third and youngest of the movements is Turabi's NIF, founded by the Muslim Brothers in alliance with several Sufi orders in April 1985. Not unlike the FIS in Algeria or the Palestinian Hamas, it is a militant Islamist movement that views itself as modernist.

Al-Sadiq al-Mahdi and Hasan al-Turabi, the leaders of the Ansar and the NIF, besides being brothers-in-law, have much in common. Both were born in the early 1930s and, after receiving a traditional Muslim education, went on to study in secular schools and universities. They both then became leading politicians in the 1960s. As leader of the Umma Party, Sadiq served as prime minister from 1966 to 1967 and again from 1986 to 1989. Turabi has led the Muslim Brothers since 1964 and, following a long period of collaboration with the Umma Party, became a close ally of President Numayri in 1977.[3] Following Numayri's downfall in April 1985, Turabi's newly founded NIF succeeded in becoming the third largest party in the 1986 elections. It then participated in the coalition government led by al-Sadiq al-Mahdi. It is in this period that Turabi and his followers became involved in the military coup which overthrew the democratically elected government and replaced it with the present military-Islamist regime under Bashir. It is this phase of the NIF's political evolution that is the topic of this study.[4]

### Islamism, Democracy and Power

Hasan al-Turabi and the NIF, despite their participation in the 1986 elections and their subsequent inclusion in the government, are committed neither to the observance of law nor to a peaceful transition to an Islamic order. In this respect, they possess much of the same self-righteousness of many modern Islamists who look down on their 'less Islamic' compatriots and seek to impose their superior version of Islam on them. In Sudan most Muslims, whether supporters of Ansar or Khatmiyya, viewed the arrogance of Turabi and his followers with growing suspicion, bordering on hostility, following Turabi's enthusiastic cooperation with Numayri and the Muslim Brothers' support of the 'Shari'a Laws' in September 1983. After Numayri's fall from power in April 1985, the Khatmiyya and the Ansar also voiced their opposition to the rigidity of the NIF regarding its position on an Islamic constitution and its refusal to compromise with the non-Muslim South. According to Turabi, the victory of Islam could only be brought about through modern Islamist movements and through the application of *ijtihad*:[5]

> [T]he modern Islamist movement looks like the only hope for rescuing modern Muslim societies from the endemic cycle of instability caused by the inherent illegitimacy of the secular political systems ruling over them.... For a worldview that remains unchallenged theoretically, that places its adherents at the centre of the universe as the divinely-sanctioned leaders of humanity, replacements are hard to find, especially if they all entailed third- or fourth-class membership in the community of nations.[6]

Islamists like Turabi claim that their movement is basically democratic in origin and only 'became revolutionary because there was very little option left. The domestic order denied them freedom of organization and freedom of expression.' In a way, the Islamist movement was 'exiled from democracy'. Since Islamists view western democracy as corrupt and hypocritical, they do not believe that they can achieve power democratically.

Indeed, even should they gain the majority in democratic elections, they do not believe that they would be granted legal recognition, let alone power. The cancellation of Algeria's December 1991 election results by the military provides them with an apt illustration to that effect. To quote al-Turabi, 'Islam seems to be inevitable' and 'if you want to avoid Islam, you have to avoid the ballot box completely because if you resort to it, Islam will win'.[7]

The alternative for Sudanese Islamists was to act by force, stage a revolution, and impose their conception of Islamic norms on society. As members of the Muslim Brothers have done in other countries, the Sudanese Muslim Brothers began to infiltrate into the Sudan Defence Force (SDF) officer corps. They first did so in 1955, in the wake of the 1952 Egyptian Free Officers' coup and with the active help of a member of the secret organization of the Egyptian Muslim Brotherhood who had escaped to Sudan following an assassination attempt on President Nasir in November 1954. However, it was a rather clumsy effort of a politically immature movement.

Following President Numayri's 'National Reconciliation' attempt in July 1977, the Muslim Brothers and Turabi undertook a concerted effort with a definite political goal and succeeded in gaining a solid foothold in the military. Their better-educated membership, experience, superior organization and relative financial affluence gained as a result of the new Islamic banking system introduced by Numayri with al-Turabi's prompting, enabled the Brethren to achieve a high degree of success in the army. Their first initiatives took the form of voluntary religious teaching and prayer services, all with the blessing of the SDF's high command. Second, they urged their graduates to join the officer corps following the conclusion of their medical, engineering or accountancy studies. Third, they searched for former Muslim Brothers and their relatives serving in the SDF and lured those that they could back into the movement.

All these efforts were undertaken during the years 1978–85. Throughout this period, conditions within both the Sudan and the SDF were ripe for revolt due to a deteriorating economy, growing corruption and renewal of the 1983 civil war. The Brethren had two principal aims: the creation of conditions within the army which would enable the Muslim Brothers to impose an Islamic state by force of arms if other methods failed, and the laying of a foundation for an Islamic army to replace the SDF. This second objective was central because the Brothers perceived the existing armies of the Muslim world as supporters of the status quo and the last resort of secularism.[8]

Thus, Turabi's tacit support of the seizure of power by a group of NIF Islamist adherents within the SDF on 30 June 1989 came as no surprise. As mentioned above, both Turabi and Bashir have continuously denied NIF complicity in the coup and to prove the point Turabi was even put under temporary arrest together with other political leaders. However, it soon became clear that al-Turabi and the NIF controlled the reins of power behind al-Bashir's throne. One telling example of the growth of NIF influence was the acquisition by the NIF of control over all institutes of higher learning. This became apparent in 1990 when Dr. Ibrahim Ahmad 'Umar, an NIF adherent and the minister of higher education, dismissed the university presidents as well as the deans of numerous faculties and reorganized higher education in Sudan's five public and private universities, doubling the number of students. This allowed NIF members, many of whom were university graduates, to benefit from the increased opportunities of employment offered by fellow Brothers within the higher echelons of power. These included senior posts in academic, financial, economic and political institutions, and diplomatic positions abroad. Academic institutes had been a Muslim Brothers stronghold ever since they were founded in the 1950s. Now that the Muslim Brothers exercised complete control, they sought to rid themselves of their competitors, whether Umma supporters, Khatmiyya adherents or communists.

In an interview published in *Trends* in 1994, Turabi confirmed his support of the 1989 military coup.[9] When asked: 'How would you respond to the charge that Sudan is an Islamic dictatorship and where do you stand *vis-à-vis* the democratic process?', he responded that Islam is based on the *shura* (consultation) and is neither a dictatorship nor a single party model: 'In Islam we don't like multi-party bias. As Muslims we don't present our views as a member of a party, or *tarika*, or *madhab*, because in front of Allah we will be individually responsible: it is not the party or group which will go to heaven or hell.' According to Turabi, 'a multi-party system in the Sudan would not be democratic because political parties or a government governed by the House of *Khatmiyyah* and the House of the *Mahdi* was a dynastic thing'.[10] Turabi also argues that initially no one rejected Bashir for his alleged dictatorial tendencies. He was welcomed by the Sudanese masses as well as by the rulers of Egypt, Saudi Arabia and the United States. It was only once they realized that he was following the path of Islam that they turned against him. This is because the West will never allow conceptions that it finds unacceptable to gain power.

Although Turabi condoned the assumption of power by force in order to secure the Islamic state, he ostensibly condemned terrorism and rejected its use by fellow-Islamists in Egypt and Algeria. 'Islamization cannot be achieved by force...Because the Islam of force has nothing to do with true Islam and force should be used [only] for self-defence'.[11] Yet he refused to condemn specific acts of terrorism committed under the banner of Islam, stating that he could not condemn someone with whom he wanted to have a dialogue. Thus, when asked whether the killing of innocent Frenchmen in

Algeria was morally justified, Turabi responded: 'If I was in Algeria and the government was persecuting me...I would think that France is guilty of supporting these persecutors, this terrorist government, and I could attack France in any way whatsòever. But ultimately, I do not think it is correct to kill an ordinary Frenchman who is visiting the country.'[12] This was as far as Turabi was willing to go in condemning terrorism. But, as is well known, Islamic-led terrorism also exists in the Sudan and Sudanese Islamists were allegedly involved in the attempt to blow up the World Trade Center in New York in February 1993. The 26 June 1995 assassination attempt on the life of President Husni Mubarak in Addis Ababa once again indicated Sudanese involvement in Islamist terrorism across its borders and triggered off an acute crisis between Egypt and Sudan. The real issue was radical Islamism, which had been behind the assassination attempt. Egypt accused the Sudanese authorities of having trained the would-be assassins and of smuggling them across its border with Ethiopia. Though Sudanese involvement was not proved, it seemed clear that the Egyptian Islamists who had plotted the assassination had been granted asylum in Sudan.

A western journalist who visited the Sudan in 1994 and interviewed Turabi and others, both Islamists and their opponents, commented: '[T]here hangs about Turabi himself an atmosphere of reflexive denial. Rather than overtly plotting the political terror, the Islamists turn their backs on it, and let it happen as a matter of distasteful necessity in revolutionary times.'[13] To put it bluntly, Hasan al-Turabi and his fellow Islamist leaders within the NIF are probably not involved in plotting or executing terrorist acts. However, they refuse to condemn them and attempt to offer justification based on their Islamist ideology.

According to al-Turabi, the Islamic system of government and public affairs has been absent from Muslim life for centuries and its implementation will take many years: 'This must be seen as the first step towards the ultimate unity of the *umma*.... Establishing an Islamic system in one country is not the end but the start of such an end.... May Allah bless the Islamic state of Sudan and make it successful as the first link which will lead to one *umma* united under a central Islamic government.'[14] In a press conference Turabi praised Bashir for having created an Islamic state and asserted that during 1995 a total civilianization of the regime would take place and 'a government of consultation [*shura*] headed by an Imam' set up.[15]

Al-Turabi advocates a democratic interpretation of Islam, based on *shura* and leading to popular consensus (*ijma*'). *Shura*, according to Turabi, guarantees the Islamic state against the misuse and abuse of *shari'a* by despotic rulers. Unlike democracy, which is founded on the sovereignty of the people, *shura* is based on the sovereignty of God as embodied in a divinely revealed textual authority. Hence while democracy suffers from the shortcomings of human reason, *shura* does not because it is based on *tawhid* (the unity of God) and on the divine texts which will ultimately end conflict and unify the *umma*. *Shura* is also the only way to achieve Islamic liberation from despotic local and western domination. Thus, Turabi calls on Muslims to use the term democracy with caution since, as manifested in the Third World, it has frequently led to coercion and the monopolization of authority.

The Muslim should reclaim democracy, in its pure Islamic form, by aligning it with *shura*. Clearly, al-Turabi only accepts the formal part of democracy and not its substance, since its ultimate determinant rests on God's revelation and not on the people's legislation. To the Islamists, *shura* is superior to western democracy since it does not suffer from the shortcomings of human reason.[16] Unlike traditional jurisprudence, which worked within the consensus of the Muslim *umma* and rejected radical reform and revolution, Turabi advocates removing all restraints inherent in traditional Muslim states in pursuit of the Islamic state. For him there are no limits on revolutionizing the structure and the mentality of the *umma*. 'No limits on revolution and freedom...are imposed; thus *ijtihad* rearranges *shari'a* without any institutional regulative principle'.[17] Turabi further emphasized the need for wide-ranging *ijtihad*, stating: 'The most serious thing we have found is that most of the Islamic literature has been written centuries ago, and much of it is irrelevant today, in the field of economy, law, politics, government, etc. Therefore a great deal of *ijtihad* is required.'[18]

Turabi's justification of the use of force while propagating so-called Islamic democracy is probably tied up with his belief in the urgent need for the adaptation of Islam to modern times. Since the establishment of an Islamic state is the most urgent goal on the Islamist agenda, how it is achieved is of less importance. Therefore, the Algerian experience is rather useful as it provides an excuse for the use of force in order to achieve power and establish the Islamic state.

## Islamism and the South: Religious and Ethnic Minorities

Civil war has burdened the Sudan since independence and serves as a case in point when discussing the pros and cons of an Islamist order. Sudan is a state whose borders were artificially created in the nineteenth century by colonialist conquerors attempting to impose a unitary form of government on a population which was ethnically diverse and culturally and religiously divided. How does the Islamist movement in Sudan confront this conflict?

Throughout the nineteenth century, attempts to Islamize the non-Muslim South were pursued both under Turco-Egyptian rule and the Mahdiyya. Likewise, when Great Britain ruled the Sudan during the Anglo-Egyptian

Condominium, it introduced the so-called Southern Policy aiming to bring Christianity to the South with the active help of various missionary societies. However, neither Muslim nor Christian missionaries made significant progress and the majority of the South has remained true to its own tribal religions. Thus when independence was finally achieved in January 1956, the predominantly Christian southern political elite agreed to join their northern Muslim compatriots in a united Sudan on the mistaken assumption that it would be a secular-federal state in which they would enjoy full civil rights. North–South hostilities first erupted on the eve of independence and, apart from a period of ten years from 1973 until 1983, relations have never been peaceful.

Abel Alier, a southern lawyer and politician who was instrumental in bringing about the February 1972 Addis Ababa Agreement and later appointed as first Vice-President of the South, wrote in retrospect: 'For the first time in 73 years since the beginning of the condominium administration Southerners were responsible for their own people'.[19] It was therefore no wonder that Alier regarded the abrogation of that treaty, on 5 June 1983, as a tragedy for the Sudan and a personal rebuff. Alier lists the underlying issues that led to this disaster. He regards Numayri's reconciliation in July 1977 with the National Front (NF), which had opposed the Numayri regime since 1969, and especially with the Mahdists and the Muslim Brothers and their respective leaders as the major cause of the agreement's collapse. Both al-Sadiq al-Mahdi and Hasan al-Turabi objected to the three southern provinces being united into one political unit. They demanded an Islamic constitution for the whole Sudan under which the head of state would always be a Muslim. The Muslim Brothers promised Numayri that if he followed its advice 'he would go down as the greatest Sudanese leader in history and would regain the following of the bulk of the Northern Sudan'.[20] Unfortunately for the Sudan, Numayri did in fact follow the Islamist's advice and thus led the state directly back into civil war in 1983.

The newly founded SPLA, under the command of Dr. John Garang, a former SDF officer, also included elements from the western Sudan, especially the Nuba Mountains, and was even supported by some northern Muslim politicians such as Dr. Khalid Mansur, a former minister of foreign affairs. It demanded the abrogation of the so-called Islamic laws as a precondition for resuming the peace talks. A compromise was agreed upon, in November 1988, between Sayyid Muhammad 'Uthman al-Mirghani, the leader of the Khatmiyya sufi order and of the Democratic Unionist Party, and the SPLA. It was reluctantly adopted by al-Sadiq al-Mahdi's government, since the Khatmiyya was a senior partner within his coalition government and the compromise enjoyed both popular and military support, especially within the senior officers' corps. It might have put an end to the civil war had it not been rejected by the NIF as a betrayal of the Islamic mission. This in turn led to the 30 June 1989 coup which brought the Sudan under the present Islamist junta.

In January 1987, while in opposition to al-Sadiq al-Mahdi's government, the NIF published its 'Sudan Charter' in which it sought to define the nature of the Sudanese state under the heading 'National Unity and Diversity'.[21] In the document's introduction, the NIF states that the Sudanese are one nation 'diversified by the multiplicity of their religious and cultural affiliations'. Since most southerners are 'non-believers', they are free to choose their respective religions, practice them and educate their children in accordance with their principles. However, Muslims constitute the population's majority and therefore have: '[A] legitimate right, by virtue of their religious choice, their democratic weight and of natural justice, to practice the values and rules of their religion to their full range – in personal, familial, social or *political* affairs.' Other religions would be granted the freedom to adhere to their values 'in private, family or social matters'. However, as noted, *political* affairs are excluded.[22] The superiority of the Muslim majority is also applied to the sphere of law: 'Thus Islamic jurisprudence shall be the general source of law: It is the expression of the will of the democratic majority. It conforms to the values of all scriptural religions; its legal rules *almost correspond* to their common legal or moral teachings. It recognizes as source of law, the principles of national justice and all sound social customs.' All matters relating to family and personal status would be conducted in accordance with the person's religious affiliation, much in line with the *millet* system applied to certain non-Muslim minorities under Ottoman rule. However, in the northern (Muslim) provinces, Islamic laws including the *hudud* would be applicable to non-Muslims as well.

In the section titled 'Ethnicity and Nationhood', the charter elaborates on the ethnic and cultural diversity of the Sudan and promises to treat all elements of the population with due respect. It states: 'But ethnicity is a natural trait not deriving from human attainment and no good as a basis for discrimination between people or citizens in socio-political or legal relations'. The charter therefore implies that ethnic or tribal origins should not be allowed to interfere with the creation of a national entity. It thus proposes that the Sudan remain united under a federal system, granting the South and other regions a large measure of autonomy with 'immunity from interference by central authorities'. This would include the rights of these regions to retain a 'reasonable share' of the income from economic projects situated in them.

Finally, the NIF calls for a cease-fire in order to allow for the preparation of a National Conference: 'The conference shall determine all the issues of substance concerning the ordering of public life in the Sudan, especially its justice as to differences of religious association and cultural

identity or as to distribution of power or wealth, and shall consider any constitutional or political matter relating thereto.'[23]

Despite these seemingly liberal statements, the NIF remained adamant
in its opposition to any attempt to compromise the Sudan's Islamic order for
the sake of a settlement with the SPLA. The NIF has put forth its own version of the events that led to the June 1989 Islamist military coup. They
argue that the weak and indecisive government in Khartoum under al-Sadiq
al-Mahdi was the main cause for SPLA victories in the field and its confidence in the political arena. The SPLA, according to 'Ali al-Hajj, refused
any attempts at a negotiated settlement and between June 1985 and June
1989 rejected eleven initiatives to settle the conflict.[24]

Al-Bashir opened a new peace initiative on 3 July 1989, three days after
he assumed power, when he offered a general amnesty to all 'rebels' and
invited John Garang to join in the formation of the Revolutionary Command
Council and the Council of Ministers as part of a move towards a final
agreement. The SPLA failed to respond and instead intensified its armed
rebellion. In September 1989, a National Dialogue Conference on peace
was called by the government. Once again the SPLA refused to attend.
Nevertheless, the conference drafted resolutions which were then presented
to the 'rebels' and recognized by them as a 'good basis for negotiations'.
But the SPLA continued to shift the agenda in order to justify their rebellion which, according to al-Hajj, was no more than inter-tribal warfare with
John Garang as the main obstacle to peace.[25] In the subsequent fights which
broke out between the various groups, thousands of civilians were massa-
cred and human rights were disregarded by the southerners themselves.
Consequently, the unified movement disintegrated and it has become quite
clear that neither Garang nor the National Democratic Association, allied to
western powers, were interested in a peaceful solution. Their aim was to
topple the government, even if it meant continued war.[26]

It is within this context that we have to understand the pronouncements
of the present regime and the NIF on the Sudan's internal conflict. The June
1989 coup was, in a way, a protest against al-Sadiq al-Mahdi's willingness
to reach a compromise with the Sudan's People's Liberation Movement
(SPLM) over the issue of Islamic law.[27] This has been openly admitted by
spokesmen of the NIF who claim that since the majority of Sudanese are
Muslims they had every right, as the lawful democratic majority, to enforce
their views regarding their most important beliefs on the non-Muslim
minority. Furthermore, if the non-Muslims refused to abide by such 'democratic' decisions, there was no reason for the majority to give way and the
southerners should be allowed to secede. The NIF, as stated above, views
the Islamic state as its prime goal and hence will not compromise even if
this implies a continuation of civil war and eventual partition.

On several occasions spokesmen of the present regime have stated that the internal conflict in Sudan was fostered by western powers. In an interview broadcast on *Radio Monte Carlo* on 17 November 1993, President Bashir accused the United States of promoting the conflict under the pretext of defending human rights and the right of self-determination for the southerners, the people of the Nuba Mountains, and other neglected regions. He stated that his government had proposed a federal solution which would exclude the South from the implementation of the *shari'a* laws. He claimed however, that 'the call for self-determination and separation has never been one of the demands of the rebellion movement.... The claims we now hear are dictated to the rebellion movement by some foreign powers that do not want to see an end to this war'.[28] Sudan's foreign minister, Dr. Husayn Abu Salih, accused the United States of promoting the southern rebels to further its own interests: 'We openly declare that the United Sates intends to intervene in the south so that the situation would become similar to that in Somalia.... The US Administration's aim is to exhaust the Sudan in the south and drag it into wars and battles and then control and dominate it.'[29] Hasan al-Turabi has also claimed the war in the South has been won and there is no longer any need for outside mediation. According to Turabi, the victory was the result of the new Islamist People's Defence Forces (PDF), which had replaced 'the unreliable and unmotivated professional army'. Turabi accused the West in general and the United States in particular of meddling in the Sudan's internal affairs and promoting trouble in certain regions. He accused the West of being motivated by its hostility to Islam rather than by a commitment to peace or democracy, since it is opposed to any Islamic government even if elected democratically and capable of bringing about peace. However, no matter what the West did, Islam would succeed because 'we are believers while they are not'.[30]

It seems at present that neither the SPLA high command nor the leaders of the present regime have made up their minds with regard to the Sudan's future. As late as 1992, the SPLA was in favor of a united Sudan and most northern politicians believed in a solution which would leave the Sudan undivided. However, during the 1994 peace talks, sponsored and mediated by the four member states (Kenya, Ethiopia, Eritrea and Uganda) of the Inter-Governmental Authority on Drought and Development (IGADD), the Sudan government declared its commitment to the southerners' right to determine their future status by referendum, following an interim period. The main difference between this offer and the SPLA's demand of self-determination was the latter's insistence on including parts of the northern Sudan, such as the Nuba Mountains and other so-called 'Marginalized Regions' within those areas that would be granted the right to determine their own future. In addition, the government has refused to adopt the term 'self-determination'. It is noteworthy, however, that they seem to prefer secession to compromise over Islam.[31]

The demand to grant this right has been on the southern agenda since the Juba conference in 1947 and has been raised repeatedly since independence. But it had never before been adopted by either the southerners or the government as official policy. It is the present Islamist regime, prompted by the NIF, which has brought about this change and which may ultimately lead to a partitioning of the Sudan. To quote a prominent southern leader: 'The fact that Islam and Arab culture dominate in the corridors of power in Khartoum today does not make them acceptable options for the whole country... Even if the North was to agree to a secular and democratic state in the near future, that would not mean the abandonment of self-determination by the South.'[32] In a recent speech, Abel Alier, president of the executive council of the Southern Sudan and vice-president of Sudan under Numayri, stated that those in the North who claim that self-determination must lead to separation have only themselves to blame since they ruled the country for 40 years and had a chance to unite it:

> Those who are scared about separation today and interpret self-determination as separation...are guilty of being in the habit of imposing their own social values on others; they pay lip service to social diversities and at the same time dig in for assimilation. These are the real separatists.... They are capable of driving the aggrieved people to the wall.[33]

Hence the abrogation of the 1972 agreement, in 1983, and the radical Islamism of the present regime may already have tipped the scales in favor of partition, leading to an independent southern state. How this will affect other regions of the Sudan remains unclear though the National Democratic Alliance (NDA), which includes all the northern opposition parties as well as the SPLM, has issued a declaration in which it committed itself to the right of self-determination as the only way to preserve unity.[34] In an interview with *al-Hayat*, in December 1995, al-Sadiq al-Mahdi stated that the Sudan's future depended on a democratic regime, based on equal rights for all citizens, and on the right of self-determination for the South. 'The separation of religion and state had to be implemented to guarantee human rights to all citizens.'[35] For al-Sadiq al-Mahdi, the leader of the Mahdist Umma Party, to declare openly in a widely circulated newspaper such as *al-Hayat* that he favors the separation of religion and state would have seemed impossible in the 1980s. Whether he and other Islamist leaders, such as Muhammad 'Uthman al-Mirghani, will remain true to such declarations once the present regime is overthrown, remains to be seen.

## Islamism in Regional and International Relations

Hasan al-Turabi defined the international aims of the Islamists at a 'Round Table' held with American scholars in May 1992.[36] When asked about the future aims of Sudan's Islamic revolution, Turabi responded that the Sudan's borders were artificial and hence the revolution is easily exported. This is especially true with respect to Sudan's relations with the Black African neighboring states. Relations with non-Muslim states are predicated upon peaceful relations governed by the *shari'a*. However, in Turabi's view, just as in Sudan's domestic affairs, the West perceives the Muslim challenge to the international status quo as a threat which has to be stopped. Therefore, Turabi insisted, 'Islam will challenge those who enjoy an advantage under the present world order' since it has no other choice. Muslims, according to Turabi, insist on equality at the international level where at present they are treated unjustly.[37]

> Those who enjoy an advantage now under the present world order…will see that Islam constitutes a challenge because if it seeks justice, then it seeks to have someone concede a little bit so that we ultimately reach an equitable equation. This is not because Islam is hostile to Christianity…. The Muslims will not allow the world to be molded in one pattern, one form of democracy, one form of economic system, one form of whatever. It is in the interest of humanity that people be allowed the freedom to develop different models.[38]

Al-Turabi further expounded on this idea in an interview with Olivier Rolin for *Le Nouvel Observateur*. Quoting from a speech made by the governor of Omdurman province – 'The orientation of Islamic civilization is leading us to establish an Islamic state in Sudan and throughout the entire world' – Rolin asked Turabi whether this was not an imperialistic position. Turabi responded by stating that Islam was neither imperialistic nor nationalistic and only sought to spread its true mission peacefully wherever it could: 'Here, now, in Sudan we are in the process of establishing a model not just for the Sudanese, but for the entire world, because now humanity is one'.[39]

Al-Turabi viewed the Gulf War as a first step in this direction since it helped Islamists to turn their movements into popular mass movements, radicalizing even those in Saudi Arabia and Egypt, whose present rulers rightly feel threatened. He predicted the downfall of these regimes in the not too distant future, though he admitted that in Egypt this might take a little longer because of the regime's entrenchment. 'Yet the Egyptian government fears the Sudanese model because Islam could prove its undoing.'[40] Turabi's election to the post of Secretary-General of the Arab and Islamic People's

Congress, in April 1992, with its headquarters in Khartoum, further raised the suspicions of moderate Muslim governments. It clearly indicated Turabi's supreme position among his fellow Islamists as the spokesman of what has become known as radical 'Islamic Pan-Nationalism', Islam opposed to the status quo. Turabi attributed his election to the Gulf War which served to unite Muslims against the West and its Muslim collaborators: 'I personally owe a lot to the Gulf War, because without it I could not have organized the Popular Arab and Islamic Convention... which is essentially Islamist, and to assign the post of Secretary-General to someone like myself who is known to be an Islamist.'[41]

In an audience with the American ambassador, who warned him that the United States would react if its interests were threatened, Turabi responded that western military threats could only help the Sudan: '[H]istorically I know that a country cannot develop if there is no challenge.... The whole of the Sudan is in military training, almost a million Sudanese are already trained, and if they have to defend this territory, they will. I know there are very powerful Zionist/Christian fundamentalist lobbies in the USA, that want to crush Islam in Sudan before it can spread.'[42]

With regard to the Arab-Israeli conflict, the NIF rejected the Madrid talks when they were first started. According to Turabi, Sudan 'was the only Arab state that said no'. But in 1993 it seemed to adopt a more pragmatic point of view when it approved, though reluctantly, the Washington Accords between Israel and the PLO. Turabi explained this shift by stating that since the Islamic government in Khartoum realized that Arafat had agreed to the Madrid formula 'as an act of necessity...we should not try to be better than Yasser Arafat himself or to embarrass him'. He further stated that the official Sudanese position left the freedom of decision making to the Palestinians themselves. In February 1993, Turabi demonstrated his claim to international-Islamic leadership when he chaired the Khartoum talks between the PLO and Hamas. It was an attempt to establish a united front for interaction with Israel and the United States. Such a role would have been unthinkable for any Sudanese Muslim leader prior to the June 1989 coup and the Gulf War. Turabi demonstrated his pragmatism when he stated in an interview with *al-Sharq al-Awsat* that the Arabs should accept Security Council Resolution 242, which entails recognition of Israel within its pre-1967 borders. According to al-Turabi, this was permissible as it would not be the first time that Muslims had relinquished a section of their land, provided that Israel also withdrew from its conquered lands.[43]

How should one interpret these seemingly moderate utterances from an Islamist leader who at the same time claims not to be guided by political considerations and who on other occasions has totally rejected compromise? In his capacity as the Secretary-General of the Popular Arab and

Islamic Conference, Turabi criticized the Washington Accords without aiming the criticism against Arafat or the PLO leadership. His basis for criticism was that these accords did not lead to the establishment of two states 'but rather to the establishment of a Palestinian municipality in Gaza and Jericho'.[44] Turabi was even more outspoken when he addressed a press conference on 5 December 1993, informing the journalists about the decisions reached at the Popular Arab and Islamic Conference which had just concluded in Khartoum: 'The conference declared its total rejection of the Gaza-Jericho agreement and called on the Arab and Islamic nations not to normalize their relations with the enemy until the Palestine people restore their legitimate rights.'[45] In an interview titled 'Our Islam for the Entire Earth', published in *Le Nouvel Observateur* in August 1994, Turabi rejected the Palestinian-Israeli agreement as an act of desperation forced on Arafat. When asked whether this was a defeat, Turabi answered: 'When you are trapped, you accept any compromise whatsoever. The Arabs are unanimous in saying: No Israel. Israel is not a democratic phenomenon. It is an example of usurpation.' His response as to whether he accepted Israel's existence was: 'How can you accept that people occupy your country, drive you out and then say it is an accomplished fact? You [France] left Algeria, why? I do not question the existence of Jews, but of Israel, yes. The Jews are free to go anywhere and the Muslims accepted them when they were persecuted in Europe.'[46]

## Conclusion

Several reports, written mainly by foreign correspondents who have visited the Sudan and met with leading personalities, indicate that many within the NIF are disillusioned with the present regime and fear the repercussions of its inevitable downfall on their movement. Whereas they continue to believe in the Islamic revolution, they have realized that its performance in the Sudan leaves much to be desired. To quote one of many such reports:

> The Islamic revolution is caught in a dilemma. If it is to deliver genuine solutions it will have somehow to abandon the cynical pursuit of power.... But if, instead, in the pursuit of *ijtihad* and modern forms of justice, it returns to purer principles of Islam, it may find impossible standards there. That is the lesson of Sudan. No one has yet shown that the modern Islamist creed is an ideology suited for governing.[47]

Whereas this and other reports are based on outsiders' impressions, their volume suggests that the regime is facing increasing pressures, probably as a result of its prolonged isolation from even its closest neighbors such as Egypt, Saudi Arabia, Eritrea, Libya and Chad. Hasan al-Turabi's response to such allegations would be that the Islamic revolution cannot be judged according to a trial period of five years. Moreover, as an active participant in Sudanese politics since independence and as a critical observer of the political bunglings of Arab nationalism, Arab socialism and other so-called secular attempts, he would most likely respond to such charges by stating that, compared to the utter failure of all the ideological and political movements mentioned above, Islamism has already proved its ability to govern. To this, one could add that Turabi and his fellow Islamists throughout the Muslim world have claimed consistently that the Islamic state cannot be judged on its performance in a single territory and only after it has spread to Saudi Arabia, Algeria, Egypt and other regions will it be able to create the modern Islamic order that will become the only real challenge to the western bloc.

One may also address the question of whether the Sudan's Islamist dictatorship is indeed heading towards an Islamic state, as prophesied by Turabi, or whether the much larger neo-Mahdist movement might once again 'rise from its own ashes' as it did both after its destruction by Kitchener in 1898 and after the Aba Island massacre carried out by Numayri in March 1970. According to al-Sadiq al-Mahdi 'the scenario is the same through succeeding Kitcheners up to the latest'.[48] However, al-Sadiq al-Mahdi can hardly be viewed as an unbiased observer. Nor can there be any conclusive answer to the question posed above, since much depends on the stability of the present regime, the length of its survival in power and its consistency in following the NIF's formula for an Islamic state. If the NIF's dream comes true and the radical Islamists maintain power into the twenty-first century, then the likelihood of a smaller, divided Sudan seems a real one.

Another alternative is the replacement of the present regime either by a military coup, a civilian revolution or a combination of both. All three alternatives have occurred before in Sudan and are therefore credible. However, even if this should happen it seems unlikely that the present regime will be replaced by one advocating the separation of Islam and politics, as suggested by the opposition leaders including al-Sadiq al-Mahdi. It is one thing to preach 'secularism' while in exile and opposition; it is quite another thing to carry it out once you assume power in a state such as Sudan. Graham Thomas' suggestion that the leaders of the Khatmiyya and the Ansar should withdraw from active politics and devote themselves to their religious missions, so that a united party of the Sudan could lead the country democratically without sectarian divisions, seems as utopian today as it did when it was preached by British members of the Sudan Political Service during the Condominium.[49]

The most likely scenario seems to be the one foreseen by al-Sadiq al-Mahdi. It is based on the assumption that the Mahdists continue to constitute the single largest Islamic grouping in the Sudan and are likely to remain so for the forseeable future. Therefore, even if the Umma Party remains true to its present moderate position *vis-à-vis* the South, it seems unlikely that it will lead Sudan towards the separation of state and religion. The Islamic state envisioned by Mahdi and his supporters, prior to 1989, is likely to remain their ideal even after the present regime comes to its end.

## NOTES

1. Quoted by Graham F. Thomas, *Sudan's Struggle for Survival* (London: Darf 1993) pp.105–6. Thomas was a senior official in the Sudanese government during the 1950s and has maintained close ties with the Sudanese elite, especially al-Sayyid 'Abd al-Rahman al-Mahdi and his offspring.
2. For details, see G.R. Warburg, 'The Sharia in Sudan: Implementation and Repercussions, 1983–1989', *Middle East Journal* 44/4 (Autumn 1990) pp.624–37.
3. For a more detailed treatment of the politics and ideology of the Ansar and the Muslim Brothers, see G.R. Warburg, 'Mahdism and Islamism in Sudan', *International Journal of Middle Eastern Studies* 27 (1995) pp.219–36.
4. For a more detailed biographical treatment, see Ahmad Muhammad Shamuq (ed.), *Ma'ajim al-shakhsiyyat al-Sudaniyya al-ma'asira* (Khartoum: bayt al-thaqafa 1988) pp.41–2, 205.
5. *Ijtihad* refers to independent reinterpretations of legal theological questions in line with modern change.
6. Abdelwahab El-Affendi, *Turabi's Revolution Islam and Power in Sudan* (London: Grey Seal 1989), pp.164–6, 183–6; quotation from p.185. El-Affendi is one of the most eloquent spokesmen of the Muslim Brothers' cause and his book is the best account of the movement's history, ideology and politics. For Islamist ideology and policies in the South, see Arthur L. Lowrie, *Islam, Democracy, the State and the West, a Round Table with Dr. Hasan Turabi* (Tampa: Florida State University, May 1992).
7. Lowrie (note 6) pp.18–21.
8. Ibid., p.21. Also see Haydar Taha, *Al-Ikhwan wa'l-'Askar, qisat al-jabha al-Islamiyya wa'l-sulta fi al-Sudan* (Cairo: markaz al-hadara al-'Arabiyya li'l-i'lam wa'l-nashr 1993) pp.61–3. Thomas (note 1) p.108 writes that Turabi proudly admitted to him that the NIF had 14 cells within the army.
9. 'Inside Sudan Turabi Speaks', Interview with Muhammad al-Turabi, *Trends* 5/5 (1994). Analysis in the following passages is based on information provided in this interview.
10. Lowrie (note 6) p.26.
11. 'Al-Turabi Criticizes Islamists' Violent Methods in Algeria and Egypt', FBIS-NES-93-220, 17 Nov. – translated from *al-Hayat*, 13 Nov. 1993.
12. FBIS-NES-94-166, 26 Aug. – quoting from Olivier Rolin's interview with al-Turabi, *Le Nouvel Observateur*, 25–31 Aug. 1994.
13. W. Langewiesche, 'Turabi's Law', *The Atlantic Monthly* (Aug. 1994) p.32.
14. 'Inside Sudan Turabi Speaks' (note 9).
15. *Sudan Democratic Gazette* 54 (Nov. 1994) p.9 (hereafter SDG). *SDG* is published monthly in London by Bona Malwal, a prominent southern politician and writer who lives in exile.
16. A.S. Moussalli, 'Hasan al-Turabi's Islamist Discourse on Democracy and Shura', *Middle Eastern Studies* 30/1 (Jan. 1994) pp.57–61.
17. Ibid., p.55 – quoted from Hasan al-Turabi, *Qadaya al-huriyya wa'l-wahda wa'l-shura wa'l-dimuqratiyya* (Jedda 1987) pp.10–11.
18. 'Inside Sudan Turabi Speaks' (note 9).
19. Abel Alier, *Southern Sudan, Too Many Agreements Dishonoured* (Exeter: Ithaca Press 1990) p.89.
20. Ibid., p.237. Bona Malwal, who served at the time as minister of information and culture under Numayri, ultimately resigned in protest against this policy.

21. National Islamic Front, *Sudan Charter* (Khartoum, Jan. 1987). The following quotations are from this document.
22. Ibid., p.2; italics are mine.
23. Ibid., p.10.
24. Dr. Ali El-Hajj, 'The Problem of the Southern Sudan and the Shifting Agenda: With Whom Can We Conclude Peace?' (Paper presented to the National Committee for the Celebration of Sudan's Independence 1956–1993, London, 8–10 Jan. 1993) pp.7–9; the author, who was born in Chad and settled with his family in Darfur in 1947, presented himself as a spokesman for Darfur although no one in Darfur regarded him as such. According to *SDG* 53 (Oct. 1994) p.3, he had been involved in attempting to convince and even bribe both southerners and Darfurians to accept the Islamist agenda since 'he feels that he has arrived in the elite Arab camp because he has embraced Islamic Fundamentalism'.
25. Ali El-Hajj (note 24) pp.9–11.
26. Ibid., pp.15–19.
27. In an interview published in *al-Hayat* (Dec. 1995), quoted in *SDG* 68 (Jan. 1996), al-Sadiq al-Mahdi explained why he had failed in his commitment to abolish the Islamic Laws between 1986 and 1989: soon after the 1986 elections he learned that the DUP and the NIF had secretly agreed to oppose any abrogation of these laws and, since they held enough votes in parliament to defeat any motion calling for an abrogation, he was forced to modify his position.
28. FBIS-NES-93-221, 18 Nov., p.22 – the interview was conducted and broadcast in Arabic on *Radio Monte Carlo*, 17 Nov. 1993.
29. FBIS-NES-93-191, 1 Oct. – quoting from an interview published in *al-Sharq al-Awsat*, 1 Oct. 1993.
30. *SDG* 55 (Dec. 1994) p.8 – quoting from an interview with Turabi in *al-Wasat,* 7 Nov. 1994.
31. P.N. Kok, 'Guest Column: NIF Accepts Self-determination by Definition', *SDG* 52 (Sept. 1994) p.10. My discussion is based on this article as well as on accounts published in *SDG* from Oct. to Dec. 1994.
32. *SDG* 53 (Oct. 1994) pp.2–3.
33. *SDG* 69 (Feb. 1996) p.10.
34. 'NDA Leadership Adopts Plan for Overthrowing NIF Regime', *SDG* 69 (Feb. 1996) pp.6, 10.
35. Quoted in *SDG* 68 (Jan. 1996) p.7; *al-Hayat.*
36. Arthur Lowrie and Louis J. Cantori (eds.), 'Islam, Democracy, the State and the West', *Middle East Policy* 1/3 (1992) pp.49–61; Summary of a lecture and round-table discussion with Hasan Turabi, University of South Florida, 10 May 1992; this is an early version of the Lowrie account (note 6).
37. Ibid., pp.52–3.
38. Lowrie (note 6) pp.30–31.
39. *Le Nouvel Observateur* (note 12) p.26.
40. Lowrie and Cantori (note 36) p.57.
41. Ibid., p.56.
42. Inside Sudan Turabi Speaks' (note 9).
43. Muhammad al-Hasan Ahmad, 'Al-zahir wa'l-batin fi mawaqif jabhat Turabi', *al-Sharq al-Awsat*, 23 Jan. 1993; the author states that Turabi's position remained ambivalent and that he continued to reject negotiations with Israel.
44. Arlit Khuri, 'Al-Turabi Criticizes Islamists' Violent Methods in Algeria and Egypt', FBIS-NES-93-220, 17 Nov. – translated from *al-Hayat*, 13 Nov. 1993.
45. BBC ME/1865, 7 Dec. 1993; quoted from *Radio National Unity* (Omdurman), 5 Dec. 1993.
46. *Le Nouvel Observateur*, pp.34–5 – the following quotations are from the FBIS version (note 12).
47. Langewiesche (note 13) p.33. The reason that all such reports are published abroad, either by Sudanese opposition members or by foreigners, is obvious since under the present regime it is dangerous for Sudanese residents to air such views in public.
48. Thomas (note 1) p.131. Quoted from a private letter that Mr. Thomas received from al-Sadiq al-Mahdi on 10 March 1992. Sadiq's reference to 'Kitchener' when referring to Numayri and Bashir is far from complimentary.
49. Ibid., p.146.

# Egypt's Struggle against the Militant Islamic Groups

## ELIE PODEH

This study deals with the militant Islamic challenge to the Egyptian regime during the early 1990s. The article analyzes the militant Islamic groups' modes of operation and the regime's counter-measures. This analysis leads to the conclusion that although the Islamic groups are a major source of instability in Egypt, their ability to overthrow the government and to establish an Islamic order is doubtful. The militant Islamic groups would be able to pose a viable alternative to the regime only if they could overcome the disputes among themselves, broaden their socioeconomic infrastructure, penetrate the army and find a charismatic leader capable of attracting and leading the masses.

## Historical Background

In the summer of 1983, Egyptian Interior Minister Hasan Abu Basha suggested that 'the phenomenon of radical religious groups is gradually disappearing'.[1] His statement followed the execution of President Anwar al-Sadat's assassins, members of an Islamic militant group called al-Jihad. Twelve years later, in June 1995, during a visit to Ethiopia, President Husni Mubarak barely escaped an assassination attempt, presumably carried out by one of the Egyptian militant Islamic groups.[2] This episode clearly demonstrated that these groups still pose a serious threat to the stability and legitimacy of the regime.

The Islamic movement in Egypt has been the subject of numerous studies.[3] The abundance of such efforts, concentrating on the historical and sociological dimensions of the Islamic movement, were primarily motivated by Egypt's political and cultural centrality in the Arab and Muslim worlds.[4] This article attempts to shed new light on the confrontation between the regime and the Islamic militant movement during the early 1990s by focusing on the latter's modes of operation and on the regime's counter-measures.

The main argument of this article is that although the militant Islamic groups are still a major source of instability in Egypt, their ability to overthrow the government and to establish an Islamic order based on the *shari'a* is very much in doubt. Moreover, several drastic measures taken by the regime against these groups during recent years (1993–95) served to undermine their infrastructures.[5] Consequently, the threat to the regime may arise from a different front: the veteran Muslim Brotherhood (al-Ikhwan al-

Muslimin), a grass-roots movement which has advocated a non-violent struggle against the regime and has therefore attracted many followers in Egypt. This last point however, is not the focus of this chapter, as it requires a separate study.[6]

John Esposito suggested three causes for the regional resurgence of Islam. First, secular nationalism has failed to provide a common identity or a strong base of legitimacy for the secular regimes in light of the residual effects of European colonialism, continued dependence on the West and the disastrous results of the 1967 War – which crippled the Arab nationalist movement. Second, many states inadequately responded to their respective societies; they failed to achieve economic self-sufficiency or to slow the rapidly widening gap between the haves and have-nots. And third, the 1973 October War and the accompanying oil embargo created a new-found sense of pride and power. Thus, the inability of the secular Arab leaders to respond to these extreme psycho-social developments fostered the development of a 'third way', an Islamic option distinct from capitalism or communism.[7] Ansari and Auda furthered the sociological analysis of the Islamic resurgence by noting that it was a consequence of 'the breakdown of traditional solidarities and communal ties under the impact of urbanization or rural migration into the cities'.[8]

In general, the Egyptian model coincides with these analyses: the legacy of British colonial rule; excessive dependence, first on the Soviet Union, and subsequently on the United States; harsh economic and social realities, a product of both 'Abd al-Nasir's nationalization and Sadat's 'open door' policies; the former's humiliating defeat in 1967 and the ideological vacuum that was created with the receding influence of pan-Arabism. Taken together, these developments have served as a catalyst for the rise of Islam in Egypt since the late 1960s.

The most significant Islamic group in modern Egypt, the Muslim Brotherhood, was founded by Hasan al-Bana in 1928.[9] The suppression of this movement by 'Abd al-Nasir in the mid-1950s (following its attempt to assassinate him) left an ideological vacuum that was filled by Sayyid Qutb, whose writings attracted many young followers during the 1960s. In his famous booklet *Ma'alim fi al-Tariq* (Milestones), Qutb called for the overthrow of the 'infidel' 'Abd al-Nasir's regime and for the formation of an Islamic state based on the *shari'a*.[10] His militant ideology, which found a receptive ear among the Egyptian dispossessed, led to his execution in 1966. Nevertheless, Qutb's ideology remained a powerful force, serving as a guide for many devoted Muslims. It also filled the ideological vacuum that resulted from the decline of 'Abd al-Nasir's pan-Arabism and the difficulties associated with Egypt's harsh economic reality; many Egyptians adopted Qutb's violent prescription for remedying the society. By 1981, the proliferation of militant Islamic groups attested to the gravity of the challenge facing the regime.

Al-Jihad, one of these militant Islamic groups, clearly demonstrated the severity of the Islamic threat when they assassinated President Sadat in October 1981. However, the Islamic movement was not in a position to seize power and, apart from a short-lived rebellion in Asyut, the transfer of authority to the vice-president, Husni Mubarak, went smoothly. With the arrest of many militant activists, the government succeeded in subduing the internal opposition.

The harsh steps against the militants were successful for only a short period. After a relative lull of three years, the Islamic militant groups reorganized according to a three-stage process. The first (1984–87) witnessed a new wave of Islamic assertiveness and scattered, small-scale violence, although it was easily quelled by Egypt's security forces. The second (May 1987–June 1992) involved an escalation of violent Islamist activity. It was sparked by the radical al-Jama'a al-Islamiyya's failed assassination attempt against Interior Minister Abu Basha. This activity was directed mainly at Christian Copts and at public figures, and clashes between the security forces and the Islamic groups spread from their strongholds in Upper Egypt to the slums of Cairo. Despite the harsh methods instituted by two successive interior ministers, Zaki Badr and 'Abd al-Halim Musa, the religiously inspired strife did not significantly subside. The third, current, phase commenced in June 1992, with the assassination of liberal writer Faraj Fuda and sporadic terrorist attacks on tourists in Upper Egypt. These were followed by a series of terrorist incidents in October that led, *inter alia*, to the death of a British tourist, signaling the beginning of an all-out confrontation between the government and the Islamic radical opposition. The death toll resulting from political violence during the years 1991–1994 is estimated at 571 with many more injured.[11]

## Mapping the Islamic Groups

Surveying the Islamic groups in Egypt is difficult due to their avowed secrecy and the government's deliberate attempt to downplay their importance. Nonetheless, the main lines of their activities can be discerned. An in-depth report in the Egyptian weekly, *Sabah al-Khayr*, suggested a division based on ideological and organizational trends: the **salafi** – al-Ikhwan al-Muslimin or the Muslim Brotherhood; **jihadi** – al-Jama'a al-Islamiyya and al-Jihad groups; and **takfiri** – the veteran al-Takfir wa al-Hijra; al-Tawaqquf wal-Tabayyun or al-Najun min al-Nar; al-Shawqiyyun and al-Najun min al-Nasr groups.[12]

They all share the goal of establishing a new social and political order based on Islam, although they differ on how this goal should be realized. Their target is to counter what they refer to as 'Westoxication'.[13] The Muslim Brotherhood, usually classified as a 'moderate' or 'conservative' Islamic movement, pointedly objects to the use of violence against the regime or the people. It believes in gradual, peaceful change inasmuch as violence is prohibited by the *shari'a*.[14] By contrast, the jihadi and takfiri groups, considered to be 'radical' militants, advocate armed struggle against the 'secular' regime by invoking the concepts of *jahiliyya* (pre-Islamic idolatrous society), *al-hakimiyya* (God's sovereignty), and *al-takfir* (branding with atheism).[15] The takfiri groups are the most extreme, regarding the whole of Egyptian society as 'infidel' (*kafir*), and therefore completely disengaging themselves from it. These ideological positions have had an important bearing on the scope of the violence employed by each faction. While the jihadi groups aim at targets associated with the regime and at foreigners, the takfiri groups make no distinction between the regime and the ordinary population. Despite important differences between the Muslim Brotherhood and the militant Islamic groups, the two sides reportedly have an implicit agreement 'not to exchange verbal abuse'.[16]

Many members of the jihadi and takfiri groups share similar backgrounds. These organizations normally recruit urban-based, young individuals from the lower-middle class and from the margins of society – the unemployed, poor and uneducated. The make-up of these organizations also includes unemployed university graduates, usually of technical and scientific education. Some are former members of the Muslim Brotherhood, have served time in prison or have an inclination toward clandestine activity. Many activists come from Upper Egypt, a region that has experienced social unrest as a result of rapid urbanization. The members of these groups are imbued, in Dekmejian's words, with 'deep conviction, sense of mission, and readiness for martyrdom'.[17]

Structural differences exist between the takfiri and the jihadi groups. Membership in the takfiri groups is insulated from society and provides a total environment of activity under the leadership of a single, frequently charismatic leader. Decision making and implementation in the jihadi groups, though, is more flexible due to the fact that the organization is headed by a collective leadership in which local leaders (*amirs*) enjoy a relatively wide latitude. This informal and uncentralized nature of the organization has enabled the jihadi groups to survive massive government crackdowns.[18]

The two most important jihadi groups, al-Jihad and al-Jama'a, share a similar ideology, and their pattern of activity appears to be similar as well. Historically, the Jama'a has dominated the fundamentalist scene ever since Sadat's assassination and al-Jihad's almost complete elimination by the regime. However, 1993 saw the reemergence of the latter as a viable force rivaling the Jama'a. Egyptian security forces arrested hundreds of dissidents accused of 'reorganizing the Jihad group', a revival attributed to two well-known leaders: 'Abbud al-Zumur (in Egyptian prison) and Ayman al-Zawahiri (who lived in Afghanistan before moving to Geneva). The new Jihad faction, or Tala'i al-Fath (Vanguards of Conquest) as it came to be known, was responsible for attempts on the lives of the interior minister and the prime minister during 1993.[19]

## Modes of Operation

Although the activity of the Muslim Brotherhood was largely overshadowed by the more militant groups, it nevertheless posed a serious challenge to the regime. This threat emanates from several sources; first, the Brotherhood is a grass-roots organization enjoying mass support among the less privileged and the less educated. The Brotherhood has exhibited its organizational capacity in building private schools, day-cares, clinics, and by offering immediate help in times of crisis (e.g., during the earthquake in Cairo in October 1992 and the severe flooding in Upper Egypt in November 1994). In addition, Islamic charitable organizations (the *jami'yyat khayriyya*), often associated with the Brotherhood, have helped to promote economic and social development in local communities. Second, the Brotherhood has skillfully transmitted its message through the media (TV, radio and newspapers) and mosques. Third, in the 1980s the Brotherhood succeeded in sending representatives to parliament by creating electoral alliances with various secular parties like the Wafd Party, the Liberal Party and the Socialist Labor Party. Finally, by the end of 1992, the Brotherhood managed to take control of most of the professional unions.[20] In such a way, it managed to establish for itself a unique place in Egyptian politics – within the system, although officially banned by it.

The activities of the Muslim Brotherhood in Egypt have largely coincided with Esposito's description of the 'quiet revolution' that has been taking place in Islamic countries in recent years. 'While a rejectionist minority had sought to impose change from above through holy wars', he claims, 'many others reaffirmed their faith and pursued a bottom-up approach, seeking a gradual Islamization of society through words, preaching, and social and political activity'.[21]

In contrast to the Muslim Brotherhood, efforts of the Islamic militants to undermine the regime have taken place along four major tracks. First, since June 1992, the Islamic militants have initiated attacks against tourists and tourist sites to cripple the economy and transmit abroad an image of Egyptian instability and insecurity. As a result, tourism revenues fell to $1.3 billion in 1993, a decline of 27 per cent in comparison to 1992. Tourist arrivals fell by 21 per cent and hotel occupancy fell by 31 per cent.[22] As the government had expectations that tourist revenues would reach $4 billion in the 1992–93 period, the impact of the loss was much greater than the figure of 27 per cent implies.[23]

Since October 1992, 21 attacks were reportedly carried out against foreign tourists, mainly by the Jama‘a, in which seven were killed and 53 wounded.[24] In early January 1993, Islamic militants issued a warning that tourists and foreigners 'must leave the country because we fear they could be killed in the conflict between us and the secular regime'.[25] The threats were inspired by Shaykh 'Umar 'Abd al-Rahman, the spiritual leader of the Islamic radical movement (residing in New Jersey), who advocated the use of violence against tourists.[26] The most serious incident occurred in late February 1993, when a homemade bomb exploded in a cafe near Tahrir Square, in the center of Cairo, killing three foreigners and injuring 18 people; the attack was later attributed to the reorganized Jihad group.[27] This incident was seen by the government as a turning point in the conflict with the Islamic militants, inviting a radical new response. Although the government invested great efforts in safeguarding tourism, Mubarak admitted that 'no country in the world can guarantee the safety of its visitors 100 per cent of the time'.[28]

The second track of action has focused on regime symbols – security officers and military judges. Mounted primarily by the Jama‘a, these were aimed at exposing the ineffectiveness and vulnerability of the Egyptian security forces. Policemen and security officials were repeatedly targeted for assassination attempts, especially in Upper Egypt. Military judges were also targeted, in revenge for death sentences issued against militants. In July 1993, for example, the Jama‘a launched 'a retaliatory attack' against the chairman of the military courts, who had handed down 13 death sentences. While he escaped unhurt, four security men were killed and six were wounded.[29]

The third track has consisted of attempts to assassinate public figures, either politicians associated with the establishment or intellectuals associated with secular-liberal ideas. Apart from assassinating Sadat, Islamic groups kidnapped and killed Shaykh Muhammad Husayn al-Dhahabi, former minister of Awqaf, in 1977; they also assassinated Assembly Speaker Rif'at al-Mahjub in 1990, and, as previously stated, Faraj Fuda in 1992. During 1993, three assassinations were attempted, unsuccessfully, by the Jama‘a or al-Jihad against information minister Safwat al-Sharif, newly appointed interior minister Hasan al-Alfi (both were slightly injured) and the veteran Prime Minister 'Atif Sidqi. The attack against Alfi was particularly alarming, for, although it failed, it was carried out in central Cairo, in broad daylight, thus demonstrating meticulous planning and training. In October 1994, on the sixth anniversary of his reception of the Nobel Prize for literature, the renowned novelist Naguib Mahfouz was stabbed.[30] The media has also served as a tool in the hands of the militants, who have used it as a means to declare their intention to assassinate Mubarak either in Egypt or during his visits abroad.[31] This step was apparently sanctioned by 'Abd al-Rahman who articulated the wish that Mubarak meet the same fate as his predecessor.[32] As formerly mentioned, the attempt on Mubarak's life, carried out in June 1995, was unsuccessful.

The fourth track has involved assaults against secular cultural targets. Since 1986, the Jama'a has attempted to hit 'sinful and corrupted' targets such as night clubs, bars, cinemas, video shops and taverns. The most serious of these incidents occurred on 9 December 1993, when gunmen opened fire inside a cinema in the Cairo suburb of Hilwan, killing a policeman and injuring seven civilians. The theater was targeted because it was showing uncensored films as part of the Cairo International Film Festival.[33]

When carrying out their terrorist operations, the Jama'a and Jihad groups were usually careful to not hurt innocent Egyptian citizens. However, a series of terrorist acts in central Cairo (May–June 1993), ended with the killing and injuring of innocent passers-by.[34] The two groups denied any involvement, fearing damage to their standings. Presumably, these were carried out by members of a small splinter groups of the takfiri branch, who view all of Egyptian society as a legitimate target.[35]

## The Regime's Response

Confronting the Islamic challenge became the government's first priority in the 1990s. President Mubarak made it clear that his primary objective was to safeguard Egypt's stability and the security of its people, promising a 'comprehensive and all-out confrontation' with the terrorists.[36] In speeches and interviews, however, Mubarak attempted to moderate the impression that Egypt had been harmed by terrorism. Moreover, he consistently disassociated terrorism from Islam so as not to alienate true believers, portraying the terrorists as criminals.[37] In his view, Islam played no role in these groups, inasmuch as they were made up of 'killers and professional criminals'.[38] Mubarak frequently described terrorism as a worldwide phenomenon, with Egyptian terrorism as one of its offshoots. He also denied that economic and social strains fostered extremism, claiming that it was Iran and Sudan which were responsible for financing and training terrorist groups.[39] Mubarak, however, was well aware that domestic problems contributed to the Islamic resurgence. He also realized that the Islamic movement was not monolithic, but was composed of competing groups. This awareness led his regime to adopt a combination of military, political and socioeconomic measures in an effort to contain the various modes of Islamic activity.

## Military Measures

The regime has used large-scale force to suppress the Islamic movement. The security forces initiated massive crackdowns on militants (estimated at over 20,000 in 1992–93[40]) in their strongholds in Upper Egypt and in Cairo's poorer neighborhoods. Additionally, they provoked clashes which resulted in heavy casualties on both sides. One such police raid led to the killing of Tala't Yasin Hammam, a leading military commander of the Jama'a, in April 1994.[41]

As the legal process in the civilian courts was protracted and sentencing, on the whole, relatively lenient, Mubarak issued a decree transferring the trials to the 'fast-track' military courts, in accordance with the Anti-Terrorism Law approved in July 1992.[42] In response to appeals by the opposition against this step, both the Constitutional Court and the Higher Administrative Court ruled that the president was entitled to refer any crime to the military judiciary system under the existing Emergency Law.[43] As expected, the military courts sped up the process and issued harsh sentences: 58 Islamic militants were sentenced to death in cases of murder and terrorism committed against political figures, policemen, Copts and foreign tourists. Between June 1993 and January 1995, 41 of the condemned were executed, the largest number of executions in modern Egyptian history.[44]

The increased use of the death penalty, however, did not improve the situation and in certain cases it even exacerbated the tension, as comrades of the condemned attempted to avenge the courts' decisions. The Jama'a explicitly warned Mubarak that he was 'digging his own grave' by executing Islamic militants.[45] Nevertheless, when a civilian court cleared 24 Muslim militants of murder charges in connection with the assassination of Rif'at al-Mahjub, the government was further convinced that the military courts constituted the preferable vehicle for dealing with Islamic militants. This verdict led the government to rely solely on the military courts and to abandon pursuing the processes through the civilian courts.[46]

The regime has relied heavily on the security forces to suppress the Islamic militants, but the Egyptian army has remained its major pillar against the militants. This was manifested in October 1993, when the defense minister declared that the army was prepared to participate in the fight against the Islamic groups: 'the armed forces are the last line of defense [and] cannot remain idle in the face of threats that may harm [the country]'.[47]

## Political Measures

Prime Minister 'Atif Sidqi's government has adopted a mixture of legal, administrative and propaganda measures intended to erode the extremists' power bases. It continued to refuse to allow the formation of parties with explicitly religious orientation. The Muslim Brotherhood, for example, though tolerated, was still officially banned. Given the Brotherhood's widespread appeal among the masses, the regime opted instead for a 'tacit alliance' with it, on the one hand, while continuing to contain its religious attraction, on the other.[48]

The regime attempted to undermine the Brotherhood's appeal by various means: (a) the High Committee for Islamic *Da'wa,* presided over by the Grand Shaykh of al-Azhar, was established in February 1983 to promote *da'wa*: the act of persuading the Muslim to abide by the tenets of Islamic law and apply them in everyday life;[49] (b) the government upgraded the ministry of Awqaf's personnel and resources; (c) the Higher Council for Islamic Affairs, established in 1960 to propagate the state ideology, was reactivated;[50] and (d) since 1985 the government has 'nationalized' private mosques. Of the approximately 170,000 mosques, only some 30,000 were administered by the ministry of Awqaf. The rest were privately run, serving local, often extremist, preachers who turned the mosques into power bases.[51] In March 1993, Mubarak repeated his call for bringing all mosques under the jurisdiction of the ministry of Awqaf and for turning them into 'collective institutions'.[52] The government did not fully implement its plan as it did not have enough state preachers to serve in the mosques.

Another measure for containing religious appeal was to tighten control over the dissemination of religious messages. The interior ministry disrupted the militants' information and communication networks by seizing unauthorized audio and video tapes issued by radical Islamic leaders and closing down distribution centers and private radio stations.[53]

In addition, the government concluded that Islamic extremists had infiltrated various state-run educational and information bodies and were using them to disseminate the Islamist message. Several steps were taken to confront this so-called 'educational terror'. First, 'preventive measures' were taken against the penetration of Islamist curricula and Islamist cassettes into schools, colleges and universities.[54] Second, the Federation of Radio and Television (FTR) abolished the popular talk show *al-Qur'an al-Karim* (the Holy Koran), because it had become a podium for radical Islam. The FTR also decided that only representatives of al-Azhar University and the ministry of Awqaf would be invited to participate in programs on Islamic culture.[55] Third, the ministry of information set up 55 information centers throughout the country to 'explain the dangers of [the] militants' thinking and [their] violence'.[56] Fourth, all press interviews with extremists were banned.[57] And, finally, the education minister stated that he would not let Egypt's schools become a 'well of extremism and terrorism', and issued a directive forbidding children under 11 to wear the veil, and thereafter only with parental approval.[58]

The People's Assembly also took several legal steps to curb Islamic activity. In April 1994, it extended the Emergency Law (initially decreed after Sadat's assassination) for three more years; it also passed the Anti-Terrorism Law, as mentioned above, to give more leeway to the authorities in dealing with the militants; in February 1993, it legislated the Professional Syndicate Law to weaken the power base of the Muslim Brotherhood, which by the early 1990s had taken over the key syndicates of the engineers, lawyers, dentists, physicians, pharmacists and merchants;[59] in October 1993, it amended the Journalists Syndicate Law, enabling the government to tighten its control over the media;[60] and in March 1994, it attempted to sponsor legislation curbing the influence of village mayors, giving the government more control over the election of local leaders.[61]

In addition, the ministry of interior and the police underwent a reshuffling, a rather routine measure in times of domestic unrest. In April 1993, 'Abd al-Halim Musa, who had served as minister of the interior since January 1990, was replaced by Hasan al-Alfi, hitherto the governor of Asyut.[62] Alfi's appointment reconfirmed that 'the road to the interior ministry job passed through Asyut' as both Musa and his predecessor, Zaki Badr, were also previous governors of Asyut. Apparently the experience acquired there in dealing with Islamic activists became a prerequisite for any interior minister.[63] The official reason given for Musa's dismissal was his decision to initiate a dialogue with the imprisoned Islamic militants, a decision made without consulting the president.[64] However, he was probably dismissed because he did not have a clear strategy against the radical Islamists. Alfi, the new minister, promptly reshuffled the police command and prepared a new plan to revitalize the police service. He also replaced nine governors, including those of the key provinces of Fayyum, Asyut and Giza.[65]

The government attempted to encourage prominent religious and political figures to openly condemn the Islamic militants, in the hope of creating a broad national-religious front to demonstrate that the militants represented a small minority. The most outspoken religious authority to criticize Islamic terrorism was the widely respected Mufti, Sayyid Tantawi.[66] In contrast, the grand shaykh of al-Azhar, 'Ali Jadd al-Haqq, maintained an ambiguous position; while he refused to term the incidents in Upper Egypt 'terrorism', he approved death sentences for Islamic militants.[67]

The government also attempted to recruit the opposition in its effort to form a national front against Islamic terrorism. At the initiative of the ruling

National Democratic Party (NDP), a declaration against terrorism and violence was drawn up and signed by several opposition parties in late March 1993.[68] In September, Mubarak proposed holding a 'broad national dialogue' involving 'all political parties and forces which adhere to democracy and reject violence and terrorism'.[69] He envisaged that such a dialogue would demonstrate the existence of a national consensus opposing Islamic terrorism and the regime's commitment to further democratization. In December, all the opposition parties and forces signed a petition accepting Mubarak's proposal for an 'open dialogue'.[70] However, the initiative was boycotted by the leading legal opposition party, the Wafd, and without the participation of the Muslim Brotherhood ended in July 1994 with no concrete results.[71]

The government acted to confront Islamic threats from abroad as well. A large number of Egyptian militants were trained as fighters during the Afghan War, possibly with the support of Iran and Sudan. At the end of the war, an estimated 800 such veterans returned to Egypt, making a decisive contribution to the local militant movement, while many others remained in the centers of radical Islam in Kabul and Peshawar, including Jihad leaders Muhammad Shawqi al-Islambuli and Ayman al-Zawahiri.[72] Seeking to remove this threat, Mubarak met the Pakistani Prime Minister, Nawaz Sharif, in Germany in March 1993 and requested that he expel a number of Egyptian extremists.[73] Restricting Islamic activity was also the main topic of a November meeting in Cairo between Mubarak and his Afghan counterpart, President Borhanoddin Rabbani.[74] In May 1993, Mubarak also decided to restrict telephone links with Muslim states that were allegedly sponsors of terrorism: Sudan, Pakistan, Afghanistan, Iran and Iraq.[75]

Within the Arab orbit, Mubarak tackled the terrorist problem in two ways: he attempted to coordinate policies with fellow Arab leaders facing the same threat and he tried to convince the oil-rich countries to help finance his confrontation against the common Islamist danger posed by Iran and Sudan. During 1993, for example, Mubarak met with the Algerian, Tunisian and Libyan heads of state with the aim of gaining their cooperation in combating Islamic terrorism.[76] An accord ensuring cooperation against terrorism was signed with Tunisia and travel restrictions were imposed on the Egyptian-Libyan border.[77] Mubarak also toured the Gulf states. Although he failed to obtain financial support, he apparently had some success in convincing Gulf leaders to desist in funding the militants.[78]

## Socioeconomic Measures

While Mubarak publicly denied any connection between the socioeconomic situation and the rising tide of Islam, he was aware that it was necessary to allocate more resources to problems which were believed to nurture Islamic terrorism: population explosion, illiteracy, widespread unemployment and a shortage of housing. Of the four, Mubarak considered rapid population growth to be Egypt's 'most serious future problem'. The country's population, estimated at 60 million, was expected to reach 70 million by the year 2000 and 91 million by the year 2013.[79] While the rate of demographic increase reportedly dropped from 2.7 per cent (1985-86) to 2.1 per cent (1992–93), the National Population Council's goal for the years 1992–2007 was to attain an average increase rate of 1.9 per cent or less, so that the population would not exceed 66 million by the year 2000.[80] The importance of this issue was reflected in the establishment of a Ministry for Population and Family Affairs in October 1993 and in the hosting of the UN International Conference on Population and Development in Cairo in September 1994.[81]

Education, unemployment and housing were also targeted as major national priorities. The number of adult illiterates, according to official sources, was 17.9 million,[82] and the government aimed to reduce this figure. The Ministry of Education was reportedly allotted LE6 billion in the annual budget of 1993, its largest allocation ever. During the course of the year, 1,500 new schools were built as part of a five year program to build 7,500 schools. Mubarak claimed that an integrated plan was drawn up to reform the educational system, embracing more schools, more teaching staff and better curricula. He also asked his newly appointed government to work on an education master-plan for the year 2000.[83]

Another priority was the creation of job opportunities for high school and university graduates as well as for unskilled workers. By 1993, unemployment reached 17 per cent, according to official figures, and over 20 per cent, by opposition and other estimates. A partial official census revealed the existence of 1.4 million unemployed university graduates alone.[84] The government's current five-year plan (1992/93–1996/97) includes the creation of 400,000 new jobs annually, mainly in the private sector.[85] In Asyut alone, the hotbed of Islamic militancy, the government created 30,000 jobs between 1992 and 1994.[86]

Another ambitious national project was the renovation or, alternatively, the demolition of shantytowns, euphemistically called 'randomly built areas' (*al-manatiq al-'ashwa'iyya*). Residents of demolished areas were to be offered alternative accommodations in newly established urban centers. This plan was intended to alleviate the problem of population density in the major cities and to eliminate a major cause of social unrest. The plan, launched in April 1993, involved 430 slums in Cairo, Alexandria, Giza, Port Sa'id, Suez, Qalyubiyya and Upper Egypt.[87] The high priority which Mubarak attached to this plan was indicated by the establishment of a

Ministry for New Urban Communities in October 1993. The president also promised incentives to Egyptian investors willing to finance development projects in the new urban centers, industrial areas or remote regions.[88]

Egypt's social programs were closely connected with economic reform. In May 1991, Egypt's economic system entered a new phase when the government signed an agreement with the IMF and the World Bank for debt rescheduling and the restructuring of the Egyptian economy. According to this agreement, the Paris Club, the consortium of creditor countries to which Egypt owed 90 per cent of its foreign debt, decided to reduce Egypt's outstanding debt by 50 per cent: 15 per cent was to be waived in July 1991, another 15 per cent in January 1993, and the remaining 20 per cent in July 1994. The rest of the debt was to be paid over a period of 25–30 years. As a result, Egypt's foreign debt was reduced from $50 billion in 1990 to $26 billion in 1994.[89] In return, Egypt was obliged to initiate a series of fiscal and structural changes in its economy, namely, reduce its budget deficit, liberalize exchange and interests rates, cut subsidies, lower customs tariffs, liberalize prices, introduce a new sales tax and encourage privatization, particularly by selling the companies of the public sector. Several of the measures adopted by the government brought about substantial economic improvement: the budget deficit dropped from 20 per cent of the Gross Domestic Product (GDP) in 1990 to 3 per cent in 1993. During the same period, inflation fell from 25 per cent to less than 10 per cent; interest rates rose above the inflation rate to over 15 per cent; the Egyptian pound held its value at about LE3.32 to the dollar; foreign currency reserves rose from $2.7 billion to $12 billion; and the balance of payments edged into a modest surplus for the first time in many years.[90] However, as a result of grave difficulties in privatizing the economy, the deadline for the third phase of the program was put off to December 1994, a deadline that the government also failed to meet.[91]

Although it seems that the economic measures were successful on the macro level, they adversely affected the lower-middle class.[92] The Mubarak regime was not oblivious to these difficulties and it therefore decided to slow the pace of privatization. Thus, although the socioeconomic measures did not alleviate the hardships of the lower-middle class in the short run, the regime hoped that their successful completion would improve the conditions of the less privileged and reduce the phenomenon of Islamic terrorism in the long run.

## Conclusion

'Abd al-Nasir's defeat in 1967 and Egypt's suspension from the Arab League in 1979 were two of the gravest challenges that Egyptian governments have had to face during the last 30 years. It was Sadat who succeeded in undoing the 'shame of defeat' by launching the 1973 War and it was Mubarak who succeeded in steering Egypt back to the center of the Arab world. In contrast to these external challenges, the Islamic threat is primarily a domestic problem – and one that calls into question the very legitimacy of the regime. Unlike in the past, achievements on the foreign front are no longer the panacea for deflecting public attention from economic and social realities. Attempting to break the vicious circle by which social and economic distress nourishes radical Islam, Mubarak adopted a combination of military, political and socioeconomic measures in order to alleviate the situation. Assessing these reforms from our narrow historical perspective, it would seem that they were partially successful as by 1995 the intensity of the violence had considerably lessened. Yet, it is still premature to estimate whether these measures will prove effective in containing the Islamic upsurge in the long run.

The Islamic groups have already demonstrated their capability to shake Egypt's stability. Their methods and their manpower resources allow them to attempt almost any operation they wish, the assassination of Sadat and the attempt on Mubarak's life serving as the ultimate examples. Nonetheless, their capacity to take over the state is doubtful, at least in the near future. This assessment is based on several assumptions: first, these groups lack an infrastructure strong enough to stay in power. Second, as long as the regime maintains the loyalty of the army and the security services – its principal pillars of support – the position of the radical Islamic groups will be tenuous at best. Third, the entire political system, including the banned Muslim Brotherhood, reject and condemn terrorism in principle. Moreover, the Egyptian people themselves appear to view with concern and anger the acts of violence which often hurt innocent bystanders.

The radical Islamic groups can, therefore, pose a viable alternative to the present regime only if they overcome the disputes among themselves, broaden their economic and social infrastructure, penetrate the army, and find a charismatic leader capable of attracting and leading the masses. Only then would the Islamic militant groups be able to exploit Egypt's ongoing social, economic and political disequilibrium.[93] In light of this evaluation, perhaps Esposito's general description of a 'quiet revolution' that has been taking place beneath the radical facade of the extremist groups,[94] is the real danger for the Egyptian regime. Fouad Ajami once observed that in Egypt 'revolutions either do not happen or, when they do, they are turned into familiar and harmless things'.[95] It remains to be seen if these words will hold true for this revolution, if it will indeed become a 'familiar and harmless thing'.

NOTES

1. Ami Ayalon, 'Egypt', in Legum, Shaked and Dishon (eds.), *Middle East Contemporary Survey* 7 (1982–83) (NY: Holmes & Meier 1984) p.425.
2. *Ha'aretz*, 5 July 1995.
3. See, for example: Morroe Berger, *Islam in Egypt Today: Social and Political Aspects of Popular Religion* (Cambridge: CUP 1970); I. Altman, 'Islamic Movements in Egypt', *Jerusalem Quarterly* 10 (Winter 1979) pp.87–108; R.S. Humphreys, 'Islam and Political Values in Saudi Arabia, Egypt and Syria', *Middle East Journal* 33/1 (Winter 1979) pp.1–19; R.H. Dekmejian, 'The Anatomy of Islamic Revival and the Search for Islamic Alternatives', *Middle East Jnl* 34/1 (Winter 1980) pp.1–12; Daniel Crecelius, 'The Course of Secularization in Modern Egypt', in John L. Esposito (ed.), *Islam and Development: Religion and Sociopolitical Change* (Syracuse: SUP 1980) pp.49–70; Saad Eddin Ibrahim, 'Islamic Militancy as a Social Movement: The Case of Two Groups in Egypt', in Ali E. Hillal Dessouki (ed.), *Islamic Resurgence in the Arab World* (NY: Praeger 1982) pp.117–37; F. Ajami, 'In the Pharaoh's Shadow: Religion and Authority in Egypt', James P. Piscatori (ed.), *Islam in the Political Process* (Cambridge: CUP 1983) pp.12–35; Ahmed Gomaa, 'Islamic Fundamentalism in Egypt During the 1930s and 1970s: Comparative Notes', in Gerald Warburg and Uri Kupferschmidt (eds.), *Nationalism and Radicalism in Egypt and the Sudan* (NY: Praeger 1983) pp.143–58; H. Ansari, 'Sectarian Conflict in Egypt and the Political Expediency of Religion', *Middle East Jnl* 38/3 (Summer 1984) pp.397–418; idem., 'The Islamic Militants in Egyptian Politics', *International Jnl of Middle Eastern Studies* 16 (1984) pp.123–44; Gilles Kepel, *The Prophet and Pharaoh: Muslim Extremism in Egypt* (London: Al Saqi Books 1985); M. Sid-Ahmed, 'Egypt: The Islamic Issue', *Foreign Policy* 69 (Winter 1987–88) pp.22–39; E. Sivan, 'The Islamic Republic of Egypt', *Orbis* 31/1 (Spring 1987) pp.43–54; U. Kuperschmidt, 'Reformist and Militant Islam in Urban and Rural Egypt', *Middle Eastern Studies* 23 (Oct. 1987); S.E. Ibrahim, 'Egypt's Islamic Activism in the 1980s', *Third World Quarterly* 10 (1988) pp.632–57; A. Sonbol, 'Egypt', in Shireen T. Hunter (ed.), *The Politics of Islamic Revivalism* (Bloomington: Indiana UP 1988); Barry Rubin, *Islamic Fundamentalism in Egyptian Politics* (London: Macmillan 1990); Gehad Auda, 'An Uncertain Response: The Islamic Movement in Egypt', in Piscatori (ed.), *Islamic Fundamentalisms and the Gulf Crisis* (Chicago: The Fundamentalism Project of the American Academy of the Arts and Sciences 1991) pp.109–30; J. Voll, 'Fundamentalism in the Sunni Arab World: Egypt and the Sudan', in Martin E. Marty and R. Scott Appelby (eds.), *Fundamentalism Observed* (Chicago: U. of Chicago Press 1991) pp.345–402; S. Reed, 'The Battle for Egypt', *Foreign Affairs* 72/4 (Sept.–Oct. 1993) pp.94–107; M.C. Dunn, 'Fundamentalism in Egypt', *Middle East Policy* 2 (1993); Abdel Azim Ramadan, 'Fundamentalist Influence in Egypt: The Strategies of the Muslim Brotherhood and the Takfir Groups', in Marty and Appelby (eds.), *Fundamentalism and the State* (Chicago: U. of Chicago Press 1993) pp.152–83; D. Sullivan, 'Islam and Development in Egypt: Civil Society and the State', in Hussin Mutalib and Taj ul-Islam (eds.), *Islam, Muslims and the Modern State: Case-Studies of Muslims in Thirteen Countries* (London 1994) pp.211–31; Gehad Auda, 'The "Normalization" of the Islamic Movement in Egypt from the 1970s to the Early 1990s', in Marty and Appelby (eds.), *Accounting for Fundamentalism* (Chicago: U. of Chicago Press 1994).
4. Saad Eddin Ibrahim wrote in connection to this that 'vibrations there [Egypt] often radiate to a much broader cultural hinterland beyond its borders', see, 'Islamic Militancy as a Social Movement: The Case of Two Groups in Egypt', in Ali E. Hillal Dessouki (ed.), *Islamic Resurgence in the Arab World* (NY: Praeger 1982) p.117. On Egypt's central position in the Arab world, see E. Podeh, *The Quest for Hegemony on the Arab World: The Struggle over the Baghdad Pact* (Leiden: E.J. Brill 1995) ch.1.
5. For a different view, see a recent article written under the pseudonym 'Cassandra', 'The Impending Crisis in Egypt', *Middle East Journal* 49/1 (Winter 1995) pp.9–27.
6. For a recent study on the Muslim Brotherhood, see Sana Abed-Kotob, 'The Accommodationists Speak: Goals and Strategies of the Muslim Brotherhood of Egypt', *International Journal of Middle East Studies* 27 (1995) pp.321–39.

7. John L. Esposito (ed.), *Voices of Resurgent Islam* (NY: Oxford UP 1983) p.11; idem., 'Political Islam: Beyond the Green Menace', *Current History* (Jan. 1994) p.20.
8. H. Ansari, 'The Islamic Militants in Egyptian Politics', *Int Jnl of Middle Eastern Studies* 16 (1984) p.123; Gehad Auda, 'The "Normalization" of the Islamic Movement in Egypt from the 1970's to the Early 1990s', in Marty and Appelby (eds.), *Accounting for Fundamentalism* (Chicago: U. of Chicago Press 1994) p.375.
9. On the foundations of Islamic fundamentalism in Egypt before and during the Muslim Brotherhood's period, see, J. Voll, 'Fundamentalism in the Sunni Arab World: Egypt and the Sudan', in Marty and Appelby (eds.), *Fundamentalism Observed* (Chicago: U. of Chicago Press 1991) pp.347–66.
10. For secondary sources on Qutb's ideology, see Emmanuel Sivan, *Radical Islam* (New Haven, CT: Yale UP 1985); Y. Haddad, 'Sayyid Qutb: Ideologue of Islamic Revival', in John Esposito (note 7) pp.67–98; and Voll (note 9) pp.369–70.
11. For various figures, see, The Economist Intelligence Unit, *Country Report,* 'Egypt', 4th Quarter 1994, p.9; Cassandra (note 5) pp.19–20.
12. *Sabah al-Khayr* (Cairo), 22 April 1993. Another interesting report can be found in *Sawt al-Kuwait al-Duwali* (London), 23 May 1991.
13. E. Sivan, 'The Islamic Republic of Egypt', *Orbis* 31/1 (Spring 1987) p.46.
14. *Al-Haqiqa* (Cairo), 2 Jan. 1993.
15. Abdel Azim Ramadan, 'Fundamentalist Influence in Egypt: The Strategies of the Muslim Brotherhood and the Takfir Groups', in Marty and Appelby (eds.), *Fundamentalism and the State* (Chicago: U. of Chicago Press 1993) p.152.
16. *Ruz al-Yusuf* (Cairo), 31 May 1993. For more details on these groups, see Ramadan (note 15) pp.157–77; Auda (note 8) pp.382–5, 401–4; Voll (note 9) pp.384–90; Ansari (note 8) pp.123–41.
17. R.H. Dekmejian, *Islam in Revolution: Fundamentalism in the Arab World* (Syracuse: SUP 1985) p.96, for more information, also see pp.102–5; Auda (note 8) p.401; Ansari (note 8) pp.131–41; Ibrahim (note 4) p.126.
18. For more information on the structure, see Dekmejian (note 17) pp.97–9; Ansari (note 8) pp.125–30; Auda (note 8) p.401.
19. *Ruz al-Yusuf*, 17 May 1993; *Jerusalem Post*, 22 Aug. 1993; *al-Hayat* (London), 5 Nov. 1993.
20. For more information on the activities of the Muslim Brotherhood, see Ramadan (note 15) pp.164–77; Auda (note 8) pp.379–81; Voll (note 9) pp.356–74, 387; D. Sullivan, 'Islam and Development in Egypt: Civil Society and the State', in Hussin Mutalib and Taj ul-Islam (eds.), *Islam, Muslims and the Modern State: Case-Studies of Muslims in Thirteen Countries* (London 1994) p.211; Esposito, *The Islamic Threat: Myth or Reality* (NY: OUP 1992) p.100.
21. Esposito, 'Beyond the Green Menace' (note 7) p.21.
22. *Country Report,* 'Egypt', 2nd Quarter 1994.
23. See Mubarak's interview in *Akhbar al-Yawm*, 11 Dec. 1993, where he claimed that Egypt had lost $2 billion of tourism income. For various figures, see e.g, *Financial Times*, 16 Feb. 1993; *Ha'aretz*, 31 March 1993; *Jerusalem Post*, 10 June 1993; *Washington Post*, 11 July 1993; *Middle East Int*, 10 Sept. 1993.
24. *Country Report,* 'Egypt', 4th Quarter 1994, p.10.
25. *Agence-France Presse* (hereafter *AFP*), 2 Jan. – Foreign Broadcast Information Service, Near East and South Asia, Daily Report (hereafter *DR*), 4 Jan. 1993
26. *Al-Musawwar*, 24–25 Dec. 1992. 'Abd al-Rahman, who had been acquitted of charges of subversion in connection with the violent, anti-government riots in Fayyum in 1989, left Egypt and entered the US in May 1990 on a tourist visa granted by the American consulate in Khartoum. In early 1993, his green card was revoked by the immigration office and he was charged with misrepresenting himself on his visa application, polygamy and crimes of moral turpitude. In early 1995, he was convicted for his involvement in the bomb explosion in the New York World Trade Center on 26 Feb. 1993, which left six dead and over 1000 wounded.
27. *AFP*, 27 Feb. – *DR*, 1 March 1993; *New York Times*, 27–28 Feb. 1993; *Ha'aretz*, 28 Feb., 1 March 1993.
28. Mubarak's speech during a visit to Ghurdaqa, *MENA*, 6 Jan. – *DR*, 8 Jan. 1993.

29. *AFP* 19 July – *DR*, 21 July 1993; *Jerusalem Post*, 19 July 1993; *New York Times*, 19 July 1993.
30. 'Egypt',*Country Report*, 4th Quarter 1994, p.9.
31. *AFP*, 8 July – *DR*, 9 July 1993; *New York Times*, 18 July 1993; *Middle East Int*, 10 Sept. 1993.
32. *Jerusalem Post*, 3 March 1993; *al-Ahali*, 8 March 1993. See also, 'Abd al-Rahman's message to his followers on the occasion of 'Id al-Fitr, *AFP*, 24 March – *DR*, 25 March 1993.
33. *MENA*, 10 Dec. – *DR*, 10 Dec. 1993; *Jerusalem Post*, 12 Dec. 1993. See also Abdel Azim Ramadan (note 15) p.163; Saad Eddin Ibrahim, 'Egypt's Islamic Activism in the 1980s', *Third World Qtly* 10 (1988) p.651.
34. *MENA*, 21 May – *DR*, 24 May 1993; *Jerusalem Post*, 23 May 1993; *Ha'aretz*, 24 May 1993; *Middle East Int*, 28 May 1993; *MENA*, 18 June – *DR*, 21 June 1993; *New York Times, 20* June 1993; *Ha'aretz*, 20 June 1993; *Middle East Int*, 25 June 1993.
35. *Sabah al-Khayr*, 22 April 1993; *Country Report*, 'Egypt', 3rd Quarter 1993.
36. Address at police academy on Police Day, Radio Cairo (hereafter *R. Cairo*), 25 Jan. – *DR*, 25 Jan. See also Mubarak's Revolution Day speech, *R. Cairo*, 22 July – *DR*, 22 July 1993.
37. *MENA*, 9 Feb., 1 April – *DR*, 10 Feb., 2 April 1993.
38. *Al-Musawwar*, 24 Sept. 1993.
39. Mubarak's interview in *Der Spiegel*, 25 Jan. 1993; *MENA*, 12, 30 March 1993, 15 Sept. 1993 – *DR*, 12, 30 March 1993, 16 Sept. 1993; *al-Jumhuriyya* (Cairo), 13 March 1993; *The Times*, 2 April 1993; *Le Figaro*, 10 April 1993; *R. Cairo*, 26 April 1993 – *DR*, 27 April 1993; May Day speech, *R. Cairo*, 1 May 1993 – *DR*, 3 May 1993; *al-Ahram al-Masa'i*, 27 May 1993; interview in *Akhbar al-Yawm*, 11 Dec. 1993.
40. For figures, see Cassandra (note 5) pp.19–20.
41. See, for example, *Financial Times, Washington Post, Ha'aretz, New York Times*, 11 March 1993; *New York Times*, 18 March; *MENA*, 18 March 1993 – *DR*, 19 March 1993.
42. *AFP*, 17 Feb. 1993 – *DR*, 18 Feb. 1993.
43. *MENA*, 23 May 1993 – *DR*, 24 May 1993.
44. *Country Report*, 'Egypt', 4th Quarter 1994, p.11; See also Cassandra (note 5) p.17.
45. *AFP*, 8 July 1993 – *DR*, 9 July 1993.
46. *New York Times*, 15 Aug. 1993; *Middle East Int*, 28 Aug. 1993.
47. Interview in *al-Ahram*, 11 Oct. 1993.
48. Auda (note 8) p.390.
49. Ibid., p.376.
50. Ibid., p.390.
51. Esposito, *The Islamic Threat* (note 20) p.98. For the figures of mosques, see *AFP*, 20 Feb. 1993 – *DR*, 24 Feb. 1993; *Jerusalem Post*, 17 March 1993. Different figures were given by the opposition daily, *Al-Sha'b*, 8 Jan. 1993: 120,000 mosques, of which 70,000 were privately-run; and by Voll (note 9) who claimed that only 20,000 non-governmental mosques existed in Egypt, see p.346. By comparison, Morroe Berger claimed that in 1962 there were only 3,006 governmental mosques and 17,218 private mosques, see *Islam in Egypt Today: Social and Political Aspects of Popular Religion* (Cambridge: CUP 1970) p.18.
52. This announcement came after a meeting with Awqaf Minister Muhammad 'Ali Mahjub, *R. Cairo*, 16 March – *DR*, 17 March 1993.
53. *Country Report*, 'Egypt', 3rd Quarter 1993.
54. *Al-Jumhuriyya* (Cairo), 15 April 1993; *Ruz al-Yusuf*, 10 May 1993; *Akhbar al-Yawm*, 1 May 1993; *al-Ahram*, 7 May 1993; *al-Wafd*, 11 May 1993; *R. Cairo*, 24 May – *DR*, 25 May 1993; *Ha'aretz*, 25 Aug. 1993.
55. *Ha'aretz*, 21 March 1993. This decision was criticized in *al-Nur*, 14 April 1993.
56. *Country Report*, 'Egypt', 1st Quarter 1994.
57. *Middle East Broadcasting Corporation Television* (MBC TV), 28 Nov. – *DR*, 29 Nov. 1993.
58. *Country Report*, 'Egypt', 4th Quarter 1994, p.12.
59. For further details on the nature of the law, see, *Al-Ahram Weekly*, 18–25 Feb. 1993, 25 Feb.–3 March 1993; Cassandra (note 5) p.15; E. Podeh, 'Egypt', in A. Ayalon (ed.), *Middle East Contemporary Survey* 17 (1993) (Boulder, CO: Westview Press 1995) p.290.
60. Cassandra (note 5) pp.15–16.

61. According to Cassandra (note 5), this step was a lesson of the Algerian experience, as Islamists first gained control of villages and towns through the ballot-box. See p.16.

62. On Alfi's nomination, see *AFP*, 18 April – *DR*, 18 April 1993; *Ha'aretz, Jerusalem Post*, 19 April 1993.

63. *Al-Majalla* (London), 4 May 1993.

64. *MENA* quoting May, 18 April – *DR*, 19 April 1993. On the mediation attempt, see *al-Majalla*, 4 May 1993; *AFP*, 15 April – *DR*, 16 April 1993; *al-Wafd*, 17 April 1993; *Ruz al-Yusuf*, 19 April 1993; *al-Ahram*, 4 May 1993; *Ha'aretz*, 20 Oct. 1993. *Al-Sha'b* reported on 13 April 1993 that the noted Shaykhs Mutawalli al-Sha'rawi and Muhammad al-Ghazzali were among the mediators. *Al-Wasat*, 3–9 May 1993, claimed that 'Umar 'Abd al-Rahman expressed 'clear opposition'to any mediation with the Egyptian government.

65. *R. Cairo*, 21 April – *DR*, 23 April 1993.

66. *Al-Ahram*, 14 Jan. 1993; *MENA*, 19, 31 March – *DR*, 23 March, 1 April 1993; *R. Cairo*, 4 May – *DR*, 5 May 1993.

67. *Al-Ahram*, 16 July 1993.

68. *Al-Ahram Weekly*, 15–21 April 1993; *al-Ahram*, 4 Aug. 1993; *Country Report*, 'Egypt', 2nd Quarter 1993, pp.10–11.

69. Mubarak's interview in *al-Ahram*, 30 Sept. 1993. See also *Country Report*, 'Egypt', 1st Quarter 1994.

70. *Al-Wafd*, 7 Dec. 1993.

71. Cassandra (note 5) p.17.

72. *New York Times*, 28 March 1993; *al-Diyar*, 9 April 1993.

73. *Country Report*, 'Egypt', 2nd Quarter 1993, p.9; *al-Ahali* (Cairo), 7 April 1993.

74. *Al-Ahram, al-Akhbar*, 19 Nov. 1993; *MENA*, 20 Nov. – *DR*, 22 Nov. 1993; *al-Wafd*, 20, 23 Nov. 1993; *al-Safir*, 27 Nov. 1993.

75. *Ha'aretz*, 18 May 1993; *Country Report*, 'Egypt', 3rd Quarter 1993.

76. *Ha'aretz*, 27 June 1993.

77. *Country Report*, 'Egypt', 3rd Quarter 1993.

78. On Mubarak's visit, see *MENA*, 9, 16 May – *DR*, 10, 17 May 1993; *AFP*, 17 May – *DR*, 18 May 1993; *al-Akhbar*, 17 May 1993; *al-Usbu' al-'Arabi*, 31 May 1993.

79. *R. Cairo*, 7 Feb., 26 April – *DR*, 8 Feb., 27 April 1993; interview of Mubarak in *al-Jumhuriyya* (Cairo), 18 Sept. 1993.

80. *Country Report*, 'Egypt', 2nd Quarter 1994; *Marches Tropicaux et Mediterranees*, 18 Dec. 1992. For additional figures, see *R. Cairo*, 7 Feb., 26 April – *DR*, 8 Feb., 27 April 1993.

81. On the ministry, see the composition of the new government, *R. Cairo*, 14 Oct. – *DR*, 15 Oct. 1993. On the conference and its critics, see *Country Report*, 'Egypt', 4th Quarter 1994, pp.10–11.

82. *Al-Akhbar*, 5 Jan. 1993. According to *al-Sha'b* (Cairo), 8 Jan. 1993, the figure was higher, 20 million.

83. *Al-Wafd*, 15 Sept. 1993; text of al-Sidqi's cabinet designation letter, *MENA*, 13 Oct. – *DR*, 14 Oct. 1993; *R. Cairo*, 14 Oct. – *DR*, 18 Oct. 1993; Mubarak's address to the People's Assembly, *R. Cairo*, 11 Nov. – *DR*, 16 Nov. 1993; Sidqi's government policy statement, 13 Dec. – *DR*, 15 Dec. 1993.

84. Cassandra (note 5) p.12. Deputy Prime Minister Kamal Janzuri stated that the number of unemployed was 1.4 million, see *al-Ahram*, 7 Feb. 1993. For other figures taken from opposition and foreign sources see *al-Wafd*, 10 Feb. 1993; *New York Times*, 4 Oct. 1993. On the census, see Sidqi's government policy statement, *R. Cairo*, 13 Dec. – *DR*, 15 Dec. 1993.

85. Cassandra (note 5) p.12. The author in fact claims that 700,000 jobs are needed to provide work for 500,000 new entrants each year and to reduce unemployment.

86. *Country Report*, 'Egypt', 4th quarter 1994, p. 9.

87. Mubarak's May Day speech, *R. Cairo*, 1 May – *DR*, 3 May; *Ha'aretz*, 12 May 1993; Sidqi's government policy statement, *R. Cairo*, 13 Dec. – *DR*, 15 Dec. 1993. Cassandra (note 5) p.21.

88. Mubarak's address to the People's Assembly, *R. Cairo*, 11 Nov. – *DR*, 16 Nov. 1993.

89. This program came on top of US debt-forgiveness following the Gulf War in the amount of $7 billion. The Arab states (Saudi Arabia, Kuwait and other Gulf states) had written off

another $7 billion of Egypt's debt. See Elie Podeh, 'A Year After Iraq's Invasion to Kuwait: The Impact of the Gulf Crisis on the Arab System' *Data and Analysis* (Hebrew) (Tel Aviv: The Dayan Center for Middle Eastern and African Studies, Dec. 1991). For further details, see Cassandra (note 5) p.11.

90. *Financial Times*, 22 April 1993; *al-Ahram Weekly*, 22–28 April 1993. See also interview with Minister of International Cooperation, Dr. Maurice Makramallah, *al-Ahram Weekly*, 5–11 March 1993. Cassandra (note 5) p.11.

91. *Country Report*, 'Egypt', 4th Quarter 1994, pp.14–20.

92. For criticism based on the gaps between the macro and microeconomic policy, see Cassandra (note 5) p.14.

93. Ibid., p.10. See also R.D. Kaplan, 'Eaten from Within', *Atlantic Monthly* (Nov. 1994) pp.26–44.

94. Esposito, 'Political Islam: Beyond the Green Menace' (note 7) p.21.

95. Fouad Ajami, 'In the Pharaoh's Shadow: Religion and Authority in Egypt', in James P. Piscatori (ed.), *Islam in the Political Process* (Cambridge: CUP 1983) p.34.

# Islamic Activism in Turkey since the 1980 Military Takeover

## ANAT LAPIDOT

This article examines the nature and strength of the Islamic movement in contemporary Turkey. It argues that the policies of the military and civilian governments, in attempting to establish a strong ideological base that could challenge the left, allowed and even promoted the activities of Turkey's Islamic organizations. Indeed, these counter-balancing efforts backfired as the Islamic movement rejected the national cause and joined the struggle for social justice. As a result, and in direct contradiction to the intentions of the military and civilian governments, there evolved an ideological alliance between Islamic circles and the left. This ideological shift along with the collapse of ideological alternatives and a background of intensifying socio-economic problems contributed heavily to the Islamic movement's electoral success in recent years.

Islam first publicly reemerged as a factor in the Turkish political scene in the 1950s as a consequence of the state's transition to a multi-party regime. Its increased importance was a result of the electoral competition between the Republican People's Party (RPP) and the Democratic Party (DP).[1] Later, the establishment of the Islamic-oriented National Salvation Party (NSP) in the 1970s, and its participation in the coalition government in 1974, seemed to indicate a significant breakthrough in a country that had long been perceived as the symbol of secularism in the Islamic world. In 1973 the NSP become the third largest party in the country, and in 1974 NSP leader Necmettin Erbakan became a deputy prime minister under RPP leader Bülent Ecevit. One year later, in 1975, Erbakan was appointed minister in Süleyman Demirel's coalition government, a move which gave his party greater influence in areas including public education and communication. This increase in political power, in addition to the general political and social instability of the time, gave rise to already growing fears among secularists regarding the strength of the Islamic movement and the role of Islam in Turkish culture and society.

In the 1980s, the Iranian revolution, the spread of Islam within Turkish communities abroad and within Turkey itself, the relatively open, government-encouraged public debate on Islamic issues, as well as numerous other indications that Islamic activity had spread into a broad range of areas, all inspired the interest of researchers, academics and others in the role of Islam in Turkey. This interest increased further after June 1985 when Turks were shocked to discover that a group of army officers, calling themselves 'the Patriotic Officers', had circulated a memorandum arguing that Turkey protected the interests of the US rather than those of Islam, and that like Israel, Turkey had become a front-line state against the Islamic nation.[2] In mid-1985, prayer rooms were built inside government ministries and the parliament. In 1985, the study of Arabic as a foreign language was introduced into Turkey's high school curriculum[3] and in January 1988 the government introduced a law proscribing the defamation of Muhammad, Allah and the religion of Islam.

The main question regarding these developments was, and remains, what caused Islam to continue to be an important factor in the social and political life of twentieth century Turkey, a country founded on the basis of an explicitly secular ideology. Many attempts have been made to answer this question by looking at the relationship between political and social factors and Islam. However, the strength of Islam in Turkey, and probably in other areas of the Middle East, cannot be explained sufficiently by a lack of political stability or democracy. These same political and socio-cultural conditions also prompted the rise of other ideologies and movements, such as those of leftist, secularists, fascists and nationalists.

## The Growth of Islamic Political Activism

While the reemergence of Islamic political activism is not a phenomenon new to the 1980s, its appearance has been viewed by many as different and much more significant than past versions. Some researchers, such as Kemal Karpat, have held that the Islamists provided the only possible alternative to the 1980 military takeover, since no other force possessed comparable popular support.[4] This was clearly demonstrated, he argued, when the clandestine radio station of the Turkish Communist Party in East Berlin denounced the coup in 1980 and then called on the followers of the Islamic NSP to lead the resistance.[5]

While Karpat may have exaggerated the power of the NSP, his argument did point to an interesting development: the expanding relationship between Turkey's Islamists and leftists.[6] During the 1980s there was an attempt to create a dialogue between Islamists, especially figures from the circle known as the 'New Muslim Intellectuals', and several well-known left-wing leaders.[7] A number of former leftists became Islamists, especially during the early years of the Iranian revolution. This relationship was expressed not only on the personal level, but also in joint publishing projects and public debates.[8] The reason for this phenomenon is not the topic of this article; however, I would argue that part of the strength of the Islamic movement in the 1980s stemmed from its ability to appeal to people from the left as well as to religious traditionalists. The constituencies of the Islamic movement and the left shared common interests. Both movements emphasized not only social equality, living standards, inflation and unemployment, all important issues in the 1970s, but also stood together on such issues as the environment, women's rights and human rights, all of which were new to the Islamic discourse. Thus with the collapse of communism in the late 1980s, the Islamic movement was able to offer the ex-communists an attractive alternative.

Although the Islamic movement was mainly based on popular appeal, its activists intellectualized Islam much more strongly than had been done previously. They published up to 60 monthly periodicals, in addition to numerous books. The Islamic movement in the 1980s developed an intellectual foundation which not only provided it with a coherent ideological base, but, even more importantly, gained it the respect of the secular audience.

Although the Islamic protest was organized, it was not completely concentrated in political parties. This made it difficult for the government to control the movement. The more independent and fragmented the movement's structure became, the more likely it was to incorporate groups that held radical, sometimes militant, views. At the same time, the more divided the movement, the more difficult it was for it to consolidate at election time.[9]

In the 1980s, as the Islamic movement expanded its ties with the main centers of government power, the more marginal radical groups that directly attacked Kemalism and demanded an Islamic state were able to operate at will. These radical elements, emerging for the first time in Turkish republican history, were primarily influenced by the Islamic revolution in Iran. Active militant groups such as Hizbü't-Tahrir[10] and the Islamic Jihad continue to exist in Turkey and have carried out a number of terrorist attacks and murders,[11] although they have been kept on the fringes of society. Several, like the urban-based Islamic Great Orient Fighters Front (IBDA-C), have a local base, but most of them have been supported by foreign elements.[12] Cemaleddin Kaplan was an example of a foreign-backed radical figure. The former *müftü* of Adana and a supporter of Khomeini, he remained an ongoing irritation to Turkish security and, until his recent death, sought to bring down the secular Kemalist Turkish republic.[13] His supporters' strategies included smuggling video cassettes of his sermons into the country to expose the masses to the idea of an Islamic state. Despite the late Uğur Mumcu's estimation of Kaplan's influence as minimal, only a few thousand supporters, others believed differently.[14]

Although most terrorist activities were supported from outside Turkey, opposition to the Kemalist state was increasingly voiced within by the end of the 1980s. This expression took different forms and was voiced by different groups. Why was this case? Apart from the reasons mentioned above, an additional explanation may be rooted in the collapse of the communist regimes at the end of the 1980s. Whereas alternative forms of political ideology, such as pan-Islam and pan-Turanism, had previously been regarded as utopian dreams, the collapse of communism provided the Turks with another seemingly realistic option – an Islamic Turkic front centered in Turkey, including the Muslims of the former Soviet Union. Such an option attracted both ultra-nationalists and Islamists, as the population of the new Central Asian republics was both of Turkic and Islamic origin. This populist vision stood in contrast to the view of the traditional elite which insisted on the continued existence of the nation state framework.

## Ideological and Organizational Aspects of the Islamic Movement

Defining the Islamic movement is a complex task. The term 'Islamic movement' has served as a framework for different organizations, each of which operates in its own way and in accordance with its own beliefs, although geared toward the same goal: the establishment of an Islamic society and polity. The current emphasis of research on Islam in Turkey is aimed at understanding Islam from above, not from below. This explains the extensive examination of the Islamic-oriented party; however, the *tarikats* [sufi orders], perhaps the most significant and influential of Turkey's Islamic organizations, have not been sufficiently evaluated or examined.

As pointed out by Sabri Sayrı, many researchers have attempted to draw a line between traditionalists and radicals.[15] The traditionalists were perceived to be the majority of the Islamic intelligentsia, politically moderate and of local origin, with Turkey as their source of identification. The radicals were commonly viewed as the fundamentalist minority, inspired by the Iranian revolution.[16]

This division does not correspond to reality, nor does it, now or in the past, represent the Islamic movement in its entirety. Therefore, it may be useful to focus on the political theories of the movement's factions. This approach reveals a more precise distinction between the two main currents of the Islamic movement. It should be mentioned that both of the currents corresponded to general trends in the Muslim world and have no distinctive ideological Turkish character.

The first current viewed the takeover of Turkish political institutions as its primary goal. Its adherents believed that once this was achieved, they would be able to transform Turkish society into an authentic Islamic one.[17] The second held the same ultimate goal, the establishment of an Islamic society; however, it proposed a different method of achieving the goal. They argued that the movement needed to establish a socio-economic as well as a religious base, and that social action would facilitate their taking full control over the Muslim community in the future.

Both currents, which together constituted the center of the Islamic movement, intended to achieve their goal, not through extra-legal activity, but through democratic institutions, to which they were opposed in principle. This too was not a solely Turkish phenomenon. The tactics of most groups who seek an Islamic solution to their societies' social and political problems changed in the latter half of the 1980s, from unalterably opposing western notions of democracy to waging democratic campaigns against their states' authoritarian regimes. In Turkey, Islamic movements came to the realization that under present conditions the best way to gain power was by participation in open elections. They learned to use the system they opposed. This is in contrast to the belief of the early 1980s that the only way to achieve power was through violent revolution. The effectiveness of the new tactics was first proven in the 1991 election, when Erbakan's Refah Partisi (Welfare Party) won 16.7 per cent of the vote. Additional proof has been provided by Islamic victories in municipal elections in Istanbul and Ankara in 1993 and, most recently, in a successful showing in parliamentary elections at the end of 1995 (see below).[18]

As in other Turkish ideological movements, both of the Islamic currents contained militant factions which promoted the use of extremist methods. Among those giving primacy to the regime's overthrow were the Hizbü't-Tahrir and the Islamic Jihad. These groups, however, are the exception, and should be considered as irritations rather than real threats to the status quo. On the other end of the spectrum, those movements giving primacy to societal change, one finds reports of violent actions by *tarikat* members, such as stone throwing and on several occasions even the killing of those who dared to eat in public during the Ramadan fast.[19]

The other ideological issue over which the Islamists are divided is the issue of nationalism and the legitimacy of the nation state. With the exception of those who accept the state-sponsored Turkish-Islamic synthesis (like the Aydınlar Ocağı, see below), most Islamists are united in their rejection of the legitimacy of the current nation state. There was, however, a disagreement on the nature of the ideal Islamic state.[20] Rejection of the state is based on the theological concept of *tevhid* (belief in one God). This idea has always been the most important principle in Islam. However, in the modern period, particularly in line with the views of the Iranian thinker 'Ali Shari'ati, *tevhid* has taken on new meaning and importance. For the purpose of the present study, the importance of *tevhid* lies in its implementation as a social and political order, that is to say, a complete rejection of all particularities and divisions of different communities of all forms. This idea was considered a religious value and commandment, hence contesting the idea of the nation state. Likewise, *tevhid* rejected any consideration of ethnic particularity, a principle which had been supported by some members of the Islamic movement. It is important to note that the Muslim community in Turkey is mostly Sunni, with a minority, estimated at between 25 to 30 per cent, of Alevis.[21] Moreover, the Sunnis are split between a majority of Turks and Kurds who observe the Hanafi legal code and a minority of Kurds who follow the Shafi'i school.

It is also worthy to note the methods adopted by the Islamists to achieve their political aspirations. Although the Islamic movement's most prominent organization is Erbakan's Refah Partisi, additional institutions are also used to promote its political ideology. Additional vehicles include clubs, parliamentary or governmental circles, such as the ANAP's Islamist wing, and publishing houses such as Girişim and Birleşik.

But perhaps the most interesting organizations within the movement are the *tarikats*, whose roles within the political and social systems have been strengthened over the last 20 years. Although the activities of the *tarikats* were officially prohibited in 1925, in many areas of the country these groups continue to be dominant. The most significant are the Kadiri, Halveti-Cerrahis, Rufai, Süleymanci, Nakşibendi, and Işıkcılar; the Nurcu, which operates similarly, may also be added to this list.[22] The *tarikats* have had considerable experience in underground activities. Since September 1980, though, they have been more open in their political involvement and have come to publicly support various political parties, such as Refah Partisi, Doğu Yol Partisi (The True Path Party) or Anavatan Partisi (The Motherland Party). In fact, many politicians have acknowledged having ties to various *tarikats*. The most famous example is that of Turgut Özal's family connection with the Naksibendi order. Some researchers believe that such ties to *tarikats* have now become the most important element of Turkish electoral politics.[23]

## Government Policies Towards Islam

The growth in number and influence of the Islamists in Turkey over the last 15 years was graphically demonstrated in the December 1995 national elections, when Refah won 5,985,322 votes, 21.32 per cent of the total votes cast. This translated into 158 seats in the Turkish parliament, making Refah the single largest party (although it did not mean that Refah was able to form a government).[24] It can be said, then, that almost 22 per cent of the population was willing to express its support for the establishment of an Islamic society. Ironically, Refah's success was the result of successive military and civilian governments policies towards Islam. Indeed, under the laws which the secular governments propagated during the 1980s, Atatürk himself would no doubt have been arrested for insulting the Prophet and hurting the feelings of the religious population.

After the military coup of September 1980, the generals' attitude towards Islam was ambiguous, on the one hand opposing Islamic radicalism and on the other promoting Islamic activities. Even though the fear of Islamic *irtiça* (reaction) was one of the reasons for the military takeover, ironically it was the generals who introduced Islam and adopted it as part of the state ideology. Moreover, as Feroz Ahmad argued, 'there is no doubt that the influence of Islam in Turkish politics and society has increased dramatically under the military government.'[25] (On the growth of Islamic activities sponsored by the government, see appendix.)

This tendency continued and even increased under the rule of the Motherland Party. The state ideology introduced by the generals and known as the Turkish-Islamic synthesis was formulated by right-wing circles, members of the Aydınlar Ocağı (Hearths of the Enlightened), which came together at the end of the 1960s against the backdrop of the leftist-dominated student riots. Their conservative theoretical formula was encouraged after the coup by the generals, who hoped to create a counterweight to the left-wing ideology which was attracting the nation's youth. The formula was later adopted by most right-wing political figures, who saw in it a potential replacement for leftist ideology with considerable voter appeal.[26] For the originators of the ideology, the members of the Aydınlar Ocağı, Islam was not merely an element of Turkish culture but a useful instrument of social control. The founders' goal was to produce an ideology which would be an alternative to Kemalism, which was blamed for the confusion that was affecting Turkey's younger generation. In addition, they hoped that the synthesis would represent an ideological protective wall *vis-à-vis* the left, which was perceived by many as being responsible for the anarchy and the wave of politically-inspired terrorism which had hit the country toward the end of the 1960s.

The Aydınlar's ideological starting point was that, contrary to religious or leftist circles, the right-wing secular majority had no collective consciousness or awareness and was therefore passive. Consequently, a leftist minority with a consolidated radical consciousness would be capable of carrying the country in a new undesirable direction. The Aydınlar invested most of its energy in producing a new collective identity for the passive majority by writing a new historical narrative. Its preoccupation with history and the emphasis placed on the study of its own version of history were intended to provide legitimacy to the government and political guidance and awareness to future generations.[27]

This approach was precisely what the generals who carried out the 1980 coup needed. The Turkish-Islamic synthesis, with its emphasis on authoritarian politics and social control through cultural and religious motifs, was cynically used by the Turkish decision-makers in their attempt to control public expressions of political consciousness, which had peaked in the late 1970s. As Toprak and Şaylan pointedly demonstrated, many of the primary institutions of Turkish cultural and intellectual life were restructured along the lines advocated by the Aydınlar Ocağı.[28] Universities lost their autonomy and the Higher Education Council (YÖK) was attached to the office of the President of the Republic.[29] The State Radio and Television Authority (TRT) was turned over to the ideologues of the Aydınlar Ocağı and, more importantly, religious and moral instruction were emphasized in the education system.[30]

The mass media, particularly television, but also radio and newspapers, were to play a major part in creating and shaping collective sentiments and values.[31] Islam as understood by the Aydınlar was a complex mixture of beliefs, values, symbols and rituals. As such, its members understood Islam not in the theological context but in the context of its role in society. Religion was seen as part of the ideological sphere of a society, helping to maintain political, cultural and economic order. This was to be achieved by linking religious terms with social and national ones, by demonstrating that the existing social, political and economic order was right because it was God-given and that changing it would be both a sin and a betrayal.

The post-1984 governments, influenced by the Turkish-Islamic Synthesis ideology, frequently attempted to use law to exert its control over the arts and sciences, but with little success. Several attempts were made to place science and knowledge under 'moral control'. A famous case is that of the Turkish Minister of Education Vehbi Dinçerler, who in 1987 tried to prevent Darwin's theory of evolution from being taught in schools, mandating instead the teaching of a religious version of creation.

The extent to which the post-1980 military regime turned to Islam was revealed in the Rabıta affair.[32] Rabıta, the Saudi-based Rabitat al-'Alam al-Islami (World Islamic League), advocated the establishment of a pan-Islamic federation based on the *shari'a*. Rabıta's ties in Turkey came to light when Uğur Mumcu, a Turkish investigative journalist, reported that a 1981 decree by the military-backed government of former Admiral Bülent Ulusu allowed Rabıta to pay the salaries of Turkish religious functionaries in Belgium and Germany.[33] Later, as Mumcu demonstrated, ANAP gave *carte blanche* to fund numerous religious organizations and projects in Turkey. Over the years Rabıta gained access to the highest reaches of the Turkish government through Saudi links with conservative politicians, among them the family of the late President Turgut Özal.[34]

The influence of the Turkish-Islamic Synthesis was especially felt in the areas of education and the media, traditionally the major battlegrounds between Islamists and secularists. The initial intention of the generals and the civilian governments was to eventually create a peaceful, controlled Islamic ideology. However, this gave a green light to religious activities in all areas of public and social life. Thus, ironically, the implementation of the Turkish-Islamic Synthesis also gave a push to the Islamic movement, helping it to grow throughout the 1980s to become the largest single party in parliament. Of course the next question to be addressed is whether the Islamic movement that has emerged is necessarily a dangerous phenomenon to the existing socio-political order.

## Conclusions

The most important change over the last 15 years in the Turkish secular-religious battle is that Islam no longer stands only in a theological context. Modern Islamic political thought is more of a social ideology and less of a theological issue. In fact, God is hardly mentioned in the writings of the modern Turkish Islamists; in contrast, discussions of the need for social justice appear often.

The second issue that deserves attention is that of the failure of successive Turkish governments to control the spread of political Islam. Turkey's military governments initially tried to use Islam to create a strong ideological base to counter the ideology of the left. Their intention was to encourage a conservative, peaceful and apolitical version of Islam. The Motherland Party, which won the elections in 1983, continued this policy, encouraging additional religious activity. They wished to create a new ideology that would act as a social cement: Islam as a tool of social control. The result, however, was very different.

Governmental policies during the last decade caused the Islamic movement to flourish. The period was characterized by relatively free religious publication and a degree of intellectual activity never before experienced in Turkey. The Islamic boom was manifested in all fields of life including the economy, politics and, most importantly, education and the media.

Finally, and most importantly, the assumption of many in the West and in Turkey that Turkish Islam, mainly Sunni, is fundamentalist-proof is a misunderstanding of contemporary Islam as well as of contemporary Turkish history. Not only does Sunni Islam, in general, have fundamentalist and radical elements in it, but the general view of Turkey as a secular state is an incorrect assumption. Atatürk's efforts to keep Islam out of politics is still commonly understood as having been a total success. This was never really the case. To be sure, the Kemalists did succeed in driving many religious groups underground; however, this often only turned them into independent units, both socially and economically. The result was the development of a strong, unpredictable movement, parts of which were exposed to radical religious and leftist ideas, especially in the 1980s, and which pose a challenge to the government. It is worth mentioning in this context that the amount of literature translated from Persian into Turkish in the last decade, especially that of the influential Iranian Islamist writer 'Ali Shari'ati, is quite considerable. Even though many believers would not accept the attempt to present a universal version of Islam, the influence of Shi'i ideas on Turkish Islamists can neither be doubted nor ignored.

Does this mean that the Turkish nation-state is in danger? It is difficult to answer this question and indeed no answer is attempted here. In order to determine the potential power of such an ideology, one must extend study to Turkey's secular community, as well. Furthermore, the extent of success of the Islamists depends to a large extent on external issues such as regional and international politics, the views of the army, the economy, etc.

The chances of the Islamists eventually achieving at least a share of power is high. For now, even though they have been excluded from the most recent, post-election coalition government, they are likely to have considerable influence on the legislative process, and parliamentary activity is bound to be influenced by their agenda. Whether they will choose to integrate themselves into the existing state-structure or seek to radically alter it, still remains to be seen.

## APPENDIX

### TABLE 1
### PERSONNEL AT THE DEPARTMENT OF RELIGIOUS AFFAIRS*

| Year | Supplementary Services | Religious Services | Management Services | Total |
|------|------------------------|--------------------|--------------------|-------|
| 1979 | 1,035 | 47,744 | 1,977 | 50,756 |
| 1980 | 1,239 | 49,831 | 2,202 | 53,272 |
| 1981 | 1,239 | 49,831 | 2,202 | 53,272 |
| 1982 | 1,239 | 49,831 | 2,202 | 53,272 |
| 1983 | 1,239 | 50,130 | 2,202 | 53,571 |
| 1984 | 1,549 | 55,890 | 3,581 | 61,020 |
| 1985 | 1,549 | 55,890 | 3,581 | 61,020 |
| 1986 | 1,639 | 61,696 | 3,682 | 67,017 |
| 1987 | 1,739 | 67,166 | 4,120 | 73,025 |
| 1988 | 1,864 | 77,725 | 4,673 | 84,262 |
| 1989 | 1,976 | 77,722 | 4,944 | 84,642 |

*Source*: The (Annual) Department of Religious Affairs Bulletin, Ankara, 1989.

TABLE 2
TURKISH PILGRIMS*

| Year | Female | Male | Total |
|------|--------|------|-------|
| 1979 | 3,409 | 7,396 | 10,805 |
| 1980 | 9,356 | 16,794 | 26,150 |
| 1981 | 10,879 | 19,591 | 30,470 |
| 1982 | 14,016 | 23,571 | 37,587 |
| 1983 | 13,737 | 22,118 | 35,855 |
| 1984 | 11,914 | 18,536 | 30,450 |
| 1985 | 13,711 | 20,017 | 33,728 |
| 1986 | 18,072 | 24,563 | 42,635 |
| 1987 | 34,346 | 45,554 | 79,900 |
| 1988 | 40,057 | 51,949 | 92,006 |

*Source*: The (Annual) Department of Religious Affairs Bulletin, Ankara, 1989.

TABLE 3
ANNUAL DISTRIBUTION OF MOSQUES IN TURKEY*

| Year | Province and Country | Sub-District, Town and Village | Total |
|------|----------------------|-------------------------------|-------|
| 1984 | 11,319 | 43,348 | 54,667 |
| 1985 | 11,770 | 45,290 | 57,060 |
| 1986 | 12,398 | 47,062 | 59,460 |
| 1987 | 12,921 | 48,611 | 61,532 |
| 1988 | 13,907 | 49,040 | 62,947 |

*Source*: The (Annual) Department of Religious Affairs Bulletin, Ankara, 1989.
• An average of 1,500 mosques are built every year.
• There is a parallel between the increase of population and the increase in number of mosques (2.5 per cent approximately). The ratio of mosques to the general population is 1:857.

TABLE 4
KORAN SCHOOLS AND STUDENTS*

| Year | # of Schools | # of Female Students | # of Male Students | Total # of Students |
|------|--------------|----------------------|--------------------|---------------------|
| 1979–80 | 2,610 | 38,329 | 30,157 | 68,486 |
| 1980–81 | 2,773 | 44,960 | 35,951 | 80,911 |
| 1981–82 | 2,946 | 58,359 | 42,909 | 101,268 |
| 1982–83 | 3,047 | 64,936 | 49,732 | 114,668 |
| 1983–84 | 3,047 | 60,175 | 42,348 | 102,523 |
| 1984–85 | 3,335 | 67,394 | 45,686 | 113,080 |
| 1985–86 | 3,662 | 78,354 | 52,520 | 130,874 |
| 1986–87 | 4,058 | 86,977 | 57,036 | 144,013 |
| 1987–88 | 4,420 | 89,099 | 53,664 | 142,763 |
| 1988–89 | 4,715 | 97,053 | 58,350 | 155,403 |

*Source*: The (Annual) Department of Religious Affairs Bulletin, Ankara, 1989.
• Approximately 234 Koran schools open annually.
• The average annual increase in the number of students in 5876.

## NOTES

1. H. Reed, 'Revival of Islam in Secular Turkey', *Middle East Journal* 8/3 (Summer 1954) pp.267–82; B. Lewis, 'Islamic Revival in Turkey', *International Affairs* 28/1 (Jan. 1952); P. Stirling, 'Religious Change in Republican Turkey', *Middle East Jnl* 12 (Autumn 1958) pp.395–408.
2. *Briefing*, 8 Dec. 1986.
3. *Hürriyet*, 6 Jan. 1987.
4. K. Karpat, 'Turkish Democracy at Impasse: Ideology, Party Politics and the Third Military Interval', *Int Jnl of Turkish Studies* 2/1 (1981) pp.1–4.
5. Ibid.
6. See also Arnold Leder, *Catalysts of Change: Marxist Versus Muslim in a Turkish Community* (Austin: U. of Texas Press, Middle East Monographs 1976).
7. The most outstanding example of leftist-Islamist relations were those between the Islamist Ali Bulaç and the leftist Murad Belge. On Ali Bulaç, see Anat Lapidot, 'Islam and Nationalism: A Study of Contemporary Islamic Political Thought in Turkey (1980–1990)', Ph.D. thesis, University of Durham 1996.
8. For an example, see an article on a conference entitled 'Din ve Siyaset', where Gencay Şaylan, a journalist, Murat Belge and Hüseyn Hatemi, a Shi'ite Islamist writer, were among the participants, in *Mülkiyetiler Birliği Dergisi* (Istanbul: Şubat 1987).
9. An example of such electoral division was the strong approval by the Nurcu members for Demirel, in contrast to the support given by the Nakşibendi to Özal and Erbakan (on the Nurcu, see below (note 22)). In Jan. 1987, a series of articles on the relations of right-wing parties with Islamic groups was published in *Cumhuriyet*.
10. According to *Hürriyet*, the fundamentalist terrorist organization *Hizbüt-Tahrir* had been operating in Turkey for some years. The organization had its headquarters in Jordan where it was established and operated since 1950. In Nov. 1982, some members and founders of its Turkish offshoot were arrested during a police operation in Ankara. Five of them were Turks and the rest were Palestinians and Jordanians. See *Hürriyet*, 19 Nov. 1982.
11. See Özek, Devlet ve Din, (Istanbul: Ada Yayınları 1982) pp. 568–9.
12. On *IBDA*, see *Nokta*, 12–18 June 1994.
13. Also known as Hocaoğlu.
14. Uğur Mumcu, *Cumhuriyet*, 10 Feb. 1987; *Rabıta*, p.207.
15. Sabri Sayrı, *The Prospects for the Islamic Fundamentalism in Turkey* (Santa Monica, CA: Rand, July 1989) p.29.
16. Ibid., pp.22–5.
17. *Refah Partisi*, election pamphlets 1987 (no details).
18. Although this was achieved by alliance with Turks.
19. For example, the killing in Van of a Turkish student during the Ramadan of 1987.
20. Even among the *Aydınlar* members, there is no determined position on this issue. Some of them leaned towards the pan-Turkic solution, which was based on ethnicity rather than on geographical territory.
21. The Alevi minority, according to the Department of Religious Affairs, consists of mainly three groups: the Haci Bektaş, the Kizilbaş and the Shi'ites.
22. The Nurcus are not a *tarika* by definition, they are more a school of thought. The way they operate, and their network, is very much similar to that of the *tarikats*. For more information, see P. Dumont, 'Disciples of the Light. The Nurju Movement in Turkey', *Central Asian Studies* 5/2 (1986) pp.33–60.
23. Gencay Şaylan, *İslâmiyet ve siyaset. Türkiye Örneği* (Ankara: V Yayınları 1987) pp.85–104.
24. FBIS-WEU, 26 Dec. 1995.
25. F. Ahmad, 'Islamic Reassertion in Turkey', *Third World Quarterly* 10/2 (April 1988) pp.750–69; quotation from p.763.
26. Şaylan (note 23) p.66.
27. On its ideology, see Süleyman Yalçin, 'Türk-İslâm Sentezi', *Türk-İslâm Sentezi* (Aydınlar Ocağı 1987).
28. See Toprak, 'Religion as State Ideology in a Secular Setting: The Turkish Islamic Synthesis',

in Malcolm Wagstaff (ed.), *Aspects of Modern Religion in Secular Turkey* (Durham: U. of Durham, Centre for Middle Eastern and Islamic Studies, Occasional Paper No.40, 1990) pp.10–15; and Şaylan (note 23). See also *Yeni Gündem*, 'Türk İslâm Masonları', 22–28 Feb. 1987.

29. The Higher Education Council was then reopened under a different name.
30. Toprak (note 28).
31. On the influence of Turkish-Islamic synthesis on state Radio and Television see *Cumhuriyet*, 19 May 1987; *Milliyet*, 13 June 1987.
32. *DT*, 21, 28 March 1987.
33. *DT*, 4 April 1987; *BBC*, 23 March 1987.
34. *FT*, 23 March 1987.

# State, Islam and Opposition in Saudi Arabia: The Post-Desert Storm Phase

## JOSEPH KOSTINER

This article reviews the status of Saudi opposition groups in the period following the Second Gulf War. The historical roots of opposition to the monarchy are traced, and it is noted that although the monarchy did successfully consolidate its authority and adapt over time, the presence of groups critical of the government and its Islamic and administrative positions have remained. Recently economic, leadership and security crises have given rise to a new opposition, unique in its combination of Islamic and 'modern' concepts. Thus far, as in the past, the regime has dealt with its opponents effectively, although the ultimate impact of this latest opposition surge remains to be determined.

The formation of the Saudi Kingdom, namely the transformation of the rudimentary, tribal Saudi chiefdom into a more organized monarchical state during the late 1920s and early 1930s, transformed the role of Islam in Saudi society. Until the late 1920s, Islamic principles practiced according to the Wahhabi creed, which dominated the core Saudi society of Najd, were all-embracing. These tenets were the *raison d'être* of Saudi expansion: the expunging of unlawful religious practices (*bid'a*) in the newly occupied territories; propagating a moral code of behavior according to the holy law (*shari'a*) aimed at establishing an exemplary Islamic polity (*siyasa shar'iyya*); and the promotion of a unifying ideology beyond tribal and regional identities. With the establishment of state institutions, the advent of political centralization and the delineation of borders, all processes which began evolving during the late 1920s, Islamic functions developed in two different forms: a state religion, consisting of a creed controlled and exercised by the state, and a 'wild' Islam of the opposition, which objected to state interests and resisted state control.

The split attested to the dispute which prevailed during this period between the Saudi leader, 'Abd al-'Aziz Ibn 'Abd al-Rahman, commonly known as Ibn Sa'ud, and a collection of tribal groups, the *Ikhwan*, fiercely loyal to Islam but resistant to the Saudi state-building process. Ibn Sa'ud sought to capitalize on their expansionist tendencies, while subjugating them to a centralizing government. There were fierce debates between the two parties, which also included the leading *'ulama'*.[1] Beginning in 1930, as Ibn Sa'ud was winning his campaign against the *Ikhwan*, it became evident that the Saudi King was designating Wahhabi Islam as the state religion.

This meant that only the senior *'ulama'* who were part of the Kingdom's establishment would wield supreme religious authority and that mandatory religious opinions would be issued by them only and not arbitrarily by any competent interpreter. It also meant that the senior *'ulama'* would not operate independently, but in the framework of state institutions in education, the judiciary and religious-services, whose budget would come from the state. Moreover, state interest, as defined by the King and the government, would take precedence over any altruist or utopian Islamic interests. Wahhabi Islam thus remained a moral code, a unifying factor and ideological motivator of society, but only in accordance with state interests and as a legitimizer of royal Saudi rule.[2]

The Saudi regime thus implemented several principles and strictures of Islam, mingled with state practices and institutions: the *shari'a* served as the main source of law and as a constitution; the Wahhabi code was adopted to govern public behavior; education and intellectual life were mainly shaped by the *'ulama'*'s preaching and sermons. Yet there was no Wahhabi doctrine for governing, as the Wahhabi tenets focused on moral, ritual and territorial expansionist issues. The political order evolved according to state interests. There were the royal family, government ministers, elite businessmen and regional governors, who together ran the regime and, in fact, held political and economic prominence over the religious clerics.

In 1929–30, the *Ikhwan* were decisively defeated as an active opposition, and their version of how to uphold Islamic principles did not dominate Saudi society. However, their convictions did remain as a latent, undercover denomination, serving various opposition groups over the years. Therefore, religious authority did not rest, at least not entirely, with the *'ulama'* of the establishment; even today, other qualified persons may interpret the holy law as they understand it, challenge the establishment's interpretation and gather together adherents of their preaching. In addition, the *Ikhwan*'s version resisted the supremacy of the incumbent Saudi government. They favored a different regime, perhaps under another government. Furthermore, their version does not view state interests as supreme, overruling other concerns. It focuses on Islamic goals, in their unmediated and pre-state forms. In their view, the exercising of the holy law and striving for an Islamic lifestyle is of the highest worth and therefore deserves priority over state interests.[3]

Two conclusions can be reached from this discussion. The first is that the vagaries of state formation provoked oppositions' responses attempting to restore what they regarded as a controlled and just rule. These vagaries took the form of the sometimes extreme intensification of modernization, evident in a westernizing lifestyle and of a centralizing, bureaucratic, even absolute, government, to the dismay of different groups in society who objected to this process. Second, both the authorities and their opponents used the language of Islam to express themselves: they accused each other of breaching the holy law, of neglecting Islamic goals and deviating from Islamic practices, even those pertaining to administrative, economic and political affairs. Thus, while Saudi Arabia emerged as a state with a puritanical and Islamic-oriented regime, the changing phases of state formation provoked opposition groups to accuse the government of unlawful Islamic conduct and to suggest new interpretations and even a new government in the name of Islam.

To be sure, outward tension between opposition forces and the government was a rare occurence in Saudi Arabia. The Saudi state was a flexible and accommodating institution.[4] Its evolution into an organized state in the 1930s, with fixed international borders, a centralizing government and a policy geared toward economic development was balanced by the maintenance of personalized, informal decision-making at the top, contacts between the rulers and the lower ranks, intermarriage between princes and commoners and cultivation of the senior *'ulama's* position. It is true that in the late 1950s, during King Sa'ud's reign (1953–64) an opposition movement developed which questioned the arrangements and exposed the anomalies of this state order. In the light of initial oil income and the advent of radical pan-Arabism, the process of decision-making and personal, arbitrary conduct of King Sa'ud was deemed obsolete. At that time, the intellectual, or even literate community in Saudi Arabia was still limited, so that an opposition movement, such as it was, emerged chiefly from among the young princes, led by Prince Tallal. They advocated a constitutional monarchy, based on liberal and socialist principles. With the exception of Prince Tallal's short period of participation in government in 1960, this movement remained a vocal, non-violent but also ineffective critic of the state order, and in 1962 Tallal and some of his associates went into exile (to Lebanon, and then Egypt) where they continued their futile calumny of the Saudi regime for some time.[5]

During King Faysal's reign (1964–75), a new stage of state building emerged, focusing on the reforms introduced to remedy the shortcomings of the earlier state order. This revised state order, continued by Faysal's successor, King Khalid (1975–82), focused on maintaining the supreme, unrestricted rule of the King, and reinforced his role through a more complex, differentiated bureaucracy. Centered on a wealthy, oil-based economy, it geared itself to the development of business and health and education services. From this framework, there emerged socio-economic stratification and educated groups. The absolute rule and socio-economic and technological change were balanced by the maintenance of both the Wahhabi moral code and patron-client, tribal and personal contacts among the different societal groups, notably between princes and commoners, all of which were effective in reinforcing a traditional and familiar lifestyle. An elaborate welfare system was introduced, guaranteeing free health insurance and free education to Saudi citizens, especially to support those elements who did not benefit from business opportunities and social change.[6]

Faysal's order was sustained for almost three decades, mainly by satisfying the major part of Saudi society. Consequently, the opposition movement of November 1979 was an exception to the relative calm and did not portend further challenges. In that instance, several hundred activists, mostly from the former *Ikhwan* tribe, 'Utayba, coalesced after military service in the National Guard while some of them were students at the Islamic University of Medina. They were motivated in several ways, as their leader, Juhayman al-'Utaybi, demonstrated in his publicized letters, which explained their anti-establishment religious convictions.

'Utaybi's group violently took over the Grand Mosque in Mecca, the holiest of all Islamic sites, on 20 November 1979. It drew support only from the manual workers of the lower classes and foreign laborers (from Egypt, Yemen and Pakistan). The vast majority of Saudi society regarded them as a violent, marginal group, whose elimination by security forces was deemed fully justified, this after two weeks of unlawfully occupying the holy Mosque. A *fatwa* of 30 leading *'ulama',* dated 24 November, which depicted them as rebels and trouble-makers, added to their negative image.[7] In additon, 'Utaybi's demands that oil should not be sold to the US and that state wealth should not be squandered, but used only to meet society's needs,[8] had little appeal in a regime that used considerable funds to upgrade its inhabitants' living standards.

At bottom, 'Utaybi's group was reacting, in an extreme fashion, to the sudden affluence and western lifestyle which had begun to emerge in the Kingdom. He attempted to delegitimize Saudi rule in the tradition of the *Ikhwan:* Ibn Sa'ud had deceived the *Ikhwan* by failing to lead them in a *jihad* against neighboring states and instead had formed an alliance with the 'Christians'. The duty of a good Muslim, contended 'Utaybi, was to fight the West and reject the socio-technological 'progress' of Saudi society. Furthermore, he argued, the authority of the main *'ulama'* was false. They were aligned, including the leading cleric 'Abd al-'Aziz Ibn Baz, with the Saudi family in a bond of corruption.[9] Like the *Ikhwan,* 'Utaybi's movement rejected the state's Islamic authority and reserved its right to interpret Wahhabi Islam in a militant form, with a call to overthrow the Saudi family, fight the West and ban the Islamic senior *'ulama'.* However, in 1979, there were no obvious and widely agreed-upon reasons in Saudi society to ban the senior clergy, fight the West and topple the Saudis. Most Saudis were basically satisfied with the prevailing mode of Faysal's order.

A challenge from a different source, Saudi Arabia's Shi'i minority who were concentrated in the Gulf region of al-Hassa, erupted shortly after the Grand Mosque takeover. Demonstrations during the Shi'i *'Ashura* festival (dedicated to mourning the deaths of the seventh century Imams Hasan and Husayn) on 28 November 1979, and again on 1 February 1980, deteriorated into riots against the authorities. They were kindled mainly by Iranian provocation, typical of Khomeini's efforts to export the newly victorious Iranian revolution. The Shi'i audacity in openly holding, for the first time in decades, the *'Ashura* festival against the wishes of the Saudi authorities, attests to the strength of Iranian influence. Furthermore, it may also attest to the fact that the Shi'i population was relatively discriminated against, in both jobs and welfare conditions. The Saudi authorities' response included harsh suppression of the riots (leading to a total of 21 dead in the two incidents) as well as an improvement in economic conditions and development in Shi'i home areas.[10] The Shi'i outburst was not repeated. It did not prove to be a well-organized opposition movement, but a short-lived event which did not threaten to derail the incumbent order.

### The Decline of Faysal's State Order

It was only in the 1990s that a more sustained, non-episodic radical Islamic opposition movement emerged. Like its predecessors, it questioned the nature of the existing state order and presented its own interpretation of Wahhabi Islam. What precipitated this development was the decline of several of the underpinnings of the state order and inherent balance which had prevailed in the Kingdom since the 1960s. The decline was catalyzed in part by the 1990–91 Gulf War, which exposed deep-rooted structural problems in Saudi society. First, Saudi leaders, who should have been the primary force in the ongoing process of state building, were both aging and losing their prestige. King Fahd, Crown Prince 'Abdallah and the person often identified as the third important leader, Minister of Defence Sultan, were all septuagenarians. King Fahd suffered from cardiac and diabetic problems, and in November 1995 had a minor stroke, compelling him to transfer authority temporarily to 'Abdallah. Their ability to lead the country was thus increasingly doubtful. Moreover, the need to rely on 500,000 foreign soldiers to cope with the Iraqi threat during 1990–91 and the expenditure of c.$80 billion from the Saudi financial reserves ($20 billion paid to Iraq during its 1980–88 war with Iran and $60 billion for Desert Storm) left the Kingdom in an economic recession and brought about a change for the worse in the Saudi people's image of the royal family as charismatic, resourceful and invincible rulers.[11]

The economic well-being, which had anchored the state order, was no longer guaranteed. The economy had been in recession since the mid-1980s, when oil prices started to decline. Unfavorable macro-economic figures in the 1990s included a price of oil per barrel at $18 or less, budget deficits of just under c.$20 billion, unprofitable investments (e.g., in wheat-growing), a declining GDP per capita from $17,000 in the early 1980s to just over $7,000 in 1995 and growing internal borrowing.[12]

In addition, social conditions, which were the proof of the regime's previously successful balancing acts, were also declining. Increased unemployment (25 per cent among university graduates), and reduced health and educational services were particularly disturbing in a fast-growing Saudi society with an extremely high birth rate (about 3.6 per cent per annum). The cultivation of a healthy, well-educated and numerically growing Saudi society became more and more difficult under new budget constraints.[13]

Changing demographic conditions, a relative economic recession, the rise of a new, educated generation in Saudi Arabia and the country's aging and somewhat incompetent rulers all shook Faysal's order and exposed its deficiencies in the 1990s. A fundamentalist opposition movement thus emerged, under new circumstances. First, the existing mode of state development, including the Kingdom's economic, social and political arrangements, was unsatisfactory to a considerable segment of Saudi society. Second, the emerging opposition was able to establish some support in Saudi society, which, even though not extensive, was at least sufficient to sustain it for some years. The third point was that the opposition leaders were able to couch their grievances in an Islamic language which, unlike in the movement of 1979, related to contemporary and relevant circumstances.

The most important characteristic of the fundamentalist opposition of the 1990s was its educational and socio-economic stratification. Its members were not identified as especially coming from the lower class, who were mainly manual workers in construction, transport and small businesses. Nor were they of a particular or dominant tribal origin, as in the case of the group who occupied the Grand Mosque in November 1979. Instead, they were of mixed origins whose common denominator was their academic background, mostly students, academics or higher education graduates working as professionals or administrators, and who could be regarded as members of the new 'middle class'.

The opposition of the 1990s, in fact, represented a new type of activist, a product of the era of affluence. As William Ochsenwald has noted, many young Saudis opted to take advantage of higher education opportunities, either in one of the seven Saudi universities or in western institutions of higher education. In their studies, young Saudis mixed lay, academic or technical studies with a religious curriculum. Moreover, a new sort of young *'ulama'* emerged, who mixed traditional tutorials with university education, gaining exposure to both secular education and currents of thought, popular among foreign *'ulama'*, such as the Muslim Brotherhood groups in Egypt and various Islamic revivalists. In addition, many *'ulama'* embarked on secular careers. A type of professional *'alim*, an educated academic knowledgeable in both lay and religious ideologies, thus emerged: a new mixture of lay-educated professionals with religious knowledge and *'ulama'* interacting with wider elements of Saudi society.[14]

The personal careers and occupations of some of the main activists in the fundamentalist opposition reflected the changes which had occurred in Saudi society. Safar al-Hawwali, a preacher who established a following of supporters and students, was a lecturer and head of the religious department at the Islamic University in Medina. Another popular preacher, Salman al-'Awda, studied both natural sciences and law and had become a lecturer in religious studies at the Imam Muhammad University, Qasim Branch in the city of Burayda. The main activists of the fundamentalist opposition office in London, the Committee for the Defence of the Legitimate Rights (CDLR) (Lajnat Difa' 'an al-Huquq al-Shar'iyya) were Muhammad al-Mas'ari, a physicist, and Sa'd al-Faqih, a lawyer and former head of the Saudi Board of Grievances.[15] In a recent study, R. H. Dekmejian showed how academics and religious sages mingled: the signatories of two petitions served on King Fahd (52 signed in May 1991 and 107 in September 1992) presenting Islamic-fundamentalist demands, consisted of about 60 per cent academics with about 45 per cent of the signatories holding religious positions.[16]

The opposition's wide-ranging socio-political critique reflected this combination of 'modern' and Islamic education, as opposed to the narrow, fanatical Islam espoused by regime opponents in previous decades. They presumed to represent the 'liberal opposition', a group of academics and officials who served King Fahd the first petition after the Second Gulf War in April 1991, asking for the establishment of a Consultative Council (Majlis al-Shura), the implementation of civil rights and appointments in the administration based on merit. In the ensuing months, however, the liberals were silenced either by government intimidation or promises of change, and subsequently disappeared from the political stage. The fundamentalists not only displayed more staying power, but also employed a more appropriate discourse to represent a wide range of academic, middle-class public opinion in criticizing the government. They aspired to act, in the words of Sa'd al-Faqih, as an 'enlightened fundamentalist trend', which had deeply 'penetrated the public, and has influence over the middle class and among intellectuals'.[17]

The fundamentalist opposition thus maintained that its resentment of Saudi rule was grounded in the government's violation of moral and efficient administration and economics, and lack of attention to strategic planning. The opposition's beliefs echoed the calls for consumer rights and a more just economy which they had acquired on western campuses. Indeed, among the first middle-class Islamic opposition activists were Saudis studying in the US, who faxed home their complaints about the corruption of Saudi leaders.[18] The memorandum of September 1992, a revision of earlier petitions, articulated the broadly based arguments against government practices. It demanded that ministers and officials be appointed without favoritism based on kinship, ethnic or regional considerations. It also demanded that overseas spending be subject to accountable scrutiny and that luxury construction and wasteful expenditure cease. In its publications, the CDLR often pointed out the high stipends for princes and the commissions they received on military transactions, while the average Saudi had to pay indirect taxes on telephone, petrol and electricity, yet ran the risk of unemployment and endured worsening water, health, educational and postal services.[19]

To be sure, the opposition had a clear Islamic agenda and a definite Islamic purpose. The yardstick for measuring the government's policies was how it followed the law, whether it ran a just and legal regime or slid into a sinful performance. To understand the opposition's preaching fully, it should be stressed that in its leaders' eyes, the remedy for the regime's failing managerial, strategic and economic conduct was the full implementation of the *shari'a* and the reintroduction of Islamic goals for Saudi authorities in the different fields of public life. In the memorandum of 1992 and other CDLR publications, it was put forth that the implementation of the *shari'a* as an integral part of the virtues of Islamic equality and morality constituted a guarantee of untainted administrative appointments, the prevention of illegal indirect taxes and controlled social services. Moreover, government ministries would have to operate according to Islamic goals, which would ensure their correct and lawful conduct.[20]

## Discrediting the Incumbent Regime

The discreditation campaign mounted by the opposition was intended to delegitimize Saudi rule by destroying its foundations. The opposition did not entirely discredit the role of tribal values in Saudi society; instead it criticized Saudi rulers' use of such values to assure their absolute rule. In one of its publications, the opposition attacked Sa'ud hegemony as evidenced by the name Saudi Arabia. The writer, M. S. Zein Al-Abdin, noted that people of a variety of tribes (i.e., Qahtan, Mutayr, 'Utayba, Shammar and others) should not really regard themselves as 'Saudi citizens'. 'I do not know how their citizenship can be Saudi while they themselves claim purer nobility and ancestry than the family of Sa'ud,' he asked rhetorically.[21] The Saudi rulers were thus portrayed as usurpers. They were also depicted as misusing tribal principles, focusing on personal preferences to further their rule. They were described as using state funds to pay rents, in order to maintain the personal wealth of their dynasty, and accused of appointing their proteges to the state's bureaucracy. According to the opposition, the Saudis also conducted internal relations according to 'negative tribal principles', notably the persistence of intra-dynastical factions within the royal family. Thus, the CDLR criticized the Saudi leaders for maintaining the rift between Fahd and his six Sudayri brothers and Crown Prince 'Abdallah. The example which they tendered was Prince Sultan's (Fahd's full brother and minister of defence) public announcement in November 1995, describing Fahd's recent health problems as a 'slight ailment', thereby trying to dispel the impression that Fahd's handover of power to 'Abdallah was permanent. This statement allegedly brought to light Sultan's refusal to acknowledge 'Abdallah as heir to the throne.[22]

The Islamist opposition also focused on several areas of socioeconomic neglect and incompetence. One concerned the corrupt and asymmetrical allocation of wealth: only the royal family, its cronies and certain 'lucky' geographical regions had enjoyed the lion's share of the huge oil wealth, while the middle and lower classes and most of the peripheral regions (bordering Yemen, Jordan and Iraq) had been neglected. Moreover, 'despite these problems, their actions do not suggest that al-Sa'ud has given the slightest thought to the above questions, since shortsightedness and self-concern guide their activities'.[23]

The opposition also pointed out the Saudi rulers' poor record in human rights. The Islamists thereby tried to discredit the regime as cruel and oppressive, as demonstrated in the arrest and torture of opposition leaders (notably, the arrest campaigns such as that launched on 13 September 1994 against Islamist preachers and academics). Moreover, the opposition was extremely vocal over the regime's attempts to prevent political freedom and criticism of the government, namely the right to pass on information and hold meetings. The opposition depicted these efforts as proof of the government's weakness; its leaders regarded any criticism as a threat to their existence. Unlike strong and credible regimes, the Saudis could not tolerate criticism. The opposition made public a long list of cases in which their leaders who had engaged in preaching against the government's foreign policy had been warned to stop and taken into custody when they refused.[24]

The Islamists' most potent efforts to discredit the regime were directed at the government's outward appearance as a lawful, Islamic regime. The opposition viewed the rulers' association with senior 'ulama', notably of the

Supreme Council of Senior Scholars, as an instrumental mechanism to initiate a suitable *fatwa* (religious opinion) to justify their policy. Sa'd al-Faqih, the deputy leader of the CDLR, viewed these *'ulama'* as *fatwa*-makers 'not out of conviction, but out of fear of the consequences of not doing so'.[25] In another opposition publication, the writer, Ehsan Ehsanullah, tried to prove that Saudi rule violated in various forms its presumption of upholding Muslim rule within the prescribed limits of the *shari'a*, namely *siyasa shar'iyya*. The Saudis, he declared, had attempted to establish a *mulk*, a secular, ruler's estate, rather than an Islamic community (*umma*). Their very rule over a kingdom was antithetical to Islam and their control of the holy places an unlawful practice (*bid'a*). The Saudi rulers also had not transformed society into a 'rightful society' (*umma wasatan*) characterized by law-abiding members of a religious community, but rather kept the inhabitants content by means of economic payoffs. Saudi rule should thus be regarded as a common power state, or sultanate; one CDLR publication referred to the Saudi rulers as 'Pharaohs', non-Islamic and idol-preaching rulers.[26]

In the CDLR's view, the regime 'can be classified at best as a mix of a mutilated form of Islam combined with tribalism and feudalism. It has even degenerated into a form of Mafia-like family rule'.[27] The illegitimacy of the Saudi regime was, in the opposition's view, plain to see, particularly since it had discredited itself in areas where the Saudi rulers hoped to legitimize and solidify their rule: reliance on tribal values, Wahhabi Islam and economic well-being for the whole Saudi society. Their multiple failures had stripped them of any meaningful legitimacy.

## Organizational and Operational Remarks: Where Does the Threat to the Regime Lie?

The Sunni Islamist Opposition represents several ideological trends. There are Hijazi *neo-Salafi* groups, oriented to a strict interpretation of the *shari'a*. These are non-Wahhabi and do not recognize the Najdi, Wahhabi *'ulama'*.[28] There are also the leading theologians, such as Safar al-Hawwali, Salman al-'Awda and 'Aid al-Qarni, their students and other middle-class followers as well as the CDLR. All were critical of the incumbent rulers' interpretation of the *shari'a* and of the senior *'ulama''s* authority. However, they have not (at least until now) established a clear ideological alternative, for a number of reasons:

(1) They lack a unifying ideological trend which would define their position within the broader Islamist fundamentalist discourse. The variations among Wahhabi and non-Wahhabi fundamentalist origins,

and the need of the Saudi-Wahhabi opposition to appeal and build bridges toward other fundamentalists and western-educated supporters, led them to draw on western ideas of good management, Muslim-Brotherhood-related concepts of justice and Wahhabi responses to unlawful government.

(2) They also lack a clear political platform: they preach against Saudi rule and the royal family, but do not call clearly for its ousting through revolutionary action or for the Saudi masses to rise up against the regime. They may yet be too unsure of popular support and power to do so. In some major events, such as after the September 1994 arrests, the number of demonstrators reached several thousand,[29] but in an unorganized, uninstitutionalized form. They seemed to be waiting for the Saudi regime to collapse on its own and, in the meantime, continued their efforts to delegitimatize the regime and exacerbate the situation.

(3) Despite their main preachers' popular appeal, circulated via cassettes, faxes and printed publications, the opposition did not produce a religious authority of stature who could match the position of the leading 'ulama', notably 'Abd al-'Aziz Ibn Baz. Thus, despite their audacious characterization of the Senior Council of Scholars as a rubber stamp for Saudi rule, they were unable to match or counterbalance its role through an opposition-led body.

In addition, the opposition movement of the 1990s was not reliant on an identified, institutionalized social group, a tribal group and/or a regionally-based group, which had constituted the hub of fundamentalist opposition in the past. Lacking this background, the 1990s opposition was bereft of the known and established tradition of fighting and violence common to tribal groups, thus depriving it of the ability to cultivate an image of bravery and sedition. However, since 1995, a growing readiness to engage in violence had become noticeable. One source for this change might have been the thousands of Saudi volunteers, 4000 *mujahidin* (holy fighters) from Medina alone, who had been despatched by the Saudi government to Afghanistan to fight the Soviet armies there. Although there is no clear evidence that Saudi *mujahidin* returned to become an armed opposition in Saudi Arabia, it should be borne in mind that this did happen in Egypt, Algeria, Yemen and elsewhere; the Saudi *mujahidin* had acquired skills and access to arms capable of turning them toward a violent course of action.[30] Another source of Saudi opposition violence might have emanated from a group led by 'Usama ibn Ladin, a Jidda-based businessman originally from Hadramawt, who had contacts with the leaders of the radical Islamist regime in Sudan. He was expelled from Saudi Arabia and denied his Saudi citizenship in

April 1994, due to his involvement in sabotage and anti-government activities in both Saudi Arabia and in Egypt. Ibn Ladin thereupon focused on publishing anti-Saudi booklets in London, in which his own, and other Saudi opposition factions, were presented as one main body.[31] In addition, from his place of imprisonment, one of the main Saudi activists, Salman al-'Awda, called for his supporters, on 30 April 1995, to stop 'studying the law' and embark on an anti-government *jihad*. 'Awda did not call for a clear uprising, but predicted 'events, incidents and happenings' which would kindle clashes between the government and Saudi demonstrators,[32] and pave the way for a broadly based *jihad* against the government.

It is unclear whether these developments led to the car-bomb explosion in a US-staffed communications center of the Saudi internal militia, the National Guard, on 13 November 1995. The perpetrators could also have been Iranian or Iraqi-despatched terrorists.[33]

Despite the gradual increase in violent incidents on the part of the Saudi Islamist opposition, terrorism did not develop into an organized and institutionalized form of activity. The lack of a violent, anti-government tradition, typical of the present supporters of the Islamist opposition, and particularly their tendency to fight the government by religious discourse on the level of moral and religious principles, has so far limited the development of a major terrorist course of action.

The main threat posed by the opposition movement should thus be understood in different terms:

(1) The opposition drew its supporters from the educated, professional circles, threatening to turn the backbone of Saudi society into a dissatisfied, alienated class, supplying new members for the active opposition ranks.

(2) The opposition possessed the ability to expose the managerial, leadership and administrative incompetence of the government and to discredit it on moral and religious grounds. This discrediting was particularly difficult for the government, as it presumed to delegitimize its two most important societal underpinnings: the religious and tribal practices on which it relied. However, as mentioned above, the opposition movements did not produce an alternative socio-political order, religious center or prominant ruling figures which could seriously challenge the incumbent government.

## The Authorities' Response

The government's response to the opposition's challenge can be classified into several categories. One central feature was the imposition of physical limitations on the opposition activists. The Saudi police initiated arrest campaigns after each outburst of opposition activity, accompanied by restrictions of movement and the banning of preachers' cassettes. The activists' movements were also put under surveillance, and meetings and gatherings were dispersed and banned. This type of response reached its peak on 9 and 13 September 1994, with the arrest of two main preachers, Salman al-'Awda and Safar al-Hawwali together with, according to the CDLR, 1,300 of their followers, in the city of Burayda in the Qasim region.[34] A separate tactic employed by the authorities was to seek to effect splits within the opposition through the tendering of material incentives.

The government also attempted to delegitimize the opposition by denoting their activities as dissident (*bid'a*) and unlawful, and by turning the chief, establishment *'ulama'* against the opposition. Thus, after the abovementioned arrests, the Grand Mufti (chief religious authority) and head of the Council of leading *'ulama'*, Ibn Baz, issued a *fatwa* declaring that unless the two leading preachers, 'Awda and Hawwali, repented of their former conduct, they would be banned from lecturing, conducting meetings and recording cassettes. Baz's *fatwa* justified their arrests, and other leading *'ulama'* followed suit.[35] Fahd himself accused the opposition of unlawfully calling itself fundamentalist, while in fact it was a usurper of the state system and acting against society.[36] However, as in several past cases, there were senior *'ulama'* who hesitated to condemn the opposition, presumably identifying, at least partially, with their preaching. In October 1994, the King announced the establishment of a Supreme Council of Islamic Affairs (al-Majlis al-'Ala lil-Shu'un al-Islamiyya), led by Prince Sultan, and a few days later the Council for Islamic Call and Guidance (al-Majlis lil-Da'wa wal-Irshad) headed by the Minister of Islamic Affairs, Religious Guidance and Endowments, 'Abdallah al-Turki. These two new bodies were made responsible for guidance of Saudis abroad, moral behavior and proper conduct of mosque functionaries, and mosque activities at home.[37] This was a clear attempt to regulate mosques, over and above the incumbent *'ulama'*'s authority.

In addition to its religious aspects, this official response echoed another category of responses aimed at upholding state authority above all other, dating back to 1992. The establishment of a 60-member appointed Consultative Council which began operating in Fall 1992 was a way of placating the professionals, who constituted 60 per cent of the members, with institutionalized advisory rights. However, the Consultative Council was merely a fig-leaf, as it was part of a basic law which stressed the King's legislative and executive authority (the judicial bodies being subjected only to the *shari'a*) and his responsibility for choosing his Crown Prince from among the royal family. Another law underlined the position of regional governors (*umara*) in the provinces. The main purpose of these laws was to reaffirm the royal family's authority and particularly that of the King, as paramount ruler (*Wali al-Amr*) over the entire country.[38]

## Conclusion

The reasons for the emergence of the Saudi fundamentalist opposition in the post-Desert Storm era can be explained by the problems of economic recession, declining leadership and security and the rise of new elites that typified this period. As such, the Saudi opposition resembled other opposition movements in the Middle East. The uniqueness of the Saudi case, however, was in its intellectual and ideological origins, namely a Wahhabi opposition school going back to the 1920s, with principles which enabled the opposition to give its own seditious interpretation to the *shari'a* and, consequently, to discredit both the senior *ulama'* and the Saudi government. In addition, their religious arguments corresponded to western ideas of managerial and administrative misconduct, attributed to the Saudi government, which appealed to educated, middle-class Saudi professionals and students. Hence, unlike the limited tribal nature of the earlier opposition movements, the present movement was based on a combination of Wahhabi and western ideas. However, this movement lacked a clear call for revolution and was not violent in nature. The government was thus able to effectively employ both administrative means and its intelligence system to fight the opposition.[39] But the opposition's drive to discredit the authorities on religious, tribal and socioeconomic grounds may have a long-term corrosive effect.

## NOTES

1. J. Kostiner, 'On Instruments and their Designers: The Ikhwan of Najd and the Formation of the Saudi State', *Middle Eastern Studies* 21 (1985) pp.298–323.
2. Compare with James P. Piscatori, 'The Role of Islam in Saudi Arabia's Political Development', in John L. Esposito (ed.), *Islam and Development: Religion and Sociopolitical Change* (Syracuse: SUP 1980) pp.123–38.
3. Kostiner (note 1); H. St. John B. Philby, 'Notes on Saudi Arabia for Dr. Hugh Scott', Philby's Papers (St. Anthony's College, Oxford University, 29 Aug. 1944).
4. See the theory of J. Migdal, *Strong Societies and Weak States* (Princeton: PUP 1988).
5. H. Lackner, *A House Built on Sand* (London: Ithaca Press 1978) pp.65, 74–89, 137–55.
6. D. Holden and R. Johns, *The House of Saud* (London: Sidgwick and Jackson 1981) pp.198–222.
7. M. Abir, *Saudi Arabia in the Oil Era* (London: Frank Cass 1987) p.159; J.A. Kechichian, 'The Role of the 'ulama' in the Politics of an Islamic State: The Case of Saudi Arabia', *International Journal of Middle Eastern Studies* 18 (1986) pp.53–71.
8. J.A. Kechichian, 'Islamic Revivalism and Change in Saudi Arabia: Juhayman al-'Utaybi's "Letters to the Saudi People"', *The Muslim World* 50 (1990) pp.1–16.

9. Ibid.
10. Abir (note 7) p.156.
11. *The Economist,* 18 March 1995.
12. *Financial Times,* Special Supplement on Saudi Arabia, 20 Dec. 1995.
13. *New York Times,* 22 Aug. 1993; *Washington Post,* 28 Oct., 18 Dec. 19'
14. W. Ochsenwald, 'Saudi Arabia' in Shireen T. Hunter (ed.), *The Revivalism* (Bloomington: Indiana UP 1988) pp.103–15.
15. M. al-Rifa'i, *al-Mashru' al-Islahi fil Sa'udiyya: Qissat al Hawwali wal-'Awda* (n.p. 1995) pp.18–20.
16. R.H. Dekmejian, 'The Rise of Political Islamism in Saudi Arabia', *The Middle East Journal* 48 (1994) pp.635–7.
17. Sa'd al-Faqih, 'Which Way for the Kingdom?', *Middle East Dialogue* 10 (May 1994).
18. *Mudhakirat al-Nasiha* (n.d., n.p.) Sept. 1992 Memorandum; *Al-Muharrir,* 14 Sept. 1992; Mas'ari's interview with *Radio Tehran,* 1 May – quoted by *BBC World,* 3 May 1995.
19. For instance, *CDLR Monitor* 66 (22 Sept. 1995); M.S. Zein Al-Abdin, *The Saudi Terror* (Birmingham Centre of Islamic Studies 1995) p.5.
20. Rifa'i (note 15) pp.21–5.
21. *Mideast Mirror,* 14 Jan. 1996.
22. *CDLR Monitor* 65 (7 Oct. 1995).
23. *Saudi Arabia: A Country Report* (CDLR Publication, 3 Jan. 1995).
24. *Saudi Record of Human Rights 1994* (LIBERTY for the Muslim World, 6 Feb. 1995).
25. al-Faqih (note 17).
26. *Saudi Arabia, A Country Report* (note 23).
27. *CDLR Monitor* (note 22).
28. See the in-depth account by R. Schulze, *Islamisher Nationalismus im 20 Jahrhundert* (Leiden: E.J. Brill 1990) pp.133–80.
29. Ehsan Ehsanullah, *Siyasa Shar'iyya, The Anthropology of Injustice, The Case of the Saudi Kingdom* (London: Hajrah Sanaullah Trust 1994).
30. *Financial Times,* 20 Dec. 1995.
31. *Al-Yamman al-Kubra,* 19 Nov. 1995; *Al-Kurbaj,* Nov. 1995.
32. *MidEast Mirror,* 30 April 1995.
33. *Financial Times,* 20 Dec. 1995.
34. *New York Times,* 22 Sept. 1994; *CDLR Press Releases* 14, 18, 23 Sept. 1994. The discussion of government responses as well as of the other issues of this article, derive from the chapters and resource material in Joshua Teitelbaum, 'Saudi Arabia', in Ami Ayalon (ed.), *Middle East Contemporary Survey* 17 (1993) (Boulder, CO: Westview Press 1995). I am grateful to Josh for his cooperation and good advice.
35. *Saudi Press Agency,* 26 Sept. – FBIS-NEA, *Daily Report,* 27 Sept. 1994.
36. *Al-Hayat,* 21 Oct. 1994.
37. *Al-Hayat,* 5 Oct. 1994; *Al Sharq al-Awsat,* 9 Oct. 1994; see Teitelbaum (note 34).
38. For the basic laws, see Teitelbaum (note 34) pp.668–701; and R. Aba-Namay, 'The Recent Constitutional Reforms in Saudi Arabia', *The International and Comparative Law Quarterly* 42 (1993) pp.295–331. See also Fahd's interview in *al-Siyasa,* 28 March 1992.
39. See Teitelbaum (note 34).

# Hizballah in Lebanon – At the Crossroads

## EYAL ZISSER

Hizballah, the Party of God, burst onto the Lebanese scene in a whirlwind of violence at the end of 1983. Since then, it has become a power with considerable clout in the Shi'i community of Lebanon. At the end of the 1980s it reached the height of its strength when it gained control of most parts of the Shi'i concentrations in Lebanon. However, since then, Hizballah has faced a series of challenges which threaten its continued activity, if not its very existence, including the Ta'if agreement, the Middle East peace process and Iran's increasing inability to support Hizballah. In the face of these challenges, Hizballah appears pragmatic, willing, it seems, to abandon its goals, at least for the time being. This, however, raises a key question: Can the organization truly change course and turn away from the ideological commitment and path of violence that have characterized it to date? Or do those aspects indeed define the organization? It is still too early to lay odds on the organization's future, but it seems that it may be in jeopardy.

Hizballah, the Party of God, burst onto the Lebanese scene in a whirlwind of violence at the end of 1983. A string of grievous attacks against Israeli and western targets in Lebanon left hundreds dead and wounded, leading to the end of American and French involvement and Israel's withdrawal from most of Lebanon soon after. These terrorist strikes mark the start of a new phase in the politics of Lebanon's Shi'i community and, indeed, for the country as a whole.

The violent struggle against the West, and particularly Israel, has since become one of the hallmarks of Hizballah activity. This development suggests how profoundly the organization has been influenced by two pivotal events in the recent history of the Middle East: Iran's Islamic revolution and Israel's involvement in Lebanon since 1982. However, internal processes in Lebanon, particularly the Shi'i community, since the 1950s, must also be considered in order to understand the rise of Hizballah.

A survey of the factors that lead to the organization's emergence lays bare one of the central dilemmas with which it has had to contend since its inception. Hizballah owes a certain debt to Iran for the support it has provided in establishing and sustaining the organization. Hizballah is committed to Iran's path and perceptions; it even adheres to Iran's dictates. Hizballah's goal is the establishment of an Islamic Republic in Lebanon, like that established in Iran in 1979. However, Hizballah has been forced to approach this objective from a Lebanese context in which it operates and to pay heed to the local circumstances that attended its birth.

This predicament, as yet unresolved, was clearly expressed by the organization's Secretary-General, Sayyid Hasan Nasrallah, in an interview in August 1994 with the organization's newspaper, *al-'Ahd*. He stated that, '[Hizballah] is indeed a Lebanese party; its leadership is Lebanese, its members are Lebanese, and its following is Lebanese, yet it has ties with another country'. Nasrallah later added in a rejoinder to opponents of the organization that, 'This phenomenon is no stranger to Lebanese reality, as every party operating in Lebanon has ties to other countries, yet no one casts doubts on their Lebanese identity'.[1]

Since Hizballah first organized its operations in 1983, it has become a power with considerable clout in the Shi'i community of Lebanon. At the end of the 1980s it reached the height of its strength when it gained control of most of West Beirut and large sections of South Lebanon. Since then, however, Hizballah has faced a series of challenges which threaten its continued activity, if not its very existence. Most important of these is the Ta'if agreement which led to the conclusion of the civil war in which the organization had flowered. The Ta'if agreement laid the foundations for the establishment of a new Maronite-Sunni order with Syrian backing. It excluded the Shi'i community from this new order, despite the fact that it constitutes a majority in the country. A second challenge is the Middle East peace process, which may force an end to the organization's struggle against Israel and erode one of its bases of legitimacy and power. Finally, Iran's increasing political and economic difficulties are liable to curtail its ability to back the organization politically, economically and militarily as generously as it has in the past.

In the face of these challenges, Hizballah appears pragmatic and enterprising, ready, it seems, to abandon its ideological goals, at least for the time being or, more precisely, to postpone their implementation to the far future. Hence, the organization took part in the Lebanese parliamentary elections in the summer of 1992, thereby conferring its de facto recognition to the Ta'if agreement which it had initially outright rejected. Hizballah is also attempting to expand its activity to social and economic spheres, thereby laying the foundations for its transformation into a social and political movement that could play a role in the existing Lebanese political order. Declarations by Hizballah leaders during the last few years also indicate a grudging readiness to accept a possible Israeli-Syrian-Lebanese peace agreement.

This state of affairs raises a key question, the answer to which will determine, to a great extent, Hizballah's ability to meet the challenges facing it today. Can the organization truly change course? Can it turn away from its ideological commitment, fervor and the path of violence that have characterized it to date? It is exactly these elements that have constituted the essence of Hizballah – their loss will strip it of its unique character, its vitality and its ability to capture hearts and minds. Such a change of course would blur the line between Hizballah and its rival for control of the Shi'i community, Amal, which preaches Shi'i integration into the existing Lebanese order, albeit with certain reforms.

On the other hand, should Hizballah stay true to its path and policies it is likely to find itself on a collision course with the Lebanese government and the Maronite and Sunni communities behind it who would like to see Hizballah and the Shi'i community it represents weakened. The trajectory fueled by adherence to its ideology would lead Hizballah to clash with Syria, which considers its own interests in Lebanon best served by the establishment of a stable, moderate regime, subservient to Syria. In addition, it means the continuation of the struggle with Israel, which regards Hizballah as a terrorist organization threatening security on its northern border as well as Israeli and Jewish targets abroad.

It is still too early to lay odds on the organization's future. However, its actions and policies during the past few years make it possible to cautiously suggest that it would be very difficult, if not impossible, for Hizballah to abandon its long-term objectives which include the practical and ideological commitment to a violent struggle with Israel and the West. Consideration of the dangers facing the organization suggest that its future is in jeopardy.

Indeed, the impasse in the Syrian-Israeli negotiations during most of 1995–96 enabled Hizballah to continue and even to escalate its military activity against Israel, thus postponing the moment of truth. Furthermore, in continuing the military struggle against Israel, Hizballah attained clear achievements, such as the understandings following Israel's operations 'Accountability' of 1993 and 'Grapes of Wrath' of 1996. These understandings recognized the right of Hizballah to attack Israeli targets in the security zone, while the mutual commitment to avoid civilian targets enabled Hizballah to portray itself as the defender of the Shi'i population in southern Lebanon. Nevertheless, these achievements were clearly short-term, and did not incur a real change in the realities threatening Hizballah in the long run.

## The Emergence of Hizballah

On 18 April 1983, the American embassy in Beirut was blown up by a suicide bomber. Sixty-one people were killed and 120 wounded. Some months later, on 23 October, the headquarters of the US Marines and those of the French forces in Beirut were attacked in a similar manner. Two hundred thirty-nine Marines and 23 French soldiers were killed; another hundred were injured. A week later, on 4 November 1983, the Israeli Army headquarters in Tyre was similarly hit. Twenty-nine soldiers and members of Israel's General Security Service were killed; tens more were wounded. Responsibility for the strikes was claimed by an unknown organization calling itself Islamic Jihad, but it soon became clear that it was the military wing of Hizballah who uses the other name when preferring not to take direct responsibility for clandestine operations.[2]

These suicide attacks marked the start of a new phase in the campaign fought by Syria and its allies in Lebanon against the Israeli and western presence there. Pressured by these strikes, the US and France withdrew from Lebanon in late 1984, and in September 1985 Israel drew back to a self-declared security zone in South Lebanon.

These attacks were significant as a manifestation of the turnabout experienced by Lebanon's Shi'i community. Once a docile and submissive minority, it had remade itself into a radical, aggressive faction waging an active struggle to gain dominance in Lebanon and, in the case of Hizballah, to achieve a more far-reaching goal, the establishment of an Islamic regime.

Hizballah's emergence was overshadowed by two cataclysmic events that took place in the Middle East at about the same time, events which facilitated the organization's establishment and early activity and which may also explain the radical, militant nature which characterized it from its start.

The first of these was the Islamic revolution in Iran, which quickly became a source of inspiration and a role model for Shi'i religious leaders in Lebanon. Furthermore, immediately after consolidating their rule Iran's new leaders showed an avid interest and growing involvement in Lebanon's Shi'i community. Iran was behind the decision of several prominent Shi'i leaders to leave the ranks of Amal, until then the principal game in town for members of Lebanon's Shi'i community. Iran also encouraged, or coerced, different and sometimes rival factions to unite into a new organization – Hizballah. This new body was to serve, at least as far as Iran was concerned, Iranian strategic interests in Lebanon.[3] Over the years since the revolution, Iran became Hizballah's primary backer: financially, militarily and politically. Iranian aid included the dispatch of Iranian volunteers to Lebanon (approximately 1,500 Revolutionary Guards have been stationed in Lebanon's Biqa' Valley since 1982),[4] the supply of arms, mostly via Syria, and economic assistance amounting to tens of millions of dollars annually, if not more. The financial aid paid the salaries of organization members, particularly the fighters, and made possible Hizballah's expansion into the spheres of education, health and welfare.[5] Hizballah also enjoyed Iran's political patronage on more than one occasion in power plays with political forces in Lebanon, and naturally with the Syrians as well. Syria had to carefully weigh the consequences of any move on Hizballah against its desire to maintain the special ties it has had with Iran since the 1980s.

The second critical event to influence Hizballah's development was the Lebanon War of June 1982. Two of its consequences had a singularly direct influence on the Shi'i community and on Hizballah in particular. First, the fall of the PLO in Lebanon freed the Shi'i community from domination. Its expulsion from Lebanon in the summer of 1982 left a vacuum which the Shi'i organizations rushed to fill, first Amal and then Hizballah. Second, although the armored columns of the IDF were initially welcomed when they crossed into South Lebanon's Shi'i villages in June 1982, when the fog of battle lifted it became clear to the Shi'is that Israel had allied itself with the Maronites to the detriment of Shi'i interests. Disillusionment with Israel led to opposition to its continued presence in Lebanon, which together with the growth of religious extremism and the spread of Iranian influence within the community soured the Shi'is' attitude toward Israel to one of hostility and hatred. Hostility grew even further in the course of the 1990s, following Israel's military operations 'Accountability' and 'Grapes of Wrath', which led hundreds of thousands of Shi'ites to flee their homes in South Lebanon. The aim of these operations was to create pressure on the Lebanese as well as the Syrian regimes, so that they might restrain Hizballah attacks against Israel.[6]

The Israeli challenge, along with the encouragement and inspiration afforded Lebanese Shi'is by Iran's Islamic revolution, gave the organization its boost onto center political stage in Lebanon. In addition to these issues, internal Lebanese factors and processes generated within the Shi'i community during the period in question, and especially the one that preceded it, must also be considered in an examination of Hizballah's development.

The transformation of Lebanon's Shi'i from a weak, passive and marginal community to a radical, aggressive entity struggling to achieve a position of predominance began in the early 1970s. This reversal was clearly the product of changes in demographics and standard of living. Due to its high rate of natural increase, the community's percentage of Lebanon's total population surged from 19 per cent in 1950 to 30 per cent by the early 1970s,[7] leading to increased emigration from rural areas in the south of Lebanon and the Biqa' Valley to shanty towns surrounding the big cities. With this came a corresponding breakdown of the community's social and traditional framework and a drop in the status of the feudal-like families of notables who had led the community previously. The exodus from the Shi'i villages brought about conditions of poverty and need, and an inevitable feeling of despair and helplessness among the uprooted.

These changes in lifestyle produced a crisis of leadership and identity.

Into the breach stepped Musa Sadr, a Shi'i cleric born in Iran to Lebanese parents, who had arrived in Lebanon in 1959. He worked to improve the lot of Lebanese Shi'is, as well as his own position, by raising the level of religious solidarity at the expense of the old allegiance to the family structure and the community's traditional leadership.[8]

Musa Sadr waged his campaign in accordance with the Lebanese rules of the game. Evidence of this was his readiness to cooperate with the Lebanese Maronite establishment in return for recognition as leader of the Shi'i community. Indeed, in accordance with his demands, the Supreme Shi'i Council was established in 1969 and Sadr chosen its leader.[9] The early 1970s saw Sadr at the height of his success, but on 13 April 1975 civil war began in Lebanon, completely changing the rules of the game. To a great extent it also undermined most of Musa Sadr's accomplishments to date.

The Shi'i community had played a marginal role in the events precipitating the outbreak of the civil war; unprepared to cope with the struggle, it ultimately found itself in an even worse position. Unlike the other protagonists in the conflict, it lacked a foreign patron to provide backing in the internal Lebanese arena. Furthermore, and again unlike the other Lebanese communities, the Shi'is lacked an organizational, military infrastructure upon which to build up a militia to protect and further its own interests.

The civil war made Musa Sadr and his campaign irrelevant within the context of the new Lebanese reality created by the war. Expertise in political maneuvering and manipulation were no longer important assets, as for the subsequent 15 years, military strength became the determining factor of the power and standing of each community and its leaders. After the outbreak of the civil war in 1975, Musa Sadr founded the Amal movement (*Afwaj al-Muqawama al-Lubnaniyya*, the Lebanese Resistance Brigades) as a military force. Its objective was to protect the political power gained by the Shi'i community during the preceding years. However, Amal was unable to gain a significant foothold as a military force; the PLO still controlled most of the Shi'i areas in Lebanon and quashed any attempt by the community to organize itself or establish any independent base of operations.[10]

In 1978, Musa Sadr visited Libya at the invitation of its leader, Mu'ammar al-Qadhdhafi. All traces of Sadr disappeared there and it appears he was assassinated by the Libyans who regarded him as an obstacle to their efforts to gain a position of influence in Lebanon. Musa Sadr's demise took place after his work of many years to improve and strengthen the standing of Lebanon's Shi'i community had already reached a dead end. It seems that not only was his political approach to solving his community's problems obsolete; his ideological, pragmatic and moderate approach had been jettisoned as well.

It was against this background that in the late 1970s critics and opponents emerged to denounce Sadr's moderation, maintaining that the Shi'i community should widen its goals. Their strength increased with Musa Sadr's disappearance and his subsequent replacement as Amal's leader by Nabih Barri, a lawyer from outside the circle of religious leaders. Another new leader was Sayyid Husayn Musawi, head of the Islamic Amal that had been established at the end of the 1970s. In June 1982, Musawi parted company from his Amal colleagues in protest over Nabih Barri's consent to take part, together with Bashir Jumayyil, in the National Salvation Committee founded by then-president Ilyas Sarkis. Other radical Shi'i factions sprouted up alongside Islamic Amal, including the Lebanese branch of the Shi'i organization al-Da'wa, The Association of Muslim Clerics of Jabal 'Amil (South Lebanon), and the Family of Brotherhood under the leadership of Ayatollah Sayyid Muhammad Husayn Fadlallah.[11]

The Lebanon War of 1982, coming close upon the heels of the Islamic revolution in Iran in 1979–80, hence found at least a portion of the Shi'i community on the threshold of extremism which would characterize it in the years to come. The emergence and growth of Hizballah was the natural and direct consequence of this trend.

Since its emergence as a political power in Lebanon, Hizballah has had to confront the central dilemma of its purpose and goals. Should it view itself as an extension of Iran in Lebanon, subservient to the will of its mentors in Tehran, or should it fashion itself into a Lebanese organization with complete independence of decision and action?

An examination of declarations made by Hizballah leaders, and especially of the background of these declarations, leaves no room for doubt as to the organization's long term goals, central to which is the establishment of an Islamic regime in Lebanon along the Iranian model as a step toward founding one united Islamic state to encompass all the Muslim world.

Indeed, one Hizballah leader, Husayn al-Musawi, elaborated in 1984:

> We are faithful to Imam Khomeini politically, religiously and ideologically. In accordance with Khomeini's teaching we strive to fight all manifestations of corruption and vanity in this world, and all who fight the Muslims . . . . Our struggle is in the east as well as the west...our goal is to lay the groundwork for the reign of the Mahdi on earth, the reign of truth and justice.[12]

The organization's ideological platform, published in February 1985, stated: '[W]e the sons of the nation of Hizballah regard ourselves as a part of the Muslim people of the world', and that, 'the supreme triumph in Iran was to bring about the re-establishment of the nucleus of the great Muslim state in the world.[13]

The platform enumerated the following practical, immediate political goals:

1. To drive Israel out of Lebanon as a prelude to its complete annihilation and the liberation of Jerusalem.
2. To force the US, France and their allies out of Lebanon and eradicate all traces of their influence in this country.
3. To subjugate the Phalangists to the rule of justice and bring them to justice for their crimes against the Muslims and Christians, perpetrated with the encouragement of the US and Israel.
4. To give full freedom of choice to our people to determine their fate and choose the form of government they desire. Since we do not hide our commitment to the rule of Islam, we call upon the nation to choose an Islamic regime, which alone can assure justice and honor for all and foil any attempt at renewed imperialist infiltration of our country.[14]

These goals are all of a piece, the cornerstone of which is the campaign to utterly destroy Israel and struggle against the West as the principal means to build an Islamic regime in Lebanon. It was, indeed, not long till this struggle became the practical, as well as ideological, focus of Hizballah activity. This was perhaps because the organization realized the possible dividends (e.g., Iranian and Syrian support) that could be extracted from a violent struggle with Israel, but primarily because the organization realized that the essence of the religious ideology guiding it (as it had guided the Islamic revolutionaries in Tehran) was the necessity for an uncompromising struggle against its enemies.[15]

Notwithstanding the above, the organization's efforts at moderation and even pragmatism in the internal Lebanese context are conspicuous in its platform, as it calls for the enabling of the residents of Lebanon to determine their path and their destiny, rather than subjecting them forcibly to an Islamic regime. The platform goes on to elaborate: 'If our compatriots are given the opportunity to freely choose a system of government for Lebanon they will prefer Islam, and therefore we issue a call to adopt the path of Islam out of free and direct choice of the people, and not by means of coercion'.[16]

It should be noted that this dilemma is manifest also in the organization's structure. From the very beginning of its activity, Hizballah endeavored to construct for itself an image of an organization based on broad and even spontaneous support within Lebanon. Nevertheless, one of the characteristics of the organization's growth was the establishment of a hierarchical organizational infrastructure, similar in many ways to the model set by the Iranian revolution. This is most obvious with respect to the decisive role that clerics play in leading the organization. Indeed, like Iran after the death of Khomeini, the organization has a spiritual leader, Muhammad Husayn Fadlallah, who serves as a source of inspiration and spiritual guidance. Beside him is the Advisory Council (Majlis al-Shura) of religious sages headed by the Secretary-General of the organization, Hasan Nasrallah. The Advisory Council is supplemented by the organization's executive committee that is in charge of ongoing political and organizational activities. Subordinate to the committee are other executive bodies, including a political bureau and cultural, educational and financial committees. The military apparatus is another major component of Hizballah, managing the military infrastructure including training bases, weapon stores and recruitment offices, as well as military activities against Israel. Another important apparatus is propaganda, in charge of the organization's publications, including its weekly, *al-'Ahd*, and other periodicals like *al-Sabil*, *al-Wahda al-Islamiyya* and *al-Muntaliq*. Hizballah also operates a television and a radio station. The organization operates in three major geographical areas: the Biqa', Beirut and South Lebanon. In each region there is a regional commander, subordinate to Hizballah's Secretary-General, and a representative of the central apparatuses.[17]

The apparent contradiction between Hizballah's true long term objectives and the mantle of moderation and pragmatism with which it cloaks itself is reflected in the internal conflict between those with a moderate pragmatic bias and those who are more radical. This conflict bears witness to Hizballah leaders' awareness of the fact that the organization does not function in a vacuum, but within the confines of the Lebanese reality which imposes certain restrictions on its freedom of action. The following factors come into play. First, Lebanese society is not homogeneous, but rather a mosaic of communities. The state's historical experience throughout the last centuries shows very clearly that no single community can subordinate the others and secure for itself a position of predominance. This is due to the nature of the communities themselves, their internal social structure and political system, their limited political and military practical power, etc.[18] Hence, the communities of Lebanon have no choice but to co-exist, no matter how problematic that may be. Any attempt by a single community to strengthen its own standing at the expense of the other communities is liable to cause the others to unite against it.

Second, the Shi'i of the eastern shore of the Mediterranean (the 'Levant') have always been a small minority among a hostile Sunni population. This is still true today. To the south lies Israel, while Syria borders to the east and north. The latter's population is mostly Sunni, ruled by the minority Alawis, but the secularist world view of the Syrian Ba'th regime as well as its historic predisposition toward caution make it a potential enemy of a radical Islamic organization like Hizballah. Third,

Hizballah does not enjoy majority support even among the Shi'i community. Most studies show that, at most, a hard core of 20–25 per cent of the community supports Hizballah with Amal favored by more than 30 per cent.[19] Some Shi'i support has gone to external elements, such as Maronite General Michel 'Awn who between the years 1988 and 1990 enjoyed widespread Shi'i backing.[20]

For most of the 1980s, the dilemma over the future course and goals of Hizballah remained a mostly theoretical problem, not requiring resolution in favor of either the 'Iranian path' or a 'Lebanese' one; the reality of Lebanon throughout the decade enabled Hizballah to run with the hare and hunt with the hounds. Moreover, the organization became ever stronger during the civil war, for two principle reasons. First, chaos reigned in Lebanon and in the complete absence of a functioning government, Hizballah was able to operate with total impunity. No real alternative stood to challenge Hizballah's radical path of violent struggle. Second, Hizballah's campaign against the Israeli presence in South Lebanon gained it Iran's generous support, great popularity among the Shi'i population and, as it served Syrian interests at the time, immunity from Syrian retaliation as well. Hizballah's strength was all the more prominent when seen against the political and especially military weakness of other forces in the Lebanese arena: the Maronites, Sunnis and even Amal, Hizballah's rival within the Shi'i community.

The end of the 1980s brought the organization its greatest triumphs. Hizballah had become an impressive organizational and military force, enabling it to achieve unprecedented territorial accomplishments: control of West Beirut, the most important Sunni center in Lebanon, and parts of the Biqa' Valley and the South. These achievements were bound up with the domestic struggle with Amal. The struggle ended without resolution, primarily because of the delicate balance of power which existed between Syria, which backed Amal, and Iran, which supported Hizballah. Hizballah's superiority in the battles, owing to the high motivation of its people and the financial and military assistance of Iran, was evident. Yet the fact remained that despite its efforts the organization did not gain a firm foothold in the community and the majority continued its support for Amal and its world view.[21]

## Hizballah's New Challenges

At the height of its success at the end of the 1980s, Hizballah was confronted with a series of challenges which threatened all of its accomplishments thus far and jeopardized its continued activity and even its very existence in Lebanon.

First and foremost of these was the signing of the Ta'if agreement on 22 October 1989. This marked the end of the civil war and laid the foundations for the formation of a new Lebanese order under Syrian patronage.[22] In essence, the accord constituted a new formula or framework for coexistence between the different communities in Lebanon, replacing the old formula of the National Covenant of 1943. However, like its predecessor, the Ta'if agreement is nothing but a Maronite-Sunni compact, intended to enable these two communities or, more specifically, the notable families of each, to maintain their control over state and society in Lebanon.[23]

The civil war was kind neither to the Maronites nor to the Sunnis. Both communities, and especially their notable families, emerged as the great losers of a war of their own making. First, with respect to demographics, during the war years the Shi'i community grew to be the largest in Lebanon, constituting, as of early 1995, approximately 35 per cent of the country's population. This state of affairs threatens the traditional status of the Maronite and Sunni communities who in the past had constituted the larger populations.[24]

Second, with respect to the political and military aspects, toward the end of the war the Maronites and Sunnis were left without external support and protection (in the Sunni case, without even a militia to protect the community's interests). The Maronites, at least the majority of the Maronite camp, were backed by Syria at the beginning of the war (1976), later by Israel (1981–82), and finally by the US and France (1983–84). By war's end they were alone. The Sunnis were initially supported by the PLO and later became totally dependent on Damascus's goodwill.

In order to prevent the Shi'i community from taking over in Lebanon, Sunni and Maronite leaders took action to end the civil war. The Ta'if agreement, a compromise arrangement which in fact assured the continuation of Maronite-Sunni authority, albeit under Syrian hegemony, was achieved with pan-Arab assistance. The agreement benefited the Maronites and the Sunnis but threatened Shi'i gains made during the war. The compensation offered Shi'is, a formal elevation of the status of Chairman of the Parliament to equal that of the Maronite President and the Sunni Prime Minister, was a slap in the face in view of the fact that the Shi'i community was now the largest in the country and, thanks to its militia, among the most powerful. Furthermore, restoration of normalcy to the country necessarily involved a return to the political system where battles would be waged by words in parliament rather than by force of arms. Traditionally, the Shi'i had demonstrated their weakness in the corridors of power as, among other things, they had difficulty manning the political offices reserved for them with educated members of the community. As a result they were handicapped *vis-à-vis* the other communities in their reach for a piece of the 'national pie'.

Beyond the blow to Shi'i standing, the Ta'if agreement constituted a concrete threat to Hizballah itself. In intending to revive the Lebanese polity, it threatened to fill the void that for so long had been exploited by Hizballah. The lack of a living, breathing Lebanese entity had enabled the organization to propose its own alternative to the distress of Lebanon's Shi'i community – the radical Islamic alternative. The Ta'if agreement resuscitated the Lebanese government, giving Amal a clear advantage as it was prepared to come to terms with a centralized authority and thus more capable of finding a place for itself within it.

Immediately after the signing of the Ta'if agreement, Hizballah made clear its reservations and opposition to it. It seems that the organization's hand was behind the assassination of Lebanese President-elect Rene Mu'awwad on 22 November 1989. Mu'awwad was killed in a car bomb explosion on his way to a military parade marking Lebanon's Independence Day.[25]

The peace process between Israel and its Arab neighbors since the beginning of the 1990s has posed another direct threat to Hizballah in that its successful conclusion is likely to cut off one of Hizballah's sources of power and legitimacy, the struggle against Israel. While it is true that as long as the political process was frozen, Syria preferred to turn a blind eye to Hizballah's activity against Israel, at times even encouraging it as another means of pressuring Israel, progress made in the peace process in recent years has put Syria in a difficult spot. Damascus has no interest in undermining its chances to regain the Golan Heights and win Israeli recognition of its predominant position in Lebanon. It is thus apparent that continued Hizballah activity against Israel in the event of an Israeli-Syrian accord, or real progress in the peace negotiations, would pit the organization not only against Israel, its enemy of long standing, but also against Syria and the Lebanese government functioning under its auspices.

Indeed, as early as 13 September 1993, during a demonstration held in West Beirut by Hizballah in protest of the Oslo Agreement between Israel and the PLO, Lebanese army and police forces opened fire on Shi'i demonstrators, killing nine. Hizballah refers to the event as the 'September 13th Massacre' and its leaders have repeatedly promised to settle the score with the Lebanese regime responsible for it.[26] It would seem, however, that these same leaders learned a lesson from the event and they have therefore avoided direct military confrontation with the Lebanese government. This clearly reflects the limitations imposed on them by the new Lebanese reality since Ta'if. Another example of Lebanese determination, with Syrian backing, to hem in and, if possible, defang the organization, is a 1994 report that Lebanese and Syrian forces in the Biqa' valley confiscated weapons from members of Hizballah.[27]

Iran's weakened status, as a result of internal difficulties, chiefly social and economic, has exacerbated the challenge facing the organization in recent years. Although Iran actively tried to distract public attention at home from domestic problems by instigating trouble abroad, encouragement of Hizballah's struggle against Israel being one example, it has found it difficult to maintain the level of financial assistance it had extended to Hizballah in the past. There have even been reports that Iranian aid to Hizballah has been cut by tens of percentage points.[28]

Faced with this quandary, Hizballah appears prepared to adopt a pragmatic, even moderate, approach to the two current challenges of the Ta'if agreement and the Israel-Arab peace process. In this context, one should first note the situation on Lebanon's domestic scene. In the framework of a series of decisions taken by the organization's second convention in April 1991, Hizballah halted its overt campaign against the Ta'if agreement and prepared to recognize it, or more precisely, to function in accordance with the political rules of the game it laid down. Thus, Hizballah took part in the elections to Lebanon's Parliament in the summer of 1992. Eight candidates on its list from the Biqa' Valley won seats in parliament; in addition, the organization mobilized the support of another four members of parliament.[29] Members of parliament on Hizballah's list, the Loyalty to the Resistance Bloc (Kutlat al-Wafa' lil-Muqawama), have been active on various pan-Lebanese issues such as the settlement of Palestinian refugees in Lebanon and Lebanese government policy on social, economic and political affairs.[30] This activity provides Hizballah and its leaders a convenient and legitimate platform from which to work against the Lebanese regime and undermine the Ta'if structure without deviating from the rules of the game dictated by the agreement. Indeed, the organization's leaders continue to fulminate against Ta'if: spiritual leader Muhammad Husayn Fadlallah announced that he 'does not regard Lebanon as a state, but rather as a collection of political islands maintaining their positions of power and authority', and that the Lebanese government had turned the country into a 'banana republic'.[31] Fadlallah went on to say that 'the Ta'if agreement was born of an American decision, wrapped in an Arab *'aqal* [headband which holds the traditional Arab headdress in place] and a Lebanese *tarboosh*', and therefore does not reflect the will of the Lebanese people.[32] Still, it is apparent that since Hizballah's anti-government censure, harsh as it may be, is confined to the framework of rules determined at Ta'if, it serves to strengthen and legitimize the agreement.

It would appear that in the long run, Hizballah's decision to take part in Lebanese politics may force the organization to reconcile itself with the Ta'if agreement. Indeed, as early as mid-1995, Prime Minister Rafiq al-Hariri was reported to have held negotiations with Hizballah supporters in the Lebanese Parliament, with the aim of integrating them into his proposed government, or at least to gain their support. These negotiations failed both because of American pressure and reservations within Hizballah itself. Nevertheless, there is clear significance in Hizballah's willingness to enter into a dialogue with Hariri and consider the possibility of joining his government.[33] Furthermore, in October 1995, President Ilyas al-Hirawi's term of office was extended for another three years. This extension generated sharp opposition from many Lebanese political figures, such as Nabih Barri, the speaker of Parliament and the leader of Amal. Hizballah clearly had its own reservations about the extension, but it avoided taking a prominent part in the opposition. Lebanese sources even reported that the organization was at that time involved in secret negotiations with Hirawi, the aim of which was to recruit Hizballah's support in favor of the extension.[34] Indeed, Hizballah's patron, Iran, declared, under Syrian pressure, that it considered the extension of Hirawi's term 'an internal Lebanese matter'.[35]

Second, Hizballah has in recent years invested significant effort in establishing a political and social power base in the Shi'i community. It has set up an expanding financial and social infrastructure: schools, clinics, mosques and even supermarkets in villages and urban Shi'i quarters.[36] Some in Lebanon have gone so far as to claim that this infrastructure was conceived of as a way to absorb the organization's fighters in the event it is forced to curtail its campaign against Israel and prohibited from carrying arms and maintaining a militia.[37] It should be noted here that this undertaking is to a great extent dependent on Iranian aid. It is also clear that the process of Lebanon's financial rehabilitation and the establishment of state institutions over time will constitute an additional obstacle in Hizballah's attempt to fill a social and economic role in the lives of the country's Shi'i.

Third, Hizballah leaders have begun laying the ideological foundations for a shift from the violent struggle for power which has thus far characterized the organization to a political battle based on moderation and pragmatism within the general framework of Lebanon's political system. This is evidenced by the 1994 publication of spiritual leader Shaykh Fadlallah's book endorsing Islamic-Christian dialogue (*Afaq al-Hiwar al-Islami al-Masihi*).[38] Also worthy of note are the remarks of Hizballah Secretary-General Nasrallah. Asked about Hizballah's ties to Iran and its long term goals, Nasrallah replied:

> The solution, in our opinion, is the establishment of an Islamic state in Lebanon and beyond, but this does not mean we must be hasty and impose such a solution by force on our country and countrymen. Therefore I cannot honestly say I do not advocate an Islamic state,

indeed no Islamic movement is uninterested in an Islamic state, but I do not wish [to impose this] by force or violence, rather we prefer to wait for the day that we succeed in convincing our countrymen – by means of dialogue and in an open atmosphere – that the only alternative is the founding of an Islamic state.[39]

Fourth, with respect to the political process, while Hizballah continues to express vehement opposition to the peace process, voicing virulent attacks against the agreements signed between Israel and Jordan and the Palestinians,[40] Hizballah leaders have shown signs that they would accommodate themselves, however unhappily, to an Israeli-Lebanese peace agreement and desist from their armed struggle against Israel. In fact, for some time now several, but not all, of the organization's spokesmen have intimated that its immediate, as opposed to long term efforts regarding Israel were not directed as in the past to wreaking Israel's total destruction, but rather to merely driving Israel out of its South Lebanon security zone. In such an event, said Secretary-General Nasrallah, 'weapons may be laid down'.[41] Indeed, the understandings reached between Hizballah and Israel in 1993 and 1996, in which Hizballah committed itself not to attack Israeli settlements in northern Israel and to limit its military activity to the security zone, may be seen as a proof of the process of Lebanonization and localization which the Hizballah has been undergoing.

Hence, since the start of the 1990s, Hizballah has embarked upon a new path. Is this path a true change of heart which will lead the organization to make real changes in its modes of operation, goals and perception of the world? Hizballah seems to have made a distinction between its long term goals, which have remained unchanged and therefore may continue to draw its support from Lebanon's Shi'i community, and its day-to-day policy, which has undergone profound changes in order to enable the organization to continue to function in the reality of today's Lebanon. In other words, Hizballah wishes to have its cake and eat it too.

What remains in question, of course, is the viability of such a distinction and its uncertain ability to ensure the continued activity and existence of Hizballah in Lebanon: it is altogether possible that such a disjunction between long term goals and day-to-day policy is beyond the powers of a radical organization like Hizballah and will ultimately consume it. The organization may not prove able to divorce itself from its radical world view, thereby provoking the various powers in Lebanon, or it may distance itself so completely that it loses its uniqueness and, with it, Hizballah's source of power and strength, the ideological magnet that draws for it the support it enjoys today. Indeed even now Amal is more popular than Hizballah among Lebanese Shi'is and this trend seems likely to grow in the future.

Hizballah's campaign against Israel in South Lebanon's security zone, still being waged into 1996, is symptomatic of the dilemma facing the organization. Attacks against Israeli targets have not abated with advances in the political process and the organization's implied readiness to accept the possibility of peace accords; indeed many believe the anti-Israel campaign has escalated as a result. It has begun to evince a more established and organized character, certainly more ambitious and daring, peaking in widespread organized attacks against IDF and SLA targets in South Lebanon carried out by large Hizballah forces. The organization has even taken to filming these attacks for use in 'public relations'.[42]

Like its Iranian model, Hizballah is also divided between moderates who lean toward recognition of the limitations imposed by the Lebanese reality and radicals who espouse continued adherence to the organization's original world view. At the head of the moderate camp stood 'Abbas Musawi, Hizballah Secretary-General, who was assassinated by Israel in February 1992 and Shaykh Fadlallah, Hizballah's spiritual mentor. Leading the radical camp are Ibrahim Amin and Hasan Nasrallah. It is possible to assert that the military escalation along the Israeli border may be related to the power struggles between these two camps over the control of Hizballah.

Hostilities with Israel have enabled Hizballah to continue to bear arms. Indeed, the Lebanese government's decision to disarm the militia was enforced against all except Hizballah fighters in South Lebanon, who continued to arm themselves, citing the needs of their campaign against Israel. It is apparent, however, that the importance of the ongoing struggle against Israel goes beyond enabling Hizballah fighters to maintain their weapons: Martin Kramer has quite rightly remarked that Hizballah owes its impact to its violence.[43] Indeed, the organization's leaders, newspapers, radio and television broadcasts all uphold the central place of the struggle against Israel in Hizballah activity. The same holds true for Hizballah propaganda among its adherents and that used to mobilize new supporters.[44] Secretary-General Nasrallah went so far as to proclaim that 'the primary focus of our activity is resistance and not the political bazaars of Beirut'.[45]

Although Hizballah leaders have alluded to the possibility of a cessation in hostilities against Israel in interviews with the foreign press, no mention of this whatsoever is ever made in local propaganda; on the contrary, they declare their ongoing commitment to the goal of 'eradicating the Zionist entity on the soil of Palestine' and that the struggle against Israel will not cease even if a peace agreement is achieved.[46] Hizballah spokesmen are deliberately vague on anything that touches on the issue of whether this is an immediate objective or a long term goal.

The escalation of Hizballah's campaign against Israel to the point where it threatened the existence of the security zone has led Israel to step up its efforts against the organization in recent years. One of the high points of Israeli operations against Hizballah was in February 1992 when Israeli combat helicopters killed Hizballah leader 'Abbas Musawi as he proceeded in his motorcade. Hizballah was quick to respond by striking at Israel's soft underbelly: in March 1992 its embassy in Buenos Aires was bombed, apparently by Hizballah members or emissaries. The organization also intensified its anti-Israel activities in Lebanon and began shelling Israeli settlements in the northern Galilee.[47] This led to Operation Accountability in the summer of 1993, in the course of which Israeli artillery shelled Shi'i villages in South Lebanon and forced hundreds of thousands of residents to flee north to Beirut. Israel's intention was to use massive air power to cause indirect pressure on the central government in Beirut, and thereby on the Syrian regime as well, to constrain Hizballah. By the end of Operation Accountability, a tacit understanding between Israel and Hizballah was reached with the help of the US and Syria; its main stipulation was that Hizballah would refrain from activity against settlements in the north of Israel and Israel would not take action against civilian targets or Hizballah targets located in civilian areas in Lebanon.[48]

Israel remained unable to effectively counteract Hizballah activity. In January 1994, for example, after the Israeli Air Force repeatedly attacked a Hizballah training camp in 'Ayn Dardara, leaving dozens of casualties, Hizballah responded with strikes against the Jewish community center building in Buenos Aires and the Israeli embassy in London. Hizballah has managed to sustain a balance of terror against Israel which, alongside the latter's reluctance to bring too much pressure to bear on Beirut lest negotiations with Damascus be slowed, has in effect handicapped Israel, as even the late prime minister Yitzhak Rabin has admitted.[49]

These Israeli limitations, as well as the lack of any progress in the Israeli-Syrian peace negotiations during most of 1995–96, enabled Hizballah to play – wisely and without disturbances– its main card in the struggle against Israel. In cases where there was an Israeli response, especially when Lebanese civilians were hurt, Hizballah did not hesitate to shell Israeli settlements in northern Israel, thus protraying itself as the defender of the population of southern Lebanon. Hizballah activity, aggravated in early 1996 against the background of the general elections in Israel, led then Israeli Prime Minister Shimon Peres in April 1996 to launch Operation Grapes of Wrath. It followed the model of Operation Accountability of July 1993. As in the previous case, this operation also ended with gains for Hizballah. While the organization had to commit itself once again to avoiding any attack on Israel proper, its right to attack Israeli forces in the security zones was recognized, this time in a written understanding.[50] Furthermore, Israeli pressure on the civilian population, which reached its peak with the killing of 107 Shi'i civilians who took refuge in a UN camp near the village of Qana in southern Lebanon, increased popular support for Hizballah. Hizballah was able to play an important and much appreciated role in aiding the Shi'i refugees, providing food, shelter and compensation for damage caused to their houses. Thus, the Israeli military operation aimed at denying Hizballah popular support achieved the opposite effect.[51] Nevertheless, it appears that Hizballah's gains were short term and will not help the organization address its long-term challenges.

It should be noted that despite the general consensus in Israel of Damascus's involvement in Hizballah attacks, it appears that the Syrians were not directly behind the strikes. Although it is well within their ability to preclude them, the Syrians prefer to turn a blind eye to Hizballah operations against Israel in an essentially cold calculation of profit and loss. At this stage of the peace negotiations with Israel, Syria has no wish to find itself in a confrontation with Hizballah, and certainly not with its patron, Iran. Instead, Syria has opted to use its influence over Hizballah as a bargaining chip in the difficult negotiations with Israel. Indeed, the Syrians have repeatedly implied that a peace agreement between the two countries would ensure quiet in Lebanon.[52] It may seem that firm Israeli military response aimed at Syrian targets in Lebanon would force the Syrians to try and curb Hizballah. However, given the potential for escalation, this is not the option preferred by the Israeli government. From the perspective of the Israeli leadership, only an Israeli-Syrian peace accord can move the Syrians to stop Hizballah activity against Israel.[53] While it is true that Hizballah leaders have intimated their readiness to accept such an accord, albeit with teeth clenched, one wonders whether a halt to anti-Israel activity, combined with other inevitable changes in Hizballah's internal, Lebanese policy is anything less than suicidal, as it would mean the end of the organization's unique position.

It appears Hizballah has heard the voices whispering that an end to its struggle against Israel would be self-destructive: Hizballah's newspaper, *al-'Ahd*, responding to remarks made by Lebanese Minister of Defense Muhsin Dallul that Hizballah will disintegrate once Israel's occupation ends, printed that 'Hizballah needs no one to speak for it as it reflects the opinion of a wide section of the Lebanese people...and is an enterprising pioneer in the life of the nation, whose existence does not depend on these or other circumstances or on [any] political developments'.[54]

## Looking Ahead

Since Hizballah first appeared on the Lebanese scene in 1983, it has become one of the most powerful forces within the Shi'i community and, in fact, in

Lebanon at large. In the late 1980s it even seemed that the organization was approaching its goal of turning the Shiʻi community under its leadership into the avant garde that would turn Lebanon into an Islamic state. However, in recent years a real threat has surfaced to confront Hizballah, its activity and its very existence. While the organization's activity, with emphasis on the struggle against Israel, has been its principal source of strength and distinction, it has also jeopardized Hizballah's future in that it is liable to provoke the other powers operating in Lebanon, primarily the Lebanese government as well as its Syrian patron, into actions that would eliminate the entire *raison d'être* of the organization: in short, its very success could lead to its own destruction. Moreover, the fundamental processes at work in Lebanon, its rehabilitation as a politically organized society, and the peace process do not bode well for Hizballah, particularly given the continued weakening of Iran. In response to these challenges, Hizballah has displayed a will to survive, even at the cost of adopting the more pragmatic approach necessary to continue to operate under the new circumstances in Lebanon. The organization has focused on building an infrastructure to facilitate its transformation from a radical, military organization to a political-ideological movement with broad based, grass-roots support. It can, however, be cautiously stated that the organization may not prove able to divorce itself from its traditional goals and methods, as such a drastic move would strip it of all its hard-won assets. The continued campaign against Israel and its recent escalation attest to Hizballah's internal difficulties as it attempts to translate from theory into practice its growing acknowledgment of the need to conform to the new Lebanese environment and adopt the more pragmatic and moderate approach required of it. Hizballah's track record over the past decade is therefore a disappointing one, since it does not guarantee the organization's future. In spite of a series of impressive successes on the battlefield and absolute political and financial backing from Iran, Hizballah has not succeeded in becoming the leading force even among the Shiʻi community in Lebanon. Still, it is too early to determine Hizballah's future course in Lebanon. The answer appears to lie in Hizballah's actions as well as in more general regional processes. As such, insofar as the Ta'if agreement and the new Syrian order in Lebanon do not secure long term quiet and stability in Lebanon and the Israeli-Arab peace process runs into difficulties, Hizballah will continue as a key player.

## NOTES

1.  *Al-ʻAhd* (Beirut), 26 Aug. 1994.
2.  See Martin Kramer, *The Moral Logic of Hizballah,* Occasional Papers No.101 (Tel Aviv: Dayan Center for Middle Eastern and African Studies, Tel Aviv U., Aug. 1987) pp.6–7;

idem., 'Sacrifice and Fratricide in Shiite Lebanon', *Terrorism and Political Violence* 3/3 (Autumn 1991) pp.36–7; idem., 'Hizballah: The Calculus of Jihad', in Martin E. Marty and R. Scott Appelby (eds.), *Fundamentalism and the State* (Chicago: U. of Chicago Press 1993) p.547. See also, Yosef Olmert, 'Lebanon', in Haim Shaked and Daniel Dishon (eds.), *Middle East Contemporary Survey* (hereafter MECS) 8 (1983–84) (Boulder, CO: Westview Press 1986) p.553.

3. Martin Kramer, 'Redeeming Jerusalem: The Pan-Islamic Premise of Hizballah', in David Menashri (ed.), *The Iranian Revolution and the Muslim World* (Boulder, CO: Westview Press 1990) pp.105–30; Shimon Shapira, *Shiite Radicalism in Lebanon: Historical Roots and Organizational, Political and Ideological Patterns* (MA thesis, Tel Aviv University May 1987); idem., *Iranian Policy in Lebanon 1959–1991* (Ph.D. thesis, Tel Aviv University 1994) pp.107–54.

4. Augustus Richard Norton, 'Lebanon: The Internal Conflict and the Iranian Revolution', in John L. Esposito (ed.), *The Iranian Revolution – Its Global Impact* (Miami: Florida International U. 1990) p.126; Shapira (note 3) pp.107, 109, 120–3, 140–3.

5. The annual Iranian financial aid to the Hizballah is estimated at between tens of millions of dollars to $350 million. Since 1992 there has been a substantial reduction in the amount. *Al-Majalla*, 15–21 Aug. 1994; *Ha'aretz*, 27 April 1994; William B. Harris, 'Lebanon', in Ami Ayalon (ed.), *MECS* 16 (1992) (Boulder, CO: Westview Press 1994) p.613; N. Hamzeh, 'Lebanon's Hizballah: From Islamic Revolution to Parliamentary Accommodation', *Third World Quarterly* 14/2 (1993) p.328; on the Hizballah's social activities, see pp.321–37; Norton (note 4) p.127; idem, 'Shi'ism and Social Protest in Lebanon', in Juan R.I. Cole and Nikki R. Keddie (eds.), *Shi'ism and Social Protest* (New Haven, CT: Yale UP 1998) pp.156–78.

6. Zeev Schiff and Ehud Ya'ari, *War in Lebanon* (Hebrew) (Jerusalem: Schocken Publishing House 1984).

7. A. Soffer, 'Lebanon – Where Demography is the Fare of Politics and Life', *Middle Eastern Studies* 18 (1982) pp.197–205; Martin Kramer, 'Hizballah: The Calculus of Jihad' (note 2) p.540.

8. See Fouad Ajami, *The Vanished Imam – Musa al-Sadr and the Shia of Lebanon* (Ithaca, NY: Cornell UP 1986); Shapira (note 3) pp.16–23.

9. Shapira (note 3) p.19; Ajami (note 8) pp.125–40.

10. Augustus Richard Norton, *Amal and the Shi'a: Struggle for the Soul of Lebanon* (Austin: U. of Texas Press 1987).

11. Shapira (note 3) pp.24–43; Kramer, 'The Moral Logic of Hizballah' (note 2) pp.2–9.

12. *Al-Kifah al-'Arabi*, 9 Jan. 1994.

13. Hizballah, *Nus al-Risala al-Maftuha alati Wajjahaha Hizballah ila al-Mustad'afin fi Lubnan wal-'Alam* (Beirut: Feb. 1985) pp.5–6.

14. Ibid., p.15.

15. See Kramer (note 3).

16. Hizballah (note 13) p.19.

17. See Anat Kurz, Naskit Burgin and David Tal (eds.), *Islamic Terrorism and Israel* (Tel Aviv: Papirus 1993) pp.43–5.

18. See Kamal Salibi, *The Modern History of Lebanon* (London: Caravan Books 1965); idem., *A House of Many Mansions* (London: I.B. Tauris 1988).

19. Norton (note 4) p.123.

20. Interview with Mansour Raad, *Middle East Research and Information Report* 162/20/1 (Jan.–Feb. 1991) pp.11–14; Norton (note 4) p.133; Harris (note 5) p.505–9.

21. See Norton (note 4) pp.130–2; Kramer, 'Hizballah: The Calculus of Jihad' (note 2) pp.547–52; Harris (note 5) pp.526–8.

22. The Ta'if agreement involves a change in the distribution of positions of political power among the Lebanese sects. The agreement stipulates an equality between Muslim and Christian delegates in parliament (as compared with a ratio of 5 Muslims to 6 Christians in the past). It leaves the presidency to the Maronites, but extends the authority of the Sunni prime minister and the Shi'i speaker of parliament, making their power equal to that of the president.

23. Harris (note 5) pp.519–25; A.R. Norton, 'Lebanon After Ta'if: Is the Civil War Over', *Middle East Journal* 45/3 (Summer 1991); S. Nasr, 'Lebanon's War: Is the End in Sight', *MERIP* 162/20/1 (Jan.–Feb. 1990) pp.4–9.
24. Soffer (note 7) pp.197–205; Kramer, 'Hizballah: The Calculus of Jihad' (note 2) p.540.
25. William B. Harris, 'Lebanon', in Ami Ayalon (ed.), *MECS* 13 (1989) (Boulder, CO: Westview Press 1991) p.524.
26. *Al-Safir*, 14 Sept. 1994; *al-'Ahd*, 9 Sept. 1994.
27. AFP (PARIS), 22 March – Foreign Broadcast Information Service, Near East and South Asia (FBIS:NES), Daily Report (DR), 22 Oct. 1994.
28. *Ha'aretz*, 27 April 1994; *Al-Majalla*, 15–21 Aug. 1994; Hamzeh (note 5) p.328.
29. Harris (note 5) pp.598–608.
30. *Al-'Ahd*, 4, 11, 18 Nov. 1994; Hamzeh (note 5) p.328.
31. *Al-'Ahd*, 8 April 1994.
32. Ibid.
33. *Al-Safir*, 7 June 1995.
34. *Al-Hayat* (London), 9 Sept., 2 Oct. 1995.
35. Ibid., 2, 22 Oct. 1995.
36. Ibid., 22 April 1994; *Ha'aretz*, 27 April 1994.
37. *Al-Hayat* (London), 23 Feb. 1994; *Ha'aretz*, 16 April 1994.
38. *Al-'Ahd*, 10 April 1994; Interview with Muhammad Husayn Fadlallah, *Middle East Insight* 10/6 (Sept.–Oct. 1994) pp.18–22; Hamzeh (note 5) p.324.
39. *Al-'Ahd*, 26 Aug. 1994.
40. See, *al-'Ahd*, 10, 24 Sept. 1993, 28 Oct. 1994.
41. *Al-Hayat*, 14 April 1994; *Ha'aretz*, 16 April 1995.
42. *Al-'Ahd*, 8, 15 March; *Ma'ariv*, 28 April, 3 May 1995.
43. Kramer, 'Hizballah: The Calculus of Jihad' (note 2) p.539.
44. *Al-'Ahd*, 15 July, 26 Aug., 4, 11, 18 Nov. 1994.
45. *Al-'Ahd*, 15 July 1994.
46. *Al-'Ahd*, 9 Sept., 28 Oct. 1994, 3 Feb. 1995; Ba'lback, 'Voice of the Oppressed', 15 Feb. – DR, 15 Feb. 1995.
47. See Efraim Inbar and Elie Rekhess, 'Israel', *MECS* (note 5) pp.517–8.
48. William B. Harris, 'Lebanon', in Ami Ayalon (ed.), *MECS* 17 (1993) (Boulder, CO: Westview Press 1995) pp.527–8.
49. *Ha'aretz*, 2, 3 May, 16 Dec. 1995.
50. Ibid., 26, 28, 29 April 1995.
51. *Al-Hayat*, 29 April, 3 May 1996; Reuters, 3 May 1996.
52. See an interview given by the Syrian Foreign Minister, Faruq al-Shar' to Israeli Television, Channel 1, 7 Oct. 1994 – DR, 10 Oct. 1994. See also *Ha'aretz*, 5 Jan. 1996.
53. *Ha'aretz*, 16, 18 June, 29 Dec. 1995. See also, Eyal Zisser, 'Syria', *MECS* (note 5) p.739.
54. *Al-'Hayat*, 9 Sept. 1994.

# Competing Brothers:
# The Web of Hamas-PLO Relations

## MENACHEM KLEIN

This article deals with Hamas' ideological and political dilemmas between the years 1988 and 1995, which include the contradiction between Hamas particularism as a Palestinian national movement and the universalism of its Islamic message; the divergence between its perception of itself as a political movement and the lack of political flexibility in its Charter; and the nature of its relationship with the PLO. The article analyzes three modes of political action developed by Hamas: competing with the PLO, preventing the outbreak of Arab civil war and opening formal communication channels with the PLO in order to discuss basic disagreements. Finally, the author shows how the implementation of the PLO-Israeli accords altered Hamas-PLO relations. No longer a competition among ostensible equals, their relationship became one of a ruling authority versus an opposition group.

Hamas (meaning zeal or enthusiasm, the acronym for *Harakat al-Muqawama al-Islamiyya*, The Islamic Resistance Movement) was founded in December 1987 at the very beginning of the Intifada, the Palestinian uprising in the West Bank and Gaza Strip against the government of Israel. Its ideology was crystallized during the first months of the movement's existence and published in its charter (*mithaq*) in August 1988.[1] The *mithaq* was Hamas' preemptive response to the PLO's forthcoming political program, which was adopted, along with the Palestinian Declaration of Independence, in November 1988 by the 19th Palestinian National Council (PNC). In this Declaration, the PLO accepted United Nations Resolution 181 of 29 November 1947 and its call to divide British mandated Palestine into two states, one Jewish and the other Arab. Such an acceptance marked an implicit recognition of Israel. The political program went even further, explicitly mentioning UN Security Council Resolution 242, which stipulates the right of all states in the region to live in peace and security within secure and recognized boundaries. These moves toward compromise were quickly and totally rejected by Hamas.

This chapter provides an analysis of Hamas' ideological and political dilemmas in the years 1988–95, that is, between the publishing of the Islamic Charter (August 1988) and the signing of Oslo II, the Israeli-Palestinian Interim Agreement on the West Bank and the Gaza Strip (September 1995). On an ideological level, Hamas had to confront three issues: first, the contradiction between its particularism as a Palestinian movement and the universalism of its Islamic message; second, the divergence between its perception of itself as a political movement and the lack of political flexibility in its Charter; and third, the nature of its relationship with the PLO, a nationalist Palestinian organization pursuing a peace process with Israel.

The September 1993 Israel-PLO Declaration of Principles (DOP) forced Hamas to sharpen its political profile, to increase its political activity, as well as to pragmatize its fundamental positions.[2] As a result, it confronted an additional set of dilemmas arising from the obvious gap between the movement's ideology and praxis.[3] This predicament was compounded by the need to cope with the other powerful actors in the region, namely the PLO and Israel, making Hamas' move to politics extremely difficult and further widening the gap between Hamas' ideology and political efforts.

### Conflicting Ideological Issues

The goal of Hamas, according to its charter, is to liberate all of Palestine from occupation by the 'Zionist enemy', from the Jordan River to the Mediterranean Sea, and in that area to establish an Islamic state. By claiming that Islam provides the only comprehensive solution to the problems of the Palestinians, Hamas gives its struggle a universal message. According to its charter, Hamas fights for the authenticity of Islam, and as such it will achieve not only a national victory for Palestine, but rather a victory for the whole Islamic nation (*al-umma*). Thus, the movement declared its intent to not only fight against the Israeli occupation of Palestine, but also against the western dominated non-Islamic world order. *Jihad* (holy war) is viewed by Hamas as an individual religious duty (*fard 'ayn*), to be carried out by every Muslim. Describing itself as the master of the Intifada, Hamas considered the uprising an Islamic way of fighting, and indeed the only way of winning the war against Israel. Moreover, arguing that Islam gave the masses the power to confront Israel, Hamas described the Intifada as the return of the Palestinian people to Islam. However, *jihad* is not only the fight against Israel. As Hamas founders learned from their parent organization, the Egyptian-based Muslim Brotherhood, *jihad* is also the purification of Muslim society and the implementation of Islamic law (*shari'a*).[4] Accordingly, Hamas' charter emphasized the need to 'accord the Islamic (young) generations in our area an Islamic education' and called for social integration. 'Islamic society is one of solidarity.... Social solidarity consists of extending help to all the needy, both materially and morally.'[5]

Hamas leaders are not so naive as to assume that they may be able to dominate the world. In their charter, they consider Palestine the main front of *jihad*. Moreover, since its inception, Hamas has 'Palestinianized' the universal claim of Islam and given the movement a national-religious-political profile. This trend may be interpreted as the Hamas leadership giving preference to 'Palestinianizing' Islam over 'Islamicizing' Palestine. 'Fatherland (*watan*) and nationalism (*wataniyya*) are...part of the Islamic creed.... If nationalism means that certain people are linked through specific material, human and territorial characteristics, then this is the case of the Palestinian Islamic Resistance Movement.'[6] Thus, as Andrea Nusse notes, Hamas is first and foremost a Palestinian movement influenced not only by Islamic heritage and codes, but also by western national ideas.[7]

There are three main expressions of Hamas' ideological efforts to 'Palestinianize' Islam. First, the movement stresses the important difference between the political conditions in Arab countries and those in Palestine. Arab countries may be ruled by secular Muslim regimes, but Palestine is occupied by Jews. Therefore, the choice that is typical to the rest of fundamentalist movements in the Arab world, whether to first fight the external enemy (Israel, the US and the West) or the internal one (the heretic regime),[8] does not exist in Palestine. Israel embodies both enemies. Second, Hamas views the Palestinian land, with Jerusalem's holy al-Aqsa mosque, as the center of its national-religious identity. And, third, the *jihad* in Palestine and the Intifada, led by Hamas, will determine the existential struggle against all enemies of Islam.

Hamas considers itself to be a political movement, but as Raphael Israeli emphasizes, its Charter was written in comprehensive terms, as expressing God's given truths. Based on Koranic quotations, the Islamic Charter does not leave room for political flexibility. 'Peace initiatives, the so-called peaceful solutions...are all contrary to the beliefs of the Islamic Resistance Movement. For renouncing any part of Palestine means renouncing part of religion....There is no solution to the Palestinian problem except by *jihad*.'[9] Recognizing the state of Israel is considered by Hamas as heresy (*kufr*), and the movement thus rejects political solutions that involve such a concession. According to the Hamas charter, Palestine is a holy land, patrimonium (*waqf*), and belongs to all Muslim generations; no one may concede any part of it.

Still, matters are even more complex. In taking part in a political interaction with Israel, which according to Hamas is forbidden, the PLO created a conflict between the two organizations and an internal problem for Hamas: how to relate to its brother's mistakes? If national identity is part of religion, how could Hamas compromise between two conflicting, sacred obligations: keeping Palestine undivided and furthering Palestinian brotherhood? Which ideological dimension was more crucial: 'Islamicizing' Palestine or 'Palestinianizing' Islam?

Hamas directed its ideological attack against Israel, the Jews and the

West, but it also targeted the PLO's policy of making peace with Israel and improving relations with the USA. In its writings, Hamas stated that the Palestinian people have been betrayed by 'certain Zionist Palestinian leaders' who exploit the gains of the Intifada by making concessions to Americans and Zionists.[10] Above all, Hamas interpreted the PLO's primary objective to be the founding of a democratic-secular state in Palestine, and opposed it. Contrary to the PLO's nationalist terminology, Hamas slogans used the language and symbols of Islam. The PLO related to the Arab-Israeli conflict in national terms and offered political solutions to it and the social ills of the Palestinians. Hamas, however, held religion to be a total alternative, one that offers meaningful answers to both internal and external dilemmas.

To be sure, Hamas differentiated between the PLO and other, non-Palestinian enemies. Hamas' charter has nothing favorable to say about Israel, the Jews or the US. But regarding the PLO, it declares: '[T]he PLO is among the closest to Hamas, for it constitutes a Father, a brother, a relative, a friend. Can a Muslim turn away from his Father, his brother, his relative or his friend? Our homeland is one, our calamity is one, our destiny is one and our enemy is common to both of us.'[11]

Reflecting on the social reality of allegiances to the organizations which cut across Palestinian families, Hamas declared that 'whoever has no brother is like a fighter who runs to the battle without weapons...no falcon can take off without wings'.[12] These metaphors expressed Hamas' dual approach to the PLO. Hamas recognized the importance of PLO efforts to politically integrate the Palestinians, forge their national identity and mobilize them against Israel. But, it also claimed that the PLO's mistakes justified Hamas' exclusive existence and usurpation of the PLO's traditional role as the sole legitimate representative of the Palestinian people. Thus, Hamas' rhetorical question of, 'can a falcon take off without wings?' has a dual meaning. On the one hand Hamas evaluated itself as having symbolic status equal to that of the PLO. According to such an interpretation, Hamas considers itself to be one of the falcon's wings, with the PLO as the second. On the other hand this metaphor could be interpreted as symbolizing Hamas' intention to replace the PLO in leading the Palestinian nation. The PLO's role, according to this interpretation, is minimal and in order to take off the assistance of Hamas is needed.

It should be stressed that in coping with its conceptual dilemma, Hamas did not ascribe equal weight to Islamic commitment and Palestinian brotherhood. By emphasizing Islam and by assigning first priority status to *jihad* against Israel, Hamas clearly displayed its preference for an Islamic Palestine and for its replacement of the PLO as the vanguard movement. However, the ideological tension within Hamas' program still remained. The PLO-Israeli negotiations that began in 1991 have sharpened Hamas' conflicting ideological goals: between its Palestinian and Islamic self-identities, the religious imperative of *jihad* against Israel, its position *vis-à-vis* the PLO and its unwillingness to compromise with Israel. These issues posed the single question of how Hamas should adapt to the changing circumstances.

## An Antagonistic Political Player, 1988–93

Between the 1988 publishing of its charter and the 1993 PLO agreement with Israel, Hamas developed three modes of political action. It adhered to them simultaneously, creating an antagonistic political style which reflected the division between a relatively pragmatic local leadership and hard-liners like Muhammad Nazal and Ibrahim Gawshah, two political leaders who, after their deportation by Israel in 1989, directed Hamas' branch in Jordan. This *modus operandi* also reflected the dichotomy between short and long term goals. The three modes of Hamas politics were as follows: competition with the PLO, prevention of the outbreak of civil war with the PLO and the opening of formal communication channels to reach an equivalent status with the PLO in order to discuss basic disagreements.

### Competing with the PLO

Since its inception, Hamas and the PLO have fought each other for legitimacy and the support of the Palestinian public. During the Intifada, the conflict between the two movements sharpened as they struggled for influence in the political street through graffiti, leaflets and the setting of different strike days.[13] In June 1990, Hamas published a brochure under the title 'Hamas: Between the Pains of Reality and the Future Hopes' (*Hamas: Baina Alam al-Waqi' wa-Amal al-Mustaqbal*), in which it questioned the PLO's claim to be the sole legitimate representative of the Palestinian people.[14] The slogan 'Hamas is the sole legitimate representative of the Palestinian people' was written often on the walls of Gaza City during 1991–92.[15] The PLO responded with the declaration that, 'each rival with the PLO is a rivalry with (our) homeland. The PLO is the state, not just a party within it'.[16]

One of the clearest manifestations of this competition can be found in the events surrounding the December 1992 Israeli expulsion of over 400 Hamas leaders to southern Lebanon. Hamas tried to translate the sympathy it had gained among Palestinians from the deportation into political power, and thus sought to force the PLO to leave the negotiation table with Israel forever. Conversely, the PLO attempted to show Hamas that political involvement with the international community and negotiations with Israel would achieve the return of the deportees. The PLO tried to capitalize on the affair and emphasized its role as the sole legitimate representative of the Palestinian people. At first, in December 1992, the PLO promised to suspend its talks with Israel in Washington until Israel returned the expellees, and thus, in January 1993, the PLO conditioned renewing talks on the latter's full implementation of the UN Security Council resolution that called for the immediate return of the deportees. But, as the competition between Hamas and the PLO intensified, the PLO began to rethink its December 1992–January 1993 position. Instead of regarding the deportation as the only issue holding up the negotiations, by February 1993, the PLO viewed it as one of the many, albeit the most important issue, delaying the reopening of the peace talks.

By March 1993, however, the PLO again shifted its position, concluding that the affair was not the primary problem on its agenda. In response, Shaykh Hamad Bitawi, one of the deportees, stated, 'We valued the step by our brothers in the PLO to suspend the talks...but after taking this step they betrayed us. In the beginning their deed can be remembered and therefore thanked, but after this they left us hanging'.[17] PLO leaders came to fear that the deportation crisis was becoming a burden, preventing efforts to achieve their primary aim of ending the occupation. Hence, they concluded that the PLO should compromise and allow for the staged return of the deportees in order to renew its talks with Israel.[18]

Though Hamas' charter does not leave any room for political activity *vis-à-vis* Israel, its competition with the PLO caused the Hamas leadership to use politics as a tactical device. Asked in September 1988 if Hamas might agree to negotiate with Israel, Shaykh Ahmad Yasin, the charismatic leader of the movement, did not quote the recently published Hamas charter, but rather put forth pre-conditions to future negotiations. First, he demanded that Israel completely withdraw from the occupied territories and allow the UN to assume temporary control until the people elected their own leadership. This leadership would then decide the future of the Palestinians and whether to negotiate with Israel.[19] Reacting to the May 1989 Israeli suggestion that the population of the occupied territories elect their leadership and authorize possible negotiations, Shaykh Yasin repeated his former pre-conditions.[20] In order to prevent his marginalization, Shaykh Yasin favored Palestinian consensus and declared that Hamas would participate in such elections.[21] With this, the Hamas leader expressed a tactically pragmatic approach to a phased settlement with Israel. Shaykh Yasin indicated a commitment on his part to stop violence in such a settlement in his response to an Israeli high commander's question of what should be done to stop the mutual bloodshed. Shaykh Yasin answered that Israel must free all Palestinian prisoners, stop IDF provocative actions against Palestinians and cancel its burdensome tax program.[22]

It should be noted that Hamas became more tactically pragmatic as the PLO took more initiative and advanced politically. The PLO's success with its Declaration of Palestinian Independence (1988), its participation in the Madrid peace conference (1991) and its signing of the 1993 agreement with Israel altered the political reality, enhanced the PLO's popular support and raised Palestinian expectations.[23] As a result, Hamas was compelled to try and adapt to the new situation. Thus, for example, as the Madrid conference began to show some results, Hamas renewed its talks with the PLO (see below). But when the PLO's political initiatives were in decline or even halted temporarily, or when Hamas gained popular support in elections for professional and student organizations, Hamas leaders assumed that they could achieve their long-range goals without adopting a pragmatic attitude. As a result, though Hamas sometimes improved its relations with the PLO, at other times the two came close to fighting a civil war.

## Preventing the Outbreak of Palestinian Civil War

Shaykh Jamil Hamameh (director of the al-Aqsa mosque and of the Islamic Committee of Science) and Shaykh Hamad Bitawi (once an *Imam* [prayer leader] at al-Aqsa mosque and now the President of the League of *'ulama'* [religious scholars] in Palestine), both among the most prominent Hamas religious leaders in the West Bank, said:

> As Palestinians we reject inner fighting among our people...the movement will not resort to violence and bloodshed in its resistance to a solution or authority that will come as an alternative to occupation. We as Palestinians will respect the struggle of our people and will continue to consider that the central enemy is the Jewish state and not the sons of our own people. We are not going to fight, the PLO and the Islamic movement are the sons of one people, one homeland, one religion and one family.[24]

In April and September 1990, following locally initiated, violent clashes between Fatah, the PLO's largest faction, and Hamas groups in the West Bank town of Tulkarm, the two organizations began high level discussions on a number of issues. Not surprisingly, no agreement was reached, except for a mutual call to stop the fighting before it became unmanageable. In June 1991, heavy fighting between PLO and Hamas activists in Nablus led Hamas leaders to condemn inter-Palestinian bloodshed. And in April–June 1992, after serious clashes, both sides published the 'Alliance of Honor' (*Mithaq al-Sharaf*), calling for democratic solutions to all disagreements and an end to mutual killing and fighting. As clashes continued, however, a new agreement to stop violent acts and to establish shared committees of inquiry, dialogue and inspection was signed on 13 July 1992.[25] The undeclared aim of these agreements was to prevent a Palestinian civil war. Evaluation of these agreements should not be based on results and full implementation, but rather on their implicit purpose of preventing a total confrontation.

## Opening Formal Communication Channels

In order to prevent Hamas from gaining an equal public status, the PLO made a point of being formally represented by a Fatah delegation. In the different rounds of their dialogue, Hamas tried to convince the PLO to accept the Hamas program, while the PLO/Fatah attempted to co-opt Hamas by suggesting that it participate in the PLO's institutions. However, no agreements have been reached since September 1991 when the PLO/Fatah refused to allow Hamas to have 40–45 per cent of the seats in the United National Command of the Intifada and in the PLO's 20th PNC. Hamas insisted on its demand that elections be held between 1990 and 1992 in the occupied territories for Palestinian institutions, professional associations, student unions and chambers of commerce, institutions in which the Islamists frequently receive 33–45 per cent of the votes.[26] Through achieving 40–45 per cent of the seats in the United National Command of the Intifada and in the PNC, Hamas hoped to change the PLO from within, by aligning with Arafat's secular opposition to create a majority coalition. In talks with the PLO/Fatah on the eve of the 20th session of the PNC, Hamas conditioned its acceptance of Arafat's suggestion to give Hamas almost as many seats as those of the Fatah delegation (35 out of 482 seats, 7.2 per cent, not including, of course, Fatah members belonging to other PLO institutions represented in the PNC, such as the Executive Committee) and on the PLO's rescinding its recognition of Israel and readiness to make peace with Israel as expressed in the 1988 Palestinian Declaration of Independence. It also asked that the PLO cancel its preparations for the Madrid conference. The PLO/Fatah rejected both conditions.

Hamas again tried to implement its strategy during the January 1993 talks with the PLO/Fatah that took place in the wake of the deportation of the Hamas activists. Insisting that the Israeli action had increased its support, Hamas again asked the PLO/Fatah to either grant it 45 per cent of the seats in the PNC or to totally abandon the negotiations with Israel, resume the armed struggle and put an end to the intra-Palestinian rivalry. In the process of discussing these issues, there arose differences between the two competing organizations over the question as to whether the PLO was the sole legitimate representative of the Palestinian people or a coalition that represented just its members, and not the Palestinian people.[27]

To sum up, Hamas' policy concerns were dominated by its confrontation with the PLO. The movement continued to compete with the PLO, raising political slogans, but it also opened formal communication channels and worked with the PLO to prevent the outbreak of a civil war. Reacting to the PLO efforts since 1988 to achieve a settlement with Israel, Hamas leaders refrained from escalating their confrontational policies and, to some extent, even adopted more pragmatic approaches. This became even more the case after the signing of the DOP between the PLO and Israel in September 1993.

## Sharpening Hamas' Political Profile

The September 1993 DOP was seen by Hamas as a surrender agreement in which the PLO relinquished many paragraphs of its covenant and its right to resist the continuing Israeli occupation. According to Hamas, the expected cooperation between Israeli and Palestinian security services against the movement would turn the PLO into an Israeli instrument, allowing Israel to use Palestine as 'a bridge for Israel to penetrate the Arab world'. 'We consider this to be a great historic act of treason and a dangerous one which will begin the dissolution of this leadership which has sold the struggle, sold the blood and sold the rights of the Palestinian people.'[28] Hamas' basic dilemma immediately after the signing was how to confront the new reality which, according to the movement, would not lead to an independent state. How should Hamas fight to nullify the DOP, which 'means to Zionize the Palestinian problem and the Arab nation, as well as the Islamic world?'[29]

At first, Hamas, as a competitor with the PLO, sought to build an alternative leadership, dismiss Arafat and dominate Palestinian politics. Thus, in September 1993, when the Popular and Democratic Fronts for the Liberation of Palestine (PFLP and DFLP)[30] joined forces with eight ex-PLO groups, Hamas and the Palestinian Islamic Jihad, a new coalition was formed: 'The Palestinian Forces Alliance'. Ironically, the new coalition suffered from the PLO's classic problems: how to find a common political platform and establish institutions for the coalition. By January 1994, the ten groups had succeeded in bridging only several of the substantial gaps between the secular-Marxist, ultra-nationalists and radical Muslim groups. The members of the Palestinian Forces Alliance agreed to a political platform based on the PLO's 1968 Covenant and the 1974 Program of Stages, and endeavored to bring about the cancellation of the DOP and rebuild the PLO's institutions and leadership. However, it proved difficult to prevent the radical Islamic elements from dominating the Alliance's institutions.

The new coalition had to decide if there would be equal representation of each organization, as the Fronts desired, which would confer a majority to the eight secular organizations, or representation according to each of the group's strength in the various sectoral bodies, in which case the popular Islamic groups would gain 40–50 per cent of the seats in the coalition's leading institutions.[31] In effect, the dispute was a replay of the long running debate between Arafat and Hamas. The result, declared Ghazi Abu-Jiab, a key figure in the leadership of the DFLP, was that 'there [was] no real alliance between the PLO opposition and Hamas. The attempt by the Damascus-based leadership to forge an alliance on the ground has proved a failure and is now over.'[32]

What was most interesting about Hamas' forming such a coalition was the movement's acceptance of the PLO Covenant (1968) and the PLO Program of Stages (1974) as the basis of a common political platform. The Islamic Charter had contradicted the PLO positions. It held that Palestine is an indivisible, holy unit and forbids employing any means of liberation other than armed struggle and the Intifada. The PLO's Program of Stages, however, accepts the adoption of political means and divides the liberation of Palestine into two successive stages. According to the PLO's Program of Stages, the achievement of 'the people's national, independent and fighting authority on every part of Palestinian land to be liberated'[33] will hopefully lead to the realization of the other goals articulated in the PLO's Covenant. Thus, Hamas implicitly used the ideological element of Palestinian brotherhood to justify deviating from its own ideals. Indeed, being the body with the largest following among the Alliance's components, Hamas hoped to dominate the new coalition and ultimately overtake the PLO and implement the Islamic Charter.

Hamas' efforts to build a counter-coalition to Arafat was based on its assumption that 'the Israeli army will not withdraw from the Gaza Strip or the West Bank'.[34] However, following the May 1994 Israeli withdrawal from most of Gaza Strip and the Jericho area, a serious debate arose within Hamas and between Hamas and its partners in the Palestinian Forces Alliance. Hamas began considering taking part in the newly-established Palestinian Authority's (PA) institutions instead of continuing to operate as a counter-leadership. The advocates of adopting such an approach were relatively moderate political leaders like Musa Abu Marzuq, the head of Hamas' political committee, and Dr. Mahmud al-Zahar, Hamas' spokesman. The logic of their argument was as follows: if reality forced Hamas to emphasize its Palestinian identity and adopt a program of stages, why should the movement reject the possibility of demonstrating Palestinian brotherhood and implementing its program of stages through the PA? Had not Hamas put the struggle against Zionism, Jews and Israel, on the top of its agenda, thus ruling out the option of Palestinian civil war? If the developing, non-Islamic political system within the PA could be seen by Hamas as a legitimate corridor to the 'Islamizing' of Palestinian, then why not use this corridor?

Assuming that the new reality created by the DOP was almost irreversible, the pragmatists within the Hamas political leadership began advocating that the movement should integrate, either partly or indirectly, into the PA without legitimizing the DOP. Could the opposition, they asked, continue to remain aloof? Might it let the PLO and Fatah gain popular support, hoping that this support would change to disillusionment and disappointment with Arafat's leadership, thus leading to a transfer of loyalty to the opposition? Or, at least for the short run, should the opposition accept that there is no hope of undermining the PLO's authority without integrating into the PA or at least cooperating with it? Indeed, the advocates of this approach were concerned less with the distant than the immediate future. They argued that the PLO leaders were determined to see the DOP fulfilled, and expressed their fear that the PLO would take, in cooperation with Israel, serious measures against Hamas if the movement continued to remain in opposition. According to this approach, the realization of the DOP would render the opposition of the Palestinian Forces Alliance academic. Moreover, they pointed out that Israelis and Palestinians in the occupied territories alike had taken heavy losses during the Intifada and that both sides were ripe for achieving a settlement even at a high price.[35]

Hamas pragmatists favored participating in the PA because the movement was unable to convince people to behave according to the Hamas' radical, puritanical interpretation of Islamic Law[36] and because of its lack of public support, as shown by reliable public opinion polls in the occupied territories. A unique phenomenon in the Arab world, the public opinion polls taken during 1994 by an independent professional institution, the Center for Palestine Research and Studies in Nablus, showed that the support for Hamas in both the West Bank and Gaza Strip in the months April, August and December 1994 was 15.9 per cent, 13.91 per cent and 16.6 per cent, while Fatah was supported by, respectively, 37.8 per cent, 39 per cent, and 43.1 per cent of the population. The polls also revealed a decline in negative attitudes toward the DOP from 39.2 per cent in May to 32 per cent in July. In November 44.2 per cent supported Arafat as leader of the PA, while Shaykh Yasin, the Hamas' leader, received only 19.7 per cent. Another indication of the limited support of the opposition is the July estimate that 53 per cent were satisfied with the way the PA was functioning, as opposed to 21 per cent who were not.[37]

Both Musa Abu Marzuq and Dr. Mahmud al-Zahar declared that the movement would participate in elections to all public institutions: from the all-West Bank/Gaza Legislative Council, to municipal councils, trade unions, etc. Furthermore, according to both Shaykh Jamil Hamameh, Hamas' coordinator in the West Bank, and an anonymous Hamas activist in the Gaza Strip, a program to establish a political party to run on behalf of Hamas had been developed in June–July 1994. Arafat tried to encourage the pragmatists among Hamas' leaders to participate in the elections to the PA Council and until April 1995 refused to let the Palestinian police and security services take firm steps against Hamas armed units that had acted against Israel. Hamas also redefined the purpose of its social and educational services, seeing them as building the infrastructure of the Palestinian state rather than of a counter-Islamic one.[38] Due to these pragmatic considerations, Hamas' local leadership in the Gaza Strip agreed with their colleagues in Fatah on a mutual, temporary, non-aggression arrangement. Moreover, negotiations were also opened between Arafat and Hamas leaders regarding Arafat's suggestion to assure four seats in the PA to Hamas, the same number of seats held by official Fatah representatives from Tunis. Arafat has also discussed giving Hamas control of the *awqaf* (religious trusts), the institution upon which Hamas traditionally based its power. But the movement refused to legitimize the DOP and accept Arafat's offer of a minority status of four seats; Fatah, by comparison, held 14 seats.[39] In November 1994, the PA and Hamas came to a limited agreement. Arafat nominated Shaykh Hamad Bitawi, the most prominent pro-Hamas religious representative in the West Bank and head of the Palestine Religious Scholars Association, as head of the religious courts in the West Bank, under the PA's *awqaf* ministry. Furthermore, the PA introduced a Vice Section (*Surtat al-Adab*) to the Palestinian police, composed of and commanded by Hamas activists, an act which allowed Hamas to serve informally as a watchdog of morality in Gaza.[40] Mahmud al-Zahar summed up his movement's pragmatic approach: 'Hamas is found among the administrative staff of the PA and its services...[but] no one is saying that our presence there means recognizing the Oslo agreements'.[41]

Hamas' partners in the Palestinian Forces Alliance reacted very negatively to its pragmatism. The Palestinian Islamic Jihad attacked Hamas for its readiness to integrate within the PA without explicitly receiving permission to operate against Israeli targets outside of the Gaza Strip and Jericho. The PFLP and the DFLP blamed Hamas for the failure to build a united armed command in the occupied territories whose purpose would be to coordinate Alliance operations against the DOP, as well as for the failure to organize a continuing popular protest in response to the massacre in Hebron of 29 Palestinian worshipers by a Jewish settler on 25 February 1994. They accused the Hamas of causing the Alliance to stumble.[42] Indeed, following Hamas' reconsideration of its attitude toward the PA, the

Palestinian Forces Alliance collapsed. Since then, operations against Israel and political statements have been undertaken by the opposition groups separately.

## Toward Defining PA-Hamas Relations

On 18 November 1994, thirteen people were killed in Gaza and scores were wounded when angry Hamas and Islamic Jihad activists clashed with Palestinian policemen after Friday prayers.[43] The violence was reminiscent of PLO-Hamas confrontations which took place prior to the signing of the DOP, albeit on a much larger scale. While Hamas blamed the PA for the killings, Fatah accused the Islamists of behaving with extreme insubordination, of putting themselves above the law and of serving Iranian interests. To preempt an Islamic revolt against the PA, the Palestinian police arrested many Islamists. The Fatah leadership, on behalf of the PA, began mobilizing its supporters, using the slogan, 'We brought about this Authority, not they, and we will protect it with all means'.[44]

Nonetheless, both Hamas and Fatah, preferring to prevent civil war, cooled the super-heated atmosphere and reached an unsigned agreement. The accord stipulated that Hamas accept that the PA police was the only force allowed to carry weapons publicly, while the PA assented to Hamas' argument that its weapons were directed against Israel. Further, the PA implicitly allowed Hamas to operate against Israeli targets with methods not contradicting the DOP. Arafat had three considerations in offering Hamas such a deal: preventing civil war, co-opting Hamas and attaining formal recognition of the PA and its police force, and using Hamas' terrorist attacks to encourage Israel to expand the PA's jurisdiction. Arafat did not want to undermine the DOP; rather, he hoped to improve his authority by using Hamas as a means to that end. Hamas political leaders considered the agreement the maximum they could achieve under the new circumstances created by the DOP. The two organizations also agreed that all demonstrations had to be coordinated with, and licensed by, the PA and that Hamas could not attack the IDF position near the Netzarim settlement in the Gaza Strip. In accordance with this agreement, a judicial investigation committee was formed to find those responsible for the killings. In addition, the two sides committed themselves to avoid bloodshed, refrain from publishing provocative leaflets and respect the free expression of political views. A reconciliation committee was formed, with the participation of high level Hamas and Fatah officials, as well as Palestinian mediators from both Israel and the occupied territories.[45]

The events in Gaza were unprecedented in terms of both the numbers of casualties and the successes of both Fatah and Hamas in mobilizing support for subsequent demonstrations. Not only were the quantitative and qualitative dimensions of the confrontation new, but its solution was unique as well. The agreement did not recycle former resolutions, but reflected the new reality created by the DOP and Hamas' acceptance of the PA as the ruling authority. Hence, Hamas demanded that the PA take responsibility for the actions of its police, unless the investigative committee came to a different conclusion. Hamas maintained its recognition of the PA's authority and its leaders told Shaykh 'Abdallah Nimer Darwish, the head of the Islamic Movement in Israel and one of the mediators between Hamas and the PA, that they had 'no interest to weaken the Chairman [Arafat], nor on being an alternative authority, but rather only to work [with the PA], hand in hand to build our homeland'.[46] Since the agreement was meant to stabilize PA-Hamas relations in Gaza, the mediators and other Palestinian political personalities in the West Bank suggested expanding the agreement, hoping to apply it to all aspects of PA-opposition relations.[47] Such an agreement was reached in Jericho on 12 December 1994 when all Palestinian organizations, except for the Islamic Jihad, agreed to forbid the carrying of arms and the wearing of masks, to keep public order, and to seek the permission of the PA two days before convening public demonstrations. Other commitments included the PA's acceptance of the right of all organizations to publish leaflets and statements (not including graffiti), and its acceptance of responsibility to punish any of its employees who violated the agreement.[48]

However, the local agreement was neither expanded to include the West Bank nor formalized to define all aspects of PA-Hamas relations. Three factors came into play: armed operations against Israel taken by the 'Izz al-Din al-Qassam Brigades, the armed wing of Hamas; Israel's pressure on Arafat to take serious measures against 'Izz al-Din al-Qassam members; and a subsequent change in PA policy towards Hamas.

Beginning in September 1993, 'Izz al-Din al-Qassam units carried out several operations against Israeli targets, including terrorist attacks against civilian buses in Hadera, Afula (both in April 1994) and Tel Aviv (October 1994); against soldiers waiting to board buses in Jerusalem (December 1994) and at the Beit Lid junction (January 1995, in cooperation with Islamic Jihad); and the kidnapping and killing of three Israeli soldiers. Due to operational factors, such as the need for Hamas armed units to find hiding places to avoid capture, as well as a high level of structural compartmentalization, 'Izz al-Din al-Qassam men operated independently, free from the control of the Hamas local political leadership. However, for operations within Israel's pre-1967 borders, al-Qassam required detailed approval of the political leaders 'outside' Palestine. Thus, Hamas political leadership 'inside' could only influence 'Izz al-Din al-Qassam commanders in a roundabout way. In fact, a consensus between the two political wings (inside and outside) was needed in order to influence al-Qassam operations.[49] Such an agreement would prove difficult to come by, as Hamas leaders 'inside' and 'outside' had different views.

The more pragmatist political leaders 'inside', like 'Imad al-Faluji, questioned the utility of 'Izz al-Din al-Qassam operations. He and some of his colleagues wondered whether, given the new political reality in the wake of the DOP, it would be better to use only political means, at least in the short term. 'Izz al-Din al-Qassam operations, they assumed, would not push Israel to the wall, but rather intensify its occupation as well as Hamas conflicts with the PA. In addition, they determined that continued violence would decrease the movement's popularity among the Palestinians. The radicals 'outside', however, held a contradictory opinion.[50]

'Izz al-Din al-Qassam operations prompted debate within the PA establishment as well. On the one hand, Major-General Nasr Yusuf, the Director-General of Palestinian National Security Forces, asked Arafat to let him use massive force against Hamas. On the other hand, PA civilian staff members recommended minimizing the use of force or, alternatively, co-opting Hamas into the PA and strengthening Hamas' moderate stream, as well as a series of measures including the limiting of Hamas' financial resources, opening a propaganda campaign against Hamas, publicizing the division between radicals and pragmatists in the Hamas leadership and raising the claim that Hamas served the interests of Iran and Afghanistan, and competing with Hamas inside the mosques by making use of religious ceremonies to explain PA positions.[51]

In addition to these internal dynamics which existed within both the PA and Hamas, the relations between the two were influenced by Israel's reaction to the attacks. Following the Beit Lid attack (January 1995), then Prime Minister Rabin clarified that unless Arafat acted seriously against Hamas and dramatically reduced 'Izz al-Din al-Qassam attacks, Israel would not redeploy its forces in the West Bank, nor let Arafat hold elections in the West Bank and Gaza Strip. For that purpose Rabin met not only with Arafat, but also with Major-General Yusuf, Colonel Muhamad Dahalan, Head of Palestinian Preventive Security in Gaza Strip, and Amin al-Hindi, Head of General Intelligence.[52]

Due to the Israeli pressure in the aftermath of the Beit Lid attack, Arafat began using his police and intelligence forces against Hamas. He intensified his efforts in April 1995 after an explosion in Gaza City killed six people, including Kamal Kahil, one of 'Izz al-Din al-Qassam's senior commanders. Hamas and Islamic Jihad responded with attacks on Israeli targets in the Gaza Strip in which tens were killed and wounded. The affair stirred controversy over exactly which of the parties were responsible. Hamas blamed the PA for cooperating with the Israeli security service against 'Izz al-Din al-Qassam units, or at least for not protecting the Hamas militants, and therefore claimed the right to retaliate. Conversely, Arafat blamed Hamas for maintaining an ammunition dump in a residential quarter and providing Israel with a reason to tighten its closure of the West Bank and Gaza Strip, delay its military redeployment, as well as postpone the Palestinian elections.[53]

Thereafter, Arafat ordered the following moves against Hamas: the arrest of more than 250 Hamas activists, including prayer leaders (*A'imma*) and prayer speakers (*Khutaba*); the closing of Hamas' weekly newspaper, *al-Watan*, and the jailing of its editor Sayyid Abu-Musamah; the establishment of military courts which sentenced 20 Hamas detainees to prison terms; the prohibition of the posting of political pamphlets on mosque walls; and at Arafat's request, Jordan's expulsion of Musa Abu Marzuq 'Imad al-'Alami (a senior member in Marzuq's political department), and limiting of the activity of Hamas spokesman Ibrahim Ghawsha. Moreover, both Furayh Abu-Middayn, the PA Minister of Justice, and Brigadier-General Ghazi al-Jabali, Director-General of the Palestinian Police Force in Gaza, requested that all illegal arms be relinquished by 12 May 1995.[54]

In April 1995, Arafat began to follow his traditional policy of divide and rule, albeit in a different fashion. Until that time, Arafat had reacted more leniently to Hamas attacks against Israeli soldiers and settlers than to those perpetrated by the Islamic Jihad, hoping to co-opt the moderates among Hamas leaders into his PA.[55] However, in the spring of 1995, Arafat altered his course. He began to arrest Hamas members while gradually releasing Islamic Jihad detainees in order to encourage a more pragmatic approach among them. In addition, with Israel's cooperation, he prohibited moderate Hamas leaders 'inside' from going to Amman to discuss with their radical colleagues there the movement's policy toward the PA.[56]

Hence, a new agenda came into being for the PA-Hamas dialogue. Hamas demanded the release of its prisoners and the dismantling of military courts. The PA responded by raising the issue of the continuation of Hamas' armed activity within PA areas. The PA, through a Fatah delegation, indicated it would release Hamas detainees if the movement stopped attacking Israeli targets within the PA territories. It also demanded that Hamas cease using the Gaza Strip as a base for the mobilization, training and preparation of al-Qassam units, the gathering of arms and explosives and the publishing of communications.[57] In other words, the PA asked Hamas to comply with Israeli demands and to entirely cease its armed activities within the PA area.

Publicly, Hamas spokesmen condemned Arafat for surrendering to Israel and explained that Hamas had respected the PA by not attacking Israelis in

PA-controlled areas, the exception being in revenge for the Israeli-instigated killings in Gaza of Hani 'Abid, head of the Islamic Jihad armed section, (November 1994) and Kamal Kahil (April 1995).[58] However, in talks with the PA, Hamas leaders in Gaza discussed the proposal to suspend all forms of 'Izz al-Din al-Qassam activity for a one year period in order not to provide Israel with reason to delay the next stage of the DOP. As part of a compromise between the PA and Hamas, as well as between Hamas radicals and moderates like 'Imad al-Faluji who wondered even prior to the talks about the utility of 'Izz al-Din al-Qassam operations, Hamas decided to suspend armed operations until 1 July, the intended deadline for an Israel-PA agreement over IDF redeployment and the Palestinian elections.[59]

## Conclusion

The three modes of Hamas politics prior to the DOP – competing with the PLO, preventing the outbreak of a civil war and opening formal communication channels – continued to characterize Hamas political activity after the signing of the DOP as well, the only difference being an increase in the level of political maneuvering. Interpreting the DOP as 'Zionizing' Palestine, Hamas concluded that in order to emphasize the Islamic elements of its Palestinian identity, the movement needed to expand the scope of its activities. Therefore Hamas initially tried to form an alternative coalition, made up of ultra-nationalist and ultra-secularist Palestinian organizations, and agreed to base the coalition's program on the PLO's pre-1988 political platform. Once this coalition disintegrated and Arafat entered Gaza, Hamas recognized that the implementation of the DOP's initial phase had inaugurated a new stage of legitimate, albeit limited, Palestinian authority, with the PLO determining the Palestinian political agenda and the opposition left basically powerless.

As Arafat and his PA began to directly influence the internal agenda of the opposition groups, Hamas was forced to confront new dilemmas. Most significantly it had to determine how to respond to the PA's curtailment of its freedom of action. Having rejected the DOP, Hamas recognized that it could not continue to compete with the PLO in the political field and subsequently turned to terrorist attacks against Israeli targets as its sole means of recourse. As a result, the competition between the two rival Palestinian organizations became internal. In other words, the implementation of the DOP altered Hamas-PLO relations. No longer a competition between ostensible equals, their relationship became one of a ruling authority versus an opposition group.

Following the signing of the DOP, Hamas and the PA established a *modus operandi* consisting of three components. First, without recognizing the Oslo and Cairo agreements, Hamas integrated itself into the PA's administrative and operational levels, but not in senior and representative positions. Second, both sides concluded several local or time-limited unsigned agreements. These types of understandings helped Hamas cope with the widening gap between its ideology and praxis and between its 'hawks' and 'doves', by not obligating itself to an over-all agreement. Third, through their communications channels, each side came to identify the other's red lines and were thus able to prevent the outbreak of civil war.

Hamas accepted the legitimacy of the PA and did not revolt when many of its members were arrested by Arafat's police. The PA, for its part, used its power carefully. Most of the arrested Hamas members were released after a short stay in jail and the PA canceled its plan to license all illegal arms. Time and again, Hamas declared that its arms were not directed against the PA but rather at Israel, although it made clear that its members would fire if the PA policemen attempted to enforce the licensing. 'We act in accordance with political and security circumstances... we have to accustom ourselves wisely', Major-General Yusuf concluded.[60] In addition, a mixture of realist calculations of its power *vis-à-vis* the PA and an idealistic-romantic religious view of Palestinian brotherhood, as well as Hamas' openness to public needs due to the grass-roots nature of the organization, led Hamas to pragmatize its core attitudes. Finally, in ideological terms, Hamas leaders concluded that threats to Palestinian brotherhood may temporarily take precedence over Islamic imperatives. Thus, Palestinian brotherhood became a mediating factor, helping Hamas adapt to the new reality created by the DOP.

The scope of this article prohibits an extended analysis of the interaction between Hamas and the PA since the end of 1995. Nevertheless, it is both pertinent and worthwhile to summarize several of the major developments that have influenced their relations. First, after close to half a year of preparations and the exchange of draft agreements, the PA and Hamas managed to hold an official dialogue in Cairo (19–22 December 1995) that concluded with a shared declaration. For the first time, the two sides released a declaration specifying the positions of Hamas with respect to the Oslo agreements, elections to the PA Legislative Council, as well as on terror attacks against Israel. In the joint communique, Hamas reasserted that it would not participate in the election and continues to reject the Oslo agreement. However, Hamas agreed not to force a boycott of the election and committed itself not to embarrass the PA with terror attacks against Israel launched from PA territory.[61]

Second, the killing of one of al-Qassam's highest commanders, Yahyia 'Ayash, 'the Engineer', by Israel in Gaza City on 5 January 1996 created popular indignation, prompting Hamas to break its agreement with the PA.

Hamas called for a boycott of the PA elections set for 20 January, but failed to persuade even its own supporters, roughly 60 per cent of whom participated in the election and helped to elect five pro-Islamist members to the PA Legislative Council.[62] Presumably frustrated by its initial failure, Hamas implemented four terrorist attacks between 25 February and 4 March in Jerusalem, Tel Aviv and Ashkelon in which about 70 people were killed and almost 120 wounded. In response to these attacks and pressure by the Israelis on the Palestinian community, PA police and security forces acted against the movement. The situation quickly deteriorated into a total clash between Hamas and the PA. PA police uncovered a secret cell planning Arafat's assassination; Hamas subsequently accused the PA of 'crossing the final red line ... in imprisoning hundreds ... raiding charitable and educational institutions' and using 'ugly Nazi crimes'. Hamas called in the PA to stop all measures it had taken against the movement 'before a disaster takes place'.[63]

Third, during the end of 1995 and the first half of 1996 Hamas' internal divisions deepened as the organization almost split between its outside and inside leaders, as well as its radicals and moderates. The members of the organization disagreed about its orientation. Should Hamas cooperate with Hizballah and Iran under the ideological supervision of the Iranian Islamic revolution or should it focus on its Palestinian profile, a position that would even enable the movement to integrate itself in to the PA under certain conditions?[64] A new political movement, the Islamic National Salvation Party (Hizb al-Khalas al-Watani al-Islami) was founded by second-tier Hamas political leaders on 27 March 1996. On 13 May Hamas' leadership decided to open negotiations with Arafat over their participation in his PA cabinet.[65] Both this web of Hamas-PA relations as well as Hamas' internal discord are unprecedented. Although there has been neither a civil war nor a collapse of Hamas into smaller units, the PA and Hamas are closer than ever before to reaching both of these points. The *modus operandi* achieved by the PA and Hamas between February and March 1996 has been seriously challenged, but has not as of yet collapsed.

## NOTES

1.  On the movement's inception, see, *inter alia*, Hisham H. Ahmad, *Hamas From Religious Salvation to Political Transformation: The Rise of Hamas in Palestinian Society* (Jerusalem: Palestinian Academic Society for the Study of International Affairs (PASSIA) 1994). For Hamas' structure and activities see, *inter alia*, Anat Kurz, Maskit Burgin, and David Tal, *Islamic Terrorism and Israel, Hizballah, Palestinian Islamic Jihad and Hamas* (Hebrew) (Tel Aviv: Tel Aviv U. 1993); Jean-Francois Legrain, 'Palestinian Islamism: Patriotism as a Condition of Their Expansion', in Martin E. Marty and Scott R. Appelby (eds.), *Accounting for Fundamentalism* (Chicago: U. of Chicago Press 1994) pp.413–427; Ori Nir, 'Scorched in the Torch of Jihad', *Ha'aretz*, 15 Nov. 1994.

2.	On nation building, see, *inter alia*, Charles Tilly, *From Mobilization to Revolution* (Reading, MA: Addison-Wesley 1978); Morris Janowitz, *Community Political Systems* (Glencoe, NY: The Free Press 1961); Karl W. Deutsch, *Nationalism and its Alternatives* (NY: Knopf 1969); A.D. Smith, 'The Nation: Invented, Imagined, Reconstructed', *Millennium* 20/3 (1991) pp.353–68; Anthony D. Smith (ed.), *Ethnicity and Nationalism* (Leiden: E.J. Brill 1992); Cliford Geertz, 'The Integrative Revolution, Primordial Sentinents and Politics in New Nations', in Cliford Geertz (ed.), *Old Societies and New States* (Glencoe, NY: The Free Press 1963) pp.105–57.

3.	On the contradiction between the two, see, *inter alia*, Martin Seliger, *Ideology and Politics* (Glencoe, NY: The Free Press 1976). For a treatment of the PLO's same problem, see, *inter alia*, M. Klein, 'The PLO as a Methodological Problem for Israeli Researchers', *British Journal of Middle Eastern Studies* 20/2 (1993) pp.164–73.

4.	Andrea Nusse, 'The Ideology of Hamas: Palestinian Islamic Fundamentalist Thought on the Jews, Israel and Islam', in Ronald L. Nettler (ed.), *Studies in Muslim–Jewish Relations* 1 (Oxford Center for Postgraduate Hebrew Studies and Harwood Academic Publishers 1993) pp.97–125.

5.	Raphael Israeli, 'The Charter of Allah: The Platform of the Islamic Resistance Movement (Hamas)', in Yonah Alexander (ed.), *The 1988–1989 Annual on Terrorism* (Dordecht, The Netherlands: Kluwer Academic Publishers 1990) pp.117, 119.

6.	Quoted in Nusse (note 4) p.108.

7.	Ibid., pp.108–10.

8.	On Islamic fundamentalism in general see, *inter alia*, Hamid Enayat, *Modern Islamic Political Thought* (London: Macmillan 1982); Said Amir Arjomand (ed.), *From Nationalism to Revolutionary Islam* (Albany, NY: SUNY Press 1984); Ali E. Dessouki (ed.), *The Islamic Resurgence* (NY: Praeger 1982); Emmanuel Sivan, *Radical Islam* (New Haven, CT: Yale UP 1985); John L. Esposito (ed.), *Voices of Resurgent Islam* (NY: Oxford UP 1983); Panayiotis J. Vatikiotis, *Islam and the State* (London: Croom Helm 1987); and the relevant chapters in the five volumes of Marty and Appelby (note 1).

9.	*The Islamic Charter*, as translated by Israeli (note 5) pp.114–15.

10.	Nusse (note 4) p.110.

11.	Israeli (note 5) p.123. Hamas even declared in its Charter that once the PLO adopts Islam as its guiding ideology, Hamas members will become the PLO's soldiers.

12.	Ibid.

13.	Israeli (note 5) pp.99–134. Paul Steinberg and Ann Mary Oliver, *The Graffiti of the Intifada, A Brief Survey* (Jerusalem: PASSIA 1990); Shaul Mishal with Reuben Aharoni, *Speaking Stones* (Syracuse, NY: SUP 1994); Meir Litvak, 'Tenu' at Hahamas: Zehut Falastinit Aheret' (The Hamas Movement: Another Palestinian Identity), in David Menashri (ed.), *Islamic Fundamentalism: A Challenge to Regional Stability* (Hebrew) (Tel Aviv: Tel Aviv U., The Dayan Center 1993) pp.57–70; Matti Steinberg, 'The PLO vis-a-vis Palestinian Fundamentalist Islam' in Y. Ariel, M. Steinberg and M. Klein (eds.), *Virtue and Necessity: Fundamentalist Trends vs. the Contemporary Middle East* (Hebrew) (Jerusalem: Leonard Davis Institute, The Hebrew U. 1989) pp.27–42.

14.	See Meir Hatina, *Palestinian Radicalism: The Islamic Jihad Movement* (Hebrew) (Tel Aviv: Tel Aviv U., The Dayan Center 1994) p.105, note 31; Litvak (note 13) pp.57–70.

15.	Ahmad (note 1) p.65.

16.	'Radduna 'Aila al-Hamasyyn, (Our Answer to the Hamas People), *Filastin al-Thawira*, 8 July 1990.

17.	Interviewed by Ahmad (note 1) p.69.

18.	*Al-Quds al-'Arabi*, 9 Feb. 1993; *al-Hayat*, 8 March 1993. This change in attitude stemmed from four developments: first, the opening of negotiations involving the US, Arab regimes, the PLO and Hamas in order to reach a compromise that could enable the deportees' return; second, Egyptian and American pressure on Israel and the PLO to reach a satisfactory solution to the affair; third, the agreement between Israel and the PLO to permit the return of veteran PLO deportees, especially well-known Fatah figures, in order to improve the PLO's status and undermine Hamas' structure; fourth, the failure of the Jan. 1993 Hamas-PLO talks in which Hamas attempted to transplant the competition with the PLO into the latter's

Palestinian National Council (PNC) (see below).

19. *Yediot Aharonot*, 16 Sept. 1988, as quoted in Kurz *et al.* (note 1) p.161.
20. Kurz *et al.* (note 1) pp.188–9.
21. Ibid.
22. *Jerusalem Post*, 21 Jan. 1989, as quoted in Kurz *et al.* (note 1) p.161.
23. See Ahmad (note 1) pp.104–5.
24. Interviewed by Ahmad (note 1) 70–1.
25. *Ha'aretz*, 14 July 1992.
26. For a survey of results in different elections during this period, see, *inter alia*, Kurz *et al.* (note 1) pp.191–3. As Ziad Abu 'Amr noted, because of the electoral system employed in these institutions, it is important to distinguish between the number of votes each trend has won and percentage of seats it has gained in each elected council. According to him, 'the Islamists usually enjoy 40 to 45 per cent of the popular vote'. See Ziad Abu 'Amr, *Emerging Trends in Palestinian Strategic Political Thinking and Practice* (Jerusalem: PASSIA 1992) pp.24–5.
27. N. Haidari, 'The PLO and Hamas: a Struggle Over Influence', *Majalat al-Dirasat al-Filastiniyya* (Arabic) 12 (Winter 1993) pp.115–44. In the same issue, see also the protocol of the Jan. 1993 talks, pp.128–44; *al-Hayat*, 1 Feb. 1993.
28. Sheih Bitawi in Ahmad (note 1) pp.110, 112.
29. Ibid., p.109.
30. The dilemmas of the two fronts and other Palestinian opposition groups *vis-a-vis* the PLO will be discussed in length in my article 'Quo Vadis? Palestinian Dilemmas of Ruling Authority Building Since 1993', *Middle Eastern Studies*, forthcoming.
31. *Al-Shira'*, 12 Jan. 1994.
32. *Middle East Report*, Nov.–Dec. 1994, p.25; Haidari (note 27).
33. Yehuda Lukas, *Documents on the Israeli-Palestinian Conflict 1967–1983* (Cambridge: CUP 1984) p.157.
34. Sheh Bitawi, in Ahmad (note 1) p.110.
35. Dan Avidan, 'The Political Initiative of Hamas', *Davar*, 29 May 1994; Yosef Algazi, 'Not on a Silver Tray', *Ha'aretz*, 20 May 1994; Emmanuel Sivan 'Between Versailles and Munich', *Ha'aretz*, 25 May 1994; Amira Hess, 'Hair Color Index', *Ha'aretz*, 17 June 1994; see also the Hamas leader Ismael Haniyya's interview in *Ha'aretz*, 29 Sept. 1994.
36. Amira Hess, 'Alcohol via the Hard Way', *Ha'aretz*, 5 June 1995; *al-Wasat*, 15 May 1995.
37. *Results of Public Opinion Polls* (Nablus: Center for Palestine Research and Studies, April–Dec. 1994); *Ha'aretz*, 16 June, 20 July, 25 Nov. 1994; M. Steinberg, 'You Can Not Applaud With One Hand Only', *Davar*, 5 Sept. 1994. It should be noted that according to these polls, a third group, 26–28 per cent of the population, preferred to identify themselves with neither Fatah nor Hamas, but rather as independents.
38. *Ha'aretz*, 19 June 1994; *Kol Ha'ir*, 24 June 1994; *al-Quds*, 26 June, 7 March 1994.
39. Z. Bar-El, 'One Plate, Many Close Friends', *Ha'aretz*, 3 June 1994. Regarding Arafat's suggestion to include Sheikh Ahmad Yasin, the charismatic leader of Hamas who is under Israeli arrest, see *Ha'aretz*, 27 May 1994; al-Haj Ahmad in an interview with Yosi Torpshtein, *Ha'aretz*, 10 June 1994.
40. *Ha'aretz*, 13, 18 Nov. 1994.
41. *Ha'aretz*, 29 Nov. 1994. See also D. Rubinstein, 'Time Out for Arafat', *Ha'aretz*, 16 June 1995; and Amin al-Hindi, *al-Watan*, 4, 13 Jan. 1995, as published in *Ha'aretz*, 8, 15 Jan. 1995.
42. D. Rubinstein, 'The New Palestinian Alliance' and Z. Schiff, 'Signals from Hamas', *Ha'aretz*, 29 April 1994; Former Shabak (Israeli General Security Service) official Sim'on Romah in an interview in *Ha'aretz*, 20 April 1995.
43. *Ha'aretz*, 20 Nov. 1994. It seems that PA police were not well trained and had no experience in dealing with such a provocative and violent demonstration. An expression of the tension between a radical Islam organization and the PA occurred a month earlier, when Arafat was kicked out of a Gaza mosque by Islamic Jihad supporters. They blamed him for cooperating with Israel in the killing of the commander of the organization's armed section.
44. *Ha'aretz*, 20 Nov. 1994.

45. *Ha'aretz,* 20–22, 24–25, 27, 29 Nov., 4 Dec. 1994. It should be noted that the Israeli-Palestinian mediating delegation included members from the primary political groups active among the Arab citizens of Israel: the political parties (The Arab Democratic Party and The Democratic Front for Peace and Equality); the Islamic movement in Israel; and Dr. Ahmad Tibi, an independent political figure who is also one of Arafat's advisers. In its composition and acts, the delegation played a mediating role between the PLO and Israel on the one hand and confronted Palestinian organizations on the other hand. These roles had been played by the Israeli-Palestinians since the Intifada. See D. Rubinstein, 'Different Existence, Another Identity', *Ha'aretz,* 13 March 1995; and, E. Rekhess, *The Arab Minority in Israel: Between Communism and Arab Nationalism 1965–1991* (Hebrew) (Tel Aviv: Hakibbutz Hameuhad 1993). However, Hamas leaders in the Amman branch, Ghawshah and Nazal, were against the agreement which the delegation helped to conclude and tried to prevent it. *Ha'aretz,* 23 Nov. 1994.

46. A. Hess, 'Trying to Stop Escalation', *Ha'aretz,* 25 Nov. 1994. The same attitude was also expressed by Mahmud al-Zahar to *al-Quds,* quoted in *Ha'aretz,* 29 Nov. 1994. The same article also notes that this attitude was attributed to Shaykh Yasin by another mediator, Israeli MK Talib al-San'a. This theme also lay behind the eight points unofficially accepted by all Palestinian organizations, published by the mediation committee in *al-Ittihad,* 23 Nov. 1994.

47. *Ha'aretz,* 5 Dec. 1994.

48. *Ha'aretz,* 15 Dec. 1994.

49. *Ha'aretz,* 13, 14 Oct., 14 Nov. 1994, 29 Jan. 18 April 1995. Mahmud al-Zahar to *Ha'aretz,* 13 June 1995.

50. *Al-Quds,* 19 Nov. 1994; G. Bechor, 'The Long Veto Arm of the Jihad' and O. Nir, 'Scorched' (note 1).

51. *Al-Hayat,* 2 Feb. 1995; D. Rubinstein, 'The Understandings and the Rules of the Game', *Ha'aretz,* 20 April 1995.

52. Z. Schiff, 'Upgrading in Gaza', *Ha'aretz,* 17 Feb. 1995; idem., 'The Terror Might Surprise Again', *Ha'aretz,* 9 June 1995.

53. *Ha'aretz,* 6, 7, 9 April 1995. On cooperation between the Israeli and the Palestinian security services see, *inter alia,* Schiff, 'Upgrading in Gaza' (note 52).

54. *Ha'aretz,* 13, 14, 28 April, 7 May 1995; D. Rubinstein, 'Hamas' Self-restraint', *Ha'aretz,* 5 June 1995; idem., 'Time Out for Arafat', *Ha'aretz,* 16 June 1995; G. Bechor, 'The Front for United Palestine', *Ha'aretz,* 7 May 1995; *al-Wasat,* 15 May 1995.

55. *Ha'aretz,* 24 Aug., 8, 11 Sept. 1994.

56. *Ha'aretz,* 11, 26 April, 7, 19 May 1995; Bechor, 'The Long Veto Arm of the Jihad', *Ha'aretz,* 25 May 1995; *al-Wasat,* 15 May 1995.

57. *Ha'aretz,* 13, 23 April , 7 May, 11 June 1995; *al-Wasat,* 5 May 1995; *al-Hayat,* 27 Jan. 1995; Schiff, 'The Terror Might Surprise Again' (note 52).

58. *Ha'aretz,* 13 April 1995; Mahmud al-Zahar to *Ha'aretz,* 13 June 1995; Rubinstein (note 51).

59. *Ha'aretz,* 16, 20 April, 11 June 1995; Rubinstein, 'Time Out for Arafat' (note 54); Mahmud al-Zahar to *Ha'aretz,* 13 June 1995. Besides stopping 'Izz al-Din al-Qassam operations, Arafat tried during the PA-Hamas talks to achieve Hamas' formal acceptance of the DOP, but was rejected even by a moderate like 'Imad al-Faluji. Moreover, even Nabil Sha'th and Hisham 'Abd al-Razzaq, who negotiated with Hamas, objected to this demand. *Ha'aretz,* 14, 16, 18 April 1995; Rubinstein (note 51).

60. Nasr Yusuf to *Ha'aretz,* 2 April 1995. According to him, the PA succeeded in licensing 400 weapons out of 1000. See also *Ha'aretz,* 29 Nov. 1994, 12, 20 April, 9 June 1995.

61. *al-Quds,* 22 Dec. 1995.

62. *Ha'aretz,* 8, 24 Jan. 1996; *al-Quds,* 22, 23, 27 Jan. 1996.

63. 'Izz al-Din al-Qassam leaflet, 3 April 1996; *Ha'aretz,* 5, 6, 7 June 1996; *al-Quds,* 22 April, 8 May 1996.

64. *al-Watan al-'Arabi,* 8 April 1995; *al-Wasat,* 18 Dec. 1995; *al-Quds,* 7 March 1996; *Ha'aretz,* 4, 6 March 1996.

65. *Ha'aretz,* 22 May 1996; *al-Quds,* 13 May 1996.

# Religious Zionism and the State: Political Accommodation and Religious Radicalism in Israel

SHMUEL SANDLER

In its earlier years Israel was spared the impact of religious radicalism. In the last two decades, however, religious doctrines have begun to claim a role in foreign policy, culminating in the 4 November 1995 assassination of Prime Minister Yitzhak Rabin. The primary aim of this study is to explore the systemic political processes and contextual factors that in the past have subdued national religious radicalism in Israel. The general argument of this essay is that the tradition of political accommodation with the religious parties fostered their participation in government coalitions, and by doing so, mobilized a large portion of the religious sector to support the state. Equally important in suppressing religious radicalism in Israel were the two main doctrines of religious Zionism, the instrumental and the redemptionist, which applauded cooperation with secular Zionism and the state, hence enabling political accommodation and avoiding a comprehensive violent confrontation. The absence of a religious party in the Rabin government brought the country's political discourse to an unprecedented level of intensity, strengthening a new blend of religious nationalism that posed a potential for delegitimization of the state.

One of the major perplexities of world politics is the revival of religious nationalism in an era of growing interdependence and integration.[1] Concurrent with this revival has been the outbreak of ethno-national conflicts; states torn by ethnic disputes include Belgium, Canada, Northern Ireland, Yugoslavia, Lebanon, Iraq, Cyprus, Ethiopia, the Sudan and India. In all of these polities, either now or in their recent histories, ethnic conflicts have coincided with religious inter-communal dissension.[2] The Middle East is one of the regions most prone to these kinds of disputes. The Arab-Israeli conflict, which from its inception was inspired by a religious dichotomy, nevertheless existed primarily as an interstate or ethno-national conflict. However, the rise of radical Islam has placed new emphasis on the religious dimension of the conflict.

Until recently Israeli politics was spared the impact of religious radicalism, although some of its political parties did adopt foreign policy positions influenced by religious doctrines. However, the vigorous opposition by religious circles to an Israeli withdrawal from Gaza and Judea and Samaria (the West Bank) culminated in the 4 November 1995 assassination of Prime Minister Yitzhak Rabin. The assassin claimed that he had been inspired religiously and believed his actions served the national cause.[3] This event serves as an indication of the magnitude and potential of religious extremism in the Jewish state.

The primary aim of this study is to explore the systemic political processes and contextual factors that in the past have subdued national religious radicalism in Israel. Such an effort is necessary in order to come to an understanding of the current potential in the state of religious radicalism.[4] The ultimate threat of religious extremism is the delegitimization of the state. My general argument is that the secular camp's tradition of political accommodation with the religious parties fostered their participation in government coalitions, and by doing so, succeeded in mobilizing a large portion of the religious sector to support the state. Involving initially the National Religious Party (NRP), this mode of political behavior was eventually extended, albeit with less success, to the ultra-Orthodox (Haredi) parties like Agudat Israel and Shas (Sephardi Torah Guardians List). Equally important in suppressing religious radicalism in Israel were the two main doctrines of religious Zionism, the instrumental and the redemptionist, which applauded cooperation with secular Zionism and the state, hence enabling political accommodation and avoiding a comprehensive violent confrontation. Even though the religious parties have returned to power, in the long run whether these accommodationist doctrines will continue to prevail depends on the willingness of secular governments to continue the practice of power sharing with the religious sector and its commitment to pursuing policies which the religious camp can live with. In exploring the phenomenon of religious extremism in Israel, we start with a theoretical introduction to politicized religion in the modern nation state.

## Modernization and Politicized Religion

According to many analysts, a common denominator of nationalism and politicized religion is that both were to have dissipated in the modern state system. In reality, however, both ethnicity and politicized religion can be seen as a response to modernity. Walker Connor and A. D. Smith, concentrating primarily on ethnic nationalism, related ethnic revival directly to modernization.[5] Similarly, Ernst Haas interpreted the appearance of nationalism in our era as a rational choice for societies going through the strains of modernization, adding: 'nationalism can hold a society together while people are being buffeted by the strains of modernization'.[6] K. J.

Holsti defined the relationship between modernization, international communication and nationalism as a reaction of a community to external penetration and threats to its autonomy and cultural uniqueness.[7] Samuel Huntington, in his classic study of changing societies, concluded that, 'modernization means that all groups, old as well as new, traditional as well as modern, become increasingly aware of themselves as groups and of their interests and claims in relation to other groups'.[8]

The modern state, due to its powerful message, presents a threat to faith; it provides functions that free man from the need to turn to God. At the same time, modernization, by creating self-awareness on the one hand and inequality on the other, promotes value expectations that exceed value capabilities. Frustrations deriving from relative deprivation may generate passions that can be directed against competing ethnic groups, either internal or external to the state.[9] Feelings of deprivation can be experienced by an entire nation when it feels that its status in the international community is inconsistent with what it is entitled to, or by a group that shares such feelings with regard to the society to which it belongs. Challenges or traumatic experiences which the state seems unable to overcome, crises of confidence in the ability of the state to contend with security issues, economic problems, or difficulties with the delivery of public services encourage segments of society to turn to ethno-religious entrepeneurs offering alternatives to the modern state. Ethnicity and religion are also able to compete with the state when it fails to provide its citizens with a basic human need: self-identity. For example, radical Islam sees itself as a defensive movement against foreign culture and perceives Arab regimes as agents of alien forces.[10] Hence, ethno-nationalism and politicized religion must be understood as simultaneously being both challenged and fostered by modernity and its derivatives.[11] Nevertheless in Israel, despite the presence of religion in Israeli political life since the inception of the state, religion did not take on a competitive, independent dimension until the mid-1970s. A partial explanation of the delay is rooted in the politics of accommodation adopted by the secular Zionist elite.

## Religion and the Politics of Accommodation in Israel

From its inception, religion played an integral role in the Zionist movement. The forerunners of Jewish national awakening were two rabbis from Eastern Europe and the Balkans, Zvi Hirsch Kalisher and Jehudah Alkalai.[12] Political Zionism, however, was established by two secularist leaders, Leo Pinsker and Theodore Herzl, while the ideologue of spiritual Zionism, Ahad-Haam, was secular as well. The first open clash between religious and secular Zionism came in 1902 when the Zionist agenda, under pressure from the spiritual Zionists, was expanded from political to cultural affairs. The incompatibility of the secular and the Orthodox world-views was resolved through the establishment of a two-tiered system of education: religious and secular.[13] However, this compromise satisfied only a portion of Orthodox Jewry, and consequently, the religious camp split into religious Zionist (Mizrahi) and non-Zionist (Agudat Israel) factions.

While the non-Zionist faction secluded itself from the majority of secular Zionists, Mizrahi cooperated with the secularist movements in developing Eretz Yisrael (the Land of Israel). Cooperation between Mizrahi and Labor extended beyond the political realm and was translated into what over the years was termed the 'historic alliance'. As long as religious issues were not involved, Mizrahi, and especially its Labor offshoot, Hapoel Hamizrahi, accepted the norms that originated in the Labor camp. However, the movements remained separated with respect to education. In the long run the decision for a two-tiered educational system implied educational autonomy for the religious sector, with an independent ultra-Orthodox educational network also being established.[14]

The religious-secular coalition became a cornerstone of political life in Israel. Coalition politics had been an integral part of the tradition that emerged during the 'state in the making' (Yishuv) era and following the establishment of the state in 1948,[15] this tradition enabled the religious parties to integrate successfully into a power sharing arrangement.

Coalition politics between secular and religious parties rarely follow Riker's 'minimum winning coalition theory'.[16] Actually, the secular-religious coalition in Israel was designed to regulate conflict between the two rival ideological camps, in accordance with the consociational model of political accommodation.[17] This system, designed to achieve consensus, should be distinguished from a majoritarian system where 'winner takes all' and the minority, as long as it stays so, usually remains outside of the government. Consensus politics, by contrast, relates democracy and stability to a representative executive. For example, while the Sephardi parties were not successful in establishing an effective presence in Israeli politics, Israel's ruling party, Mapai, made sure that the government included Ministers of Sephardi origin.

The NRP (previously Mizrahi/Hapoel Hamizrahi) constituted a pillar of Israeli government coalitions until 1977. Ben-Gurion preferred the NRP over other parties within the Labor camp, such as Ahdut Ha-Avodah and Mapam, which until 1955 were excluded from the government. As a rule, Ben-Gurion formed coalitions with parties which did not espouse an independent line in foreign policy, like the Progressives and the NRP, and excluded Socialist parties which supported a pro-Moscow line. Nationalist Herut was kept out of the government.

The NRP suited the mold of the other 'core' coalition parties. These parties were willing to compromise their ideological disagreements on religion or on socioeconomic questions for the sake of state building. The NRP differentiated between accepting the secular state on a normative and an instrumental level. While acknowledging that the secular state was not the ideal state, religious Zionism accepted the authority of the state institutions and identified with the civic symbols and most of the rituals of the new state. To the National Religious public, the state constituted an early stage on the road to redemption. In contrast, Agudat Israel only conditionally accepted the state. Rejecting the possibility that redemption could come via secular Jews, they valued life in the Land of Israel as a religious virtue, but continued to perceive their life in the *state* of Israel as a continuation of exile.[18]

From a political perspective, the NRP's participation in the coalition provided it with access to economic resources and political symbols that gave it an advantage over its opponents within the religious camp. In electoral terms, Mizrahi viewed Agudat Israel as its main competitor. Mapai, on its part, had an inherent interest in the success of a moderate religious party in a camp where it was unable to make major inroads. In short, the NRP was a vehicle for mobilizing support among religious voters for a Mapai-dominated government.

A crucial aspect of the Mapai-NRP partnership, as indicated above, was that power sharing was limited to the religious domestic domain. Foreign policy was the domain of Mapai and its leader David Ben-Gurion. Following the June 1967 War, however, a new division developed in Israeli society with implications for foreign policy: the question of the future of the newly acquired territories, some of which included the heartland of historic 'Eretz Yisrael'. To many, regaining the Land of Israel was the essence of Zionism, and thus no part of it could be traded in exchange for a peace treaty, as suggested by the Labor-dominated governments.[19] Since many of the supporters of the Land of Israel ideology were concentrated in the NRP's constituency, the coalition between Labor and the NRP became troublesome. In fact, the collapse of the Yitzhak Rabin government in 1977 and the coming to power of a Likud-led coalition was related to the growing gap between Labor and the NRP. During the subsequent years, the NRP became more nationalistic, increasingly basing its ideology on religious sources. The 'historical alliance' between Labor and the Mizrahi movements was replaced by a partnership between right-wing, secular nationalist and religious parties.

Following Likud's emergence as the largest party in 1977, the NRP gave Menahem Begin the needed parliamentary margin to oust Labor from its leadership position. This defection transformed the Israeli political map.

The similarity in the positions on territorial issues held by Likud and the NRP implied that power sharing between right-wing secular and religious Zionists would now be based on ideological affinity rather than merely on political accommodation between ideologically distant camps. The strength of this new alliance was successfully tested in 1984 and again in 1990 when the NRP refused to join a Labor-led government without the Likud. Consequently, in 1992, when Rabin and Labor returned to power, they made only limited efforts to bring the NRP into the government[20] and, for the first time in the history of the Jewish state, the NRP remained in opposition for a full four-year term of the Knesset. In place of the NRP, Rabin formed a coalition with Meretz, a left-wing party and Shas, which then became the representative of the religious sector. This turn of events confirmed the decline of the tradition of political accommodation and partnership that had been the pre-1977 norm between religious and left-wing, secular Zionism.

### The Ideological Context of Religious Zionism

The religious sector of Israeli society, both the modernist and the *haredi*, comprises an estimated 20–25 per cent of the Jewish population.[21] Given the large size of the population, in addition to the NRP's effective control of the state's religious schools, it is not surprising that the religious sector plays a significant role in Israeli public life. However, the ability of the Mizrahi movement to combine religion with Zionist ideology, accompanied by its participation in the state-building process, provided it with a greater role in Israeli society than the other religious parties.

A central motif in the development of religious Zionism was modernity, that is, *inter alia*, the belief that an individual, or collective, can act to influence its own fate. Thus, whereas ultra-Orthodoxy stipulated that Jews cannot hasten the coming of the Messiah, religious Zionism proposed active redemption. This position and the Mizrahi movement were supported by modern Orthodoxy in the US, as well as in other communities in the Jewish Diaspora, which was more liberal than the non-Zionist ultra-Orthodox groups. The ideological basis for political cooperation between Mizrahi and secular Zionism was established by Rabbi Jacob Reines, who founded Mizrahi in 1902.[22] Rabbi Reines articulated an instrumental doctrine that advocated cooperation with secular Zionism due to pragmatic factors, namely the rescue of Jewish people from the expanding anti-Semitic onslaught in Europe. The settling of the Land of Israel was sacred, but foremost was the goal of founding a polity that would provide security to the Jewish people. On this basis, Reines supported Herzl who looked into the possibility of establishing a Zionist colony in eastern Africa (Uganda).

Reines' position was predominant in the NRP, despite a short interval in which Rabbi Meir Bar-Ilan and other Mizrahi leaders adopted an independent foreign policy line during the British-inspired Palestine-partition debate of the late 1930s (Mizrahi objected to partition on ideological grounds).[23] However, once the state had been established, the NRP had no ideological difficulty in cooperating with the state's secular elite in a partitioned Land of Israel.

As pointed out above, the NRP began to change its tradition of passivity on foreign policy issues after the Six Day War, when withdrawal from parts of the newly acquired Land of Israel was placed on the political agenda. The decline of the instrumental approach was gradual, and it was not until the mid-1970s that the NRP leadership adopted an uncompromising, hawkish policy with regard to the territories. Gush Emunim (Bloc of the Faithful), a movement that originated in the national religious camp and was established following the Yom Kippur War, demanded the expansion of settlement efforts to the entire Land of Israel and accused the Labor movement of abandoning the spirit of pioneering. The movement defined itself as the new vanguard of the Zionist revolution.[24]

These new attitudes in the national religious camp were to a large extent molded by the theological doctrines of one of the main ideological schools within religious Zionism: the teachings of Rabbi Avraham Yitzhak Kook and his son Rabbi Zvi Yehuda Kook. These two, more than anyone else, have influenced the recent ideological discourse of religious Zionism, and particularly of Gush Emunim. Although their approach transformed the political attitude of the NRP constituency, as far as attitudes toward the state are concerned it cannot be defined as a radical religious doctrine.

A basic theme in the teaching of Rabbi Avraham Kook, developed further by his son, is the idea of holiness. In accordance with the cabalistic tradition that sparks of holiness were spread throughout the universe,[25] the Rabbis Kook held that even those Jews who are not observant are unknowingly motivated by an inner divine spark. Therefore, they put forth, Jews redeeming the Holy Land were themselves holy. Advancing a unitary approach to the universe, Rabbi Kook argued dialectically that the secular and the holy complement each other while awaiting unification. By leaving the Diaspora and redeeming the land through agriculture and physical labor, Jews advanced the union between the secular material world and the holy spiritual one.[26]

Such philosophy provided an alternative rationale for cooperation with secular Zionism. While Reines grounded secular religious cooperation on an instrumental foundation, Kook idealized it. Collaboration with secular Zionism was sanctified, redeeming the land was holy, and the forthcoming Jewish state would, therefore, be an ideal one (not in the Hegelian sense) because it would be the state of the Jewish people in the Land of Israel. Moreover, Kook also drew on a messianic idea, defining the process that was taking place in the Land of Israel as the beginning of redemption. According to him, the Balfour Declaration was a divine sign that redemption had begun, though the real signs had appeared four decades earlier when Jews first began their resettlement of the Land of Israel and their flourishing agricultural efforts. Even the unfolding of events in world history indicated that Jewish redemption was near.[27] In short, alongside a universal religious vision of redemption, Rabbi Kook articulated a unitary doctrine of Jewish sacredness: the all-embracing holiness of the Jewish people, the Land of Israel and the Jewish state.

The enunciated doctrine of religious nationalism, to use Juergensmeyer's conceptual framework,[28] was competitive with that of secular nationalism. The National Religious camp and the students of Mercaz Harav (the rabbinical college established by Rabbi Kook) adopted many of Kook's themes. Mizrahi regarded him as one of its founding spiritual leaders. Religious Zionism viewed the renewal of Jewish sovereignty as equaling the beginning of redemption. The state of Israel was holy, as were its institutions, regardless of who was in power.

The Six Day War was a major event in the formation of religious Zionist thought. Rabbi Zvi Yehuda Kook, who emerged as the most accepted interpreter of his father's writings, applied his father's ideas to explain the events that took place during and subsequent to the war.[29] For the religious community, the liberation of what had been, historically, the holiest parts of the Land of Israel, the reunification of Jerusalem, and the astonishing victory of the IDF over a combination of Arab armies was a heavenly sign. For many religious Jews and especially for the disciples of Mercaz Harav, the messianic era was progressing as predicted by the late Rabbi Kook and as reemphasized by his son. It was only natural, then, that in 1968 the first group to renew the Jewish presence in Gush Etzion and Hebron came from Mercaz Harav. However, the nationalist revival extended beyond the closed circle of Rabbi Kook's graduates, encompassing most of the national religious community. An additional factor in this sweeping change is the socio-political context of that community.

## The Socio-political Context of Religious Zionism

A primary social motif in explaining the new stance among the NRP constituency is that of relative deprivation, in terms of status and values. Adhering to an ideology combining both traditional religion and modernization, the national religious movement found itself between the ultra-Orthodox and the secular segments of Israeli society. In many aspects of public daily life, people identifying themselves as national-religious made up an integral part of the larger, secular Israeli society. However, they were distinct in matters of religious observance and schooling. Despite accepting the symbols of Israel's secular state, the religious Zionists were also deeply attached to the values cherished by ultra-Orthodox Jewry, in contrast to the ultra-Orthodox who did not identify with the values of the state. This posture was particularly problematic for the national-religious youngster who sought recognition and approval according to the standards of both secular Zionism and Orthodoxy.

One attempt to reconcile this dilemma was the establishment of Yeshivot Hesder, a program that combined compulsory military service with Talmudic studies. The Hesder soldier-student was brought up by his rabbis to strive for excellence in both military service and religious studies, even if doing so required performing a double job in non-complementary areas. Even religious women, though totally exempt from compulsory military service, enlisted in the army or volunteered for nonmilitary national service. Thus, a highly-motivated community with a strong national identity evolved. It was committed to the values of both Judaism and secular Zionism. Nonetheless, these youth felt deprived in their status by both the secular and the ultra-Orthodox communities and consequently began to search for a role in which they could excel. The defense and settlement of Eretz Yisrael fulfilled this role well, as it enabled religious youth to demonstrate their dedication to both nationalism and religion.[30]

Religious youth, through interaction with both political and spiritual Zionism, became exposed to Zionist historiography, hence developing an ethno-national ideology. Modernization implied exposure to the study of Jewish history, a component absent in the traditional educational curriculum of Orthodoxy which was based primarily on study of the Talmud, neglecting even the study of the Bible. The prevalent Talmudic interpretation of Jewish history supported a passive approach to Jewish renaissance. Major 'heroic events', such as the Maccabian (167 BCE) and Bar Kochba (132–135 CE) rebellions, were seen in religious contexts. In contrast, the modern Orthodox curriculum included, in addition to Talmud and Torah, study of the other books of the Bible, Jewish history and the geography of the Land of Israel. These studies articulated a voice of an ancient past of political independence. The Six Day War and the conquest of the entirety of the Land of Israel were understood as analogous to the processes of the Bible and compared to the heroic events of Jewish history. Hence, they came to be interpreted as national rather than just religious occurrences.[31] The fusion of history with religious doctrine reinforced nationalism, producing a stronger and more robust ideology than what was by then a somewhat spent and exhausted doctrine of secular Zionism.

It was in the wake of the 1973 Yom Kippur War, however, that religious Zionism received its full-fledged nationalistic flavor, especially in the form of Gush Emunim. Religio-nationalist themes had a widespread appeal, even among non-religious segments of Israeli society, despite that the population at large did not become more religious.[32] The prevalent atmosphere of doubt following the war strengthened ethno-nationalism in Israel and prompted the development of Gush Emunim. The appeal of the movement was related to the crisis in Israeli society that further expressed itself in Labor's defeat in the 1977 elections. Gush Emunim saw itself as the Zionist response to Arab and PLO international successes following the Yom Kippur War. As Janet O'Dea (Aviad) writes: 'The wide tolerance and even encouragement which the movement...received from the Israeli population [is explained by the fact that] Gush Emunim represent[ed] a re-crystallization of attitudes, a resolute stance around certain ideas, and a reconstruction of social solidarity in face of anomie experienced after the Yom Kippur War'.[33] When the state, party and elite that stood for secular nationalism seemed to collapse, religious Zionism felt that it had been called forward to assume leadership. For the graduates of the Hesder Yeshivot, raising the national flag was another way of demonstrating their spiritual and moral superiority.

However, Gush Emunim was inspired by an additional rationale. Justification for cooperating with secular Zionists like the ultra-nationalist Herut seemed more harmonious with the redemptionist approach of Rabbi Kook then the instrumental approach of Rabbi Reines. The rise to power of an ethno-national government led by Menahem Begin justified, to the disciples of Rabbi Kook, the setbacks and ordeals of 1973. Moreover, as a modernized ideological movement, religious Zionism believed in an active role for the human being in the cosmic order.[34] In the ensuing years, it was Gush Emunim that led the settlement drive in the West Bank, or as it was now officially renamed by its Biblical titles, Judea and Samaria. Gush Emunim became the ideological vanguard of the Likud government's settlement efforts in the regions of Judea, Samaria and Gaza.[35]

The appearance of Gush Emunim corresponds with contemporary theories of ethno-nationalism. While inspired by Kook's religious thought, its adherents were motivated by feelings of relative deprivation in terms of values and status and activated by modernity. The acquiring of a Jewish historic landscape awakened among religious Zionists primordial aspirations that correspond to a definition of ethno-nationalism. Indeed several new, non-religious parties, representing the ethno-national idea, aimed their message at that segment of society. Right-wing parties, such as Likud, Tehiya (Renaissance), Moledet (Homeland) and Tzomet (acronym for Rejuvenated Zionism), competed quite successfully with the NRP for the national religious vote. In contrast, the Kach Party, headed by Rabbi

Meir Kahane, would fit a radical religious definition, as it vehemently attacked the legitimacy of the democratic-secular state. Kach was disqualified from participating in the 1988 elections because of its extreme program recommending the transfer of Israeli Arabs outside Israel and its anti-democratic ideology. Kach received its limited electoral support from both national-religious extremists and low income elements motivated by economic hardship.[36]

Religious Zionism was valued by the Likud leadership. The NRP, despite the steady decline in its number of Knesset seats, had been a major partner in Likud governments and had been given control of the always-important Ministry of Education. However, it was at this point, an apex for religious Zionism and the settlement movement, that a rupture with the state occurred.

### The Jewish Underground and Religious Zionism

Undoubtedly, the closest religious Zionism came to radicalism was the appearance in the late 1970s of the Jewish Underground. Many of its members were also involved in Gush Emunim. The Underground propagated themes and undertook actions that challenged the state. Prior to analyzing the ideological gist of the Underground, we must address the events that triggered the development of the movement. The significance of this phenomenon with respect to religious Zionism will close our analysis.

Even though it would be difficult to pinpoint the precise point in time that the Jewish Underground was formed, our attention should focus on the aftermath of the Camp David Accords. In this agreement, Prime Minister Begin committed Israel to withdrawal from all of Sinai and the removal of its Jewish settlements. He also recognized 'the legitimate rights of the Palestinians', pledging that Israel would grant them autonomy. These positions served as the background to the appearance of an illegal organization. Despite his oath to promote settlement and open the West Bank to Jewish inhabitation, the discrepancy between Begin the opposition leader and Begin the head of state left many of the religious Zionist community uncertain of what the implications of the change of government were for Jewish redemption. Prior to his election, hope had been placed on the ascendance of Begin; however, the 'betrayal' of the Likud left some in despair as the return of Labor definitely did not render hope to their cause. While the mainstream of Gush Emunim took advantage of the Likud settlement drive in Judea and Samaria that was unfolding before them, and the more dogmatic wing established the militant, but legal, Movement to Stop the Withdrawal from Sinai, a small, covert group asserted that something radical was required to stop the peace process with Egypt. Thus, extreme elements on the margins of the settlement movement organized terror acts against Arabs in the West Bank. Some envisioned that such an initiative might even be able to stop the withdrawal process. An even more extreme proposal was the 'Removal of the Dome of the Rock Mosque', an event that would certainly induce tumultous reactions in the Arab and Muslim worlds as well as force a halt to the peace process.[37]

Another catalyst to the development of the Underground was the settlement drive itself. In bringing the two diverse ethnic communities into closer physical contact, it placed new emphasis on the existential threat that each population represented to the other.[38] The subsequent increase in tension resulted in bloodshed, epitomized by the murder of six Yeshiva students in Hebron in May 1980. For the Jewish side, this act evoked the memory of the 1929 Hebron massacre of Jews by Arabs. Moreover, the establishment of the National Guidance Committee (identified with the PLO) following the Camp David Accords and Prime Minister Begin's proposal for Palestinian autonomy were also perceived by a segment of the population as a prelude to the establishment of a Palestinian state in Judea and Samaria.[39]

As a result of internal discord with respect to operational objectives, the Underground movement was composed of two branches. The first aimed to destroy the Dome of the Rock Mosque and the second focused on avenging Jews and deterring acts of terror against Jewish settlers in the territories. The leaders of both of the branches, Yehuda Etzion and Menahem Livni, had been members of Gush Emunim. Etzion had been a student of Rabbis Zvi Yehuda Kook and Yehuda Amital (a more dovish rabbi and founder of a centrist religious movement named Meimad), while Livni was a student of Rabbi Moshe Levinger from Kiryat Arba. Etzion's primary concern was destroying the mosque. Livni, who had originally been brought in as part of that plan, objected to it, instead directing actions against the Arabs in the territories. His activities included the maiming of Arab mayors, terror attacks against members of the National Guidance Committee, the attack on the Islamic College in July 1983, and an unsuccessful attempt to blow up an Arab bus on 26 April 1984. This last action was spoiled by the General Security Service (GSS), who subsequently apprehended members of the Underground.[40]

The Jewish Underground must be distinguished from other underground movements, such as the Lifta Gang or the group led by Yoel Lerner, both planning to destroy the mosques on the Temple Mount, because several of the leaders of the Underground were at least partially influenced by the Kook doctrines and were offshoots of Mercaz Harav. The most articulate of those leaders was Yehuda Etzion. In compiling a doctrine that combined both religious and activist elements, he falls in a religious-Zionist frame of reference. However, as asserted by Eliezer Don-Yehiya, there is one central motif in which he departed from Rabbi Zvi Yehuda: the sanctity of the state.[41] According to Etzion, a Jewish State that was not progressing toward the rebuilding of the Temple, the renewal of the 'kingdom of Israel' and the restoration of the Sanhedrin (the Rabbinical Israelite Court) did not carry any sanctity. For Etzion, the fact that the Jewish State let the Dome of the Rock stand was proof that it was not progressing down the road to redemption.

Etzion was primarily inspired by the writings of and his conversation with Shabtai Ben-Dov. Ben-Dov, who died in 1979, had been active in Lehi and his radical doctrines had been influenced by the nationalist poetry of Uri Zvi Greenberg (1894–1981). Another of his influences can be traced back to cabalistic rabbis. This tradition also influenced other leaders in the Underground such as Yeshua Ben-Shushan, an army officer swayed by mystical sources, and Dan Beeri, a Christian convert to Judaism. On certain occasions, Etzion and his colleagues criticized both Mercaz Harav and Gush Emunim for their lack of activism and their unwillingness to act to push forward redemption.[42]

The dividing line between Gush Emunim and Mercaz Harav on the one hand and the Jewish Underground on the other is their perception of the role of the State of Israel in the redemption process. Just as Ehud Sprinzak has distinguished between the theology of Kook and Kahane along their approach to the state,[43] it would be accurate to use the same issue to decouple the Underground from religious Zionism.[44] For both Kahane and Etzion, the State of Israel has no inherent sanctity unless it adheres in full to the role destined to it by their conception of the divine command.

Etzion was publicly condemned by his teacher Rabbi Yoel Bin-Nun, a leader of Gush Emunim, and Rabbis Yehoshua Zukerman and Zvi Tau, at that time the two most prominent rabbis at Mercaz Harav.[45] Rabbi Shlomo Aviner, considered a direct disciple of Rabbi Zvi Yehuda Kook, objected to the whole concept that the restoration of Temple was a precondition to redemption, stating that the order is actually the reverse.[46] The wave of criticism, uproar and condemnation that swept the whole settler movement also suggests that the Jewish Underground was not a direct outgrowth of religious Zionism.

Yisrael Harel, a Gush Emunim leader and the founding editor of *Nekuda*, the journal of Gush Emunim, in a post-mortem analysis asserted that the disclosure of the Underground was the event most responsible for the collapse of Gush Emunim.[47] In the ensuing years, the settlement movement, embodied in Moetzet Yesha (the Council of Judea, Samaria and Gaza), directed its settlement drive in cooperation with the government. The movement, however, faced another crisis following the defeat of the Shamir government in the 1992 elections.

## The Rabin Government and the Limits of Political Accommodation

Gush Emunim's view of itself as a vanguard was not appreciated by Labor, which had always perceived itself as fulfilling that role. This competition explains, in part, the harsh animosity of the Labor elite to the national religious movement and the settlers of Judea and Samaria. The Labor-NRP alliance that had until 1977 characterized Israeli politics had long since broken down, with each side seeing the other as diametrically opposed to its core values – leaving little basis for cooperation. As a result of the distance between the two parties in 1992, Labor made no sincere effort to enlist the NRP, instead choosing a coalition with the ultra-orthodox Sephardi Shas.[48]

The attempt by the Rabin government to substitute the NRP with Shas bore limited success. Labor's main problem with Shas was that its voters had made it clear that they preferred a Likud prime minister.[49] The majority of the Likud, even after the passing of its long-time head Menahem Begin, radiated the message of being the anti-establishment party. This complemented the cultural trends of Sephardi politics. The immigrants from Asia-Africa had voted in increasing numbers through the 1960s and 1970s for the opposition party not only because it allowed them to express their identity and resentment against their inferior socio-economic status, but also because from their perspective, Herut, and later Likud, while representing their ethnic interests, were also associated more strongly with traditional Jewish values than the socialist Labor establishment. In addition, the vote for Likud may have been influenced by anti-Arab attitudes prevalent among Sephardim.[50]

Nevertheless, the extent of Sephardi ideological commitment to the integrity of the Land of Israel is unclear. Sephardim have been under-represented in Gush Emunim, although they do comprise a substantial percentage of the settlers in Judea and Samaria.[51] However, Rabbi Ovadia Yosef, the spiritual leader of Shas, ruled that territorial compromise was religiously acceptable since it was for the sake of peace and the saving of life.[52]

Labor and other parties of the Left tried to take advantage of the Sephardi population's more flexible position on the territories. In the 1992 campaign, Labor stressed that the Likud government's program of investing in the West Bank settlements was made at the expense of the heavily Sephardi 'development towns'. Labor adopted this tactic (ultimately only partially successful) to prevent the building of a tacit coalition between Gush Emunim and the Sephardim – a political union which had been one of

Labor's chief obstacles over the years; the former provided the vanguard while the latter kept the Likud in power. The Sephardim did not oppose the establishment of the settlements; however, they resented the Labor-affiliated kibbutzim and moshavim which were products of the Labor movement and competitors for the slicing of the national pie.

The devotion of Sephardi Israelis to the Jewish state required the leaders of Shas to disassociate themselves from the non-Zionist attitudes of the Ashkenazi ultra-Orthodox parties.[53] Labor Party leaders, like Shimon Peres, were aware of this dynamic, and, grasping the significance of a partnership with some force in the religious camp, they sought to bring Shas into a Labor-led coalition. In contrast to the Ashkenazi Haredi leader Rav Eliezer Shach,[54] who could not forgive Labor for its secularization of Jewish society, and the NRP, which demanded that its position on the Land of Israel be taken into account, the leadership of Shas was ready to cooperate with Labor. Therefore, in 1992, despite a parliamentary majority based on the support of Meretz and parties with predominantly Arab constituencies, Labor chose to bolster its coalition with the inclusion of Shas. In order to maintain the arrangement, Rabin and Labor went so far as to amend two of Israel's basic laws: 'Basic Law: Human Dignity and Liberty,' and 'Basic Law: Freedom of Occupation' – the latter of which had been found by the supreme court to contradict the prohibition of importing non-Kosher meat. In both, a paragraph was added stating that its purpose was 'to anchor in the Basic Law the values of the State of Israel as a Jewish and democratic state'.[55]

In general, Rabin continued the traditional practice of consensus politics in religious affairs.[56] He followed the pattern of previous Labor governments: accommodation in domestic matters, such as religion and state, but not in foreign policy. However, the Labor Party, and Israel in general, had changed significantly since the last Labor-led government. Labor's foreign policy positions were significantly to the left of those held by the party in 1977,[57] while Israeli society was even more expansively divided along religious-secular lines. Nevertheless, Shas' leadership was ready to step into the traditional role of the NRP sharing power with Labor, even though such a move compromised the Sephardi community's hawkish foreign policy outlook.

Rabin made only a limited effort to court the NRP and its six Knesset seats (the same number held by Shas) because NRP participation presupposed power sharing in the foreign policy domain as well. Labor's move might also have been based on its awareness that Shas represented not only the religious sector but also a Sephardi constituency. Indeed, Rabin's wooing of Shas was so enthusiastic that he was willing to ignore the accusations of corruption that had been levied against the Shas Party leadership.[58] Such behind the scenes maneuvering notwithstanding, Shas was ultimately unable to deliver its followers. Despite the fact that Shas' leaders favored territorial compromise, its supporters disagreed with Labor's peace process policies. After less than two years, the Sephardi party formally left the Rabin coalition, although it continued to support the government on many occasions in the Knesset. Shas lacked the doctrines of religious Zionism that justified cooperation with a secular government.

In retrospect, the absence of a religious party in the government strained the socio-political climate in Israel and brought the country's political discourse to an unprecedented level of intensity. Since the September 1993 Oslo agreement, the normally hyper-active Israeli political arena had become fever pitched, especially among the settlers. The most extreme expression of violence came on 25 February 1994, when Dr. Baruch Goldstein, a supporter of Rabbi Kahane, gunned down 29 Palestinians in the Tomb of the Patriarchs in Hebron. Right-wing demonstrations against the peace process – predominantly attended by religious Zionists – moved beyond expressions of political preference and came to represent the anxiety of the settlers that their whole enterprise was on the verge of collapse. On some occasions, opposition rallies became violent.

The government's decision to move ahead with the peace process caused further intensification of right-wing demonstrations. In the summer of 1995 a group of rabbis from the national religious camp called upon IDF soldiers to disobey possible orders for the evacuation of the settlements in Judea, Samaria and the Gaza Strip. Then, rumors spread that some national religious rabbis had charged Prime Minister Rabin with being a *rodef* (one whose actions endanger the lives of others), an accusation that sanctioned his execution. The climax came on 4 November, with the assassination of Prime Minister Yitzhak Rabin by Yigal Amir.

Following his studies at an ultra-Orthodox Haredi Yeshiva high school, Yigal Amir went to Kerem B'Yavne Hesder Yeshiva, the hesder yeshiva most closely associated with the *haredi* camp. Upon completing his army service and studies at Yavne, Amir entered the Law School at Bar-Ilan University, an institution once associated with the NRP. It seems that Amir carried with him all the frustrations of the *haredi* community in addition to those of the national religious camp. In his testimony before the Shamgar committee, the government-appointed body charged with investigating Rabin's assassination, Amir testified that his upbringing was a mixture of national religious and *haredi* education.[59] In addition, it is possible that Amir, of Yemenite origins, may have also felt alienated from the state because of the difficulties the Yemenites experienced during the early years after their immigration to Israel.[60]

The amalgamation of ultra-Orthodox religious doctrines with the ideas of nationalism, as represented by Yigal Amir, may indicate a potential for the type of religious extremism which, up until recently, the Jewish state had been able to avoid. Indeed, Yigal Amir, more than Etzion, may depict the archetype of the Israeli religious extremist. As long as the traditionally passive ultra-orthodox were distinct from the politically active religious nationalists, the Jewish state was generally devoid of violent extremists like Amir. However, if the ultra-orthodox denial of legitimacy of the secular Jewish state and repugnance for its society is combined with radical forms of nationalism, a combination also demonstrated by the Jewish Underground, religious radicalism may be in the making at the margins of Israeli society.

Based on previous practices, the participation of the NRP in the Labor-led government might have calmed the religious extremism of its rabbis and thus possibly have prevented the association of the national religious movement with the radical path which some members of its community were taking. Rabin's successor, Shimon Peres, understood the importance of the mechanism of political accommodation and invited Rabbi Yehuda Amital, the leader of Meimad – a centrist religious Zionist movement – to join his cabinet. This party, which emerged in response to the radicalization of the NRP, failed to cross the one per cent threshold of the 1988 elections and did not run in 1992. Moreover, Peres, in contrast to Rabin, refrained from verbally attacking the settlers. Ehud Sprinzak, the foremost expert on the Israeli extreme right wing, has noted that Rabin's personal style contributed to the hostility of the national religious circles toward him.[61]

## Conclusion

In the late 1960s, ethno-nationalism began to change the nature of religion in Israeli politics, as well as of religious Zionism itself. An integral cause of this change was the meeting of Jewish Israeli society and the historic Land of Israel – especially Judea and Samaria – which came in the wake the Six Day War. For the NRP, the fusion of modernity and religion was compounded by a feeling of relative deprivation. The new political identities which grew from this combination went hand in hand with parallel processes that were taking place throughout Israeli society. The ethno-nationalist Likud won the 1977 election, the more hawkish NRP became a permanent ally of the Likud, and as a result the gulf between the Labor Party and its former national religious ally came to be wider than ever before.

The power-sharing practices of the Israeli political system has dissuaded the national religious camp from radical opposition to the state. This inclination toward collaboration, however, was not only the result of the policies of the secular parties; it was enabled by the advent of two streams from within the national religious camp as well. Both the Reines and Kook doctrines, one instrumental and the other idealistic, supported cooperation with secular Jewish nationalism (Zionism). The Kook teachings, as represented by Kook's son, Zvi Yehuda, pushed the national religious community toward more radical positions. However, these positions primarily addressed the future of the territories, not the legitimacy of the state. This distinction stands as the litmus test for religious radicalism and deviation from the tenets of religious Zionism. The most extreme exhibition of anti-state movement was the Etzion-led Jewish Underground.

In retrospect, the combination of ethno-national and religious themes in Israel's public life denoted a threat to the delicate balance between religion and state. The assassination of Yitzhak Rabin indicated that such a threat was real, and that the potential for further acts of political violence existed particularly in the absence of political power sharing. The effects of the assassination on the national religious community are, as yet, unclear. It is entirely possible that a new approach may emerge among the religious community which rejects the accommodationist perspectives of the Reines and Kook doctrines, especially in response to the continued secularization of Israel. However, the victory of the Likud-religious parties' alignment in the May 1996 elections has reinstated the religious-secular power sharing tradition. Hence, the threat that religious Zionism will adopt religious maxims rejecting the legitimacy of the secular Jewish state is very low.

## NOTES

1.  Several of the most important works in contemporary nationalism are: Ernest Gellner, *Nations and Nationalism* (Ithaca, NY: Cornell UP 1983); Dov Ronen, *The Quest for Self-Determination* (New Haven, CT: Yale UP 1979); and John Breuilly, *Nationalism and the State* (NY: St. Martin's Press 1982).
2.  See D. Rothschild, 'Ethnicity and Conflict Resolution', *World Politics* 22/4 (Summer 1970); D. Horowitz, 'Dual Authority Polities', *Comparative Politics* 14/3 (April 1982) pp.329–49; I. Duchacek, 'Antagonistic Cooperation: Territorial and Ethnic Communities', *Publius* 7/4 (Fall 1977) pp.3–29; C. Enloe, 'Internal Colonialism, Federalism, and Alternative State Development Strategies', Ibid. pp.145–75; David C. Rapoport, 'The Importance of Space in Violent Ethno-Religious Strife' *Nationalism & Ethnic Politics* 2/2 (Summer 1996) pp.258–85.
3.  See the interview with PM Rabin's assassin Yigal Amir in *Ha'aretz*, 17 Jan. 1996, p.A2.
4.  The definition of the Fundamentalism Project of the American Academy of Arts and Sciences included national religious and ultra-Orthodox movements in Israel as having global fundamentalist tendencies. I chose not to use this frame of reference. The complex association between fundamentalism and modernity, as pointed out by Mark Jurgensmeyer, and so basic in the Israeli context, contributed to my reservations for using fundamentalism as a conceptual framework. See Mark JuUrgensmeyer, *The New Cold War? Religious Nationalism Confronts the Secular State* (Berkeley: U. of California Press 1993) pp.3–6. We excluded from this study *haredi* Agudat Israel which never accepted de-jure the legitimacy of the Jewish state and even though it joined the government coalitions, refused to participate

officially within a secular Zionist government. The Agudah was a movement rejecting modernity; it abstained from active pursuit of religious-political goals.

5. W. Connor, 'The Politics of Ethno-nationalism', *Jnl of Int Affairs* 27/1 (1973); and Anthony D. Smith, *The Ethnic Revival in the Modern World* (Cambridge: CUP 1981).

6. Ernst B. Haas, 'What is Nationalism and Why Should We Study it?', *Int Organization* 40/3 (Summer 1986) pp.707–44; See also, idem., 'Why Collaborate? Issue-Linkage and International Regimes', *World Politics* 32/3 (April 1980) pp.358–405.

7. Kalevi J. Holsti, 'Changes in the International System: Interdependence, Integration, and Fragmentation', in Charles W. Kegley and Eugene Witkopf (eds.), *The Global Agenda: Issues and Perspectives* (NY: Random House 1992) p.211.

8. Samuel P. Huntington, *Political Order in Changing Societies* (New Haven, CT: Yale UP 1968) pp.37–8. Although modernization, by definition, is supposed to erode primordial loyalties, Huntington also discovered that the 'early phases of modernization are often marked by the emergence of fundamentalist religious movements'.

9. Chong-Do Hah and J. Martin, 'Towards a Synthesis of Conflict and Integration: Theories of Nationalism', *World Politics* 27/3 (April 1978) pp.361–86.

10. Emmanuel Sivan, *Radical Islam: Medieval Theology and Modern Politics* (New Haven, CT: Yale UP 1985).

11. For the appearance of the term ethnicity at the modern juncture, see Nathan Glazer and Daniel P. Moynihan (eds.), *Ethnicity, Theory and Experience* (Cambridge, MA: Harvard UP 1975) p.1.

12. The best study of these two rabbis can be found in Jacob Katz, *Jewish Nationalism, Essay and Studies* (Hebrew) (Jerusalem: Hasifriya Hatziyonit 1983) pp.263–356.

13. On the formation of political Zionism and its main tenets, see David Vital, *The Origins of Zionism* (Oxford: Clarendon Press 1975), especially chs.5, 9. On the cultural debate see David Vital, *Zionism: The Formative Years* (Ibid. 1982) ch.7.

14. On religious education and politics see Eliezer Don-Yehiya, *Cooperation and Conflict Between Political Camps: The Religious Camp, the Labor Movement and the Education Crisis in Israel,* dissertation submitted to the Senate of Hebrew University (Sept. 1977).

15. On the relationship between the Israeli political system and the Yishuv, see Dan Horowitz and Moshe Lissak, *The Origins of the Israeli Polity* (Chicago: U. of Chicago Press 1977) ch.7.

16. William Riker, *The Theory of Political Coalitions* (New Haven, CT: Yale UP 1962).

17. See Eliezer Don Yehiya, 'Religion and Coalition', in Asher Arian (ed.), *Elections in Israel, 1973* (Jerusalem: Israel Academic Press 1975).

18. Aviezer Ravitzki, 'Exile in the Holyland: The Dilemma of Haredi Jewry', in Peter Medding (ed.), *Studies in Contemporary Jewry* 5 (Oxford: OUP 1990).

19. Shmuel Sandler, *The State of Israel, The Land of Israel* (Westport, CT: Greenwood Press 1993) pp.141–9. See also Amnon Rubinstein, *From Herzl to Gush Emunim and Back* (Hebrew) (Tel Aviv: Schoken 1980).

20. E. Inbar, 'Labor's Return to Power', in Daniel J. Elazar and Shmuel Sandler (eds.), *Israel at the Polls, 1992* (London: Rowman & Littlefield 1995) pp.37–9.

21. In the late 1970s, the religious observant population was estimated at 23 per cent, the secular 40 per cent, and the remainder traditional. See Y. Ben-Meir and P. Kedem, 'An Index of Religiosity for the Jewish Population in Israel', *Megamot* 24/3 (Feb. 1979) pp.353–62. In the early 1990s, 14 per cent of Israeli Jews defined themselves as 'strictly observant' and another 24 per cent 'observant to a great extent'. Only 20 per cent defined themselves as 'totally non-observant'. See Shlomit Levy, Hanna Levinson, and Elihu Katz, *Beliefs, Observances and Social Interaction Among Israeli Jews* (Hebrew) (Jerusalem: Louis Guttman Israel Institute of Applied Social Research 1993) p.1. Another index for measuring religiosity is the distribution of students in elementary schools. The percentage of students attending the state-religious and the 'independent' (ultra-Orthodox) was 25.8 per cent in 1985. See Dan Horowitz and Moshe Lissak, *Trouble in Utopia: The Overburdened Polity of Israel* (Hebrew) (Tel Aviv: Am Oved 1990) p.93, table 2.

22. For a biography of Rabbi Reines, see Geula Bat-Yehuda, *Man of Lights* (Hebrew) (Jerusalem: Mossad Harav Kook 1985). From the large variety of books Rabbi Reines wrote,

see especially *A New Light on Zion* (Vilnus, Lithuania: Reem 1901). For a political interpretation of Rabbi Reines's thought, see E. Don Yehiya, 'Ideology and Policy Formation in Religious Zionism: The Ideology of Rabbi Reines and Mizrahi Policy under his Leadership', *Hatzionut* 8/3 (1993) pp.105–46.

23. On the attitudes of Mizrahi during the partition debate in 1937, see Shmuel Dothan, *Partition of Eretz Israel in the Mandatory Period, The Jewish Controversy* (Hebrew) (Jerusalem: Yad Yitzhak Ben-Zvi 1979) pp.55–8; and Itzhak Galnoor, *Territorial Partition, Decision Crossroads in the Zionist Movement* (Jerusalem: Magnes Press 1994) pp.136–8, 164–6.

24. On the origins of Gush Emunim, see E. Don-Yehiya, 'Jewish Messianism, Religious Zionism and Israeli Politics: The Impact and Origins of Gush Emunim', *Middle Eastern Studies* 23/2 (April 1987) pp.225–7; and E. Sprinzak, 'Gush Emunim: The Iceberg Model of Political Extremism', *Medina Umimshal* 17 (Hebrew) (Spring 1981) pp.22–49.

25. Rabbi Avraham Kook wrote that three main types of holiness are found in the universe. They reveal themselves in a concentrated manner in the Jewish people (man), the Land of Israel (space), and the Jewish holidays (time). Zvi Yaron, *The Philosophy of Rabbi Kook* (Jerusalem: World Zionist Organization 1974) pp.87–9.

26. Ibid. ch.6, especially pp.107–9, 121–3.

27. Ibid. pp.272–3, 277–80.

28. Juergensmeyer (note 4).

29. Three weeks before the Six Day War, Rabbi Zvi Yehuda Kook gave a sermon in which he lamented the fact that parts of the Land of Israel and Jerusalem were under Arab rule, and he predicted that this situation would soon be changed. This made a great impact on his disciples. See Gideon Aran, 'A Mystic-Messianic Interpretation of Modern Israeli History: The Six Day War in the Religious Culture of Gush Emunim', in Shlomo Deshen, Charles S. Liebman and Moshe Shokeid (eds.), *Israeli Judaism: Studies of Israeli Society* 7 (New Brunswick, NJ: Transaction 1995) p.202.

30. On the Yeshivot Hesder, see M. Bar-Lev, 'The Hesder Yeshiva as an Agent of Social Change in Israel', *British Jnl of Religious Education* 11 (1988) pp.38–46; Michael Rosenack, 'Jewish Fundamentalism in Israeli Education', in Martin E. Marty and R. Scott Appleby (eds.), *Fundamentalism and Society: Reclaiming the Sciences, the Family and Education* (Chicago: U. of Chicago Press 1993) pp.374–414; S. Cohen, 'The Hesder Yeshivot in Israel: A Church-State Military Arrangement', *Jnl of Church and State* 35/2 (Winter 1993) pp.113–30.

31. See Eliezer Don-Yehiya, 'Hanukkah and the Myth of the Maccabees in Ideology and in Society', in Deshen, Liebman and Shokeid (note 29) pp.318–9. On modernization and religious Zionism, see Arye Fishman, 'Religious Kibbutzim: Judaism and Modernization', in Deshen, Liebman and Shokeid (note 29) pp.173–96.

32. The new culture was termed by Amnon Rubinstein as a mixture of 'Dizengoff' and Judea and Samaria – not a more Orthodox Israel. *From Herzl to Gush Emunim and Back* (note 19). Don-Yehiya and Liebman have identified the emergence of a more traditional civil religion, though one very distant from Orthodox Judaism, see *Civil Religion in Israel* (Berkeley: U. of California Press 1983), especially the concluding chapter. See also idem., 'Israel's Civil Religion', *Jerusalem Quarterly* 23 (Spring 1982).

33. Janet O'Dea [Aviad], 'Gush Emunim: Roots and Ambiguities, The Perspective of the Sociology of Religion', *Forum* 2/25 (1976) p.45. Coming from a person who would soon become a leader of 'Peace Now' and one who could not be suspected of sympathy to this movement, this observation is even more significant. See also Don-Yehiya (note 24) pp.231–2.

34. On the active element in religious Zionism, see Ravitzki (note 18) pp.89–125, especially pp.96–8.

35. On the settlements of Gush Emunim, see Meron Benvenisti and Shlomo Khayat, *The West Bank and Gaza Atlas* (Jerusalem: The Jerusalem Post 1988); J. Portugali, 'Jewish Settlement in the Occupied Territories, Israel's Settlement Structure and the Palestinians', *Political Geography Quarterly* 10/1 (Jan. 1991) pp.26–53.

36. Following the late Rabbi Meir Kahane's electoral success in 1984, a theory was advanced that the Sephardim hated the Arabs because they were competing with them for employment. See G. Shafir and Y. Peled, '"Thorns in Your Eyes": The Socio-Economic Characteristics of

the Sources of Electoral Support of Rabbi Kahane', *State, Government and Int Relations* 25 (Hebrew) (Spring 1986) pp.115–30. For a more balanced view of the origins of the Israeli extreme right see Ehud Sprinzak, *The Ascendance of Israel's Radical Right* (NY: Oxford UP 1991). See also M. Shamir, 'Kach and the Limits to Political Tolerance in Israel', in Daniel J. Elazar and Shmuel Sandler (eds.), *Israel's Odd Couple* (Detroit, MI: Wayne State UP 1990) pp.159–68; and Etta Bick, 'Fragmentation and Realignment: Israel's Nationalist Parties', in Elazar and Sandler (note 20) pp.67–102.

37. For a full account by one of the members of the Jewish Underground, see Haggai Segal, *Dear Brothers: The West Bank and the Jewish Underground* (Jerusalem: Keter 1987). See also P. Rawking, 'Terror from the Heart of Zion: The Political Challenge of the Jewish Underground in the West Bank', *Middle East Focus* 7/5 (Jan. 1985) pp.9–13, 22–3.

38. S. Sandler, 'The Protracted Arab-Israeli Conflict: A Temporal-Spatial Analysis', *The Jerusalem Journal of International Relations* 10/4 (Dec. 1988) pp.54–78.

39. On the formation of the National Guidance Committee see Shmuel Segev, *Maariv*, 6 June 1980; Ya'acov Chavakuk, *Maariv*, 16 May 1980. See also Rafik Halabi, *The West Bank Story* (Konigstein, Germany: Athenaum 1981) p.122; and Shmuel Sandler and Hillel Frisch, *Israel, the Palestinians and the West Bank* (Lexington, MA: Lexington Books 1984) pp.92–5.

40. See Nadav Shragai, *The Temple Mount Conflict* (Jerusalem: Keter 1995) pp.96–122.

41. E. Don-Yehiya, 'The Book and the Sword: The Nationalist Yeshivot and Political Radicalism', in Martin E. Marty and R. Scott Appleby (eds.), *Accounting for Fundamentalism* 4 (Chicago: U. of Chicago Press 1993) pp.280–1.

42. For a recent criticism see D. Beeri, 'The Routes have Parted', *Nekuda* 193 (March 1996) pp.38–42.

43. See, for instance, E. Sprinzak, 'Violence and Catastrophe in the Theology of Rabbi Meir Kahane: The Ideologization of Mimetic Desire', *Terrorism and Political Violence* 3/3 (Autumn 1991) pp.48–9.

44. For an opposing view, see Naomi Gal-Or, *The Jewish Underground: Our Terrorism* (Tel Aviv: Hakibutz Hameuchad 1990).

45. For reactions, see especially *Nekuda* 73 (25 May 1984), 74 (1 June 1984), 79 (2 Nov. 1984). For a summary of reactions, see Shragai (note 40) pp.127–31. Also see Don-Yehiya (note 41) pp.279, 284.

46. Shlomo Aviner, *Shalhevetya* (Bet-El: Sifriyat Hava 1989). See also a dialogue between Aviner and Etzion in prison in Shragai (note 40) pp.130–1.

47. Yisrael Harel, Bar-Ilan University Department of Political Science seminar (20 March 1990).

48. In contemporary politics, the Sephardi–Ashkenazi division has been related to the geo-cultural roots of the two communities. See Daniel J. Elazar, *The Other Jews, The Sephardim Today* (NY: Basic Books 1989) ch.1.

49. On the electoral behavior of Shas supporters, see H. Herzog, 'Midway Between Political and Cultural Ethnicity: An Analysis of the Ethnic Lists in the 1984 Elections', in *Israel's Odd Couple* (note 36) pp.105–8. See also Eliezer Don-Yehiya, 'Religion, Social Cleavages, and Political Behavior: The Religious Parties in the Elections', in Daniel J. Elazar and Shmuel Sandler (eds.), *Who's the Boss in Israel: Israel at the Polls 1988–1989* (Detroit, MI: Wayne State UP 1992) pp.110–17. In 1984, a tie emerged after the elections that resulted from Shas joining Shamir's camp, thus forcing Peres to form a national unity government. See Daniel J. Elazar and Shmuel Sandler, 'The Two-Bloc System – A New Development in Israeli Politics', in *Israel's Odd Couple* (note 36) pp.12–14.

50. Peres and Shemer explained the clear ethnic-electoral nexus by the Sephardi–Arab variable in 'The Ethnic Factor in the Elections to the Tenth Knesset', *Megamot* 28/2–3 (Hebrew) (1984) pp.316–31. The findings of Arian and Shamir that hawkishness, especially on the territorial issue, was the clearest indicator influencing the Israeli voter's behavior also support this explanation. 'The Ethnic Vote in Israel's 1981 Elections', Arian and Shamir (eds.), *The Elections in Israel* (Tel Aviv: Ramot 1982) p.106.

51. In general, Ashkenazim and native born Israelis were more prominent in ideological movements like Gush Emunim and Peace Now. However, Jews of Asian or African (Sephardi) origin are well represented in the settlements of Judea and Samaria. A public

opinion poll jointly conducted by the Begin-Sadat Center for Strategic Studies and the Center for Palestine Research and Studies (Jan. 1996) found that 40 per cent of settlers in the West Bank were either born in Asia/Africa (10.2 per cent) or in Israel to families whose fathers were born in Asia/Africa (29.4 per cent). In addition, the same poll found that 21.2 per cent of West Bank settlers are native Israelis whose families were born in Israel, as well.

52. A major source of Shas's strength was the leadership of former Chief Rabbi Ovadia Yosef, the spiritual leader of the movement. Unlike his Ashkenazi *haredi* colleagues, Rabbi Yosef served as chief rabbi and thus implicitly endorsed the Zionist state. He was not afraid to challenge many of the Ashkenazi rabbis' halachic decisions and rule independently. When doing so he was relying on Sephardi traditions, a fact that gave him special stature among Sephardim. This independence was expressed following the 1992 elections, when Rabbi Yosef refused to conform to the demands of the venerable Rabbi Eliezer Shach, one of the original founders of Shas and a spiritual leader of Ashkenazi ultra-Orthodoxy, and ordered Shas to join the Labor government.

53. On *haredim*, see Samuel C. Heilman and Menachem Friedman, 'Religious Fundamentalism and Religious Jews: The Case of the Haredim', in Martin E. Marty and R. Scott Appleby (eds.), *Fundamentalism Observed* (Chicago: U. of Chicago Press 1991) pp.197–264.

54. For an interpretation of Rabbi Shach's views, see Baruch Kimmerling's article in *Ha'aretz*, 30 March 1990.

55. On the debate in the cabinet and legal interpretation of the Basic Law: Freedom of Occupation, see *Ha'aretz*, 29 Nov. 1993, p.4a. See also *Ha'aretz*, 24 Oct., 12, 19 Nov. 1993. See also comments by Dedi Zucker and Eliezer Schweid on 'The State of Israel: A Jewish and Democratic State', *Constitutional Reform in Israel and its Implications* (Jerusalem: Jerusalem Center for Public Affairs) pp.4–14.

56. One indication of the status quo was in the budgets of religious affairs. On the share of Shas and Agudat Israel in the 1994 budget see *Ha'aretz*, 22, 26, 27, 28 Oct. 1993.

57. Efraim Inbar, *War and Peace in Israeli Politics. Labor Party Positions on National Security* (Boulder, CO: Lynne Reiner Publishers 1991).

58. *Ha'aretz*, 12, 13 Dec. 1993; See also *Ha'aretz*, 16 Dec. 1993, pp.9a, 1b.

59. *Ha'aretz*, 17 Jan. 1996, p.2A.

60. In the early 1950s, many of the hospitalized children of immigrant Yemenite families dissapeared. It has recently come to light that some of the children were possibly adopted by Ashkenazi families without the consent or knowledge of their parents. See a series of investigative reports by Yigal Mashiach, *Ha'aretz*, Weekend Magazine (Supplement), 15, 22, 29 Dec. 1995; 5, 12, 19 Jan., 2 Feb. 1996.

61. Ehud Sprinzak in a conference at Tel Aviv University, 18 Jan. 1996.

# The Nature of Islamic Fundamentalism in Israel

MUHAMMAD HASAN AMARA

This article focuses on the nature of Islamic fundamentalism in Israel. The interplay of Islamic fundamentalism's attitude toward the Israeli-Palestinian conflict and the extent of the movement's integration into Israeli political life is explored. In addressing these themes, the history of Israeli Islamic fundamentalism is reviewed from the pre-state period through the present, as are effects of both internal and external factors on the movement's development. In general, the movement has followed a pragmatic line, although its future endeavors and nature will undoubtedly be influenced by the continuing peace process.

Marty and Appleby look at fundamentalism 'as a strategy, or set of strategies, which beleaguered believers attempt to preserve their distinctive identity as a people or group. Feeling this identity to be at risk, fundamentalists fortify it by a selective retrieval of doctrines, beliefs, and practices from a sacred past.'[1]

The formation of Islamist movements is attributed to a number of factors: (1) sociocultural and economic disequilibrium, which are associated with rapid urbanization and modernization; (2) opposition to state authority; (3) opposition to foreign occupation; and (4) the degree and 'weight of dependency in the world economic systems'.[2] Usually, more than one factor is needed for the formation of an Islamic movement.

A number of theories have been put forward for explaining the return to Islam. The 'crisis theory' claims that the Islamic awakening is a result of political or military crises, internal political crises such as unsuccessful leadership, or severe political and economic crises.[3] The psychological need to 'find an absolute and simple solution to all these crises turned many believers to religion'.[4] However, this theory was severely criticized because the return to Islam was not confined only to crises. Indeed, the 'success theory' developed in reaction to the 'crisis theory'. According to this view, success in the Islamic arena (mainly political) brought about massive support to Islamic groups (i.e., the perceived Arab victory in the 1973 October War[5] and the success of the 1979 Iranian revolution).[6] This theory was criticized on the grounds that the roots of Islamic fundamentalism are deeper and go back further into history than the 1970s. A third theory was the 'evolution theory'. According to this theory, the present Islamic revival is another stage of Islamic reaction to the modernization processes that have occurred in Muslim societies during the last two centuries.[7] Though sophisticated in comparison with the other two theories, it is difficult to see the connection between Islamic trends in various parts of the world such as Indonesia, Yugoslavia, Iran or the former Soviet Union Muslim republics,[8] owing to the huge historical, cultural, social, and geographic differences among them.

Therefore, it is too simplistic to adopt only one theory to explain the complex and multi-faceted phenomenon of Islamic fundamentalism all over the world. While various movements share goals and principles, it is the unique context of each movement that deserves the greatest attention. Marty and Appleby[9] conclude that fundamentalist groups around the world are characterized by ambiguity in their discourse. This holds true for Islamic fundamentalist movements. 'One certain conclusion is the relative degree of ambiguity in both ideology and structure, coherence and organization, that has characterized these various groups.'[10] The natural question that arises is whether this conclusion is also true of the Islamic movement in Israel.

The aim of this article is to examine the nature of Islamic fundamentalism in Israel by looking at two major issues: the attitude of the Islamic movement toward the Israeli-Palestinian conflict and the extent of its integration into Israeli political life. However, as the Islamic movement is also influenced by external environments, it needs to be viewed within the larger context: in relation to fundamentalism in general, fundamentalist groups in the Arab and Islamic worlds, and Islamic movements in the West Bank and Gaza Strip. Though every fundamentalist group is unique and has elements distinguishing it from other groups, there is good reason to expect a number of shared goals and principles.[11]

The Islamic fundamentalist movement in Israel was established in 1983 after the release of Shaykh 'Abdallah Nimer Darwish, the spiritual leader of the movement, from an Israeli prison (he had been convicted for inciting violence against the State of Israel). Initially, the activities of Islamic activists followed the pattern of 'Islamization from above'. The movement was organized in small militant groups with the aim of toppling the dominant Israeli-Jewish order and destroying Jewish dominance and turning Israel into a Muslim state with the Jews relegated to minority status. The group comprised between 60 and 100 male activists who had returned to Islam, most of them under the age of 25 and all from the area known as the Little Triangle. The Little Triangle is located between the West Bank of the Jordan River and the coastal region. On 3 April 1949, a cease-fire agreement was signed on the Island of Rhodes between Israel and Jordan.

As a result, the Jordanian forces withdrew from the Little Triangle area and the Arab villages in it were turned over to Israeli rule on 8 May 1949. Most of the activists from this area came from lower middle class backgrounds and lacked higher education. They considered themselves the successors of 'Izz al-Din al-Qassam (see below). However, the early arrest of its members in January and February 1981 brought drastic change to the activities of the movement. After his release from prison in 1983, Darwish declared that the movement's members would act within Israeli law and avoid any public calls to establish an Islamic state. Since 1983, we have witnessed a process of 'Islamization from below', whereby the Islamic movement concentrates on sociocultural, religious and educational projects.

## Historical Background

Islam as a religious, political, sociocultural and educational phenomenon was not new to the Arab society of British-ruled Palestine.[12] We can roughly trace the activity of the Islamic groups in Palestine to the 1920s, in the context of growing clashes between Jews and Palestinians. The political leadership of the Palestinians emphasized the holiness of Jerusalem to Islam[13] and used this principle primarily as a means of recruiting international Muslim sympathy for the national struggle against the Zionist movement.[14] In the late 1920s, a number of branches of a-shabab al-Muslim, the Muslim Youth, were established in Palestine. The Muslim Youth, inspired by the Egyptian Muslim Brotherhood and led by Shaykh 'Izz al-Din al-Qassam, employed force against both the British and the Jews. Though al-Qassam's group was destroyed and al-Qassam himself killed by British forces, his followers, who were primarily students, played an important role in building Shabab Muhammad (Muhammad's Youth).[15] This group declared its fight against both the British and the Jews to be a holy war (*jihad*) against invaders and conquerors, and played an active role during the Arab revolt of 1936–39.

However, the suppression of the revolt, the scattering of al-Qassam's followers and the rise of Arab nationalism brought about a change in emphasis in Muslim activities.[16] More than a score of branches of the Muslim Brotherhood were established in Palestine toward the end of the Second World War and between 1945 and 1947. However, in contrast to the Muslim Brotherhood in Egypt which was politically active on the national scene, the Muslim Brotherhood in Palestine confined most of its activities to local issues, mainly in the sociocultural and educational domains.[17]

The first Arab-Israeli War in 1948 and the establishment of the State of Israel had a profound effect on Palestinian Arabs. More than half became refugees within former mandatory Palestine, with the bulk falling under

Jordanian or Egyptian control. Approximately 160,000 Palestinians came under Israeli rule. This profound change in political environment was accompanied by other changes as well, most noticeably in the social and economic spheres of life.[18] As a result of losing much of their agricultural land, many Arab villagers in Israel became laborers in the Jewish economic sector.[19] The structure of the family unit also changed as there was a decline in the influence of extended families and *hamulas* (clans) over their members and an increase in the strength of the nuclear family.[20]

The political upheaval of 1948 also brought about great changes in the organization of the Islamic community in Israel. Whereas during the British Mandate, the Mufti (the official interpreter or expounder of Islamic law) and the Supreme Muslim Council possessed broad authority regarding religious issues, under Israeli rule most of the authority of the Supreme Muslim Council was transferred to Israeli agencies.[21] The destruction of the Supreme Muslim Council, the flight or expulsion of many religious scholars and the essentially secular nature of the state of Israel led to the ascendance of non-religious schools in the educational system of Israeli Muslims.

### Internal and External Environments

Though the Islamic fundamentalist movement in Israel, known as the Muslim Youth, was officially founded in 1983, a number of factors in the 1960s and 1970s contributed to its formation. In this section, the internal and external environments contributing to the formation of the Islamic movement in Israel are discussed. The subsequent two sections are devoted to a detailed discussion of the particular circumstances and activities of Islamic awakening in Israel.

A number of both internal and external factors in the 1960s and 1970s contributed to the formation of the Islamic fundamentalist movement in Israel. The main internal factors were the discrimination against Palestinians in Israel in the civil and national domains, the modernization and urbanization processes taking place in the Arab sector and the influence of contact with Israeli Jews. One of the consequences of modernization and contact with Jews was the internalizing of aspects of western culture, some of which had previously been alien to Muslim society in Palestine. Modernization and urbanization led to socioeconomic changes and the Arab sector, mainly rural, began to acquire urban characteristics. However, in the 1960s and 1970s, in spite of the acquisition of urban characteristics and an increase in the standard of living, local councils were not able to introduce sufficient services and infrastructure needed in order to accommodate these emerging changes.[22] The traditional *hamula*, which had initially been strengthened after 1948, gradually weakened. Nakhleh[23] argues that urbanization, changes in the Arab economy and the resultant decline in its political power weakened the ability of the traditional *hamula* to control its members. By the early 1970s, this led to increased factionalism in inter-village politics.[24] In the civil domain, Arabs experienced increased inequality and discrimination at the same time that they became more aware of their status and the effects of unfavorable discrimination. In the national domain, the definition of Israel as a Jewish state made it extremely difficult for its Arab citizens to identify with its symbols which are representative of the Jewish majority, such as the flag and the state's national anthem.

In the 1950s and 1960s, Nasserism and Ba'th Socialism (both of which were secular movements) were the most popular ideologies in the Arab world, including among the Palestinians in Israel. Nevertheless, several regional developments during the 1960s and 1970s contributed to the formation of an Islamic fundamentalist movements in Israel: the defeat of the Arab countries in the Six Day War, the success of the Islamic revolution in Iran, the growth of fundamentalism in the Arab countries (e.g., Egypt and Jordan), and the increasing influence of the Islamic movements in the West Bank and Gaza Strip.[25]

The Six Day War in 1967 served as a crucial point and was one of the main factors leading to the formation of the Islamic movement in Israel. The war changed the political conditions in Israel and in the region. Israeli Palestinians were once again confronted with their Palestinian identity, this time through contact with Palestinians in the occupied territories. Past relations were renewed and extensive contact with religious leaders, scholars, and preachers became possible; preachers from the West Bank and Gaza Strip came to give lessons regarding Islamic subjects in Israeli Palestinian mosques.[26] It also became possible to buy books of religious content which were not available in Israel. A good number of Israeli Palestinians went to study religion in West Bank universities and colleges, returning with qualifications which had been missing in Israeli Palestinian society since 1948. Furthermore, the people in the West Bank and Gaza Strip were on average more observant in their religious practices. The contact between the two Palestinian communities across the Green Line had some influence, with Israeli Palestinians becoming more religious: for example, they began carrying out more personal religious duties.[27] In addition, Israeli Muslims gained access to holy sites such as the Dome of the Rock and Al-Aqsa Mosque in the Old City of Jerusalem.

To sum up, developments in both the internal and external environments contributed to the formation of the Islamic movement in Israel. Internally, processes of modernization and urbanization that took place in the Arab sector following the establishment of the state of Israel increased the awareness of Israel's Arab citizens of the state's continuing discrimination against them. In the 1960s and 1970s, the changes in the external environments contributed to Islamic awareness among Muslims in Israel.

## Islamic Awakening: 1970s

Though the overall prevailing internal and external environments can help understand the major incentives for the formation of the movement, it is important to discuss where the movement was first established, the particular circumstances and the first organized attempts to seek change.

The formation and initial growth of the Islamic movement occurred in the Little Triangle,[28] for a number of reasons. First, all the Arabs in the Triangle are Muslims and the political, social and familial ties with the West Bank that existed before 1948 were more multi-faceted and stronger than in any of the other Arab zones in Israel. Many settlements in the Little Triangle had been 'daughter villages' to 'mother villages' in the West Bank.[29] In addition to the proximity of the Little Triangle to the West Bank, there were actually many border villages that were able to maintain contact, primarily through smuggling, throughout the separation period that continued until the occupation of the West Bank by Israel in 1967. The restoration of open interaction between the Little Triangle and the West Bank as a result of the Six Day War provided an opportunity for mutual exchange.

Second, following the establishment of the state of Israel the social, political, and educational weight and leadership of the Arab community shifted from Jerusalem, Jaffa, and Haifa to the Galilee and the importance of Galilee's urban (for example, Nazareth) and semi-urban areas increased. The Muslim communities in the Little Triangle remained more traditional than those in the Galilee, 'where the Christian community influenced the rest of the population in thinking patterns, in higher education, and inevitably in political awareness'.[30] As a result, the Communist Party played a more important role in the social domain and in promoting political awareness in the Galilee than in the Triangle. Rakah (the Communist Party) was the most successful movement on the local and national levels, although Arab votes were mainly an expression of their opposition to Zionism rather than of a belief in Communism.

Several developments (such as the celebration of Land Day, first marked in 1976, in which Israeli Arabs participated in massive protests against the confiscation of Arab lands and the continued discrimination with respect to civil rights, the perceived victory of Arab forces against Israel in the October War of 1973, the rise of the PLO in the international political arena, and the Iranian revolution) weakened the support of the Zionist parties in the Arab sector during the 1970s and 1980s. In the Galilee the political vacuum in the Arab sector was filled, to a large degree, by the Communist

Party. Conversely, in the Little Triangle, it was filled partly by the Communist Party and partly by the Progressive List for Peace and Democracy (PLPD), established in 1984. However, by 1988 the PLPD had weakened and the party basically disappeared from the political scene by the 1992 elections. It seems that by the mid-1980s conditions in the Little Triangle were more ripe for the participation of the Islamic fundamentalist movement in political life than they were in the Galilee.

## The Islamic Movement Since the Early 1980s

Shaykh 'Abdallah Nimer Darwish, the spiritual leader of the Israeli Arab community's Islamic fundamentalist movement,[31] was born in Kafr Qassem, a village in the Little Triangle. In his youth, he was active in the Communist Party. However, in 1965 he left it, shifting to Islam as a religious, ideological and political framework for action. From 1969 to 1972, he attended the Islamic college in Nablus. Following graduation, he worked as an elementary school teacher and *Imam* (preacher) in mosques. According to Darwish, the Islamic movement began around 1972 when he started preaching in Kafr Qassem and gained a good number of followers.[32] His reputation as a religious leader gradually began to spread to the neighboring villages (such as Kafr Bara, Jaljulia, Tira and Taibeh). By 1978, his influence was felt in Jatt, Baqa' Al-Gharbiyya, and even Umm-el Fahm, and at the end of the decade had reached the faraway Bedouin settlements in the Negev and Galilee.[33] Darwish was fired by the government from his teaching position in 1979.[34] By the 1970s, his ideology was based on two main positions: antipathy to western culture and imperialism, and the understanding of Islam as the most complete, liberal, and humanist way to life available to mankind.[35] As such, only Islam could remedy the problems and injustices of humanity. His sermons attracted many Muslims who had been alienated by the discrimination they felt from Israeli society and were searching for identity.

After being released from prison in 1983, Darwish declared that the movement's members would act according to Israeli law and avoid any public calls to establish an Islamic state. Since 1983, a process of 'Islamization from below' has occurred, whereby the Islamic movement has concentrated its efforts on socio-cultural, religious and educational aspects of Arab life. The leaders of the movement selected the name, the Muslim Youth Movement (harakat a-shabab al-Muslim) to indicate that most of its activists are young and that their religious message is directed primarily at the youth. They have essentially followed the model of the Egyptian Muslim Brotherhood, founded by Hasan al-Bana in 1928.[36]

One of the major aims of the Islamic movement in Israel is to encourage Muslims to return to Islam and practice it in the private and public domains. They concentrate on youth education and stress the teachings of Islam, while rejecting alien, secular western culture. The movement attains its support through community programs and social activism. Darwish and other religious leaders believe that the Israeli government has done little to improve the conditions of Arabs in Israel.[37] Their conclusion is that in the face of the Israeli government's neglect, Arab citizens need to take care of themselves.

Therefore, many associations established in different settlements have collected *zakat* and *sadaqa* (alms and charity). They use the money to support the needy or to establish communal projects. Annual volunteer camps have become a marked sign of the movement in various Arab localities. The participants have put fences around playgrounds and cemeteries, constructed shelters at bus stops, and built rooms in schools, kindergartens and mosques. These activities have increased the popularity of the movement among the Arab public and even those who are not members of the movement have contributed to it. As the Arab local councils and municipalities received little money from the Israeli government in comparison with the Jewish sector, the Islamic movement's ability to undertake projects and initiatives without official help thus stood in marked contrast to the poor performance of 'official bodies'. This generated increased support and admiration for the movement.

One of the characteristics of the Islamic movement in Israel is the young age of its leadership. Most of them are in their thirties and forties (such as Ra'id Salah of Umm-el-Fahm, Kamal Rayyan of Kafr Bara, and Kamal Khatib of Kafr Kanna). They are educated (either in Islamic colleges in the West Bank or at Israeli universities), fluent in Hebrew, knowledgeable of Israeli society and motivated to change the conditions of the Arab sector. There is no accurate estimate of the size of the movement's membership, but its success in local elections may provide some insight. The Islamic movement first participated in elections for local governments in 1989. It was victorious in six of the 14 municipalities and councils, winning 46 seats. In the area of the Little Triangle, they won 25 seats out of 116 (21.5 per cent), in the Galilee 14 out of 267 (5.2 per cent), with the rest of the seats gained in the Negev and mixed cities. In the 1993 elections, the Islamic movement maintained its position, again winning in six municipalities and councils and controlling 50 seats.[38]

Although Darwish is the movement's most important religious and spiritual leader and in general his basic explanations regarding Islamic society are accepted, there is no agreement within the movement in regards to two major issues: the solution to the Palestinian question and the extent of integration into Israeli political life.

## Integration in the Political Life of Israel

Participation in the municipal elections was accepted by all of the movement's religious leaders. Their participation was seen as a means for influencing local politics, enhancing their power at the local level, and confirming their belief that the Islamic movement could run the local councils more efficiently and offer better services than tradition *hamulas* and Communist leaders.

However, there was no agreement among the leadership regarding participation in the Knesset (Israeli Parliament) elections. The issue was raised in March 1990 within the framework of the debate on the legitimacy of participation of representatives of the movement in the Follow-up Committees for the Arab Community's Affairs.[39] A call for establishing a unified Arab party to run for the next Knesset elections without the Communist Party was issued in a number of Arabic language newspapers. According to *Kul-Al-Arab*,[40] a meeting took place between 'Abd el-Wahab Darawsha (the head of the Arab Democratic Party) and 'Abdallah Nimer Darwish regarding the formation of an electoral bloc.

Darwish repeated, in an interview to *Nida'a Aswar* on 22 June 1990, his support for establishing one Arab party in order to put an end to divisions in the Arab sector. He made it clear that his movement did not insist on acceptance of the slogan 'Islam is the Solution' for the establishment of the unified list. The condition he stipulated was a commitment to protect the rights of Israeli Palestinians; he did not rule out the participation of the Communists. However, these discussions did not lead to their participation in the 1992 Knesset elections.

A number of explanations may be offered for the Islamic movement's decision not to participate, such as that they were cautious about putting the extent of their support to a real public test. However, a more logical explanation is that their participation in the Knesset elections would mean a de facto recognition of Israeli sovereignty and commitment and loyalty to the laws of the Jewish State. Their participation in the municipal elections have a different meaning; they were within the framework of the movement's aspiration to influence the local Arab population. This could be understood as one of the ways to achieve self-rule for the Arabs.

Many prominent leaders objected to the direct participation of the Islamic movement in the Knesset elections. Shaykh Kamal Khatib of Kafr Kanna suggested that the implications on the *shari'a* of the need to take an oath of allegiance to Israel might serve as a justification for not participating in the elections.[41] Another prominent leader, Shaykh Ra'id Salah, declared that 'the Knesset represents a form of legislation which is contrary to what God ordered and taught'.[42] Nevertheless, the issue is still on the agenda of the movement. It seeks, to quote Shaykh Ra'id Salah: 'to mix between the Islamic sources and the sharp political vision'.[43] Salah's statement indicates a readiness to compromise and a desire to find solutions which would enable the movement to find a bridge between the teachings of Islam and the existing political situation in Israel.

Recent reports show that the Islamic movement seriously considered running in the Israeli Knesset elections in 1996. Darwish's position, which backs the movement's participation in the Knesset elections, is gaining more support. In a February 1995 meeting, religious leaders were equally divided on participating in the next Knesset elections. Consequently, they decided to take the issue to the thousands of the movement's members to reach a final decision.[44] The pro-election religious leaders declared that their plan was to form an all-Arab slate of candidates for the next parliament. Their list would combine Islamic fundamentalists as well as veteran Arab politicians. Ahmad Tibi, who has served for the last year as an adviser to PLO leader Yasir Arafat, is the most prominent leader slated to join the list. They also mentioned the name of Talab Al-Sani', a member of Arab Democratic Party, as a potential candidate.[45]

Although the Islamic movement has decided not to run in the Knesset elections as an independent list, they have, for the first time, decided to allow their members to exercise their rights and vote.[46] This decision clearly shows that the movement now feels confident enough to embark on elections together with other Arab politicians, but not confident enough to strike out on its own. When elections serve the movement's purposes, they have no problem in finding solutions in Islamic teachings and accommodating the prevailing political reality. The final decision not to run in the next parliamentary elections as an independent list was probably, this time, based on political calculations rather than on the ideological tension between the *shari'a* and Israeli law.

### The Israeli-Palestinian Conflict

There is ideological tension, and even a paradox, between the movement's slogan 'Islam is the Solution' and its acceptance of Israeli law. This tension is evident in the disagreement among the religious leaders of the Islamic movement in Israel regarding the solution to the Israeli-Palestinian conflict.

The movement offers Islamic solutions to the Palestinian question. In the publications of the movement, we find statements such as 'the Palestinian problem with its Muslim *umma* (community) is merely an Islamic problem, which can only be solved by fundamental Islamic solutions,'[47] or 'that Palestine is not merchandise, but it is Islamic *waqf* (property). It is not the property of the Palestinians only or Arabs only but all the Muslims'.[48] These declarations, which were written by Israeli Muslim activists, are congruent with the general Islamic teachings. An examination of these declarations shows they are not different from the statements made by other Islamic movements in the West Bank and Gaza,[49] Jordan,[50] Egypt and elsewhere.

The main message that emerges from reading the Islamic movement's journals (e.g., *Sawt al-Haq wal Huriyya* and *Assirat*) is that the Palestine problem is an Islamic problem and its solution is based on Islamic perception and teachings. However, there is no clear articulation of the essence and framework of the Islamic solution.[51] For example, vague expressions such as 'the just solution which yields to all parties their rights' are used in addressing the Arab-Israeli conflict.

Militants not currently influential among the movement's membership, such as Fathi 'Ali Nasir and Fahmi Abu Mukh[52], prefer to find models of emulation among the radical Islamic movements which utterly reject any compromise or even dialogue with the Jewish State.[53]

In contrast, Darwish represents a moderate line, stating that the Palestinian people reject terror and the use of violence and favor finding a negotiated solution with the Jewish people.[54] He believes that a compromise between Israel and the Palestinians will be achieved through education, rather than violence.

Though Darwish and his followers are pragmatic in their approach towards the Palestinian problem, they do not rule out the possibility of establishing a Palestinian state which is Islamic and Arab from 'the sea to the river'. He recognizes, however, that international public opinion sees such an advocacy as an attack on Jewish existence.[55] When asked in a symposium about a Muslim state, Darwish said 'if the Israeli army will be predominantly Muslim, we will think of an Islamic State here'. Even Darwish has sometimes used ambiguous wording. For example, he once stated: 'Yes to a political solution which gives me part of my rights today and leaves to the coming generations the final solution'.[56]

Though Darwish and other religious leaders (such as Ibrahim Sarsur and Kamal Rayyan) accept the two-state solution, they have not accepted the 1967 border. Sarsur, for instance, stated: '[W]hy should I be committed to 1967 borders? And what if the negotiating parties agree to the borders of [the UN's] 1947 partition?'[57] In explaining the slogan 'Islam is the Solution' and its relevance to the Palestinian question, Sarsur also stated, '[W]e as an Islamic movement in Israel agree that Jews have the right to live in Israel, which is part of Palestine! Even Salah al-Din al-Ayyubi (Saladin) agreed to let the Crusaders stay in the country in the coastal area. Can I say that he gave up part of the land of Palestine on behalf of the Crusaders?'[58]

Clever justifications are given by Islamic leaders in Israel when they are questioned about their position of 'Islam is the Solution' and its implications for the existence of the State of Israel. In Sarsur's words, 'we are not the Islamic movement in Jordan or the territories! We live under different conditions. For them there is the possibility to fight the occupation in their way and save themselves. We have the possibility of finding other ways and explanations. As a Muslim, nowadays I accept the existence of the State of Israel as de facto'.[59] By 'finding other ways', the Islamic movement probably means that within the constraints of the political reality, the movement should behave according to Israeli law.

Regarding the necessity of *jihad*, Sarsur states: 'What is *jihad*? *Jihad* has many forms. There are seven or eight degrees, or even twelve. The military *jihad* is one of them, and the last. If I improve life in the village, and establish work camps, this is *jihad*'.[60]

Similar to the lack of agreement regarding the Israeli-Palestinian conflict, there is also no agreement regarding the Declaration of Principles agreement between Israel and the PLO. The movement's journal, *Assirat,* severely criticized the agreement and called the PLO leaders traitors. However, Darwish, who participated in a 'solidarity demonstration' in support of the agreement in Nazareth immediately after its signing in Washington, supported the deal and praised mutual recognition between Israel and PLO.[61] Yet, he and other prominent religious leaders have expressed reservation and dissatisfaction with the Jerusalem issue. Shaykh Ra'id Salah on several occasions even refused to meet with Yasir Arafat, before finally accepting an invitation from Arafat on 9 August 1994.[62]

It is obvious that with respect to the Israeli-Palestinian conflict, the pragmatic line is dominant, namely the acceptance of a two-state solution. However, sometimes the movement's declarations are ambiguous in order to mask its lack of complete commitment to a compromise and its continued aspiration for an Islamic state, positions held even by those who articulate the pragmatic line.

## Conclusion

The Islamic movement holds primarily a pragmatic line regarding integration in the political life of Israel and the Israeli-Palestinian conflict. However, major questions remain unanswered. Will the Islamic movement continue to follow a strategy of 'Islamization from below' until it reaches full maturity? Will this result in its full participation in all spheres of life in Israel, including the elections to the Knesset? Or, will the Islamic movement work to strengthen its power base among the Arab community and then attempt to seek separation from Israel, or to use Sela's and Zilberman's term, bring about 'enclaving' within the state of Israel?[63]

In spite of the popularity of the movement among a considerable number of Israeli Muslims, it is still too early to predict one direction or another. The movement is still very young and the process of Islamization among Israel's Arab citizens will be influenced by developments in both the internal and external environments. The movement's development will depend on the evolving civil-status of Israeli Arabs, developments in the West Bank and Gaza, and the progress of the Middle East peace process.

First, the Arab-Israeli peace process is likely to have considerable impact on the development of the movement. The Arab minority status is influenced, among other things, by the Israeli-Arab conflict. Peace between Israel and the Arab states, and even more importantly the Palestinians, will accelerate the process of Arab integration into Israel. If Israel moves to end discrimination against its Arab citizens and offers the possibility of equality in many domains, this may contribute to a wider integration of the Arab community into the life of the country. A wider integration of the Arab community in Israeli life may subsequently lead the Islamic movement either to segregation from secular life or to complete political integration (as is the case of the Israeli Jewish religious parties) and weaken its strong claims against civil discrimination in Israel.

Second, the success of an emerging Palestinian entity in the West Bank and Gaza would signify the victory of the PLO and other secular forces. This might result in the weakening of the Islamic movements in the territories. It should be remembered that Hamas gave confidence and aspiration to the Islamic movement in Israel.

Third, Israel at peace with the Arab world could result in cooperation between Israeli and Arab governments in suppressing radical Islamic movements. More importantly, the Islamic movements might lose credibility among the masses in fighting their regimes on the basis that Israel is the most dangerous enemy to the Arab world, though Islamic movements, along with secular movements as well, would continue to object to normalization with Israel.

At any rate, the Islamic movement in Israel will continue to seek to dominate the National Committee of Arab Local Council Heads, in order to obtain larger budgets from the government, strengthen its level of popular support, and provide it with the capability to compete with secular nationalists and Communists at the local level. It can also be assumed that the relationship of the movement to the Israeli authorities will resemble that of Jordan, as opposed to Egypt or Algeria. The movement will most likely continue to participate in the local government elections, criticizing the Israeli government and its treatment of the Arab sector, but still working within acceptable limits and carefully evaluating the Israeli reality.

Although the main trend in the Islamic movement in Israel is characterized by pragmatism, the discourse even among the pragmatists is characterized by ambiguity. It seems that ambiguity is a strategy both for survival and to avoid being committed to particular momentary circumstances, leaving permanent solutions for some future time when conditions may have become more propitious for the realization of Islamic ideals. In this regard, Israel's Islamic movement is similar to the other Islamist movements in the region.[64]

## NOTES

1.  Martin E. Marty and R. Scott Appleby (eds.), *Accounting for Fundamentalism* (Chicago: U. of Chicago Press 1994) p.1.
2.  James Piscatori, 'Accounting for Islamic Fundamentalism', in Marty and Appleby (note 1).
3.  See Richard P. Mitchell, *The Society of Muslim Brothers* (Oxford: OUP 1993); S.E. Ibrahim, 'Anatomy of Egypt's Militant Groups: Methodological Notes and Preliminary Findings', *International Journal of Middle Eastern Studies* 12 (1985) pp.423–53; and Emmanuel Sivan, *Radical Islam* (New Haven, CT: Yale UP 1985).
4.  Thomas Mayer, *The Awakening of Muslims in Israel* (Hebrew) (Giv'at Haviva: The Institute for Arabic Studies 1988).
5.  For example, the use of *Allahu Akbar* (God is Great) by Egyptian soldiers crossing the Bar-Lev Line as their battle cry, achieving 'relative breakthrough' in the Arab-Israeli military balance, was interpreted by Islamists as the factor for Egyptian 'victory'.
6.  See John L. Esposito, *Islam and Politics* (Syracuse, NY: SUP 1983); and Daniel Pipes, *In the Path of God: Islam and Political Power* (NY: Basic Books 1983).
7.  See John Obert Voll, *Islam, Continuity and Change in the Modern World* (Boulder, CO: Westview Press 1982); and Gilles Keppel, *The Prophet and the Pharaoh* (London: Isaki 1985).
8.  See, for instance, Yousif Alqirdawi, *The Islamic Awakening between Apostasy and Extremism* (The West Bank: n.p., n.d.).
9.  Marty and Appleby (note 1).
10. Piscatori (note 2) p.371.
11. Marty and Appleby (note 1).
12. See Mayer (note 4); and Ibrahim Malik, *The Islamic Movement in Israel: Between Fundamentalism and Pragmatism* (Hebrew) (Giv'at Haviva: The Institute for Arabic Studies).
13. In respect to the holiness of Jerusalem in Islam, see Hava Lazarus-Yafe, 'The Holiness of Jerusalem in the Tradition of Islam', in E. Shaltiel (ed.), *Chapters on the Contemporary History of Jerusalem* (Hebrew) (Tel Aviv: Yad Ben-Zvi and the Ministry of Defense 1981) pp.127–9; and Emmanuel Sivan, 'The Holiness of Jerusalem in Islam in the Crusades', in Joshua Prawer and H. Ben-Shamai (eds.), *Jerusalem Book, the Crusader and the Ayyoban Period 1099–1250* (Hebrew) (Jerusalem 1991).
14. Mayer (note 4).
15. It is interesting to see that al-Qassam's name has been given to a militant group (associated with Hamas, the Islamic movement in the West Bank and Gaza Strip) and Shabab Muhammad's name to a group of Israeli Muslims active in the Islamic movement.
16. Mayer (note 4) p.28.
17. Ibid.
18. See, for instance, Majid Al-Haj, *Social Change and Family Processes: Arab Communities in Shefar-Amr* (Brown University Studies in Population and Development 1987); Yosef Ginat, *Labour as a Factor for Change in the Arab Village* (Hebrew) (Tel Aviv: The Pinhas Sapir Institute for Development 1980); H. Rosenfeld, 'Change, Barriers to Change, and

Contradictions in the Arab Village Family', *American Anthropologists* 70 (1968) pp.732–52; and S. Smooha, 'Control of Minorities in Israel and Northern Ireland', *Comparative Studies in Society and History* 22 (1980) pp.256–80.

19. See Elia Zureik, *Palestinians in Israel: A Study in Internal Colonialism* (London: Routledge and Kegan Paul 1979).
20. See Al-Haj (note 18).
21. See Aharon Layish, *Women in Islamic Law in a non-Muslim State: A Study Based on Decisions of Shari'a Courts in Israel* (NY: John Wiley and Israeli University Press 1981).
22. See Yoram Bar-Gal and Arnon Soffer, *Geographical Changes in the Traditional Arab Villages in Northern Israel* (Durham, England: Center for Middle Eastern and Islamic Studies, University of Durham 1981).
23. K. Nakhleh, 'The Direction of Local-Level Conflict in Two Arab Villages in Israel', *American Ethnologist* 2/3 (1975) pp.497–516.
24. A case in point is the success of the Communist Party at the local and national level, primarily in the 1977 Knesset elections.
25. Mayer (note 4).
26. See Al-Haj, 'The Political and Social Consequences of the Meeting between Palestinians across the Green Line', in Arnon Soffer, *Twenty Years since the Six Day War* (Hebrew) (Haifa: The Arab-Jewish Institute for the Study of the Middle East 1988).
27. Mayer (note 4).
28. See Benny Morris, *The Birth of the Problem of the Palestinian Refugees 1947–1949* (Hebrew) (Tel Aviv 1991).
29. See Shmueli Avshalom *et al.*, *The Little Triangle: Transformation of an Area* (Hebrew) (Jerusalem: University of Haifa Institute of Middle Eastern Studies 1985).
30. Reuven Paz, *The Islamic Movement in Israel after the Elections to the Local Government* (Hebrew) (Tel Aviv: Tel Aviv University, The Moshe Dayan Center for Middle Eastern and African Studies-Shiloah Institute 1989).
31. See Muhammad Mi'ari, 'The Islamic Movement in Israel', *Shu'un Filastiniyya* (Arabic) (14 March 1991) pp.215–16.
32. Ibid.
33. Ibid.
34. Mayer (note 4) p.40.
35. Ibid. p.37.
36. Ibid.
37. Ibid. p.65.
38. See As'ad Ganem and Sara Ostaski-Lazar, *The Elections to the Arab Local Government, Nov. 1993: Results and Analysis* (Hebrew) (Giv'at Haviva: The Institute for Peace Research 1994).
39. A body established in 1974 that is composed of Arab local government representatives. Its aim is to advance Arab affairs in various fields and pressure the government into allocating more funds to the Arab sector.
40. *Kul al-'Arab*, 23 March 1990.
41. Ibid. 27 April 1990.
42. *Al-Sinara*, 16 March 1990.
43. Ibid.
44. *Jerusalem Post*, 19 Sept. 1994; *Al-Hamishmar*, 15 Feb. 1995.
45. *Jerusalem Post*, 19 Sept. 1994.
46. *Kul al-'Arab*, 2 June 1995.
47. *Sawt al-Haq wal Hurriya*, 19 Jan. 1990.
48. *Assirat*, 12 Nov. 1989.
49. See Ziad Abu 'Amr, *Islamic Fundamentalism in the West Bank and Gaza: Muslim Brotherhood and Islamic Jihad* (Bloomington: Indiana UP 1994); see also his interview in the *Jerusalem Post*, 30 Sept. 1990.
50. See *Assirat*, 15 Sept. 1989; and *Sawt al-Haq wal Hurriya*, 27 Oct. 1990.
51. See Malik (note 12).
52. Fahmi Abu Mukh was the founder and general officer of the radical group 'the Jihad family',

*usrat Al-jihad,* which aimed to achieve its goals through violence. The members of the group were caught and Farid was sentenced to 15 years (see Mayer (note 4)). Fathi Ali-Nasir, from Nazareth, was the leader of the Islamic Association in Ramla prison. In May 1985 both of them were released in 'The Jibril Deal', in which 1150 Palestinian prisoners were released in exchange for 4 Israeli soldiers.

53. Mayer (note 4) p.58.
54. Ibid. p.62.
55. *Nida'a al-Aswar,* 26 June1990.
56. Ibid.
57. *Kol Ha'ir*, 19 Jan. 1991.
58. David Grossman, *Present Absentees* (Hebrew) (Tel Aviv: Hakibbutz Hameiuhad 1992) p.178.
59. Ibid. p.180.
60. Ibid. p.181.
61. See *Davar,* 23 Sept. 1993; and *Jerusalem Post*, 19 Aug. 1994.
62. *Jerusalem Post* (note 61).
63. Avraham Sela and Ifrach Zilberman, *Israel's Arab Community in the Context of the Peace Process* (Hebrew) (Jerusalem: Israel-Palestinian Peace Research Project, Working Paper Series No. 22. Truman Research Institute 1992). It puts forward a suggestion that the Islamic movement in Israel is attempting to bring about 'enclaving' within the state. In other words, their involvement in local politics is a strategy by which the movement intends to make the Arab sector autonomous. This prospectus lacks sophistication, since there is not enough evidence of the Islamic Movement's intentions to do so, and in advancing such an idea the various internal and external factors affecting the Arab society should be taken into account. First, the Arab society is not homogeneous and the majority do not support the Islamic movement. Second, the great dependence of the Arab sector on the Jewish economy makes the notion unrealistic.
64. Piscatori (note 2).

# The Islamic Challenge in North Africa

## BRUCE MADDY-WEITZMAN

This article analyzes and compares the growth of Islamist movements and regime responses in the three core Maghrib states – Morocco, Algeria and Tunisia. In spite of the many points of commonality and their geographical proximity, the particular sociopolitical and historical circumstances of each of the three states have varied widely, producing a different state-society/regime-opposition dynamic in each case, resulting in very different political outcomes. Algeria has been, and remains, in many ways, *sui generis* in the Arab world. Consequently, even if the Islamists do eventually come to power there, one should avoid adopting any simplistic Islamic 'domino theory' for the region.

Algeria's sudden, wholesale embrace of a western-style program of political liberalization during 1989–91 was unprecedented in the Arab world. It included the unqualified legalization of explicitly Islamic political parties. No other Arab regime had dared to make such a move and the consequence was far-reaching: the implosion of the Algerian polity. Algeria became a place that conformed, ironically, with Moroccan sociologist Fatima Mernissi's linguistic-cultural definition of the *gharb* (West): a place where 'all terrors are possible'.[1] Sweeping victories by the newly-founded Front Islamique du Salut (FIS), initially in municipal and then in the first round of parliamentary elections, triggered a military *coup d'état* in January 1992. The maneuver included the deposition of President Chedli Benjedid, the cancellation of the electoral process prior to the second round of parliamentary elections, the arrest of thousands of Islamist activists and the state's descent into chaos. Brutal warfare between the Algerian military and armed Islamist groups has taken between 20,000 and 40,000 lives and rent asunder the already tattered fabric of Algerian society.

Despite the enormous cost of the violence, the *denouement* is still not in sight. Algeria's current situation is an uneasy and unstable stalemate. Whatever the course of future events, it seems that the successful 'reimagining' of the Algerian political community and the establishment of even a minimal social contract is at best a distant prospect.[2] In the meantime, a proper analysis of the depths of the Islamic challenge in Algeria and a comparison of the Algerian experience to that of Morocco and Tunisia is in order. For not only is the Maghrib different than the Mashriq (Arab East), but the dissimilarity of experience *within* the Maghrib leads one to caution against adopting any simplistic Islamic 'domino theory' for the area.

## Roots of the Contemporary Crisis

Let us begin with a few general observations. The ideological roots of modern day Islamic fundamentalism are not solely of recent origin: the *salafiyya* current of Islamic reform and purification surfaced in the Maghrib in the period between the two world wars. One can argue that more than in the Mashriq, Islam in the Maghrib was one of the core values, or central points of reference, for Algerian, Moroccan and Tunisian nationalist movements that opposed European domination. In Algeria, the crystallization of a modern national identity that occurred between the two world wars was considerably shaped by the Islamic reformist movement led by Shaykh 'Abd al-Hamid bin Badis. This movement promoted both the purification of Islamic practices from 'polytheism' (maraboutic practices) and the implementation of an educational network that would stress that Islam and the Arabic language, and not the culture of France, are at the core of modern Algerian identity.[3] Similarly, *salafi* activity in Morocco played an important role in the shaping of the nationalist movement. Started in the 1920s, it came to be personified by 'Allal al-Fasi, the religio-nationalist leader of the Istiqlal Party.[4] And likewise in Tunisia, Islam 'as a component of Tunisian identity and a legitimizing value...suffused the first generation nationalist movement [in the decades prior to World War I] and...persisted even into the age of Bourguibist secularism'.[5]

In contrast to the general *salafi* current, political Islam in North Africa was not a 'pan' movement. Nor, again in contrast to the Mashriq, was pan-Arabism ever a competing ideology. Thus, the legitimacy of the state in North Africa has never been in doubt: 'the state appears more as an appropriately adjusted transfer of technology than as an alien institution'.[6]

State power grew exponentially during the post-independence generation, intruding decisively into every sphere of society. However, in the words of the Tunisian scholar Abdelbaki Hermassi, by the 1980s policies which had once been seen favorably as constituting the *etatization* of society, increasingly began to look like the *privatization* of the state as a small number of individuals began to accumulate great wealth from their privileged positions. This occurred despite a period of state retrenchment and austerity under the direction of international financial institutions.[7] In addition, the amount of resources available for development were sharply cut by the economic contraction of the post-oil boom era. This effect was felt across the Arab world, both among the petroleum-based economies, including Algeria, and the 'labor-exporters' like Egypt, Jordan and even Tunisia. What resulted was the obvious inability of Arab regimes, maghribi and mashriqi alike, to deliver the social, economic, political and *psychic* goods to their expanding, increasingly youthful, urbanized and literate populations. This failure caused a profound sense of crisis (*azma*) among wide sectors of the population and endless debate among intellectuals over what should be done (spawning a cottage industry of sorts, or *azmatology*, in the words of Muhammad Guessous, a Moroccan sociologist).[8]

The Maghrib's proximity to Europe caused its youthful population (two-thirds of which were under 30 years of age) to be especially vulnerable to psychic dislocation, particularly since North Africa had already been widely penetrated by the *gharb* (primarily France) during the prior 150 years. A proliferation of satellite dishes and powerful television transmitters brought images of Europe's material glitter into people's living rooms, raising expectations and provoking demands that had no chance of being fulfilled, thus opening the way to profound disillusionment. In Mernissi's words:

> [W]hat strikes me as a sociologist is the strong feeling of bitterness in the people [of the Muslim countries] – the intellectuals, the young, peasants. I see bitterness over blocked ambition, over frustrated desires for consumption – of clothes, commodities, and gadgets, but also of cultural products like books and quality films and performances which give meaning to life and reconcile the individual with his environment and his country....In our country (Morocco) what is unbearable, especially when you listen to the young men and women of the poor class, is the awful waste of talent. '*Ana daya*'' (My life is a mess) is a leitmotif that one hears constantly.[9]

This crisis, which took root during the 1970s and gathered strength during the 1980s, spawned a new kind of dissent, articulated most forcefully by Islamist movements. Their discourse was centered not on issues or strategies of development, but on matters concerned with justice and cultural identity.[10] Given the dual legacies of popular Islamic practice and the Maghrib's penetration by the modern *gharb*, it is not surprising that maghribi fundamentalists often found themselves alienated from their own societies and sought guidance and inspiration from movements situated outside the Maghrib, such as the Egyptian-based Muslim Brotherhood, Iran's Islamic revolution and Sudan's Hasan al-Turabi. This interaction marks a departure from pre-modern historical patterns.

### Morocco

In spite of the strong similarity in the development of their Islamist movements, the particular sociopolitical and historical circumstances of each of the three Maghrib states have varied widely. This has produced a different state-society/regime-opposition dynamic in each case which subsequently led to very different political outcomes. Witness Morocco:

apart from Saudi Arabia, no other Arab regime has so thoroughly draped itself in the mantle of Islam. King Hassan II, who has both reigned and ruled since 1961, is constitutionally the *Amir al-Mu'minin* (the Commander of the Faithful), deputized by virtue of his descent from the Prophet Muhammad to lead the Moroccan Islamic *umma* in all matters, both temporal and spiritual.[11] His own erudition in religious matters, displayed in dialogues with religious scholars on Moroccan television, reinforces this dual role.

One can argue against the oft-made claim that the Moroccan monarchy is the central religious institution of Moroccan life and that Hassan's longevity rests less on blind obedience and belief in his special sacredness (*baraka*) than on his astute use of all the levers of power at his disposal, including repression.[12] As Hassan himself told his biographer/interviewer, 'one doesn't maintain order by wielding croissants'.[13] At the same time, it seems reasonable to conclude that the Moroccan regime has been a relatively successful 'modernizing monarchy' because it anchored itself in Moroccan political and sociocultural traditions. This enabled it to avoid some of the harsher social, political and psychic dislocations experienced by radical, revolutionary Arab regimes.[14]

One such tradition is the institution of the monarchy itself. The ruling Alawite dynasty alone is almost 350 years old. More prosaic factors which have promoted relative political stability include a liberal economy and multi-party politics. Hassan has described his political strategy as 'homeopathic democracy'. It is a process of controlled, well-managed change, meant to maintain social peace and the preeminence of his rule while simultaneously promoting economic development and the general welfare. Hassan has declared his ultimate goal to be a 'bipolarized democracy', in which two parliamentary blocs alternate power with the monarch serving as the ultimate arbiter and source of authority.

To be sure, the monarchy's reliance on existing elites, economic and political, carries the danger of stagnation, a lack of attention to social and economic distress, and disaffection among the educated classes. The slow pace of change undoubtedly breeds cynicism among the educated and does little to promote feelings of empowerment among the urban poor. His IMF-directed policies of structural readjustment, involving debt rescheduling, cuts in subsidies, liberalizing capital movements and the beginning of privatization of state firms, have won considerable praise from both the Paris Club governments and international and commercial lending agencies. Macro-economic figures have responded accordingly: the budget deficit, which in the early 1980s had reached 12 per cent of the GDP, was cut to less than 2 per cent in a decade, foreign investment rose fourfold between 1988 and 1992, and annual growth rates have been generally impressive. On the micro-economic level, however, the picture is quite different. Gaps between the rich and poor, in a society where the average per capita income is c.$1,000, have increased. Urban unemployment runs between 20 and 30 per cent. And two years of severe drought in 1992–93, followed by the 'drought of the century' in the winter of 1994–95, have exacerbated the plight of the rural areas and reinforced long-standing trends of urban migration.

Like many Middle Eastern governments, Hassan initially allowed a certain amount of freedom of action for budding Islamist movements in order to counterbalance opposition from the radical left. But although he continues to allow non-political activities, since the 1970s he has severely restricted their ability to operate politically and has adopted a strategy of manipulation and co-optation.

The regime's efforts to control Islamism were made easier by the fact that Moroccan Islamists are not of one stripe. Indeed, one researcher counted no fewer than 23 politicized religious associations in the early 1980s.[15] However, these are divided into three groups. The first is explicitly reformist, but not overtly political, concentrating on matters of individual piety and righteousness and criticizing corruption. As such, it has been the least restricted. Its leading figure, before his death in the late 1980s, was an elderly mosque preacher in Tangier named Fqih al-Zamzami. Venerated by peddlers, laborers and shopkeepers, cassettes of his sermons are sold in most cities. His three sons have tried to follow in his footsteps.[16] At the other extreme is a small group known as al-Shabiba al-Islamiyya (Islamic Youth). It draws its membership primarily from student and high school movements and has advocated the violent overthrow of the regime. Its leader, 'Abd al-Karim al-Muti', is in exile somewhere in Europe. A faction of the group, led by 'Abdallah Benkirane, chose a non-confrontational, reformist posture similar to that advocated by Zamzami. In recent years, under the banner of the harakat al-islah wal-tajdid bel-Maghrib, Movement for Reform and Renewal in the Maghreb (HATM), it has attempted to become an overt participant in Morocco's political process while at the same time retaining its pragmatic approach.[17]

The third movement is lead by Morocco's most well-known Islamist, 'Abd al-Salam Yasin, a former school inspector in the Education Ministry. His movement, al-'adl wal-ihsan (Justice and Charity), is officially outlawed. Yasin's followers are both more educated and more radical than Zamzami's. In 1974, Yasin openly challenged Hassan's legitimacy as well as the legitimacy of any monarch in Islam. He later admitted to having prepared his burial shroud for the occasion.[18] (King Hassan felt confident enough not to have him executed and has merely kept him under various forms of detention for most of the time since.) During the Gulf War, 30,000 of Yasin's followers mustered under their own banner as part of a massive anti-war demonstration. This demonstration provides us with the only public indication of the movement's strength. The government recently proposed easing the restrictions on Yasin in return for a commitment that he and his followers would work within the existing system. Yasin declined the offer. The proposal itself perhaps indicates that the authorities recognize the potential strength of the Islamists and the need to defuse the movement by co-optation. Sporadic violent clashes on university campuses during recent years between Islamists and leftist groups attest to the former's continued militancy.

Moreover, an incident in the summer of 1994 provides evidence that Morocco is not entirely immune to the radical, violent Islamic current manifesting itself in Algeria and Egypt. On 24 August two Spanish tourists were shot and killed in the lobby of a hotel in Marrakesh. This was the first and so far only violent attack against foreigners. The government response was to immediately blame persons in the Algerian intelligence services for being behind the perpetrators. This precipitated a renewal of Algerian-Moroccan tensions and the closing of the border between the two states. Two weeks later, four alleged perpetrators of the act were arrested. They turned out to be a group of young French-Moroccan and French-Algerian fundamentalists, possibly connected to the remnants of Muti''s al-Shabiba al-Islamiyya. In the late 1980s, they had organized themselves into a group to advance the cause of Islamic revolution. Their activities included weapons training in Peshawar, Pakistan near the Afghan frontier, smuggling weapons to Algerian Islamists via Morocco, and a number of robberies in France to support themselves and their cause.[19] Their alleged head, a Moroccan named Tariq Fellah, was arrested in Germany in December 1994. In January, the group of four plus 14 others were put to trial in Fes for the hotel shooting plus a number of other violent acts carried out during 1994. Official Algerian involvement was never confirmed and the incident serves to highlight the common danger posed by Islamist radicals to both the Moroccan and Algerian regimes. Nevertheless, the swift arrest and trial of the group confirms anew that the Moroccan Islamists' ability to pose a serious challenge to the regime is currently extremely limited.

## Tunisia

Tunisia's Islamists have enjoyed a higher international profile than their Moroccan counterparts, but suffer from even greater repression. As in other instances in the Middle East, the protests of the Tunisian Islamists can be seen partly as a response to socioeconomic dislocations stemming from the complex processes of modernization and development. Also contributing is the existence of a clogged political system. However, the most important factor has been the 'psycho-social alienation' that has resulted from the government's pursuit of a western liberal model of modernity.[20] This model has been the objective of President Habib Bourguiba since the state became independent in 1956.[21] Notwithstanding Bourguiba's efforts to legitimize his policies in Islamic modernist terms, his initiatives have led to a greater degree of secularization than in any other Arab country. One example of such a policy is the Personal Status Code, which guarantees equality between men and women in matters of divorce and forbids polygamy. A second example is the relatively large number of women in managerial and executive positions. The current president, Zayn 'Abidin Ben 'Ali, who assumed power in November 1987, softened some of Bourguiba's strident secularism and placed greater emphasis on Tunisia's Arab-Islamic heritage. As part of this policy, the regime permitted the Islamists to participate in the 1989 elections. Officially, they captured 14 per cent of the vote and came close to winning a majority in several urban areas. The Islamists have claimed that the real level of support was between 30 and 32 per cent.[22] The regime was quick to take notice and cracked down harshly, banning the newly formed Islamist al-Nahda, Renaissance Party, and taking advantage of several violent acts perpetrated by Islamists to imprison thousands of activists. Severe reprimands from international human rights organizations have not deterred the regime from this course.

For now, Ben 'Ali continues to rule Tunisia with a firm hand and, unlike in Morocco, political pluralism remains in its infancy. All but 19 of the 163 seats in Tunisia's parliament are held by the ruling Rassemblement Constitutionnel Democratique. This is an improvement, since the previous parliament contained no opposition deputies. Economically the Tunisians have followed a course similar to Morocco's, instituting structural reforms and even obtaining good results. Tunisia's small population, reinforced by the lowest rate of population growth in the Arab world, its educated middle class, high rate of literacy, relatively large percentage of women in the work force and traditional orientation toward Europe make the state a less fertile ground for Islamists. Nonetheless, the groundswell of support for Islamist movements during the 1970s and 1980s indicates that Tunisia is not immune from region-wide currents.

Like their counterparts elsewhere in North Africa and the Sunni world in general, Tunisia's Islamists have been influenced by Egypt's Muslim Brotherhood and the teachings of Sayyid Qutb and Pakistan's Mawlana Mawdudi.[23] Nonetheless, there was considerable talk during the 1980s within Islamist circles of developing a specific 'Tunisian Islam'.[24] Part of the rationale behind this thinking was the rejection of the predominant Islamist view that legitimacy is solely within the divine purview and the support of the idea of popular will as the source of legitimacy.[25] The Islamic notion of *shura* (consultation), declared Rashid Ghannushi, who is the movement's leading figure, legitimizes multi-party politics, the alternation of power and the protection of human rights.[26] The problem, he stressed, was the repressive Ben 'Ali regime in Tunisia, and most Arab governments for that matter, which rejected all notions of civil society (*al-mujtama' al-madani*). Ghannushi's avowed goal to promote a modernist-Islamic synthesis in opposition to the Tunisian regime's 'superficial modernity', makes him one of the more interesting and original of contemporary Islamist thinkers.[27]

To be sure, Ghannushi's views are not entirely congruent with western liberal values. As he stated in one interview, state-building must begin with the recognition of the Arab and Islamic identity of the *umma*. Without first agreeing on this central pillar, the 'cultural context' of state-society relations, there is no hope of having a state authority. Once the identity question is solved, he continued, then democracy can be practiced.[28] He did not address the place in society of those who fall outside the bounds of Arab-Islamic identity.

Ghannushi frequently speaks from his London exile of the need to open up a *hiwar* (dialogue) with the West, rejecting the 'clash of civilisations' notion put forth by both Samuel Huntington and numerous Islamists. At the same time and in contrast with other Tunisian Islamists, his rhetoric has become increasingly radicalized during recent years.[29] His condemnations of the allegedly perfidious western domination of the New World Order, praise for Sudan's regime as a state founded on Islamic concepts and efforts to promote the cause of Algeria's FIS have weakened his credibility and appeal to western governments. In a wide-ranging conversation with a journalist from the *New York Times*, he repeatedly placed primary blame for excesses committed by Islamic regimes on western 'rejectionist attitudes' and justified the murder of Arab and Muslim intellectuals who had embraced secularism, referring to several as 'the devil's advocate... Pharaoh's witches'. He continued by putting forth that 'The educated who put their brains and their talent in the service of an oppressive regime have made their own decisions. They must bear the responsibility for their choice'.[30] Ghannushi has also repeatedly emphasized that western hostility to Islam is due to the activities of Zionism which, in order to retain its existing level of aid and support, is striving to convince the West that following the collapse of Communism and the failure of Arab nationalism, Islam is the new evil force in the world.[31] Speaking in closed sessions at radical Islamic conferences, his rhetoric has been even more fiery: 'Zionism does not only target Arabs and Muslims. It targets goodness... the entirety of values that have crystallized in humanity. Every evil in the world, the Zionists are behind it. This is no exaggeration. There are so many evils in the world, and behind which are the Children of Israel.'[32]

Speaking in London, Ghannushi expressed the hope that the Algerian crisis would soon be resolved in the Islamists' favor. He continued by saying that it would be followed by a 'swift end' to the deadlock in Tunisia, 'either as a result of an initiative by the regime itself, which we would prefer, or due to massive popular pressure, which is more likely to happen. However, should Algeria continue to bleed slowly, the political situation in Tunisia will move in the same direction, but slowly too.'[33] However, it seems that Ghannushi may have been overly optimistic. The immediate future for the Islamists in Tunisia does not appear to be a promising one.

## Algeria

As for Algeria, nowhere was the *azma* more acutely felt. The socioeconomic dimension is obviously crucial in explaining Algeria's slide into chaos. A generation of misguided and mismanaged 'state capitalist' policies, the worldwide slump in the hydrocarbon sector beginning in the mid-1980s, rampant corruption, rapid population growth and high unemployment all served to fuel the breakdown of the ruling FLN (Front de Libération Nationale) regime and the rise of the Islamists. Taken alone, however, a socioeconomic explanation for Algeria's woes is still not sufficient. From a historical perspective, the sudden, dramatic swing to the Islamist camp and resulting war for Algeria's soul needs to be understood as the latest chapter in a pattern of extreme changes and dislocations which have marked Algerian history: the general absence in pre-colonial times of a relatively strong central authority and unified political tradition (as compared to Morocco); the thoroughgoing destruction of existing elites by the colonial power; the terrible bloodletting during the war of independence between 1954–62, not just between Algerian Muslims and the Europeans, but within the Muslim community as well; and the superimposing of a mobilizing, revolutionary ideology and authoritarian leadership on the newly independent state which left no room for other visions or political activity.

Throughout the post-independence years, the ruling authorities in Algiers, like their counterparts elsewhere in the Maghrib and Mashriq alike, sought to manipulate Islam in the service of the regime.[34] Measures taken included enacting a personal status code in 1984 that adhered closely to Islamic precepts, banning alcohol in some cities, making Friday the day of rest, promoting religious education in the schools and accelerating the implementation of an Arabization program in schools and public institutions. At the same time, the FLN regime, first under Houari Boumediène and subsequently under Chedli Benjedid, sought to wed Islam to the governing socialist, revolutionary ideology and prevent any independent manifestations of Islamic political activity, whether urban-reformist or rural-popular.[35] Algerian Islamists, for their part, had to go to Tunisia, Morocco or Cairo for proper Islamic training, because Algeria lacked an Islamic institution of high caliber.[36] It is thus not surprising that Algeria has not produced Islamist theoreticians comparable to Khomeini, Turabi, or Ghannushi. Indeed, the 'thinness' of Islamist clerics, in both numbers and learnedness,[37] might make it more difficult for the Islamists to govern effectively, should they come to power. This scenario is markedly different from Iran where the religious classes were able to swiftly step in and establish sophisticated networks of power, even down to the neighborhood level.

Notwithstanding the regime's efforts to monopolize and manipulate Islam, signs of an Islamic revival outside of authorized state structures were widespread during the 1970s and 1980s:[38] violent clashes between leftists and radical Islamists occurred on university campuses; Mustafa Bouyali, an ex-FLN fighter in the war of independence, attempted to promote an armed insurrection in the countryside between 1984 and 1987; and the regime placed hundreds of activists in detention, including a number of the future founders of the Front Islamique du Salut (FIS). Islamists also expanded their grassroots activities in the social welfare sphere.[39] Nonetheless, nearly all observers believed that the authorities still had matters well in hand. The literature analyzing Algeria during the period is devoid of any reference to 'Abbasi Madani, the most prominent personage of the soon to be established FIS, or any sense that the Islamists had reached a critical mass.[40] Obviously we cannot demand clairvoyance, and the situation did become increasingly more dynamic and fluid after 1988. Nevertheless, it is a fact that scholars and observers, many of them 'secular-modern' Algerians, were slow to recognize the budding power of the Islamists.

This tendency continued even following the FIS's success in the 1990 municipal elections. Many sought to explain away the movement's success as a mere protest against a discredited and corrupt FLN regime, which to a large extent it was, or as a result of voter apathy or the boycott of the municipal elections by other political parties. But what in the end stands out as most salient was the FIS's ability to repeatedly mobilize large-scale support in competitive, highly-charged electoral contests, even after its top echelon was imprisoned in June 1991, and then its capability to mount a sustained armed uprising beginning in January 1992. The two more moderate, 'gradualist' Islamist parties, Hamas, led by Mahfoud Nahnah, and al-Nahda, headed by Shaykh 'Abdallah Djaballah, were completely overwhelmed by the FIS and attained only minimal support in the elections.

One keen observer of Algeria, Hugh Roberts, explains the FIS's appeal in the context of modern Algerian history. In ideological terms, he states, the FIS has developed the Islamic aspect of the FLN's governing vision, rather than repudiating it entirely.[41] In fact, the FIS explicitly claims to be the new bearers of the FLN's torch and the authentic inheritors of the FLN's legacy. The FIS-FLN connection is further strengthened by the fact that Shaykh 'Abbasi Madani, first among equals of the FIS leadership, was an early member of the FLN and was even imprisoned for his activities on behalf of the FLN for most of the period between 1954 and 1962. Also like the FLN, the FIS maintains a sort of collective leadership, befitting its status as a 'front' and helping it to gather together a number of streams and groups that supported Algerian Islamism. But what is most important is that the FIS remained a political body, giving primacy to political action over religious activities.[42]

Its two most prominent figures prior to their imprisonment in June 1991, Madani and 'Ali Belhadj, epitomize the two faces of FIS. Madani is in his mid-60s and holds a doctorate from the Institute of Education at the University of London. Although unswerving in his insistence on the establishment of an Islamic state governed by the *shari'a* and on the need to reinstitute allegedly Islamic norms, such as the separation of men and women in the workplace, his tone prior to imprisonment was relatively benign and his commitment to political pluralism, while ultimately tactical, at least left room for a dialogue with the other political forces in Algeria. In this regard, he told one interviewer that pluralism was absolutely necessary for a just society. 'We are not angels', he said, 'we make mistakes...there were different views and opinions even among the Prophet Muhammad's associates...we'll make Algeria a Hyde Park not only for free expression but also for choice and behavior'.[43] While Madani was talking about Hyde Park, 'Ali Belhadj, a 28 year-old preacher based in a mosque in the teeming Bab el-Oued quarter of Algiers, was exerting a powerful appeal to the masses of deprived and frustrated youth. His militant message was unadorned: combat the 'French' (meaning Algeria's secular forces), transform Algeria into an Islamic state immediately, by elections, if possible, and if the authorities reject the peaceful transfer of power, by force, and exact retribution on all those who have committed crimes against the people.[44]

If the FIS's mobilizing capacity in the street and in the electoral arena was impressive, no less significant has been the Islamists' ability to survive a brutal, unrestrained crackdown by the Algerian military authorities since January 1992, and even to respond by inflicting heavy punishment of their own. One can perhaps partially ascribe the Islamists' resilience to the movement's very nature as a 'front'. This structure enabled the movement to attract not only PhDs like Madani, preachers like Belhadj and the intellectuals of the so-called 'algerianization current', but also ex-army officers, radical militants who had already served prison terms for violent anti-regime actions in the 1980s as part of the Bouyali group, various *'jama'at'* (societies), whose spiritual and military leader, Shaykh 'Umar al-'Alami, was killed by the security forces in April 1993, members of the *takfir wal-hijra* group,[45] modeled after, and perhaps connected to the Egyptian radicals of the same name, and the so-called 'Afghans', Algerian veterans of the Afghanistan War against the Soviet-backed regime in Kabul.

The armed struggle against the regime has been conducted by two loosely organized bodies. The larger is the Mouvement Islamique Armé (MIA), more recently known as l'Armé Islamique du Salut, which functions as the unofficial armed wing of the FIS. The second, a smaller Islamist coalition of different armed networks, is the Group Islamique Armé (GIA). The GIA is more 'purist' in its advocacy of unbridled violence and has been responsible for some of the more shocking acts of murder and terror during the last 18 months. These have included the burning of schools, the slitting of the throats of 'immodestly' dressed women, car bombs in crowded city streets, and the hijacking of an Air France jetliner. The GIA's approach may constitute an Islamic version of Frantz Fanon's teachings on the cleansing, purifying properties of violence.

The decentralization among the armed groups renders the Islamists more prone to infighting. This was particularly evident in the case of the so-called 'war of the leaders' in 1993 that pitted the MIA's 'Abelkader Chebouti against the GIA's 'Abdelahaq Layada. Following the latter's arrest by Moroccan authorities in the Algerian-Moroccan border area and subsequent handing over to the Algerian authorities, Chebouti gained the advantage. However, one report described this as a double-edged sword, since Layada is likely to repay Chebouti's alleged betrayal in kind.[46]

Decentralization, or even fragmentation, may be a weakness for the Islamists. However, it is also, in some respects, a strength, complicating the efforts of the governmental authorities to defeat them. The number of Islamist fighters may come close to 10,000 and they clearly have considerable backing within the population. This popular support is often reinforced by the harsh repressive measures of the authorities.

Questions have been raised about the degree of control that the Islamist civilian leadership exerts over the MIA. Makhloufi, for example, was removed from the FIS Higher Council in July 1991, owing to his utter opposition to the democratic process as a means for creating an Islamic state. Chebouti, although close to 'Ali Belhadj, was never a member of the FIS or its Consultative Council. One of Madani's preconditions for a meaningful dialogue with the government is that the entire leadership, including the military wing, be pardoned and allowed to engage freely in consultations among themselves. The government has rejected this demand and consequently its efforts to conduct a substantive dialogue with Madani in the fall of 1994 floundered. In a more recent development, FIS representatives took part in a dialogue of eight opposition parties, held in Rome in January 1995, and signed a joint statement calling for the 'progressive return of civil peace' based on the relegalization of the FIS and the freeing of jailed FIS activists in return for a gradual end to violence, negotiations for the establishment of a transitional government to prepare for multi-party elections and the formation of an independent commission to investigate abuses of human rights.[47]

As for the GIA, its leaders have repeatedly been killed by the security forces and its current inner workings remain shrouded in mystery. Further complicating the picture is the widespread belief that the GIA is thoroughly penetrated by the regime's intelligence units. Some have gone so far as to blame those within the regime who oppose a dialogue with the Islamists for some of the GIA's violent acts.[48] Another case of Middle Eastern conspiracy theory at play?[49] Perhaps. However, there are important components of the regime, both military and civilian, led by chief of staff Mohammed Lamari, Generals Nezzar and Belkheir, and former PM Redha Malek, who suspect that President Liamine Zeroual's pursuit of dialogue with the Islamist political wing will inevitably open the door to an eventual Islamist takeover. Known as the 'eradicators', they advocate a one-track policy of crushing the Islamist threat with whatever means necessary and may very well pose a threat to Zeroual's hold on power. Still another complicating factor is the increasing unrest in the Berber stronghold of Kabylia, the only area in which the FIS failed to triumph in the 1991 elections. An Islamist triumph or even a deal between the regime and the FIS is viewed by many Kabylians as posing a threat to their interests, which center on demands for the recognition of *Tamazight* as an official language alongside Arabic, the right to promote and develop *Tamazight* culture, secularism, democracy, and perhaps even communal autonomy. Given the current crisis, self-conscious Berber activism increasingly has the scent of at least a proto-nationalist current.

By now it should be evident that a successful 'reinvention' of the Algerian political community is a long way off. Even if the intermittent efforts at dialogue eventually bear some fruit, bringing an early end to the violence and putting together an interim national pact or power-sharing arrangement seem to be almost impossible tasks. What is left of the state, that is the military and security apparatus, bureaucracy, and civilian politicians, still possesses considerable coercive power. So do the Islamists. Despite the numerous political parties on the scene, the January 1995 Rome declaration does not yet portend the emergence of a democratic 'third force' which would occupy the middle ground between a noxious, repressive regime and an equally noxious, radical opposition. Nor do the smaller, more moderate Islamist alternatives to the FIS have any political following.

Throughout the three years of civil war, most observers continued to believe that the Islamists would eventually gain the upper hand. One alternative possibility which was mooted was the partial disintegration of the political system and state structures and the possible emergence of multiple power centers in different geographical regions, a kind of 'warlordism'. Up until now, however, the military's ability to survive and maintain power during the years of bloodletting vividly contrasts with the disintegration of the Iranian military during the last days of the Shah. One key variable to watch will undoubtedly be the regime's ability to block any attempts at disrupting the petro-chemical complexes which provide it with the finances necessary to stay afloat (again the Iranian experience comes to mind). Another crucial variable will be the position of the western powers, particularly France. Algerian-French relations have always been brittle, a legacy of their historically tortured relationship. Tensions between the Algerian regime and the French government rose anew in December 1994–January 1995, following the hijacking of an Air France jet in Algiers by Muslim militants, its subsequent flight to France, and eventually its storming by French commandos. The event occasioned bitter, mutual recriminations by both state officials and the media. The Rome agreement by Algerian opposition groups drew a favorable reaction from France's Foreign Minister, Alain Juppé, to the Zeroual government's dismay.[50] Both French and American officials hoped that stimulating renewed political dialogue would help to jump-start the process and lead to a lessening of violence. At the same time, a public policy of support for dialogue could threaten to erode the strength of the regime. As it happened, French policy in 1995, under its newly elected president Jacques Chirac, was geared to bolstering the Algerian authorities, even at the expense of increased Islamist terrorism inside France itself. France continues to perceive the existing regime as the lesser of two evils. Along with its fellow European Union Mediterranean littorals, Spain and Italy, France fears a massive wave of Algerian emigration across the Mediterranean in the event of an Islamist triumph. This, of course, is a scenario to be avoided at all costs.

## Assessment

An Islamist FIS triumph, should it come, will surely embolden Islamist groups in other countries. However, there is enough evidence of diversity within the Maghrib to avoid a simplistic application of that old American concept, the domino theory. Much will depend on the attitudes and behavior of the Islamist leadership after coming to power. Undoubtedly, it would be beset by the enormous task of consolidation and stabilization of power. Such a task, to be sure, did not prevent Islamic Iran from simultaneously looking outward and adopting a revisionist foreign policy. Once again, however, the differences in the two sets of circumstances outweigh the similarities. Morocco does not pose the kind of threat to, or provide the kind of opportunity for, Algeria that Iraq did for Iran; the FIS leadership does not contain anyone with the personal stature of Khomeini; and Algeria does not possess the geopolitical weight of Iran.

Moroccan-Algerian relations would likely be tense in the event of an Islamist triumph. To be sure, there was never any love lost between Morocco and the radical FLN regime and the Moroccans have always expressed confidence that they are immune from the kind of upheaval besetting Algeria. Moreover, Morocco's King Hassan has already hedged some of his bets, having suggested that it would have been preferable had the Algerian electoral process been carried out to its conclusion, if only to point out the inability of the fundamentalists to fulfill their promises.[51] Nonetheless, Hassan's own combination of Islam, monarchy, and modernity is anathema to Algeria's Islamists. Morocco's cooperation with the Algerian authorities in tracking down and extraditing Islamist guerrillas using Morocco as a sanctuary, most notably the GIA's Layada,[52] is not likely to be forgotten by an Islamist government. One can certainly envisage a continuation of the traditional Algerian-Moroccan rivalry for regional preeminence.

Tunisia may be more vulnerable, owing to its small size, its long border with Algeria, its dependence on tourism (a target of Islamist extremists in Egypt), and the encouragement which an FIS triumph would give to Tunisia's Islamists. Tunisia's vulnerability was further demonstrated in a February 1995 cross-border attack by Algerian Islamists, in which a number of Tunisian border policemen were killed. Since then, Algerian and Tunisian security forces have cooperated in attempting to root out Islamists on both sides of the frontier. Tunisia has eagerly sought support from other Arab regimes in combatting Islamic extremism, particularly in the annual meetings of Arab Interior Ministers. Even more importantly, western support for its traditional Moroccan and Tunisian allies will be vital if they are to stave off Islamist challenges. As for the attitudes of the regimes themselves in Tunis and Rabat, their innate tendencies to maintain firm grips on power and block Islamist political activism have only been reinforced by the Algerian experience.

A final note of caution is perhaps warranted. The degree of political stability in North Africa during the next decade will undoubtedly be influenced by the outcome of the Islamist-regime confrontation in Algeria. Still, in retrospect, Algeria has always been *sui generis* in the Arab world. It had the least distinct historical identity in pre-colonial times of any of the Maghrib's geopolitical units and indeed perhaps even of all the Arab lands.

It experienced the most thorough colonization, the most brutal, violent struggle for independence, the closest application of the Soviet/Eastern European model of development and political organization, and now, the most comprehensive collapse (Lebanon excepted). Other Arab regimes never imitated the Algerian model of development. Nor did Algeria ever really project power beyond its borders, apart from the vacuum in the Western Sahara. If historical patterns are any guide, perhaps an Islamist triumph in Algeria, if it is to come, will have less of a revolutionary impact in the region, at least initially, than one might expect. One can also expect that Algeria's neighbors, together with the regimes of the Arab world and the West, will seek to contain an Islamic Algeria with a combination of blandishments and inducements. In any case, the real challenge facing Arab regimes in the Maghrib and beyond will continue to come from within. The degree of mutual aid and succor among the Islamists (more of an Islamic 'global village' than an 'internationale'),[53] while not negligible, does not represent an irresistible force. Modern states, singly and in alliances, possess considerable capacities of their own.

## NOTES

Thanks to Remy Leveau, Francis Ghiles, Norman Stillman, Gideon Gera and Ofra Bengio for their constructive comments at different stages in the preparation of this article. Naturally, I alone am responsible for any shortcomings in the final product.

1. Fatima Mernissi, *Islam and Democracy: Fear of the Modern World* (Reading, MA: Addison-Wesley 1992) pp.13–14. The *gharb*, Mernissi writes, is 'the place of darkness and the incomprehensible, always frightening. *Gharb* is the territory of the strange, the foreign...the place where the sun sets and where darkness awaits. It is in the West that the night snaps up the sun and swallows it; then all terrors are possible. It is there that *gharaba* (strangeness) has taken up its abode.' As she also points out, in Arab-Islamic spatial terms, the land of the setting sun, the Far West, is *al-maghrib al-aqsa*, with not dissimilar connotations.
2. Benedict Anderson, *Imagined Communities* (London: Verso 1991).
3. Jamil M. Abun-Nasr, *A History of the Maghrib in the Islamic Period* (Cambridge: CUP 1987) pp.334–5.
4. Ibid. pp.38–91; idem., 'The Salafiyya Movement in Morocco: the Religious Bases of the Moroccan Nationalist Movement', in Albert Hourani (ed.), *St. Antony's Papers, Middle Eastern Affairs* 3 (London: Oxford UP 1963).
5. Michael Hudson, *Arab Politics: The Search for Legitimacy* (New Haven, CT: Yale UP 1977) p.379.
6. Remy Leveau, 'Reflections on the State in the Maghreb', in George Joffé (ed.), *North Africa: Nation, State and Region* (London: Routledge 1993) p.247.
7. Abdelbaki Hermassi, 'State and Democratization in the Maghreb', in Ellis Goldberg, Resat Kasalen and Joel Migdal (eds.), *Rules and Rights in the Middle East* (Seattle, WA: University of Washington Press 1993) pp.106–7.
8. Kevin Dwyer, *Arab Voices* (Berkeley: University of California Press 1991) p.15; Ali El-Kenz, *Algerian Reflections on Arab Crises* (Austin: University of Texas Press 1991).
9. Mernissi (note 1) p.56.
10. Hermassi (note 7) pp.111–12.

11. Remy Leveau points out the irony that the term *amir al mu'minin* did not appear in the initial text of the 1962 constitution. Ironically, 'it was the representatives of the [political] parties who reintroduced divine right among the instruments of power'. 'Islam et controle politique au Maroc', cited in Francois Burgat and William Dowell, *The Islamic Movement in North Africa* (Austin: University of Texas Press 1993) p.167, n.3.

12. Henry Munson, *Religion and Power in Morocco* (New Haven: Yale UP 1993), makes such a cogent argument, taking issue with Clifford Geertz's classic, *Islam Observed: Religious Development in Morocco and Indonesia* (New Haven, CT: Yale UP 1968); and, Elaine Combs-Schilling, *Sacred Performances: Islam, Sexuality and Sacrifice* (NY: Columbia UP 1989).

13. *Hassan II: Le Memoire d'un Roi. Entretiens Avec Eric Luarent* (Paris: Plon 1993) p.103.

14. Along the lines laid forth by John Entelis, *Culture and Counterculture in Moroccan Politics* (Boulder, CO: Westview Press 1989). The term 'modernizing monarchy' is taken from Hudson (note 5).

15. Mohammed Tozy, 'Champ et contre champ politico-religieux au Maroc', cited by Burgat and Dowell (note 11) p.170.

16. Munson (note 12) pp.153–8.

17. E.E. Shahin, 'Under the Shadow of the Imam', *Middle East Insight* 11/3 (Jan.-Feb. 1995) pp.42–3.

18. Burgat and Dowell (note 11) pp.166–7.

19. For the details of their activities, see *Jeune Afrique*, 12–18 Jan. 1995.

20. Susan Waltz, 'Islamist Appeal in Tunisia', *Middle East Journal* 40/4 (Autumn 1986) pp.651–70.

21. Nikkie Keddie makes the important point that Bourguiba's policies, e.g., the adoption of the Personal Status Code in 1956, were not simply blind imitations of western codes (unlike Attaturk in Turkey), but contained features from the *shari'a*. 'The Islamist Movement in Tunisia', *The Maghreb Review* 2/1 (1986) p.26.

22. Burgat and Dowell (note 11) p.234.

23. For the essence of their thinking and activities, see Yvonne Y. Haddad, 'Sayyid Qutb: Ideologue of Islamic Revival', and Charles J. Adams, 'Mawdudi and the Islamic State', in John L. Esposito (ed.), *Voices of Resurgence Islam* (NY: Oxford UP 1983) pp.67–133; and, Emmanuel Sivan, *Radical Islam* (New Haven, CT: Yale UP 1985).

24. See statement by Ahmad Enneifer, one of the Tunisian 'progressive Islamists' who separated from Ghannushi, in Burgat and Dowell (note 11) pp.217–18.

25. Norma Salem, 'Tunisia', in Shireen T. Hunter (ed.), *The Politics of Islamic Revivalism* (Bloomington: Indiana UP 1988) p.164.

26. 'Rached Channouchi: Penseur et Tribun', interview, *Les Cahiers de L'Orient* 27 (1992); *The Observer*, 19 Jan. 1992, quoted in Shahin (note 17).

27. For a detailed study of Ghannushi's thinking on key issues, see Khaled Elgindy, 'The Rhetoric of Rashid Ghannushi', *Arab Studies Journal* (Spring 1995) pp.101–19.

28. Interview in *al-Shira'*, 24 Oct. 1994.

29. Michael Collins Dunn, 'The Al-Nahda Movement in Tunisia: From Renaissance to Revolution', in John Ruedy (ed.), *Islamism and Secularism in North Africa* (Washington, DC: Georgetown UP 1994) pp.149–65.

30. *New York Times*, 9 Jan. 1994.

31. *Al-Shira'*, 24 Oct. 1994; text of speech at the Royal Institute of International Affairs (RIIA), Chatham House, London, 9 May – *MSANEWS*, 23 May 1995.

32. Speech at conference of Islamic Committee for Palestine, cited by S. Emerson in testimony to United States House of Representatives International Relations Committee, Subcommittee on Africa, 6 April 1995.

33. *RIIA* speech (note 31).

34. Mohammed Tozy, 'Les tendances de l'islamisme en Algerie', *Confluences Mediterranée* 12 (Autumn 1994) pp.51–4.

35. Boutheina Cheriet, 'Islamism and Feminism: Algeria's "Rites of Passage" to Democracy', in John P. Entelis and Phillip C. Naylor (eds.), *State and Society in Algeria* (Boulder, CO: Westview Press 1992) pp.171–215; Mohammed Tozy, 'Islam and the State', in I. William

Zartman and William Mark Habeeb (eds.), *Polity and Society in Contemporary North Africa* (Boulder, CO: Westview Press 1993) pp.108–9,199–20.

36. Mohammed Arkoun, 'Algeria', in Hunter (note 25) p.180.
37. According to the Minister of Religious Affairs (in 1981), three-fifths of the *imams* in official mosques were not sufficiently qualified to comment on the Koran and the Sunna accurately. Jean-Claude Vatin, 'Popular Puritanism Versus State Reformism: Islam in Algeria', in James P. Piscatori (ed.), *Islam in the Political Process* (Cambridge: CUP 1983) p.112; in the same volume, cf. Michael C. Hudson, 'The Islamic Factor in Syrian and Iraqi Politics' pp.73–97.
38. Vatin (note 37) pp.99–101.
39. Rabia Bekkar, 'Taking Up Space in Tlemcen: The Islamist Opposition in Urban Algeria', *Middle East Report* 22/6 (Nov.-Dec. 1992) pp.11–15.
40. Mohammed Arkoun, 'Algeria', in Hunter (note 25) pp.171–86.
41. Hugh Roberts, 'A Trial of Strength: Algerian Islamism', in James P. Piscatori (ed.), *Islamic Fundamentalisms and the Gulf Crisis* (Chicago: The American Acadamy of the Arts and Sciences 1991) p.144.
42. Remy Leveau, *Le sabre et le turban* (Paris: François Boulin 1993) pp.194–7; Hugh Roberts, 'From Radical Mission to Equivocal Ambition: The Expansion and Manipulation of Algerian Islamism 1979–1992', in Martin E. Marty and R. Scott Appelby (eds.), *Accounting for Fundamentalism* 4 (Chicago: University of Chicago Press 1994) pp.428–89.
43. *Al-Watan* (Kuwait) 22 June 1990 – *FBIS-NES, Daily Report* (DR), 27 June 1990.
44. Roberts argues forcefully that 'Abassi's and Belhadj's views complemented rather than contradicted one another. For the richest, and at times most provocative analysis of regime-Islamist dynamics in Algeria up until the 1992 military coup, see Roberts, 'From Radical Mission to Equivocal Ambition' (note 42) pp.428–89.
45. The name evokes the Prophet Muhammad's rejection of infidel society and exodus with his followers from Mecca to Medina in the year 622 AD.
46. For various, and often contradictory accounts of the activities and organizational aspects of the Islamist groups, see *al-Watan al 'Arabi*, 30 April, 25 June – *Joint Publication Research Service* (JPRS-NEA), 13 May, 30 July 1993; *al-Majalla*, 12 May 1993; *Intelligence Newsletter*, 3 June 1993; *Le Nouvel Afrique Asie*, 9 May 1993 – *JPRS-NEA*, 27 May 1993.
47. *Le Monde*, 13 Jan. 1995; *Financial Times*, 14–15 Jan. 1995.
48. See, e.g., analyses by Qusay Darwish, *al-Sharq al-Awsat*, quoted in *Mideast Mirror,* 13 July 1994, and, Muhammad al-Shawi, *al-Wasat*, 25 July, quoted in *Mideast Mirror*, 22 July 1994.
49. Daniel Pipes, 'Dealing With Middle Eastern Conspiracy Theories', *ORBIS* 36/1 (Winter 1992) pp.41–56.
50. *Financial Times*, 3 Jan. 1995; *Le Monde*, 18 Jan. 1995.
51. *Le Figaro*, 22 Feb., quoted by *Radio Rabat*, 22 Feb. – *DR*, 24 Feb. 1992; *Al-Sharq al-Awsat*, 13 Jan. – *DR*, 14 Jan. 1993.
52. *Al-Hayat*, 11 June – *JPRS-NEA*, 9 July 1993; see also the criticism of Morocco's treatment of FIS activists in its territory by a Parisian-based FIS leader (*Reuters World Service*, 3 June 1994).
53. I owe this distinction to Dr. Martin Kramer.

# Islamic versus Other Identities in the Greater Middle East: Comments on the Ex-Soviet Muslim Republics

## JACOB M. LANDAU

The six newly independent, ex-Soviet Muslim republics share many characteristics. Common to all are identity conflicts based on ethnic ties, cultural traditions and attitudes to Islam. Most ethno-nationalist groups have been mythologizing their past history and culture. Islam remains, however, the most important factor determining identity throughout the area, although in diverse ways. Realizing this, most political elites take an unfavorable view of the flow of extreme religious propaganda from Iran and Saudi Arabia and of the incursions from Afghanistan. Aware of the revival of Islam, some political leaders of the new states strive to encourage various patterns of moderate religion as a bulwark against militant Islam.

Taken together, the six ex-Soviet republics offer a special case in the history of the search for political identity. All of them were as surprised as the rest of the world by the collapse of the Soviet Union and were hardly prepared to deal with the new situation. While there are many instances in modern times of nations in search of a state, each of the six is a state in search of a nation. Azerbayjan in the Caucasus, and the five in Central Asia – Uzbekistan, Kazakhstan, Turkmenistan, Tajikistan and Kyrghyzstan – are remarkably diverse, ethnically, culturally and regionally.[1] Nevertheless, they share several important characteristics: they have a common religion; for 70 years they were a part of the Soviet Union; and they achieved almost universal literacy in Russian, which effectively meant a high degree of Russification and communist indoctrination. In turn, Sovietization was expressed in an intensive secularization campaign, promoting non-belief and denigrating – sometimes persecuting – Islam.[2]

Since the official Islamic institutions were bureaucratically imposed and controlled by the regime,[3] a sort of parallel, semi-clandestine folk-Islam survived in the Sufi, i.e., mystic and other fraternities in the shadowy area between the legal and the illegal. Islam and other ideologies, such as nationalism, found it increasingly difficult to compete openly with Communism, which was supported and propagated by the state, the party and the media. All this has been changing since the Soviet liberalization policies were introduced in 1988 and even more so since independence in

1991. Parallel Islam, no longer in need of furtiveness, has moved nearer to official Islam, while the rivalry between religious and other ideologies has been assuming a somewhat different character.

### Identity Conflict since Independence

In the late 1980s, in the atmosphere of *perestroika* and *glasnost* as encouraged by Mikhail Gorbachev, the overall situation started to change, as proponents of Islam, nationalism, pluralism, liberalism, market reform and other ideas began – cautiously at first – to propound their views.[4] This process has become evident, in varying degrees, in all six republics since independence and provides proof of the search for identity. The Homo Sovieticus continues, indeed, to exist even after the dismemberment of the Soviet Union. The issue of his or her identity, particularly complex for Soviet Muslims – involving sympathies, attachments and allegiances at various levels – remains problematic. It has now become focal in each of the republics, as their inhabitants must determine their identity for themselves rather than having it decided for them by Moscow as before. Although economic and political affairs seem more immediately pressing, questions about self-perception and identity change are nevertheless increasingly being posed. Individuals and groups ask themselves whether they are Muslims, Turks, Azeris, Uzbeks, Kazakhs, and so forth.[5]

In order to understand better the general background of the current discourse about self-perceptions, characteristically specific to each of the six republics, one has to remember that their independence, although formally recognized, is not as complete as many both in the republics and outside have been led to believe. Within the newly formed Commonwealth of Independent States, Russia has clearly been aiming to re-integrate, in one way or another, all the states of the former Soviet Union. Its own role remains paramount, even hegemonic, in relation to the Muslim and other republics for demographic, economic and military reasons.

Some ten million Russians live in the six Muslim republics, about a sixth of their entire population; in Kazakhstan, almost 40 per cent of the population is either Russian or Ukrainian. Further, in many of the important cities and towns throughout the republics, Russians form an absolute majority and consider Russia as their protector. Economically, the Muslim republics depend on Russia for their markets, spare parts for their industries and – to a large extent – their currencies, some of which are still based on the ruble. Militarily, Russian forces have been called in by Tajikistan to stem incursions from Afghanistan, and Azerbayjan also called for Russian military support in order prevent a total defeat by Armenia in the Nagorno-Karabakh War. These Russian forces are there to stay and may even be called in by others as well, since all six republics have small armies with antiquated weapons. Indeed, their own military forces are altogether insignificant and inadequate for any task beyond maintaining internal order.

Russian political, military and economic agents have continued to cooperate closely with local officials who had been their former associates in the state bureaucracy, the Communist Party, the KGB, the police or other organizations. These elements, the only ones with some experience in public administration, have assumed power in the new republics, even where general elections have been held. The only state president who had not been active in the Communist bureaucracy is Askar Akayev of Kyrghyzstan, but even his own circle unavoidably includes former Communist officials. In all the Muslim republics, such people form the new – and not so new – ruling elites. They are responsible for decision-making in practically all spheres of life, under strong-handed regimes largely reminiscent of totalitarianism, and even if some have abjured Communism, one cannot say how wholeheartedly. When a nationalist government was elected in Azerbayjan, headed by Abulfaz Elçibey, its opponents, reportedly supported by Russia, staged a military coup and President Elçibey was forced to flee to his power base in the autonomous Azerbayjan province of Nakhichevan on the Turkish border.[6]

With communism – sometimes labeled 'socialism' or some other term – firmly implanted in the ruling elite of each of the six republics, other ideologies aiming at shaping the populations into distinct identities are in direct conflict, overtly and covertly, with communism no less than with each other. These ideologies include Islam, nationalism, Pan-Turkism (advocating a political, cultural or economic union of all groups of Turkic origins), or local Pan-ideologies, such as Pan-Azerism (preaching a united state made up of independent Azerbayjan and the province of Azerbayjan in Iran), Pan-Uzbekism (intending to rally all Uzbeks everywhere with Uzbekistan), and others. Of all these ideologies, the most prevalent are nationalism and Islam.

Nationalism is a potentially important force in each of the six new republics, although not necessarily to the same degree everywhere. To use a term borrowed from the title of Benedict Anderson's 1983 book, their 'imagined communities' are perceived differently not only among the populations of the separate republics, but also by the various groups that comprise each state. Due to the artificial boundaries previously imposed by the Soviets, each of the republics contains various autonomous groups, differing in ethnicity, culture and language – even without counting immigrant groups such as Russians, Ukrainians, Germans and others. Thus, Uzbekistan is composed of 75 per cent Uzbeks and 15 per cent Tajiks, as well as others, resulting in friction between the two largest communities. In various ratios, this differentiation is also applicable to the other five republics. Under these conditions, two or more ethnic-cultural communities in each republic influence self-identification.

Efforts by more comprehensive nationalisms, such as Pan-Turkism, to foster a common national identity including the diverse groups from all of the republics (in the case of Pan-Turkism, this is with the exception of Tajikistan where about 75 per cent of the population is Iranian rather than Turkish) have so far failed. Elçibey, who considered himself both an Azeri nationalist and a Pan-Turkist ideologue, was ousted precisely because his opponents were apprehensive of the spread of such ideologies. The only political party active on nationalist – and, partly, Pan-Turk – premises in several of the republics, Birlik (Union, or Unity) has been harassed, then banned, and seems now to be of little consequence.

Despite such repression – or, perhaps, due to it – national awareness based on ethnic ties is developing to some extent at a popular, rather than an elite, level. Azerbayjan is a case in point, probably influenced, in part at least, by the popular sentiment aroused during its six-year war with Armenia. In the other republics as well, there are similar indications of budding or growing nationalism, chiefly in situations of inter-ethnic conflict. Most nationalist groups, perhaps all of them, are busy mythologizing their past, in order to create common denominators for national pride – a phenomenon familiar to quite a few other nationalist movements. However for the time being at least, national consciousness based on ethnicity and culture has not produced nationalist movements in the West-European tradition. Rather these tendencies, as in Uzbekistan, are particularist and self-assertive, frequently marked by cultural features, chiefly passionate devotion to their respective languages as well as to their *ethnie* (to use a French term introduced in this context by Anthony D. Smith). Thus, Uzbekness has become the order of the day for some Uzbeks, although it is not easy to determine precisely the amount of political and social support it gets.

## Islam in Politics and Society

This leaves us with Islam as a factor determining identity, with varying impact, over most of the area we are discussing. Its hold on Azeri and Central Asian societies, following decades of officially imposed atheism, indicates that it is a political factor of considerable potency. Further, the importance of Islam lies also in the fact that, with the exception of immigrants from European Russia and such small groups as Armenians, Jews and a few others, the entire population is Muslim, mostly Sunni, except for Azerbayjan, where about 70 per cent are Shi'i. The Sunni-Shi'i cleavage is not the only one marking the diversity in Islam throughout the six republics and, to some extent, within each of them. Islam means different things to different people. Traditionally, Islam has been stronger in the rural areas (but not among the nomad tribes) and, organizationally, more conspicuous in the urban ones. It has been less visible – or, at least, less publicly articulate – in Kazakhstan, Turkmenistan and Kyrghyzstan, all Islamized relatively late (in the 18th and 19th centuries).[7]

In Uzbekistan and Tajikistan, on the other hand, Islam is more active politically. In the former, as James Critchlow, an expert on contemporary Uzbekistan, tells us, 'in no area of Uzbek life has the social change of recent years been more spectacular than in that of religion'.[8] One sign of this is groups like the Islamic Renaissance Party, set up in the town of Namangan in 1990, which demand the establishment of an Islamic republic. This presence induced Islam Karimov, president of Uzbekistan and not religiously-minded, to take the oath of office on the Koran.[9]

In Tajikistan, the impact of the 1979 revolution in Iran and of Soviet intervention in neighboring Afghanistan soon afterwards was quite marked. The fact that one of the most successful commanders among the Afghan *mujahidin* was a Tajik, Ahmad Shah Mas'ud, who later became powerful in the new government of Afghanistan, was duly noted in Tajikistan. Since independence, publications and cassettes of a fundamentalist Islamic character have been distributed in Tajikistan,[10] and the Islamic Renaissance Party has been championing the Islamization of society more vociferously there than in the other republics, albeit clandestinely at times.[11] In the mid-1991 uprising against the Communist Party of Tajikistan, and even more so in the recent civil war there, the party played a visible role.[12] It may also have had a hand in the Islamic-motivated protests and demonstrations against Rahman Nabiyev's elections as state president.[13]

All this does not imply, of course, that an Islamic ideology, insofar as it can be pinpointed, is widespread as such, although the current governments fear that a trend towards Islam – and chiefly fundamentalist Islam – is imminently spanning the diversity in Caucasian and Central Asian Islam.[14] Therefore, most political leaders take an unfavorable view of the flow of extremist propaganda from Iran and the incursions of Islamic militants from Afghanistan, as well as of the economic penetration, with an avowed Islamic motivation, coming from Saudi Arabia and Pakistan. Hence most rulers attempt to counter these moves by a delicate balancing act between Iran, Russia and Turkey.[15] As a secular state and society based on western models, Turkey appeals to many of the ruling elites in five of the six republics, which have willingly accepted its economic-technological assistance and the cultural-educational cooperation it has offered, up to and including formal decisions to change their script from the Cyrillic to the Latin alphabet.[16] The exception is Tajikistan. With its strong affiliation to Persian culture, it has cooperated less with Turkey and, encouraged by Iran, opted to return to the Arabic script that was in use before the Soviet period. This will not only open up to its population the cultural treasures of Tajik and Persian literature and language, but also, by promoting the study of Arabic, facilitate the reading of the Koran and major Islamic works.

However, over time popular attitudes matter more than those of the rulers. In all six republics, the great mass of the population which had – and still has – strong reservations regarding Communism and its offshoots, apparently understands Islam better and finds it easier to identify with it as a complete way of life than nationalism, a somewhat foreign concept not essentially rooted in local traditions. While no detailed statistical information is available about the number of practicing believers,[17] it does seem that many people have at least a diffuse cultural sense of being Muslims. After all, Islam was the most powerful factor marking them off from the rest of the Soviet Union. Thus, they are not impervious to Islamic political activism in Iran and Afghanistan.

To elaborate, it is important to remember that, whatever the diversity of its expressions, Islam continues to influence the lives of many people in the six republics as a major component of their national culture. Even under Soviet domination, during the late 1980s there were signs of an Islamic revival, along with a certain resurgence in nationalism, both of which caused some concern to the Soviet leadership of the time.[18] However, as noted above, it is impossible to estimate, even at present, the figure of the religiously observant, although it is known that the overall number of religious organizations and their incomes are on the rise, that thousands of new mosques are being built and others repaired every year, and that numerous *mazars*, or burial places attributed to saints, are increasingly being visited by believers coming on pilgrimage from distant places.[19] Again, while informed sources report large crowds praying in the mosques, one cannot of course determine how many do this out of real conviction and how many others perform the ritual out of habit only; nor can one guess the number of those praying at home or work. Islamic festivals, however, seem to be often observed; the performing of pilgrimages to holy places has increased; circumcision is reported to be almost universal; and the wearing of religious symbols is frequent.[20] Folk Islam, as expressed in the Sufi fraternities, is also very much in evidence. At least in some cases, such as Uzbekistan, new regimes are encouraging folk Islam, apparently seeing it as a barrier to fundamentalist Islam.[21]

Since most Muslims in the republics live in villages, and those who have migrated to the towns maintain their ties with the rural environment, a traditional outlook persists and encourages the attachment to Islam. There is a potentially receptive audience for broadcasts to Tajikistan, for instance, from neighboring Pakistan and, even more so, from Iranian radio, which spreads the message of militant Islam through much of Central Asia. All these attempt to consolidate Muslim public opinion in the republics into an Islamic identity that would repudiate the mostly non-believer elites, on the premise that only Islamic social teachings can provide a remedy for the disruption of society caused by Soviet Marxism and western liberalism. The Islamic Renaissance Party is committed to these ideas and to solving all social problems according to the Koran and *hadith*. Indeed, it openly declares its intent to set up an Islamic regime in each of the republics. Its main activity has been in Uzbekistan, chiefly in the Ferghana Valley; in Daghestan and the Northern Caucasus; in Tajikistan, where it was banned; and to a lesser extent elsewhere in Muslim Central Asia, mostly in clandestine ways.[22] Its program, although not politically radical, emphasizes Islam's priority in every decision-making process. This is a rare example of Islamic elements in various republics collaborating within one single party. At the moment of writing there is still little coordination among Islamic groups in different regions of the Caucasus and Central Asia.[23] An exception may be seen in the assistance offered by Muslim volunteers from Daghestan and elsewhere in the Caucasus to their co-religionists in Chechniya, in January 1995, against the Russian military forces.

Militant fundamentalist Islam is not yet an integral part of the political scene in the six republics. Nor is there any certainty that it will grow in power and impact.[24] However, considering the widespread identification with Islam in the entire area, it was a source of anxiety to the Soviet Union and continues to be one today to its successor states. Just before the final disintegration of the Soviet Union, Gorbachev publicly attacked Islam in a famous speech delivered in 1986. In the subsequent years, Soviet Muslims were imprisoned for religious activities; and Islamic demonstrations, supposedly protected by the new *glasnost*, were harshly dealt with. The fear of fundamentalist Islam carried over to the independent Muslim republics. Their current ruling elites, some of whom seem to be running out of time in government due to the worsening economic situation in their respective states, are forced to contend simultaneously with a revival of national cultures and a revitalization of Islam. Another problem facing the political leaders is that they rule with little legitimacy, their control coming from above rather than through support from below. Public manifestations of religious adherence by several of these political leaders have failed to persuade Azeris and Central Asians that these acts are more than lip service.

Intellectuals in the republics have been doubting the feasibility of co-existence between communism (even in a reformed version), on the one hand, and nationalism and Islam, on the other. Some of the less conservative intellectuals favor nationalism as a means of nation building and forging ties with other secular groups. Some of the more conservative, however, prefer strengthening religion in order to promote a bond with Islamic groups in their own republics and abroad; several of their teachings are strongly reminiscent of political Pan-Islam, aiming at uniting politically all Muslims everywhere.[25] The on-going debate among such intellectuals and others demonstrates the identity crisis which pervades some of their thinking.[26]

## Conclusion

It is difficult to obtain definitive information on the precise situation in a wide and extremely fluid region which is undergoing rapid change and, even more so, to foresee its uncertain future. The only safe prediction is that due to the multi-varied character of the population in the republics, it will probably take years before it creates some definite identity for itself. A keen observer, Graham E. Fuller of the Rand Corporation, has said, in a work published in 1992,[27] that nationalism in each of the republics is assuming a more local, moderate and pragmatic image. This does not necessarily apply to Islam, since its proponents' call to 'Islamize modernity' clashes with their opponents' appeal to 'modernize Islam'.

One may suggest, however, that two broad options are open. Islam, heterogeneous as it is in the six republics, may still assume a more radical stance, causing states to draw closer to Islamic movements elsewhere in order, for instance, to obtain political support and financial assistance. In this case, militant Islam may serve as an alternative to nationalism, without automatically contradicting it. However, should the Islam of the new republics tie up with the non-radical Islamic states, such as those on the Gulf, moderation, rather than militant extremism, could determine the future character of Islam in one or more of the six republics. In the latter case, it seems quite likely that a national-religious symbiosis may yet emerge and that Islamic nationalism, of one sort or another,[28] will shape a relatively new identity there.

NOTES

1.  Background data may be found in numerous works, including Alexandre Bennigsen and Marie Broxup, *The Islamic Threat to the Soviet State* (London: Croom Helm 1983); Shirin Akiner, *Islamic Peoples of the Soviet Union* (London: Kegan Paul International 1983); Alexandre Bennigsen and S. Enders Wimbush, *Muslims of the Soviet Empire: A Guide* (London: C. Hurst 1985); Karl Grobe-Hagel, *Russlands 'Dritte Welt': Nationalitätenkonflikte und das Ende der Sowjetunion* (Frankfurt a/M: ISP Verlag 1992); Yalçin Toker, *The Great Awakening* (Turkish) (Ankara: Toker Yayinlari 1992); Roland Götz and Uwe Halbach, *Politisches Lexikon GUS* (Munich: C.H. Beck 1993); B. Zakir Avsar *et*

al., *Turkey and the Turkic Republics on the Threshold of A New Century* (Turkish) (Ankara: Vadi Yayinlari 1994).

2. Consider the facts and their evaluation in Peter Heine and Reinhold Stipek, *Ethnizität und Islam: Differenzierung und Integration Muslimischer Bevölkerungsgruppen* (Gelsenkirchen: Andreas Miller 1984) pp.87–101.

3. Tadeusz Swietochowski, 'Islam and Nationality in Tsarist Russia and the Soviet Union', in Henry R. Huttenbach (ed.), *Soviet Nationalist Policies: Ruling Ethnic Groups in the USSR* (London: Mansell 1990) pp.221–34; Edward Lazzerini, 'Through the Contact Lenses Darkly', in Shirin Akiner (ed.), *Political and Economic Trends in Central Asia* (London: Tauris 1994) pp.173–4.

4. One of the consequences of increasing openness in the domain of religion was the increasing number of complaints by believers, for instance of mosques kept under lock and key or of church bells not permitted to ring. See Azade Ayse Rorlich, 'Islam and Atheism: Dynamic Tension in Soviet Central Asia', in William Fierman (ed.), *Soviet Central Asia: The Failed Transformation* (Boulder, CO: Westview 1991) p.187.

5. See Graham E. Fuller, *Central Asia: The New Geopolitics* (Santa Monica, CA: Rand 1992) pp.3–6; Ahmed Rashid, *The Resurgence of Central Asia* (London: Zed Books 1994) 243 ff. For a specific case, the search for identity in Azerbayjan, see Eva-Maria Auch, 'Ewiges Feuer' in Aserbaidschan: Ein Land zwischen Perestrojka, Bürgerkrieg und Unabhängigkeit', *Berichte des Bundesinstituts für ostwissenschaftliche und internationale Studien* 8 (1992) pp.31–42.

6. G. Reza Sabri-Tabrizi, 'Azerbaijan and Armenian Conflict and Coexistence', in Anoushiravan Ehteshami (ed.), *From the Gulf to Central Asia: Players in the New Great Game* (Exeter: University of Exeter Press 1994) pp.146–67.

7. However, there are some signs of Islamic political activity in Kazakhstan, too, such as those of Alash, the local Islamic party, whose moves the government is watching closely. See R. Wright, 'Islam, Democracy and the West', *Foreign Affairs* 71/3 (Summer 1992) p.142; cf. B.B. 'Wir sind die Partei Allahs: ein Interview mit dem Mufti von Mittelasien und Kasachstan', *Osteuropa Archiv* 41/4 (April 1991) A187–A191.

8. James Critchlow, *Nationalism in Uzbekistan: A Soviet Republic's Road to Sovereignty* (Boulder, CO: Westview Press 1991) p.168.

9. Rainer Freitag-Wirminghaus, 'Die Zukunft der Islamisch geprägten Staaten: Der Zerfall der Sowjetunion und die Islamische Welt', *Der Bürger im Staat* (Stuttgart) 42/2 (June 1992) p.107.

10. Ahmad Taheri, 'Die Komsomolzen der Propheten', *Die Zeit* (weekly), 24 April 1992.

11. See G.G. Kosach, 'Tajikistan: Political Parties in an Inchoate National Space', in Yaacov Ro'i (ed.), *Muslim Eurasia: Conflicting Legacies* (London: Frank Cass 1995), esp. pp.124–40; Olivier Roy, 'Le Renouveau Islamique en URSS', *Revue du Monde Musulman et de la Méditerranée* 59/60 (1991) pp.140–1; A. Hetmanek, 'Islamic Revolution and Jihad Come to the Former Central Asia: The Case of Tajikistan', *Central Asian Survey* 12/3 (1993) pp.367–74.

12. Further details in Hetmanek (note 11) pp.365–78; and Muriel Atkin, *The Subtlest Battle: Islam in Soviet Tajikistan* (Philadelphia, PA: Foreign Policy Research Institute 1989) pp.1–66. For Islam's role in the civil war, W.G. Lerch, 'Moskau ist an Ordnung und Berechenbarkeit interessiert', *Frankfurter Allgemeine Zeitung*, 22 July 1993, p.1.

13. 'The Return to Islamism', *Nokta* (Turkish) (Ankara/Istanbul weekly), 18 Oct. 1991, pp.78–9. For Nabiyev's response, see *Cumhuriyet* (Istanbul daily), 25 Oct. 1992, p.9.

14. Details in U. Halbach, 'Islam, Nation und politische Öffentlichkeit in den zentralasiatischen (Unions-) Republiken', *Berichte des Bundesinstituts für ostwissenschaftliche und internationale Studien* 57 (1991) pp.29–40.

15. For more details, see Ali Banuazizi and Myron Weiner (eds.), *The New Geopolitics of Central Asia and Its Borderlands* (London: Tauris 1994); V.F. Piacentini, 'Islam: Iranian and Saudi Arabian Religious and Geopolitical Competition in Central Asia', in Ehteshami (note 6), pp.25–46.

16. On Turkey as a secular model for the six republics and its relations with them, see G.M. Winrow, 'Turkey and the Former Soviet Central Asia: National and Ethnic Identity', *Central*

*Asian Survey* 11/2 (1992) pp.101–11; Erol Mütercimler, *The International System and the Model of Relations Between Turkey and the Turkic Republics on the Threshold of the 21st Century* (Turkish) (Istanbul: Anahtar 1993); Jacob M. Landau, *Pan-Turkism: From Irredentism to Cooperation* (Bloomington: Indiana UP 1995) ch.7.

17. See, however, data in Halbach (note 14) pp.16–19.
18. Alexandre Bennigsen, 'Islam in Retrospect', *Central Asian Survey* 8/1 (1989) pp.89–109; Yaacov Ro'i, 'The Impact of the Islamic Fundamentalist Revival of the Late 1970s on the Soviet View of Islam', in Yaacov Ro'i (ed.), *The USSR and the Muslim World: Issues in Domestic and Foreign Policy* (London: Allen & Unwin 1984) pp.149–77.
19. Cf. S.P. Poliakov, *Everyday Islam: Religion and Tradition in Rural Central Asia* (Armonk, NY: M.E. Sharpe 1992) pp.95–104.
20. Rorlich (note 4) pp.196–7; Rashid (note 5) 246ff.
21. Catherine Poujol, 'Ouzbekistan, an II de l'indépendance: un constant contrasté', *Revue du Monde Musulman et de la Méditerranée* 68-69/2-3 (1993) p.166.
22. Kosach (note 11); Halbach (note 14).
23. Y. Ro'i, 'The Islamic Influence on Nationalism in Soviet Central Asia', *Problems of Communism* 39/4 (July-Aug. 1990) pp.63–4.
24. Oliver Roy, *The Failure of Political Islam* (Cambridge, MA: Harvard UP 1994).
25. H. Bräker, 'Die Islamische Türkvölker Zentral Asiens und die sowjetisch-chinesischen Beziehungen', *Berichte des Bundesinstituts für ostwissenschaftliche und internationale Studien* 37 (1984) pp.11–14.
26. See also Nancy Lubin, 'Islam and Ethnic Identity in Central Asia: A View from Below', in Ro'i, *Muslim Eurasia* (note 11) pp.53–70.
27. Fuller (note 5).
28. 'Islamic nationalism' has recently been discussed in a number of studies, mostly written by non-Muslims. One of the most coherent exposés is Z.I. Levin's, *Islam and Nationalism in the Countries of the East Across the Frontiers: the Ideological Aspect* (Russian) (Moscow: Nauka 1988).

# Islamic Extremism and the Peace Process

## EFRAIM INBAR

This article first discusses the negative attitude of Islamic radical groups toward Israel and the peace process. It then presents an assessment of the long run potential of the Islamic radicals, as well as their present politico-military capabilities to harm the peace process. The article focuses on the capacity of Islamic radicals to subvert or intimidate the pro-peace Arab regimes, wage war and develop nuclear capabilities. It ends with some observations on how the activities of Islamic extremists influence the ongoing political debate in Israel on the future of the peace process.

This article offers a strategic analysis of the effects of Islamic extremism in the Middle East on the peace process between Israel and the Arab world.[1] Islam is one of the world's great religions, having greatly contributed to all aspects of human society. The subject of this essay, however, is the political consequences of a specific version of Islam, the radical, which is not the most prevalent, though certainly a source of danger. As a student of international relations, rather than sociology of religion or Arab culture, I will take the liberty to make a few generalizations. I follow the English author, Ben Jonson, who observed, 'The fact of twilight does not mean you cannot tell day from night'. Therefore, I will discuss the political implications of a variety of radical Islamic political entities, focusing on their policy advocacy and capabilities, rather than on their social and theological differences.

In the Middle East, the following Islamic entities are involved in campaigns of varying degrees against Israel and the peace process: Iran and Sudan; opposition groups in countries such as Egypt, Jordan and Turkey; and organizations engaged in direct armed conflict with Israel, such as the Hizballah in Lebanon, and the Islamic Resistance Movement, better known as Hamas, and the Islamic Jihad, in the Land of Israel (Palestine). While different in many aspects, these actors share a commitment to imposing Islamic law (*shari'a*) in their countries, and to demonstrating a principled or religious-motivated opposition to the existence of Israel and the continuation of the peace process. Furthermore, all are known to support or condone extreme and violent methods to achieve their goal. Their emergence is little connected to Arab-Israeli relations, though enmity to Israel certainly enhances their general appeal. Islamic extremism and those who espouse its ideas are responses to the failure of Arab regimes and societies to cope with the challenges of population growth, urbanization and the management of resources. Indeed, domestic issues are prominent on the political agenda of the proponents of radical versions of Islam, although they maintain a revisionist international outlook.[2]

First, this article discusses the negative attitudes of Islamic radical groups toward Israel and the peace process. Next, it presents an assessment of the long run potential of the Islamic radicals, as well as their present politico-military capabilities to harm the peace process. The article focuses on the capacity of the Islamic radicals to subvert or to intimidate the pro-peace Arab regimes, to wage war and to develop nuclear threats. It ends with some observations on how the activities of Islamic extremists influence the ongoing political debate in Israel on the future of the peace process.

**Predispositions and Goals**

Islamic writings, as with holy texts of a religion, can be used for a variety of political purposes. In the case of Muslim extremists, Islamic texts are used to justify the theological rejection of the notion of a sovereign Jewish state in the geographical confines of the Islamic world (*Dar al-Islam*).[3] It is true that, in general, Muslims treated Jews whom they ruled benevolently, but this historic precedent does not relate to the emergence of a sovereign Jewish state. For the extremists, such a state is religiously unacceptable and constitutes an affront to God's worldly order. For example, in its covenant Hamas presents the Arab-Israeli struggle not in national or territorial terms, but as a historically, religiously, culturally and existentially irreconcilable conflict between Islam and Judaism, between truth and falsehood.[4]

These negative attitudes toward the Jewish state, in particular, and Jews, in general, are supported by anti-Jewish statements found in the Koran and in classic Islamic texts. A Koranic example of such a sentiment can be found in *sura* II v. 58: 'And abasement and poverty were pitched upon them (the Jews), and they were laden with the burden of God's anger; that, because they had disbelieved the signs of God and slain the Prophets unrightfully; that because they disobeyed, and were transgressors'.[5] This verse has served occasionally for the depiction of Jews in negative terms. Jews were described as traitors, breakers of agreements and distorters of sacred texts. For example, in the fourteenth century, a religious decree (*fatwa*) reiterated the notion that the Jews were the enemy of God since they were 'branded with the marks of wrath and malediction of the Lord...'. In addition, the famous historian Ibn Khaldoun, living in the same century, claimed that the Jews were infected with corruption and deceitful plotting.[6] Nowadays, Hamas leaflets refer to the Jews as the brothers of apes, the killers of Prophets, bloodsuckers, the descendants of treachery and deceit, who spread corruption in the land of Islam.[7] Shaykh Mohammed Fadlallah, the spiritual leader of Hizballah, said that 'the struggle against the Jewish state, in which all Muslims are engaged, is a continuation of the old struggle of the Muslims against the Jews' conspiracy against Islam'.[8]

Another important element of the *weltanschauung* of Islamic extremists is their antagonism toward the West.[9] Peoples colonized by the West generally tend to feel a mixture of resentment and envy toward their previous rulers.[10] Radical Islamic ideology, in particular, displays great hostility toward the West, its culture and values.[11] According to Bernard Lewis, 'Islam was never prepared, either in theory or in practice, to accord full equality to those who held other beliefs, and practiced other forms of worship'.[12] Islamic fundamentalists are confident that their struggle is for the glory of God, while all their opponents, Muslims or infidels, are fighting against God. Their anti-western outlook is also the result of the belief that the West and its colonialist heritage, as well as its neo-colonialist presence, are corrupting the Islamic way of life.

Israel, rightly or wrongly, is seen as an alien extension of the West into the Middle East. Accordingly, the Jewish state is perceived to be a tool in the western scheme to dominate the region. Islamic and Marxist explanations (the latter is still fashionable in certain Arab intellectual circles) converge in portraying Israel as a 'lackey of western imperialism'.

In addition to providing for great animosity towards Israel, radical Islamic thinking and fervor support the intellectual framework for protracted conflict, such as the Arab-Israeli dispute. By arming themselves with a long-range historical perspective, radical Muslims can easily explain present failures as temporary setbacks.

As noted, Islamic extremist groups have demonstrated a great commitment to achieving prescribed goals with little concern for the methods used. Such attitudes are generally congruent with the rules of the Mideast political game.[13] Use of force between states, as well as subversion against neighboring regimes, is an acceptable practice. Islamic extremists have displayed a willingness to pay a high price for their actions, including the loss of many lives. Indeed, *jihad*, holy war, is often invoked in the service of goal achievement, and those sacrificing their lives in the process are accorded martyr status (*shaheed*) with special privileges in the afterlife.

The objectives of Islamic extremists concerning Israel is very clear. Their goal is Politicide. Coined by the late Yehoshafat Harkabi in the 1960s as a description of the PLO's goal to eliminate Israel, politicide denotes the campaign to destroy a political entity.[14] For example, the president of the Islamic Republic of Iran, Rafsanjani, during his visit to France in September 1994, said that Israel is an illegitimate phenomenon just like the Nazi conquest of France. He added that the Jews should go back to their countries of origin.[15] In reaction to the Washington Declaration, Shaykh Youssouf Alshami of the Islamic Jihad said that the declaration's significance was only that a few Palestinians were allowed to return to their homeland. He said, 'the borders of Palestine are from Ras Nakura (at the Lebanese border) to Rafah, from the sea to the Jordan river... did anybody hear before 50 years about a nation called the Jewish people?!... the present balance of power cannot last forever, and in politics nothing is impossible'.[16] A Hizballah tract issued by the group's office in Beirut reads, 'Our confrontation with the Zionist entity must end with its obliteration from existence. This is why we do not recognize any cease-fire agreement, any truce, or any separate or non-separate peace treaty with it'.[17]

Politicide is a radical goal, somewhat unusual in world politics, but less so in the Middle East. In addition to Israel, Lebanon, Kuwait and Jordan have been, or still are, objects of politicide. In this region, international borders and existing political entities, which were the creations of British and French colonialism, do not command the respect of all Mideasterners. In accordance with pan-Arabism, which is no less of a transnational ideology than extreme Islam, the Arab countries must unite into a single political structure. Radical Islam does not only challenge the structure of a specific state, but the entire Mideast international order.

The Islamic extremists are adamantly opposed to the peace process. This process involves the recognition of the state of Israel and a formal end to the state of war between Arabs and Israelis, in order to bring about a qualitatively different type of relations between the protagonists. The normative aspect of the peace process, which lends legitimacy to the Jewish state, is probably the most disturbing from the radical perspective. Indeed, in a move designed to oppose the October 1991 Madrid Peace Conference, Iran convened a parallel meeting of Islamic extremist groups. The purpose of the Islamic conference was to reach a joint strategy to fight the peace process.

Furthermore, the peace process is anathema because it is American-sponsored and enhances the American presence in the Middle East. For example, the Islamic opposition in Jordan boycotted President Clinton's address to the Jordanian Parliament, following the ceremony of the signing of the peace treaty between Israel and Jordan. According to Hazam Mansour, the Islamists' spokesman, 'Clinton is the enemy of the Arab and the Islamic nation'.[18]

What Islamic extremists fear is American-Israeli cultural and economic domination of the region, and a subsequent corruption of Islamic values. Because of the great importance they ascribe to linkages between politics and culture, their opposition to the peace process and its perceived politico-cultural implications is high on their agendas.

Indeed, the peace process is in their – mostly correct – analysis an expression of the zenith of American power in international affairs and an ebb in the political standing of the failing and corrupt secular elites in the Arab world. In their perception, Israel is being accepted as a *fait accompli* due to weakness and because of their inability to eradicate the Jewish state. The religious radicals are fully aware of the deficiencies of the present Arab political systems and the consequences for effective action in the international arena.

Yet, precisely because of sensitivity to the political arena, a temporary cease-fire with the Zionist entity, under certain circumstances, is not entirely ruled out by all Islamic extremists. Rafsanjani, in contrast to Hamanai, the ideologue of the revolution, declared that, despite the fact that Iran opposes any agreement with Israel, the Palestinians have a right to decide on this issue, and Iran would not stand in their way.[19] There are even voices within Hamas that call for some accommodation. Musa Abu Marzuk, the chairman of its political executive, said that his organization is willing to live in peace with Israel if it returned to the 1967 borders, including with regard to Jerusalem, paid reparations to the Palestinians and held free elections in the territories.[20] In February 1996, Hamas even seemed willing to enter into cease-fire negotiations with Israel. Indeed, a truce with Israel does not require too excessive theological creativity. The truce between Mohammed and the Quraish tribe of infidels – later violated – can serve as a precedent.

To sum up, Islamic radicals have expressed a strong desire to destroy Israel, and to obstruct the American-sponsored peace process. While they are ready to make considerable sacrifices to achieve their goals, there is also a potential for temporarily adjusting to the prevailing power structure. We will turn now to an assessment of their capabilities.

## Capabilities

This section analyzes the ability of the radical Islamic entities to disrupt the peace process by waging war, engaging in low intensity conflict (LIC), using subversion to replace those leaders who are willing to participate in the peace process or intimidating the ruling elite to adopt anti-peace policies.

### *Conventional War*

The Islamic states do not yet pose a serious conventional military challenge to Israel, to its neighbors or to the peace process. Sudan is not much of a military power; Iran is rebuilding its military might, but its ability to project power to the Arab-Israeli arena is extremely limited for the time being.[21]

Moreover, neither Iran nor Sudan is territorially contiguous with Israel. This geographic fact prevents them from waging a conventional, large-scale military attack, or even a war of attrition against Israel. Furthermore, the fighter airplanes in the arsenals of the two states do not have the operational range to attack targets into Israel, and no air refueling is available to extend their range.

Yet, Iran can serve, to some extent, as a strategic hinterland for Syria, despite the absence of a common border. We may even envision an Iranian expeditionary force in case of a Syrian-Israeli war. In fall 1995, Iran received from North Korea the Nodong missile, with a range of 1000 km. It will allow Iran to attack targets in Israel with conventional warheads and enhance Iran's capability to project power in the whole region, as well as to interfere in the Arab-Israeli arena. However, despite the rhetoric of the Islamic regime, Iranian foreign policy has been cautious.[22] Therefore, intervention of the kinds mentioned is not very likely and, even if played out, of limited military consequence.

A conventional war by an Islamic state against one of the Arab states which supports the peace process is also unlikely. The ability of Iran to launch a ground attack against these neighbors of Israel who signed peace treaties is negligible at best. Iran could project military power in the Gulf area, but an outright war against one of the Gulf monarchies because it opened diplomatic relations with Israel is highly unlikely.

*The Nuclear Threat*

Radical Islam poses a threat also in the area of missile and nuclear proliferation. Iran is currently attempting to acquire both capabilities to buttress the country's hegemony in the Gulf area and to enhance its stature in Central Asia and the Middle East. It renewed the nuclear program started in the days of the Shah but frozen by Khomeini. US Secretary of Defense William Perry expressed his concern that Iran might purchase or steal a nuclear bomb from the ex-Soviet republics 'in a week, a month, or five years – everything is possible'.[23] Furthermore, the US was unable to stop the sale of Russian nuclear reactors and sensitive technology to the Islamic republic. Similarly, the May 1995 renewal of the Nuclear Proliferation Treaty (NPT) regime, which is far from being a foolproof security arrangement, would hardly constrain the Iranian efforts in this area.[24]

In light of the great hostility that Iran has shown to Israel, the possession of such capabilities may elicit Israeli preemptive attacks against the Iranian nuclear infrastructure similar to the 1981 air raid against the Iraqi nuclear reactor. Israel has purchased from the United States a number of F-15I jetfighters to allow, *inter alia*, exactly for such a military option. Such an attack might heighten Arab threat perceptions and have repercussions on the peace.

Furthermore, a nuclear Iran would also increase the pressures for enhanced Arab nuclear activities. Revolutionary Iran may decide to be cautious and not initiate a nuclear duel with Israel, which does not challenge Iran's hegemony in its immediate environment. Yet, the incentive for an Arab nuclear bomb is more of a problem for Israel than a direct Iranian nuclear threat. The absence of such a bomb was one of the reasons for the Arabs to come to terms with Israel, while the introduction of nuclear weapons to an Arab arsenal would have a most destabilizing effect on the Arab-Israeli arena. There are difficult problems – technical and political – in applying the model of the nuclear relations between the Soviet Union and the US to the Middle East.[25]

Furthermore, Iranian acquisition of a nuclear bomb would put an end to one of the common goals between Israel and all Arab states – the prevention of such a scenario. The fear of nuclear proliferation in the Middle East has been one of the reasons for several Arab countries to lend support to the peace process, which includes a multilateral forum on Arms Control and Regional Security. There were hopes in the US, Israel and in several Arab capitals to use this forum to treat the issue of nuclear proliferation in the region.[26]

The successful completion of the Iranian nuclear program would also be an affront to the US and its perceived hegemonic role in the region and the world. The American-sponsored peace process may well be affected by a changed evaluation as to American will and capacity to influence the implementation of its preferred policies: counter-proliferation and an Arab-Israeli detente.

## Low Intensity Conflict (LIC)

The Islamic states do engage, however, in a war by proxy against Israel. They support LIC operations conducted by organizations based along Israel's borders (Lebanon and Gaza) and within Israeli-ruled territories and the Palestinian Authority (PA).[27] Such activities are relatively cheap and therefore not too taxing for the Iranian, and even the weak Sudanese, economies.

At the end of 1992, Hamas signed an agreement of cooperation with Iran. The latter committed itself to train Hamas members and to grant the organization generous financial support.[28] Sudan also provides training to Hamas and the Islamic Jihad. Hizballah, in Lebanon, is also under Iranian tutelage and is allowed freedom of action by Iran's secular ally, Syria. It fights the Israel Defense Force (IDF) and the South Lebanese Army, and occasionally launches Katyusha attacks on Israeli border communities. Moreover, in early 1993, Iran supplied Hizballah with Soviet-made anti-tank Sagger missiles. These significantly increased Hizballah's firepower and ability to harm Israeli forces and allies. According to then Israeli Deputy Defense Minister, Mordechai Gur, the Hizballah began to fire shoulder surface-to-air missiles against Israeli helicopters in fall 1994.[29]

The war of attrition in South Lebanon resulted in 23 Israeli casualties in 1995 (21 in 1994, 26 in 1993, but only 13 in 1992) and has become a political burden for the Israeli leadership. Despite the growing sensitivity to casualties in this sector, Israel's response has generally been low key and limited to strikes at Hizballah targets. The Syrians in Lebanon, who can restrict the activities of the Hizballah, seem immune to Israeli retaliation because of Israel's desire to project a moderate image toward the Arab world in order to advance the peace process. Indeed, high ranking officers in Israel's Northern Command have often complained that the politicians are tying their hands in the struggle against Hizballah.[30]

Hamas and the Islamic Jihad specialize in terrorist acts against Israeli military and civilian targets: shootings, knifings and suicide bombing. They have also kidnapped IDF soldiers. Terrorist attacks (mostly by Islamic activists) led to 67 Israeli fatalities in 1994, a 15.5 per cent increase from 1993. In a period of two and a half years, since the September 1993 agreement, over 200 Israelis have been killed in terrorist activities. Suicide bombers are by definition undeterred, a fact which makes defense against such acts all the more difficult.

A significant portion of the political leadership of these two organizations presently resides in Syria and enjoys considerable freedom of action there. This facilitates contacts with Iran, which has had excellent relations with Syria for many years. The establishment of the PA also enhances their capacity for action, as long as this new entity is unwilling or unable to monopolize the use of force in its territory. Indeed, some of the terrorist acts perpetrated by the two organizations were planned in the area under the PA jurisdiction, and the perpetrators found refuge there. The availability of explosives has also increased since the arrival of the PLO to Gaza and Jericho.

The main rationale for the terrorist acts of Hamas and the Islamic Jihad is to keep alive the flames of the Palestinian/Islamic struggle against Israel's existence; to defy and embarrass the PA; and to provoke Israel to take harsh measures against Palestinians under its or the PA's jurisdiction. Hamas and Islamic Jihad also believe that their actions will lead to further Israeli withdrawals, as well as to the derailing of the peace process.

From a purely military point of view, terror is not a major problem for Israel, as it does not threaten its basic existence. In the short run, terrorist attacks have a limited impact on the Israeli economy and society, though it can drastically change the mood of the country for short periods of time. The political ramifications of such terrorism for Israel are more complex and are discussed in the next section. The measures needed to combat Islamic terrorism – intelligence and counter-insurgency – are relatively cheap, particularly if compared to large-scale military operations that include the use of the air force and armored units. This strengthens the disposition not to view Palestinian terrorism as a major strategic problem.

## Subversion

Other Islamic groups are actively engaged in subversion against Arab regimes participating in the peace process. Iran and Sudan lend various forms of support to Islamic groups everywhere and make the struggle against them more difficult. The continuous success of the present regimes in prevailing over the Islamic fundamentalists should not to be taken for granted.

In recent years, Egypt has been under growing pressure from its radical Islamic opposition. Egyptian Christians (Copts) and foreign tourists have become the targets of terrorist attacks. Such attacks have spread gradually from the south to the north, even reaching the capital, Cairo. They have included attempts on the lives of senior governmental officials, and the Egyptian security forces have also been increasingly harassed by the Islamic activists. The consequences of this campaign were felt in economic and political terms. Decline in Egypt's tourism reached an annual loss of $500,000,000. The regime's overall stability has been called into question, as well.[31]

The Mubarak regime has undertaken great efforts to contain the Islamic threat at home, including arresting Islamic extremists en masse, actively hunting and eliminating such radicals, and executing those Islamic activists found guilty of terrorism by the military courts, which have had such matters under their jurisdiction since 1992. Yet, Egypt is plagued with enormous social and economic problems which foster social unrest and enhance support for the Islamic alternative. The ultimate prerequisite for an Islamic takeover is the ability to infiltrate Egypt's army and the security forces, the mainstay of the present regime, and to organize a successful coup. Egypt, to a lesser extent than other Mideastern states, is a 'one-bullet regime'. Yet, a successful political assassination could bring about a succession struggle and political instability. A successful Islamic revolution in Egypt, the most populous Arab country, would reverberate throughout the region. It would change the Middle East and would probably put an end to the peace treaty between Israel and Egypt – a cornerstone of the current peace process.

Such an event in Turkey – although much less likely – would also result in a political earthquake throughout the region. Notably, the Islamic Welfare Party (Refah) was very successful during the March 1994 municipal elections. Refah, which is well financed and mainly supported by disaffected migrants to large cities, obtained 19 per cent of the overall vote and won control of 27 provincial capitals, including the two largest cities, Istanbul and Ankara. Moreover, in the national elections of December 1995, the Islamic party received a plurality in parliament and eventually became part of the governing coalition.[32] In contrast to Egypt, but closer to the situation in Jordan, the Islamic opposition in Turkey is part of the political system, a position which probably has a moderating effect.

Hashemite Jordan also faces a strong fundamentalist opposition; the Islamic Action Front (IAF) is the largest Jordanian opposition group. Thus far, King Hussein has successfully tamed the Islamic opposition.[33] By changing the electoral rules before the November 1993 elections, Hussein reduced the Islamic opposition's parliamentary power from 34 seats (received in the April 1989 elections) to 21 in the 80-seat lower house, although they maintained their hold on 15 per cent of the popular vote. Subversive groups in Jordan, which seek to overthrow the monarchy, include the Army of Mohammed and the Young Voice of Islam. Their links to the Iranian regime were established at the trials of their activists. The death of King Hussein may bring about a period of domestic instability. If the Muslims take the palace, Jordan would probably revoke its October 1994 peace treaty with Israel and might become a staging area in a revived Eastern Front. The Islamic opposition is openly and vehemently against the peace treaty. Hamza Mansour, its spokesman, even compared the relations with Israel to AIDS.[34]

The PLO is also challenged by an Islamic opposition, which rejects the Oslo agreements: Hamas and the Islamic Jihad.[35] Significantly, the tensions between the two have not yet resulted in a civil war, though several clashes between the PA police and the Islamic radicals have already occurred. Hamas is believed to have a considerable following in Gaza and in the Hebron area; its network of institutions is involved in providing educational, social and religious services.[36] Arafat was not ready to enter a confrontation and has allowed Hamas to keep its arms, while the latter agreed not to display them in public. While several Islamists ran for the Palestinian Council in the January 1996 elections, Hamas and the Islamic Jihad formally boycotted the elections, after which Arafat's political position seemed to have improved. He was better able to secure a monopoly over the use of force in his nascent entity, but continued to prefer cooptation rather than confrontation.[37]

A series of terrorist attacks in the winter of 1996 reinforced Israeli demands from the PA to do more in curbing Islamic extremists' freedom of action. As the Israeli pressures on Arafat to rein in Hamas and Islamic Jihad continue to mount, particularly as a condition for the transfer of additional areas to his control, a showdown between the PA and the Islamic opposition might be in the offing. If the PA fails to demonstrate effective control over the territory under its jurisdiction, Palestinians as well as Israelis will question the wisdom of dealing with Arafat. A politically-fragmented Palestinian entity, which is not a far-fetched scenario, will place strains on the Palestinian track of the peace process.

## Intimidation

Islamic radicals do not have to be in power in order to harm the peace process. They can intimidate rulers to refrain from becoming too close to Israel through the use of several means, including attempts at their lives. We are reminded of the assassination of Anwar Sadat and the recent attempt to assassinate Mubarak. Indeed, Mohammed Barjawi, a Hizballah MP in Lebanon, criticized King Hussein for his peace treaty with Israel and added that 'there will always be somebody to assassinate traitors'.[38]

Even less radical measures can have a harmful effect on the peace process. The expectations of economic prosperity brought on by the peace process, exaggerated in any case,[39] can be significantly curtailed by Islamic terrorist attacks on Israeli and/or western tourists and businessmen in Egypt, Jordan or the Palestinian-held territories. Instability is not attractive to foreign investment, as demonstrated by the difficulties which the PA has faced in realizing the foreign aid commitments of the donor countries and enticing foreign investments for Palestinian industries.[40] Additional economic setbacks could further complicate matters, as improvements in the terrible economic conditions in Gaza are an important test of the PLO's decision to make a deal with Israel. Without significant advances in the standard of living there, the impoverished population may withdraw its support for Arafat and opt for the Islamic opposition.

It is noteworthy that the political leadership in Egypt and Jordan were not deflected from their diplomatic course *vis-à-vis* Israel, despite strong Islamic opposition. Similarly, Turkey has considerably improved its relations with Israel, showing little regard for the anti-Israeli disposition of the growing Turkish Islamic movement.

## Impact on Israel

A somewhat simplistic analysis of Israeli politics juxtaposes two competing visions concerning the future of the Middle East and Israel's road to peace;

it is actually a multi-dimensional continuum.[41] The most famous proponent for the vision propagated by the Left is Israel's former prime minister, Shimon Peres, who wrote a book about the emergence of a peaceful and economically prosperous new Middle East. He wrote, 'instead of visions of blood and tears there will rise visions of happiness and beauty, life and peace'.[42] Accordingly, the peace process is an important part of this historic process, by including the acceptance of Israel as a member of the emerging new Middle East. It is argued that the new strategic reality is more benign than in the past, therefore allowing Israel to enjoy lower threat perception than in the past.[43]

The contrasting picture, as seen by the Right, is of a Middle East remaining as a zone of turmoil;[44] unstable and war-prone. The Right points out the unbending hostility of the Islamic radicals and their rhetoric against the existence of the Jewish state, which evokes among Israelis traditional existential fears. The Left makes efforts to dismiss such fears as a failure in seeing the new emerging reality. The Right also stresses the fragility of the peace treaties and the need to cautiously evaluate the emerging regional trends, and even slow down the peace process with the Palestinians and the Syrians. The Islamists' determination to reverse the peace process blends well into these calls for greater caution regarding the calculated risks Israel is taking in attempting to reach formal peace agreements. The Right holds that it is possible that these will be violated by Arab countries under new Islamist leadership.

The Right also warns that the peace process will not bring the sort of economic rewards that the Left promises, and thus, it is a mistake to expect political stability in the Arab world.[45] Past attacks on Israeli tourists in Egypt and the boycott on Israeli products and on contacts with Israelis have reduced the attraction of the peace process in Israel. Similar behavior in Jordan could indicate to Israel the limitations on its attempts to integrate into the region.

The rebuttal from the Left is that the growing appeal of Islamist groups can be countered with educational and economic improvement, which will reduce the support of the poor and the deprived for the Islamist platform. The Left also argues that a reallocation of resources in the Arab world at the expense of defense expenditures is possible only in the context of a peace process, while massive foreign aid can be mobilized only if the political climate changes in the Middle East. Furthermore, the Left in Israel stresses the urgency of successfully concluding the peace process to preempt a possible deterioration in the political standing of the present Arab leaders who are contemplating peace with Israel. Their survival is also dependent upon their ability to provide a better life for their people. Therefore, Israel and the West have an interest in providing economic aid. The emphasis on the importance of economic factors in the peace process and the developing Middle East is the result of two intellectual influences: socialism and liberalism.[46] The Laborite leadership, Peres in particular, has socialist ideological roots, which have been gradually replaced or complemented by liberal ideas coming from the US.

The terrorist acts perpetrated by the Islamic extremists have had mixed effects on Israel. Over the years, the Jewish state has developed social mechanisms which routinize the impact of armed conflict.[47] This is a cushion which minimizes the socio-economic and political repercussions of terror. In the short run, Israeli positions are hardened by terrorist attacks, while in the long run, these attacks have influenced Israeli public opinion in the dovish direction, that is, a greater willingness to withdraw from Israeli-ruled territories.[48] Israeli society has become war-weary; it is less willing to pay the price involved in the continuation of the protracted Arab-Israeli conflict. Moreover, increasing terrorism seems to have elevated the costs of holding onto the territories, and an increasing number of Israelis consider withdrawal from part or all of the territories a positive step (in the framework of a negotiated settlement). Israelis understand that one reason for the successful terrorist acts is the accessibility of Israeli cities as a result of its control of the territories. It is the Left that claims that separation between Arabs and Jews by withdrawing from heavily Arab-populated areas could minimize the chances for successful terrorist acts. In this respect, Islamic terrorism pushes the Israelis toward greater willingness to part with the territories and to make a deal with the Palestinians. Yet, the emergence of terrorist havens in PA-controlled zones may lead Israelis to reconsider the direction of the peace with the Palestinians.

A similar dynamic seems to occur on the Syrian track of the peace process. Hizballah's costly war of attrition in South Lebanon is bringing about a softer Israeli negotiating position, which makes a deal with Syria closer. Israeli sensitivity to casualties pushes the Left to question the need for a security zone in South Lebanon and to accept a Syrian role in Lebanon. Indeed, Rabin pointed out that an agreement with Syria is needed to put an end to the costly armed conflict in South Lebanon.[49] In addition, hints by the Labor-led government of willingness to cede the Golan Heights have eroded the large majority of Israeli opposing any withdrawal from the strategic plateau.

The cumulative effect of terrorism was one factor which undermined the popularity of the Yitzhak Rabin-led government, as well as Rabin's own reputation as 'Mr. Security'. The government's initial line about terror casualties being 'the victims of peace' was not well received and was therefore dropped. Support for the Rabin government fell to a record low by the winter of 1995.[50] Similarly, the series of terrorist attacks in February and

March 1996 brought an erosion in the popularity of Rabin's successor, Peres; and it was it easier for the Likud to point out the shortcomings of the Labor approach toward the Palestinians. Yet, these attacks had only limited influence on the outcome of the elections two and a half months later (May 1996) – an eternity in Israeli politics.[51]

The nuclear threat emanating from Iran, which the Labor government has strongly emphasized, has similarly generated mixed responses. The Left sees in the peace a panacea to all regional problems, including nuclear proliferation. The fear of nuclear proliferation also fits well with the dovish predisposition to hurry 'before the window of opportunity closes'. Furthermore, since Israel is relying less than before on unilateral measures and might not be in the position to eliminate the Iranian nuclear threat on its own, the Labor-led government hoped to build an international coalition to prevent the fruition of the Iranian nuclear program. Labor-led Israel wanted the Arabs to join the effort.[52]

While in favor of international action to prevent Iran acquiring a nuclear bomb, the Right claims that the Arabs have a good reason to do so without any Israeli concessions. Furthermore, right-wing politicians are much more skeptical concerning the effectiveness of an international effort and the American willingness to play a leading role. Therefore, the nuclear specter is another indication that existential threats are still around. The possibility of a nuclear bomb in the hands of Islamic extremists is a nightmare for all Israelis. The extremists do not hide their politicide goal, and there are serious difficulties deterring a determined opponent with a low sensitivity to cost.[53] The chances for stable deterrence in a nuclearized Middle East seem to be slim.

## Conclusion

Religion is of great political consequence and cannot be easily discarded as a relic of the past, or the haven of the ignorant and poor. Max Weber was wrong in writing about the 'Entzauberung der Welt', by which he meant that the modern world is disenchanted and is no longer seeking sacredness. He minimized the impact of religion. Yet, traditional patterns do not fade away easily. Consequently, what we see today is indeed a new version of the impact of religion on politics, but much of its underlying logic is going to remain with us and not disappear. Religion may well be the opium of the people, but Marxist and liberal thinking, which both underscore the importance of economic factors in domestic and international conflict, have proven wrong in heralding the politics of reason.

The radical Islamic threat is here to stay and will not disappear as a result of economic and social engineering by the existing corrupt and inefficient secular elites, even if much western aid is poured into the Middle East. The Islamic fanatics are intent on dismantling the Jewish state, though they cannot presently do much more than harass Israelis and the supporters of the peace process in Arab countries. The greatest damage can be done to the Palestinian Authority, which is the weakest link in the peace process. The potential for great havoc in the near future exists. It lies primarily in a possible Muslim takeover in Egypt and in a nuclear device in Iran.

The fortunes of the Muslim radicals are dependent primarily upon the interplay of indigenous developments. Neither Israel nor the West can do much about the regional environment. Determination to defend the well-being of innocent citizens and vital interests can command the respect of Islamic foes, who are capable of adapting in the face of superior power. Moderation on their part regarding Israel, the peace process and the West is a possibility that cannot be totally dismissed, but this can happen only in a domestic environment which makes the Islamic radical platform no longer appealing. Only then, a rather unlikely prospect in the near future considering the tremendous domestic problems confronting Middle Eastern societies, will Islamic extremism cease being the threat it constitutes today.

## NOTES

I thank Bruce Maddy-Weitzman, Shmuel Sandler, the participants of the Program on International Political Economy and Security (PIPES) Seminar at the University of Chicago, and Jordan Steng in particular, for their useful comments.

1. For studies of radical Islam, see *inter alia*, Emmanuel Sivan, *Radical Islam: Medieval Theology and Modern Politics* (New Haven, CT: Yale UP 1985); David Menashri (ed.), *The Iranian Revolution and the Muslim World* (Boulder, CO: Westview 1990); James Piscatori (ed.), *Islamic Fundamentalism and the Gulf Crisis* (Chicago: American Academy of Arts and Sciences 1991); Ziad Abu-Amr, *Islamic Fundamentalism in the West Bank and Gaza* (Bloomington: Indiana UP 1994); Gabriel Ben-Dor, 'The Uniqueness of Islamic Fundamentalism,' in this volume, pp.239–52. The notions 'Islamic radicalism' and 'extremism' refer to the nature of the goals and the means of the political entities discussed in this article and are used interchangeably. Fundamentalism refers primarily to theological issues and is beyond the scope of this article.
2. P.W. Rodman, 'Co-opt or Confront Fundamentalist Islam', *Middle East Quarterly* 1/4 (Dec. 1994) p.64.
3. See Raphael Israeli, *Fundamentalist Islam and Israel* (Lanham: University Press of America 1993).
4. See Raphael Israeli, 'The Charter of Allah: The Platform of the Islamic Resistance Movement (Hamas)', *Israel Affairs* 2/1 (Autumn 1995) pp.273–93.
5. *The Koran Interpreted*, trans. by Arthur J. Arberry (NY: Macmillan 1979) p.36. See also Moshe Maoz, *The Image of the Jew in Official Arab Literature and Communications Media* (Jerusalem: Shazar Library 1976) p.9.
6. Maoz (note 5) pp.9–10.
7. Esther Webman, *Anti-Semitic Motifs in the Ideology of Hizballah and Hamas* (Tel Aviv: The Project for the Study of Anti-Semitism, Tel Aviv University 1994) pp.18–19.
8. M. Kramer, 'The Jihad Against the Jews', *Commentary* (Oct. 1994). For a recent study of

Hizballah, see Eyal Zisser, 'Hizballah in Lebanon – At the Crossroads', in this volume, pp.90–110.

9. For the Muslim historical and psychological perception of the West, see Graham E. Fuller and Ian O. Lesser, *A Sense of Siege. The Geopolitics of Islam and the West* (Boulder, CO: Westview / A Rand Study 1995) pp.27–80.

10. Otare D. Mannoni, *Prospero and Caliban. The Psychology of Colonization* (NY: Praeger 1964).

11. B. Lewis, 'The Roots of Muslim Rage', *The Atlantic* (Sept. 1990) pp.47–60.

12. Ibid, p.56.

12. Ibid, p.56.

13. For a recent treatment of the rules of the game in the Middle East, see Y. Evron, 'Gulf Crisis and War: Regional Rules of the Game and Policy and Theoretical Implications', *Security Studies* 4/1 (Autumn 1994) pp. 115–52.

14. Yehoshafat Harkabi, *Fedayeen Action and Arab Strategy*, Adelphi Paper No.53 (London: IISS 1969).

15. *Ha'aretz*, 13 Sept. 1994, p.A7.

16. *al-Quds*, 26 July 1994.

17. *The Middle East* (Feb. 1992) p.13.

18. G. Bechor, 'The Voices of Allah,' *Ha'aretz*, 26 Oct. 1994, p.B2.

19. *al-Quds*, 8 June 1994.

20. *al-Quds*, 24 April 1994.

21. For their order-of-battle see the recent volumes of *Military Balance* (London: IISS).

22. For an elaboration of this point, see Haggay Ram, 'Exporting Iran's Islamic Revolution: Steering a Path between Pan-Islam and Nationalism', in this volume, pp.7–24.

23. *Ha'aretz*, 6 Jan. 1995, p.A1. For the Iranian motivations, see S. Chubin, 'Does Iran Want Nuclear Weapons?', *Survival* 37/1 (Spring 1995) pp.86–104.

24. For the weaknesses of the NPT, see Gerald Steinberg, 'Arms Control in the Middle East: Global Regimes vs. Regional Dynamics', in Efraim Inbar (ed.), *Regional Security Regimes. Israel and Its Neighbors* (Albany, NY: SUNY Press 1995) pp.175–97.

25. See E. Inbar, 'The Nuclear Mirage in the Middle East', *Midstream* 27/3 (March 1981) pp.3–6; Yair Evron, *Israel's Nuclear Dilemma* (Ithaca, NY: Cornell UP 1994).

26. Egypt tried to force the issue by insisting on an Israeli adherence to the NPT, before its extension, instead of waiting for the establishment of a regional structure. For the chances of establishing such a regional security arrangement, see E. Inbar and S. Sandler, 'The International Politics of a Middle Eastern Arms Control Regime', in Efraim Inbar and Shmuel Sandler (eds.), *Middle Eastern Security. Prospects for an Arms Control Regime* A BESA Study in Mideast Security (London: Frank Cass 1995) pp.173–85.

27. For their terrorist activities, see Anat Kurtz *et al.* (eds.), *Islamic Terror and Israel* (Hebrew) (Tel Aviv: Papyrus and JCSS, Tel Aviv University 1993); M. Burkin, 'Terrorist Activity from Lebanon and the Threat to Northern Israel', in *The Middle East Military Balance. 1993–1994* (Boulder, CO: Westview Press for the Jaffee Center for Strategic Studies 1994) pp.131–47.

28. Meir Litvak, 'The Hamas Movement: A Different Palestinian Identity', in David Menashri (ed.), *Islamic Fundamentalism: A Challenge to Regional Stability* (Tel Aviv: Dayan Center, Tel Aviv University 1993) p.68.

29. *Ha'aretz*, 1 Nov. 1994, p.A3.

30. E. Rabin, 'We Have Played This Game Several Times,' *Ha'aretz*, 12 July 1993; R. Ben-Yishai, 'Lebanon: Why Does Israeli Government Show Restraint?,' *Yedi'ot Aharonot*, 12 Aug. 1994. For the general Israeli reluctance to use force because of the peace process, see E. Inbar and S. Sandler, 'Israel's Deterrence Strategy Revisited', *Security Studies* 3/2 (Winter 1993/94) pp.346–48.

31. See *inter alia*, Barry Rubin, *Islamic Fundamentalism in Egyptian Politics* (NY: St. Martin's Press 1990); E. Podeh, 'The Struggle of the Egyptian Regime Against the Islamic Challenge', *Ma'arachot* (Hebrew) 36/4 (June 1994) pp.40–8; and his 'Egypt's Struggle against the Militant Islamic Groups', in this volume, pp.43–61.

32. For their political program and anti-western attitudes, see the interview with the secretary-

general of the party, Oguzhan Asilturk, *Turkish Daily News*, 22 Nov. 1994, Section Two, p.1; see also Anat Lapidot, 'Islamic Activism in Turkey since the 1980 Military Takeover', in this volume, pp.62–74.

33. L. Tal, 'Dealing with Radical Islam: The Case of Jordan', *Survival* 37/3 (Autumn 1995) pp.139–56; See also G. Kramer, 'The Integration of the Integrists: a comparative study of Egypt, Jordan and Tunisia', in Ghassan Salame (ed.), *Democracy Without Democrats?* (London: I.B. Tauris 1994) pp.200–26.

34. Bechor (note 18).

35. For the relations between the PA and Hamas, see Menachem Klein, 'Competing Brothers: The Web of Hamas-PLO Relations', in this volume, pp.111–32.

36. There are great difficulties in polling Palestinians. According to the poll results of the Center for Palestine Research and Studies (Nablus) released on 31 May 1994, support for Islamic groups in Gaza is approximately 20 per cent. Most other estimates are higher, but there seems to be a gradual erosion in the Islamic appeal in Palestine.

37. Arafat allowed Hamas to open an information office and to publish a magazine, and released from prison many Hamas activists. See *Ha'aretz*, 29 Jan. 1996, p.A5.

38. *Ha'aretz*, 28 Oct. 1994, p.A3.

39. Eliyahu Kanovsky, *Assessing the Mideast Peace Economic Dividend*, BESA Mideast Security and Policy Studies No.15 (Ramat Gan: BESA Center for Strategic Studies 1994).

40. Z. Schiff, 'After Nezarim', *Ha'aretz*, 15 Nov. 1994, p.B1.

41. For the continuum in Israeli attitudes on national security and the Arab-Israeli conflict, see E. Inbar and G. Goldberg, 'Is Israel's Elite Becoming More Hawkish?', *International Journal* 45/3 (Summer 1990) pp.632–5; Efraim Inbar, *War and Peace in Israeli Politics* (Boulder, CO: Lynne Rienner 1991).

42. Shimon Peres with Arye Naor, *The New Middle East* (NY: Henry Colt 1993) p.46.

43. For reduced threat perception and other components of the new Israeli strategic thinking, see E. Inbar, 'Contours of New Israeli Strategic Thinking', *Political Science Quarterly* 111/1 (Spring 1996) pp.41–65.

44. For this term see Max Singer and Aaron Wildavsky, *The Real World Order. Zones of Peace/Zones of Turmoil* (Chatham, NJ: Chatham House 1993). For Benjamin Netanyahu's view, see his *A Place Among the Nations* (Hebrew) (Tel Aviv: Yedi'ot Aharonot 1995).

45. Kanovsky (note 39).

46. For the relations between economic ideas and international relations see R.Gilpin, 'Three Models of Future', *International Organization* 29/1 (Winter 1975) pp.37–63.

47. Baruch Kimmerling, *The Interrupted System* (New Brunswick, NJ: Transaction 1985).

48. Giora Goldberg, Gad Barzilai and Efraim Inbar, *The Impact of Intercommunal Conflict: The Intifada and the Israeli Public Opinion* Policy Studies no.43 (Jerusalem: The Leonard Davis Institute for International Relations, The Hebrew University 1991); Asher Arian, *Security Threatened. Surveying Israeli Opinion on Peace and War* (Cambridge UP and the Jaffee Center for Strategic Studies, Tel Aviv University 1995).

49. *Ha'aretz*, 30 Sept. 1994, p.A3. For the Syrian track, see E. Inbar, 'Israeli Negotiations with Syria', *Israel Affairs* 1/4 (Summer 1995) pp.89–100.

50. See the poll results in *Ma'ariv*, 6 Jan. 1995, p.1; *Yedi'ot Aharonot*, 10 March 1995, p.1.

51. The analysis of the elections is beyond the scope of this article. Netanayahu's razor-thin victory is primarily related to more effective campaigning and organization, and to a better ability to capture the center of the Israeli political map than Labor.

52. E. Inbar and S. Sandler, 'The Changing Israeli Security Equation: Toward a Security Regime', *Review of International Studies* 21/1 (Jan. 1995) pp.41–59.

53. See Inbar and Sandler, 'Israel's Deterrence Strategy Revisited' (note 30) pp.342–3; Gabriel Ben-Dor, 'Arab Rationality and Deterrence', in Aharon Klieman and Ariel Levite (eds.), *Deterrence in the Middle East*, JCSS Study no.22 (Boulder, CO: Westview 1993) p.97; Adam Garfinkle, 'An Observation on Arab Culture and Deterrence: Metaphors and Misgivings', in Inbar (note 24) pp.201–29.

# Radical Islam and the Struggle for Influence in Central Asia

## ROBERT O. FREEDMAN

The threat of an Iranian-style Islamic takeover of the newly independent states of Central Asia is currently more of a potential than actual threat to the secular rulers of these countries. Nonetheless, economic, environmental and nationality problems render these rulers vulnerable to a future Islamic potential challenge. The threat of Islam has been used by local leaders to justify dictatorships and intervene in neighboring countries, while foreign governments, such as Turkey and Israel, have sought to exploit the threat of Islam in Central Asia to strengthen their support from the United States. By contrast, Iran has downplayed the Islamic factor in its foreign policy toward these new republics and as a result has enhanced its relationship with Russia, which seeks to establish its hegemony over the region.

In the aftermath of the collapse of the Soviet Union, the emergence of six independent Muslim states which had been constituent republics of the former USSR, gave rise to the fear, in Moscow as well as Washington, that Iranian-backed Islamic radicalism was on the verge of sweeping into the new Muslim states. This essay will examine the role of radical Islam[1] in the politics and foreign policies of the new Muslim states of Central Asia (Uzbekistan, Kazakhstan, Turkmenistan, Kyrgyzstan and Tajikistan) and analyze the impact of the Islamic issue on the competition for influence taking place in the region. While the primary competitors are Russia, Turkey and Iran, mention will also be made of the policies of Israel and the United States. It is interesting to note that the policies of the Central Asian states of Iran and Turkey as well as of Russia are motivated to a greater or lesser degree by fear of Islamic radicalism and the threat it presents to the region (whether or not the threat is perceived correctly). This article argues that while initially many in Moscow feared that a surge of Islamic radicalism would sweep the region, their fears were unfounded and in the three year period following the collapse of the Soviet Union, Russia has managed to reassert a modicum of control over the region. Turkey, which initially saw the new Muslim states as an area in which it could exercise influence – and in the process obtain large amounts of US aid to fight Islamic radicalism – became bogged down in its own domestic problems and so far has proved incapable of challenging Russia in Central Asia. At the same time Iran, under the leadership of its pragmatic President Ali

Akbar Hashemi Rafsanjani, proved more interested in assuring its supply of sophisticated arms from Russia than in seeking to promote Islamic radicalism in Central Asia, which, in any case, was not yet ripe for it. Finally, Israel, also concerned about Islamic radicalism which could threaten its own interests in Central Asia, sought to aid the states in the region economically while at the same time seeking to reinforce its ties with the United States by taking the lead in the fight against Islamic radicalism.

## Central Asia's Vulnerability to Islamic Radicalism

In the aftermath of the collapse of the Soviet Union, the leaders of the newly independent Muslim states of Central Asia faced a number of serious problems, of which Islamic radicalism was far from the top of the list. Perhaps the most serious was the near economic collapse that, with the exception of Turkmenistan,[2] affected all of the countries of the region. Under the Soviet Union, the Central Asian republics primarily supplied raw materials (cotton, grain, oil, natural gas, etc.) to the other republics in the Former Soviet Union (FSU) (Kazakhstan, which has an industrial base, was a partial exception), while importing manufactured goods under the centralized planning system run by Moscow. After 1991, to a large degree, the sources of supply were cut off, as were some of the markets for Central Asian products, and the Central Asian economies have had a difficult time adjusting to the new market conditions that are, albeit slowly, beginning to take effect throughout the FSU. Compounding this difficulty were the already serious problems of unemployment and underemployment (except in Turkmenistan) that existed in the last days of the USSR and were only exacerbated by the rapid rise in population throughout the region. The situation was made even worse by soaring inflation rates that beset the new Central Asian states, cutting the populations' already limited purchasing power and leading to popular discontent.

Another set of problems facing the new leaders were ecological ones. The drying up of the Aral Sea due to overuse of water from the Syr Darya and Amu Darya rivers had led not only to water shortages but also to the blowing of poisonous salts over sections of Kazakhstan, Uzbekistan and Turkmenistan.[3] In addition, the overuse of pesticides and fertilizers, due to the Soviet effort to increase agricultural production, had led to the poisoning of the soil. This had caused damage to the health of significant numbers of the rural population. Further contamination was caused by Soviet nuclear tests in Kazakhstan. Although these economic and ecological problems can be blamed on the old Soviet leadership in Moscow, unless action is taken by the Central Asia leaders to solve them, they are liable to provide political ammunition for the opponents of the new regime, including Islamic radicals.

Another set of very serious problems facing the new Central Asian leaders relates to the issue of nationality. Caused in part by Russian immigration to the region over the past century as well as the way the Soviets deliberately drew the borders of the republics (especially that between Uzbekistan and Tajikistan), the interspersal of populations poses a series of delicate problems for the Central Asian states as they seek to forge national unities based on the dominant nationality of their respective states. This problem is most acute in Kazakhstan where due to losses during collectivization and the immigration of Russians over the last 100 years, Kazakhs are a minority within their own state (41.9 per cent) while Russians (37 per cent), Ukrainians (5.2 per cent) and Germans (4.7 per cent) comprise almost half the population.[4] Given the fact that the bulk of the Russians live in the northern part of Kazakhstan near the border with Russia, Kazakh leader Nursultan Nazarbayev faces the dual problem of preventing the breaking up of his country and the inclusion of its northern section in a 'greater Russia' if he antagonizes the Russian population too much, while at the same time needing to fulfill the needs of his Kazakh base of support. A similar, albeit somewhat less serious problem is found in Kyrgyzstan where the Kyrgyz are 52.4 per cent of the population and the Russians 21.5 per cent. Kyrgyz leader Askar Akayev is also hampered by the fact that most of the skilled jobs in his country are held by Russians and the Kyrgyz economy, already in very difficult straits, could collapse if the Russians were to depart en masse. For this reason, he is making major efforts to entreat his Russian population to stay, even promising to establish a Slavic university for the children of the Russian community. In both states, the presence of the Russians, who are seen as the old colonial overlords in Central Asia, provides political ammunition not only for nationalist opposition but also, potentially, for an Islamic opposition. The Kyrgyz have an additional nationality problem to face as well, given the fact that 12.9 per cent of the state's population is Uzbek, and the Uzbeks and Kyrgyz have already clashed, with lethal results, in the volatile Fergana Valley, shared by Uzbekistan, Kyrgyzstan and Tajikistan.

The other three Central Asian states have much less of a Russian minority problem: 9.8 per cent in Turkmenistan, 8.3 per cent in Uzbekistan and 3.5 per cent in Tajikistan (where it is rapidly dropping because of the country's ongoing civil war). Tajikistan, however, has a major Uzbek minority problem (25 per cent) and faces a serious problem of Uzbek irredentism. For their part, while Tajiks are only between 5 and 10 per cent of the population of Uzbekistan,[5] they are concentrated in the important Uzbek cities of Bukhara and Samarkand. As discussed below, one of the reasons Uzbek leader Islam Karimov intervened in the Tajik civil war was to prevent the quasi-democratic government experiment in Tajikistan from threatening, by example, his highly authoritarian regime in Uzbekistan, and generating irredentist claims to Samarkand and Bukhara.

In the face of these economic, ecological and nationality problems, each of the leaders of Central Asia is seeking to create a new national identity.[6] The question, however, is what will its underpinnings be? Underlying Central Asia is a Persian cultural heritage, but superimposed on top of it is a Turkic linguistic heritage that exists in every state except for Tajikistan, where Persian remains the national language. The 'national' heritage is perhaps the most recent of all, in that it was partially created by the Soviet Union as Stalin pursued a 'divide and rule' policy among the Central Asian peoples. Given this mix of Persian, Turkish and national identities, where does Islam fit in and can it be used to threaten the existing regimes? To answer this question it is necessary to briefly examine the political situation in each of the Central Asian states and assess how their leaders are handling the Islamic issue.

Kazakhstan and Kyrgyzstan are the least Islamized of the Central Asian states, with Islam having penetrated the two nomadic peoples only about 200 years ago. Soviet leaders, seeing Islam as an ideological rival to communism, succeeded in stamping out most overt practices; in both countries Islam is more of a folk or cultural phenomenon than a theological one.[7] This is fortunate for the leaders of the two countries, both more or less western-style democrats (Akayev more than Nazarbayev, who had been a communist-era apparatchik), because an assertive Islam might further hasten the departure of the Russian population of the two countries, which neither Nazarbayev, for political reasons, nor Akayev, for economic ones, can afford. In any case, both Nazarbayev and Akayev, while saying they are proud Muslims, publicly denounce Islamic radicalism.

Islam was far more developed in Turkmenistan, Uzbekistan and Tajikistan than in Kazakhstan or Kyrgyzstan at the time of the Russian revolution of 1917. Nonetheless, while the Soviet leaders were unable to completely eliminate Islam as an independent movement, particularly in rural areas, they did succeed, through a centralized government-controlled religious administration, in controlling it for the most part. They managed to limit Islam to a cultural phenomenon, although the Soviet press complained from time to time that even Central Asian communists participated in such Islamic rituals as circumcision. With the onset of *perestroika*, however, and especially since the collapse of the Soviet Union, there has been an Islamic revival.[8] Mosques have proliferated and *madrasas* (religious schools) have expanded. Perhaps more ominously for the regimes, Islamic renaissance parties emerged, posing a problem for authoritarian leaders like Uzbekistan's Karimov, Turkmenistan's Sapurmarad Niyazov and Tajikistan's Emamali Rakhmonov. Of the five

Central Asian states, Turkmenistan is by far the best off economically due to its relatively small population and large reserves of natural gas. Due to its continuing tribal structure, it is also the most stable. Niyazov has proclaimed himself a cultural Muslim and has sought good ties with neighboring Iran, but does not permit independent Islamic political activity. As long as the economy of Turkmenistan remains strong and Niyazov is able to maintain himself in power, Islamic radicalism may find little fertile ground in Turkmenistan.

The situation is far more complex in neighboring Uzbekistan. By far the largest in terms of population of any of the five Central Asian states and suffering severe problems of inflation, overpopulation and unemployment, Uzbekistan appears vulnerable to the threat of Islamic radicalism despite the fact that the country has rich reserves of oil and natural gas and is a major producer of cotton. Karimov, aware of the threat posed by Islamic radicalism, which he constantly overstates to gain Russian and western support, has adopted several tactics to deal with the problem.[9] First, he banned the Islamic Renaissance Party, along with all other political parties in Uzbekistan. Proclaiming the theme of 'stability', Karimov pointed to the chaos in neighboring Tajikistan (which, ironically, he helped to promote) and claimed that economic development had to come before democracy in Uzbekistan lest Islamic radicals seize power. He has also moved to outflank the Islamic opposition by acting as the patron of cultural Islam. He organized the extensive refurbishment of the Islamic complex at the Shrine of Sufi leader Khaja Bahudin Nakshband near Bukhara and held a major international Islamic convocation there during the spring of 1993 on the 675th anniversary of Nakshband's birth. Karimov also organized the refurbishment of the tomb and Islamic complex of Abdallah al-Bukhari (a famous gatherer of *hadiths* [prophetic traditions]) outside of Samarkand, and held a major international ceremony there with Muslim leaders from around the world in October 1993. Interestingly enough, just as Soviet leaders used the official Islamic establishment, the Islamic spiritual directorate, to help control Central Asian Muslims, Karimov is using it to both gain political legitimacy and expand Uzbek influence. In an interview, the executive director of the Islamic spiritual directorate noted, 'We hope to contribute to the new ideology of independence of Uzbekistan, since we feel the center part of this ideology should be Islam ... in the future we expect the Muslims of all of Central Asia to be under our direction'.[10]

In evaluating Karimov's efforts to outflank the Islamic radicals, one can make several preliminary observations. First, Karimov's efforts, for the time being at least, seem to have been successful as he has managed to drive both religious and non-religious political opposition underground. Nonetheless, if Karimov continues to prohibit all public opposition activity, the only place where the opposition may be able to gather will be in the mosque. If this happens a situation not unlike that in Iran from 1974 to 1978 may develop, where the mosque was used to help topple the regime. Of course, the situation in Uzbekistan is different from Iran, where for hundreds of years the Shi'i religious establishment was independent of, and often in conflict with, the regime. It is also unlike the Sudan where religious political parties were active well before the state became independent in 1955.[11]

Tajikistan provides a special case since Islamic forces, albeit initially not radical ones, have played a role in that country's ongoing civil war.[12] Essentially, the communist era leadership of Tajikistan was drawn from the Tajik provinces of Khojand (Leninabad) in the north (an area heavily populated by Uzbeks) and Kulyab in the south. Once the Soviet Union collapsed, the Tajik leader, Rahman Nabiyev, was challenged by a group of democrats and moderate Islamists, whose bases of support were outside Khojand and Kulyab, particularly in the eastern provinces of Garm and Pamir, as well as in the capital, Dushanbe. This loose alliance succeeded in overthrowing Nabiev in the fall of 1992. This in turn alarmed Uzbek leader Islam Karimov who feared the infection of the model of a democrat/Islamic alliance into Uzbekistan where he was being challenged by similar kinds of democrats and moderate Muslims. Leading the Islamic movement in Tajikistan was Qadi (Judge) Akbar Turajanzode, who took pains to dispel the idea that he or the majority of his Islamic Renaissance Party were Islamic radicals. Thus he refused to run for president in the Tajik elections and called for a secular democratic state with full respect for human rights. While he acknowledged that some members of the Islamic Renaissance Party wanted an Islamic state, he indicated that such a state was not desirable both because of the secular nature of the population whose Islam was much more of a cultural than a religious identity, but also because an Islamic state would scare away the foreign investment which Tajikistan needed so badly. Also, in a possible slap at Iran, whose Persian language and culture Tajikistan shares (although not its Shi'i form of Islam), Turajanzode noted, 'Let the sins of society not be attributed to Islam'.[13]

Despite the moderate position of Turajanzode, Karimov claimed that the Tajik leader and his followers were 'fundamentalists'. He then intervened militarily with the help of Russia, whose leaders at the time (Fall 1992) were almost paranoid about the threat of Islamic radicalism, and restored to power the old-line communists, now led by Emamali Rakhmanov. While many of the democratic opposition fled to Moscow or to the West, much of the Islamic opposition fled across the Tajik border into Afghanistan where they became radicalized by Afghan *mujahidin* (primarily by the forces of Afghan Tajik leader Ahmad Shah Mas'ud, who is engaged in his own rivalry with the Afghan Uzbek leader, Rashid Dostam). Some of the Tajik refugees, given military training and weapons by the *mujahidin*, then mounted attacks back across the border into Tajikistan. In the process, they killed a number of Russian soldiers guarding the Tajik border and drew Moscow into the heart of the fighting. This posed a serious problem for the Russian leaders. On the one hand, as noted by deputy defense minister Boris Gromov, they had no desire to become too deeply involved in another Afghanistan-type war. Nonetheless, Gromov warned against the withdrawal of Russian border guards from the Afghan-Tajik border, saying it would lead to 'a lack of stability in Central Asia' that would spread to Russia and open 'channels for the flow of narcotics and weapons'.[14] Deputy foreign minister Anatoly Adamishin, Yeltsin's diplomatic troubleshooter, warned on his return from Tajikistan in early November 1993 that if Russia left Central Asia 'it will turn into a continually bubbling cauldron that will boil right next to our own borders, next to the Volga, if you wish'.[15] The Russian ambassador to Uzbekistan, interviewed in early October 1993 in Tashkent, warned of the spread of Islamic 'fundamentalism' from Tajikistan into Russia.[16]

This summary of the Tajik civil war and the role of Islam in it, reveals how the perceived (or deliberately misperceived) role of Islam can be a factor not only in internal politics in a Central Asian state, but also in the international politics of the entire region. The next section will examine the policies of Russia, Turkey, Iran and Israel in Central Asia, and the way each has dealt with the Islamic issue.

## The Politics of External Powers in Central Asia

### Russia

In the immediate aftermath of the collapse of the Soviet Union, Russian leader Boris Yeltsin was so preoccupied with the need to establish good relations with the United States and consolidate Russia's position as the primary successor state of the former Soviet Union (and acquire its seat on the United Nation's Security Council) that he paid little attention to Russia's relations with the other newly emergent countries of the FSU. His opponents on the center and right of the Russian political spectrum, however, soon seized on his lack of attention, claiming that Yeltsin was ignoring what had become a vacuum of power in what they called the 'near abroad', and that outside powers could move in to assert their influence in what should be Russia's natural sphere of influence. Politics aside, Russia indeed did have clear interests in Central Asia. Those included the approximately ten million Russians who suddenly found themselves outside of the boundaries of their new homeland, many of whom perceived themselves as threatened by the new situation where virtually overnight their status had been transformed from ruling class to threatened minority. Consequently they appealed for support from the Russian leadership which, under prodding from the Russian right, soon began to champion their cause. A second Russian interest was economic. Millions of Russian workers, particularly in the textile industry, depended on raw materials from Central Asia and when these were interrupted following the collapse of the USSR, many found themselves unemployed. A third strategic interest took two forms. In the first place, particularly in 1992, there was a widespread fear of Islamic radicalism penetrating from Central Asia into Russia itself (there are 19 million Muslims in Russia). In addition, there was the concern that regional powers, such as Turkey and Iran, or even the US, might exploit the new geostrategic situation to extend their influence into Central Asia. Thus *Pravda*, by then a spokesman of the nationalist part of the Russian political spectrum, commenting on a visit by US secretary of state James Baker to Central Asia in February 1992, complained that Baker was doing more than the entire Russian foreign ministry and that the US was drawing the Islamic states of the former Soviet Union into the orbit of US policy and away from Russia, 'their closest neighbor and natural ally'.[17] US actions were linked by the Russian right to those of America's NATO ally, Turkey. Because of its Turkic cultural and linguistic ties to Azerbayjan, Uzbekistan, Turkmenistan, Kyrgyzstan and Kazakhstan, Turkey was seen as seeking to create a Turkic alliance on the southern periphery of Russia, using such devices as the Black Sea Economic Cooperation Zone, which it created, and the Economic Cooperation Organization in which it shared leadership with Iran.[18] This Russian concern was not baseless, as exemplified by the comments of the late Turkish President Turgut Özal, who noted in March 1993: 'Whatever the shape of things to come, we will be the real elements and most important pieces of the status quo and new order to be established in the region from the Balkans to Central Asia. In this region, there cannot be a status quo or political order that will exclude us'.[19] While some in Moscow feared Turkish political expansion into the Caucasus and Central Asia, others were concerned by the threat of 'fundamentalist' Islam emanating from Iran that could infect not only the Muslim states of the former Soviet Union but also the Muslims who lived in Russia. For this reason, they saw the secular Islamic model of Turkey as a useful counterweight to Iranian Islamic radicalism.[20]

By the beginning of 1993, however, the Yeltsin leadership was beginning to change its view of the threat of Islamic radicalism in Central Asia. Except for the civil war in Tajikistan, which had not yet caused large numbers of Russian casualties, Islamic radicalism did not appear to be a serious problem, and the basically secular outlook of the local leaders, as well as their ability to hold onto power, had become clear. At the same time, under heavy pressure from nationalist elements in both the parliament which he disbanded by force in October 1993 and the even more right-wing parliament that was elected in December 1993, Yeltsin began to take a much more assertive role toward the states of the former Soviet Union (except for the Baltic states) seeking to bring them under Russian control. In part this was due to the prohibitive costs of constructing a new defense perimeter around Russia to replace the one which protected the former Soviet Union and which was located, primarily, in the newly independent states. Additionally, the new policy was aimed at protecting the Russians living in the non-Russian republics who, if forced to return to Russia, would create a major refugee problem which the severely burdened Russian economy would have a hard time dealing with. In large part, however, Yeltsin was seeking to co-opt the nationalist agenda for his own political purposes. Russian policy, beginning in early 1993, sought to place Central Asia under Russian control. Tactics used included manipulation of the Russian ruble in an effort to get the new states limited hard currency reserves under Russian domination; the blocking of pipelines and other transportation links to force such Central Asian states as Kazakhstan to bow to the Russian will; the signing of military cooperation agreements to reestablish the old Soviet defensive perimeter; and the urging of the Central Asian states to allow 'dual citizenship' for Russian citizens.[21]

While these measures have worked, to a greater or lesser degree, in the short run, it appears doubtful whether Russia has the economic capacity to provide the kind of capital assistance the Central Asian states need to develop. In addition, the greater the overt Russian presence, the more vulnerable the Central Asian regimes become to accusations by Islamic radicals and other opposition elements that they are subservient to Moscow. In any case, while Moscow in the short run has succeeded in reestablishing a modicum of control over Central Asia, its long range capabilities remain in question and its very presence in the region may strengthen Islamic radicalism.

*Turkey*

When the Soviet Union collapsed, Turkish President Turgut Özal and part of the Turkish elite saw the opportunity of expanding Turkish influence into Azerbayjan and throughout Central Asia. Such a development would have the added benefit of enhancing Turkey's relationship with the United States in the wake of the Cold War, as Turkey would serve as a bulwark against Iranian-inspired Islamic radicalism. Özal's initial optimism led him to pledge more than $1 billion in credits for the newly independent Central

Asian states in such areas as banking, education and transportation. In addition, Turkey established direct air communications with the region; Turkish television beamed programs to the Turkish-speaking countries and Turkish businessmen established numerous joint ventures. Yet while this assistance was welcomed by Central Asian leaders (and Azerbayjan), it did not lead to the rapid expansion of Turkish influence. In the first place, having just rid themselves of one 'big brother' the Central Asians had no desire to replace it with another and sought to maximize their ties with a number of states to avoid dependence on any one.[22] Second, as noted above, the economic problems of these states (with the exception of Turkmenistan) were so great that Turkey simply did not have the economic capacity to meet their needs, especially as its own economy was reeling from a 70 per cent annual inflation rate. Third, with the resurgence of the Kurdish uprising in southeastern Anatolia, Turkish attention was diverted from Central Asia to more pressing needs at home. Similarly, Turkey was distracted by the fighting in the former Yugoslavia, pitting Bosnian Muslims, supported by Turkey, against Serbs and, initially, Croats; the continuing conflict with Greece over Cyprus; and, above all, the war between Armenia and Azerbayjan.[23] Finally, the death of President Özal, ironically, just after he had completed a tour of Central Asia in March 1993, also seemed to weaken Turkish efforts to gain influence in the region, while Turkish leaders had to be disappointed that the Central Asian Muslim leaders did not back the Turkish position on such issues as Cyprus.

A final problem for Turkey lay in Moscow's use of economic warfare to gain political obedience. By closing pipelines to Kazakh exports of oil and natural gas and pressuring Azerbayjan to reroute the oil expected from its Caspian offshore oil fields (which were to be developed by a consortium of western oil companies) through Russia, rather than through Turkey, Moscow further limited Turkish influence.[24] While Turkey responded to this pressure by threatening to limit Russian oil tanker shipments through the Bosphorus and Dardanelles Straits, Russia, in turn, planned a pipeline circumventing the straits and passing instead through its traditional ally, Bulgaria, and Turkey's enemy, Greece, to the Mediterranean.

Despite, as of 1995, Moscow's having the upper hand in the influence competition Turkey has not given up. At the end of October 1994, Turkey hosted the leaders of the Turkic states of the former Soviet Union, with Turkish President Süleyman Demirel noting that 'instead of one, there are seven Turkish flags since the collapse of the Soviet Union' – a remark that reportedly greatly irritated the Russians.[25] While Moscow may have taken comfort from one paragraph of the conference's final declaration – that the heads of state reaffirmed their belief in a social order based on *secularism* – the Russians could not have been too happy with another paragraph in which the heads of state welcomed the construction of natural gas and oil pipelines to provide Europe with these fuels *via Turkey*.[26]

In sum, initial concerns in Moscow that Turkey would create a pro-Ankara bloc of Muslim/Turkic states of the former Soviet Union have not come to pass. The Russian leadership, noting that the threat of Islamic radicalism was not as great as it initially feared, has exploited the economic weaknesses of the Central Asian states, the ongoing conflicts in Georgia and Azerbayjan, and the economic and foreign policy problems facing Turkey to successfully rebuild Russian influence at Turkey's expense. Nonetheless, Turkish cultural ties to Central Asia remain strong, and should its economy improve and it be able to solve its Kurdish problem, Turkey may again be a formidable competitor to Russia in Central Asia.

## Iran

In order to understand Iranian policy in Central Asia, it is first necessary to understand the Russian-Iranian arms sales relationship. Confronted by American power in the Gulf following the end of the Gulf War; American-armed GCC states like Saudi Arabia; a temporarily defeated Iraq which had fought an eight year war against Iran from 1980 to 1988 and whose leader Saddam Hussein continued to harbor hostile intentions toward Iran; and Turkey with which relations were, at best, mixed, Iran clearly had need of modern armaments. Its only source of such advanced weaponry as MiG-29 fighters and SU-24 bombers was first the Soviet Union, and then Russia. Because of Iran's need for Russian arms, the Iranian leader, Hashemi Rafsanjani, was careful not to alienate Moscow. Thus when Azerbayjan declared its independence of the Soviet Union in November 1991, Iran, unlike Turkey, did not recognize its independence until after the USSR collapsed. Indeed, Iran feared the possible irredentist pull of an independent Azerbayjan on Iran's Azerbayjani population – particularly when Abulfaz Elçibey was in power between June 1992 and June 1993, despite the fact that Iran and Azerbayjan share the Shi'i form of Islam. Similarly, despite occasional rhetoric from other Iranian officials,[27] Rafsanjani has so far ensured that Iran maintains a relatively low Islamic profile in Azerbayjan and Central Asia, emphasizing cultural and economic ties rather than Islam as the centerpiece of relations. In part, of course, this was due to the fact that after more than 70 years of Soviet rule, Islam was in a weak state in the countries of the former Soviet Union, the leaders of the Muslim successor states were all secular Muslims and the chances for an Iranian-style Islamic revolution were very low. Indeed, some skeptics argued that Iran was simply waiting for mosques to be built and Islam to mature before trying to bring about Islamic revolutions.[28] Nonetheless, the Russian leadership basically saw Iran as acting very responsibly in Central Asia and this was one of the factors that encouraged it to continue supplying Iran with modern weaponry, including, in 1992 and 1993, submarines, as well as to promise a nuclear reactor despite strong protests from the United States.[29] Other reasons for Moscow to seek a good relationship with Iran included the hard currency which it received from the arms sales – a very scarce commodity badly needed by the hard-pressed Russian economy; a hope that Iran could help procure the release of Russian POWs in Afghanistan; and the fact that, given the hostility between the United States and Iran, Iran served as a country in the critical Gulf region where Russia could exercise influence.

To be sure, there were areas of tension between Russia and Iran. As Armenia, tacitly backed by Russia, mounted an offensive against Azerbayjan in the late summer of 1993, thousands of Azeris fled toward the Iranian border, leading Iran to mobilize on its borders – an action that elicited a limited warning from the Russian foreign ministry.[30] A far more serious problem in Russian-Iranian relations was the situation in Tajikistan. As Russian casualties on the Tajik-Afghan border rose in 1993, Russian diplomacy sought a political settlement to the war. The Russian government took several steps. In addition to mobilizing the support of the Central Asian states to help defend the Tajik border (although, at most, they were to send only token forces), Russian diplomats sought a dialogue between the Tajik rebels and their government opponents. Since Turajanzode was in exile in Iran, such a move necessarily meant bringing Iran into the diplomatic process. Indeed, in his visit to Tehran in late March 1993, foreign minister Kozyrev discussed the Tajik situation 'in detail' with his Iranian hosts.[31] He stated that Russia was seeking to use Tehran's influence to persuade the Tajik opposition to enter negotiations with the Tajik government, although Kozyrev also pointedly noted that 'since Iran is not a member of the CIS (Commonwealth of Independent States), Russia does not recognize Tehran's right, the right Moscow has, to play a direct role in Tajik affairs'.[32] While in Tehran, Kozyrev signed a Russian-Iranian agreement under which the two countries pledged 'not to use force or the threat of force against each other, not to let their territories be used in launching aggressions, subversive or separatist actions against the other side, or against states friendly to it' – the latter statement a clear reference to Tajikistan.[33] By the spring of 1994, with the aid of Iran, Russia managed to get talks started between the opposing Tajik sides, although Russia continued to suffer casualties in the fighting along the Tajik-Afghan border. By mid-1995, Russia had partially defused the situation, though there was still no agreement between the Tajik government and the rebels. Meanwhile, throughout the conflict the Rafsanjani regime maintained a low profile and helped Moscow diplomatically, thus, for the time being at least, reinforcing the Russian-

Iranian relationship. Iran has taken a similar low profile position toward Russia's invasion of Muslim Chechniya. Nonetheless, should Iran give aid to the Tajik rebels or Chechens or other Muslims in the Caucasus, Russian-Iranian relations would suffer a serious blow.

While Russian-Iranian cooperation appeared evident in Tajikistan (although some Russians complained that Iranian elements, perhaps not under Rafsanjani's control, continued to aid the Tajik opposition),[34] other problems did affect the relationship. First, as Russia reasserted its influence over Azerbayjan, the prospect of Russian troops returning to the Iranian border could not have been welcomed by Tehran. Second, as Russia moved to consolidate its defense relationship with Kuwait in November 1993, Iran took umbrage, with *Tehran Radio* warning Kuwait against concluding military pacts with states located outside the Near East because such agreements amounted to 'interference in Kuwait's internal affairs and could cause conflict in neighboring countries'.[35] Two weeks later a Moscow Persian language radio broadcast warned Tehran that the favorable prospects for the development of Russian-Iranian relations could be greatly harmed 'if Iran proposes political conditions, for example, concerning Tajikistan or Russia's military-technical cooperation with the Arab countries of the Persian Gulf'.[36]

Nevertheless, what is potentially the most serious problem in Russian-Iranian relations lies in Iran's offer to provide both the Central Asian states and Azerbayjan with transportation links for the export of their raw materials, particularly oil and natural gas. Russia has been exploiting its control over oil pipelines and railroad systems in order to help it regain political control in Central Asia. Nonetheless, except for a rail link already under construction between natural-gas rich Turkmenistan and Iran, Iran's offer seems primarily to be a problem for the future. In part, this is due to the weakness of the Iranian economy, which is suffering from a high inflation rate (58.8 per cent in June 1995 by the Iranian government's own figures)[37] as well as by a heavy burden of foreign debt. Under these circumstances, it is unlikely that Iran can provide the funds for railroad and pipeline construction. In addition the US has, *de facto*, aided Yeltsin in his efforts to regain control over Central Asia by publicly discouraging Kazakh leader Nursultan Nazarbayev from exporting its oil via Iran, and has also pressured the Azeri regime of Gaidar Aliev to rescind its offer to Iran of a 5 per cent participation in Azerbayjan's Caspian Sea oil consortium. While the US has encouraged alternate transportation routes for Central Asian and Azeri oil through Turkey, the continued conflict between Azerbayjan and Armenia over Nagarno-Karabakh and the continuing unsettled conditions in Georgia (the two possible routes to Turkey) make the Russian routes the only viable ones for the near future. In addition, Iran, which was furious at losing its 5 per cent share of the oil consortium, has joined Russia in claiming that no oil can be shipped without the agreement of all the Caspian littoral states, thus further strengthening Russian influence in both the Transcaucasus and Central Asia. Clearly, a rich and powerful Azerbayjan, Muslim or not, is not in Iranian interest, whether under Popular Front leader Abulfaz Elçibey or ex-communist Aliev; and, for the time being at least, Iran seems willing to join Russia in curbing Azeri freedom of action. It should also be noted that the Central Asian leaders, as well as those of Azerbayjan, remain suspicious of Iran, despite its low key Islamic policy. Kazakh leader Nazarbayev noted, after a visit by Rafsanjani, that their talks were held 'in accordance with the basic principles of respect of independence and sovereignty of each state, non-interference in internal affairs, (and) respect of the choice of each nation, including political, economic and *religious* matters'.[38]

In sum, so long as Iran does not 'meddle' in Transcaucasia or Central Asia in a major way or push Islamic radicalism there, and so long as it continues to be able to pay for its purchases of Russian weapons with hard currency, Russian-Iranian relations can be expected to continue to progress in a proper, if not a particularly close manner. This is despite the ideological differences between the two countries.[39] Nonetheless, given the growing instability in Iran and the growing challenge to its president, Hashemi Rafsanjani, by Iranian leaders advocating the export of Islamic radicalism to Central Asia, as well as the continuing political instability in Russia, both the future of Russian-Iranian relations and the future Iranian role in Central Asia are difficult to predict.

## *Israel*

Unlike Russia and Iran which border Central Asia, or Turkey which has close ethnic, linguistic and religious ties to it, Israel is physically, ethnically and religiously removed from the region except for the approximately 200,000 Jews who lived there at the time of the collapse of the Soviet Union. Nonetheless, Israel has clear interests in Central Asia, not least of which is the perceived need to combat radical Islam.

The central Israeli concern when the USSR collapsed was the fear that the nuclear weapons of Kazakhstan might be sold to Israel's Middle East enemies Iraq, Iran and Libya. A second concern was the fate of Central Asia's 200,000 Jews whom Israel hoped would continue to be allowed to emigrate to Israel. A third concern was that the newly independent states of Central Asia, being Muslim, would support Israel's Islamic enemies in the United Nations and other diplomatic forums. Finally, Israel, which had begun to develop economic ties in Central Asia in the final years of the

Soviet Union, hoped to be able to further develop these ties, particularly because it could offer assistance in the agricultural sector, in the areas of irrigation, water management and cotton growing-assistance that were in great demand in Central Asia. Underlying Israel's policy toward the region was the fear that if radical Islamist forces seized power, all four of Israel's concerns would become reality. Consequently, Israeli diplomacy worked actively in the region to try to block such an eventuality.

The most important target for Israeli diplomacy was in Kazakhstan, and it was there that Israel scored its most important political success. In mid-January 1992 Israel's communications minister, Rafael Pinhasi, made a three-day official visit to Kazakhstan to promote cooperation in telecommunications.[40] On 1 April 1992, a Kazakh delegation led by the Kazakh minister of trade signed an agreement with the Israeli government under which Israel would help Kazakhstan develop agriculture and live-stock breeding, train specialists and cooperate in the joint development of modern industrial technology.[41] One week later, Israel and Kazakhstan established full diplomatic relations, and Nazarbayev, in talks with Israel's ambassador to Russia, Aryeh Levin, stated that Kazakhstan was interested in securing loans and modern agricultural know-how. He also affirmed Kazakhstan's interest in a peaceful settlement of the Israeli-Palestinian conflict.[42] Four days after meeting with Levin, Nazarbayev met Simha Dinitz, head of the Jewish Agency, to discuss plans for economic cooperation in the spheres of entrepreneurship, banks, financial systems and investment policy as well as long-term cooperation in the areas of science and culture.[43]

But far more significant was the issue of the ultimate fate of Kazakhstan's nuclear weapons. Possibly in an effort to quell rumors that Kazakhstan had sold such weapons to Iran, Nazarbayev gave an interview to one of Israel's major newspapers, *Yediot Aharonot*, in which he said: 'As for the nuclear weapons in our possession, you need not worry. They are meticulously guarded, and it is absolutely impossible to sneak them across our borders'.[44] Nazarbayev also offered to help mediate the Arab-Israeli conflict.

Israeli-Kazakh relations hit a new milestone in September 1992 when the Kazakh prime minister, Sergei Tereschenko, arrived in Israel for a three-day official visit. During his visit, Tereschenko repeated Nazarbayev's assurances on Kazakhstan's nuclear weapons: 'Nuclear weapons will not be sold, not to Iran or any other country. Kazakhstan is peace-loving. Israel has nothing to worry about.'[45] The Kazakh prime minister also praised the work being done in Kazakhstan by Israeli companies in the areas of large-scale cotton cultivation, farm mechanization and irrigation. He asked for Israeli help in manufacturing finished products and marketing them abroad.[46] On the final day of his visit, Tereschenko signed an aviation agreement providing for a weekly flight from Alma Ata to Israel.[47]

Israel's priority in developing ties with Kazakhstan was reflected in February 1993 when the Israeli parliament approved loan guarantees of 55 per cent for two major investment projects totaling $220 million.[48] In April 1993 Nazarbayev received an Israeli delegation headed by science and economic minister Shimon Shitreet and energy minister Amnon Rubinstein for discussions on Israeli aid to Kazakhstan's agricultural, food and pharmaceutical industries, gas and oil production, education, satellite communications and power engineering.[49] In June 1993, the Knesset increased the percentage of loan guarantees to 65 per cent.[50]

One of the salient aspects of Israeli relations with Central Asia is the important role that Central Asian Jews, both within and beyond the region, are playing. Kazakh Prime Minister Tereschenko, during his visit to Israel in September 1992, introduced a Jewish member of his delegation as 'the first capitalist in Kazakhstan'.[51] Given both the large number of Jews who emigrated to Israel from Central Asia and the large number of Jews still residing there (around 150,000), this 'Jewish connection' may turn out to be a major asset in Israel's dealing with Central Asia, assuming that Islamic radicalism does not triumph in the region. As Sadik Safaev, first deputy of the Uzbek ministry of foreign economic relations noted: 'Many Jews have relations here if they emigrated recently. Over 2,000 years these people did a lot for this country. Uzbekistan welcomes activity from Israeli firms'.[52]

As in Kazakhstan, Israeli firms helped pave the way for Israel's diplomatic relations with Uzbekistan. Perhaps the most successful of these was Shaul Eisenberg's pilot project in drip irrigation, which enabled Uzbekistan – with the help of Israeli specialists – to increase cotton production by 40 per cent while reducing water usage by two-thirds and fertilizer and pesticide use by 10–20 per cent.[53] Given Uzbekistan's extremely limited water availability and the ecological damage due to overuse of pesticides and fertilizer, Israeli help could be of critical importance. Indeed, as the Israeli ambassador to Uzbekistan noted, 'Our business ties are the key to our influence in Uzbekistan, because we are providing the kinds of goods and services which the Uzbeks need'.[54]

Perhaps the pinnacle of Israel's relations with the Central Asian states came in January 1993 when the president of Kyrgyzstan, Askar Akayev, made an official three-day visit to Israel. In an interview, Akayev clarified his reasons for the visit: 'My aim is to join Israeli technology with the raw materials we have at our disposal and to create industries. You have created the highest cotton yields in the world. We have rather good agricultural land but we have a backward technology in food processing. We would certainly want Israeli help in these areas.'[55]

In a surprise move, Akayev, who in the interview described himself as a 'proud but secular Muslim', announced the establishment of the Kyrgyz embassy in Jerusalem, the first Islamic and only the third country to do so (the others have their embassies in Tel Aviv because of the continuing dispute over the legal status of Jerusalem). Although Akayev coupled his announcement with support for the independence of the Palestinian people, he also called for Jerusalem to be 'a united and indivisible city' – a statement his hosts were very happy to hear.[56] Upon returning home, however, Akayev, under heavy international pressure, backed away from his promise to open the Kyrgyz embassy in Jerusalem.[57]

During the visit, Akayev signed agreements with Israel on agriculture, trade and the power industry and visited Jerusalem's main mosques as well as Yad Vashem, the Holocaust memorial.[58] He also stated that Jews had the 'sacred right' to return to their homeland, although, like other leaders of the former Soviet Union, he appealed for the Jews of his country to stay: 'I'll be frank. We do not like to part with the Jews of Kyrgyzstan who have shared our history'.[59] He also noted that his chief legal adviser was a Jew, as was his minister of construction, and that Jews were prominent in the professions and in education.[60]

Whereas Israel made major strides in developing its relations with Kazakhstan and Uzbekistan, the two most important countries in Central Asia, as well as with Kyrgyzstan, it was less successful with Tajikistan and Turkmenistan. Before the outbreak of the civil war in Tajikistan, Israel had established an irrigation system near Dushambe (the capital) as well as a cotton-growing project, but these projects have been put on hold because of the war.[61] In Turkmenistan, Israel exhibited high-tech products, which were praised by the country's *Imam*, and offered a master plan for Turkmenistan's irrigation system, but was not able to establish diplomatic relations with the energy-rich state until the fall of 1993.[62] Since then, Israel's relations with that country developed rapidly and in the fall of 1994 then foreign minister Shimon Peres paid a visit to Turkmenistan.

In an effort both to curb the threat of Iran and to capitalize on Israeli agricultural prowess, the United States has joined with Israel in establishing a pilot program under which the United States would provide $5 million to enable Israeli agricultural and public health experts to help the five Central Asian states.[63] US interest in the project was highlighted by the fact that, under the project's ground rules, a joint US-Israeli team would work together to 'sharpen technical assistance priorities and define potential priorities and define potential projects'. This was followed in the fall of 1994 with a three-way US-Turkey-Israel project to aid both Turkmenistan and Uzbekistan.[64] These projects offered a double benefit for Israel. Not only would they enable Israel to play a still more effective role in Central

Asia, but they also underlined Israel's continuing importance to the United States as a 'strategic ally', an importance that had been called into question with the end of the Cold War. Given Russia's shared concern about the growth of Islamic radicalism in Central Asia, Israeli economic activity in the region can be seen as a plus for Moscow as well, because unlike Turkey and Iran (or the US), Israel is not seen as a major competitor with Russia for influence in the region. However, Moscow may not be too happy with the inclusion of Turkey in the US-Israeli technical assistance effort in the region.[65]

In sum, Israel made important strides in Central Asia, particularly in Kazakhstan, Uzbekistan and Kyrgyzstan, in the first three years following the collapse of the Soviet Union. Nonetheless, the high level of volatility in the region and the rapidity of change make any long-range forecasts for Israeli success most difficult to assess. Concern about the threat of Islamic radicalism, while at the present time not seen as too serious a problem,[66] continues to motivate Israeli policy-makers.

## Conclusions

There are two central conclusions that can be drawn from this analysis of radical Islam and its role in the struggle for influence in Central Asia. The first is that radical Islam does not currently pose a serious threat in any of the Central Asian states. In part this is due to the still underdeveloped nature of Islam in Central Asia as well as to the fact that all the current leaders of the region proclaim themselves to be 'secular Muslims', openly denounce radical Islam, and in some cases, such as Uzbekistan and Tajikistan, even imprison or exile Islamic leaders. Another cause for the current absence of a genuine radical Islamic threat in Central Asia is the deliberate effort by Iran to downplay Islam in Iran's relations with Central Asia, promoting instead cultural and economic ties. While, in part, this may have been due to the lack of prospects for a radical Islamic revolution in Central Asia, it appears that the most important reason was that the Islamic leader did not want to jeopardize his country's arms supply relationship with Russia.

Yet, one cannot rule out an Islamic threat to the region in the not-too-distant future. The leaders of the region, with the partial exception of Turkmenistan, face daunting problems of overpopulation, unemployment and underemployment, ecological near-disaster, rapid inflation and nationality conflicts. If these problems are not dealt with adequately, opponents of the regimes in power, including Islamic radicals, could exploit them. Second, while Hashemi Rafsanjani is currently directing Iranian foreign policy in Central Asia, his position in Iran may be weakening, and he is under attack from those who believe that Islamic issues, not state interests, should determine Iranian foreign policy. Should Rafsanjani's opponents come to control Iran's foreign policy, then it is possible that Iran will make a major effort to promote Islamic radicalism in Tajikistan and elsewhere in Central Asia, whatever the cost to Russian-Iranian relations. Finally, if the political leaders of Central Asia do not allow the development of political parties and refuse to allow political opposition to operate publicly, then such opposition might begin to gather in the mosques, with the result that it is then likely to move in the direction of radical Islam.

A second conclusion to be drawn from this study is that while Islamic radicalism is not currently a threat in Central Asia, the promotion of the perception of such a threat has been useful to the leaders of a number of states both inside and outside of the region. Chief among these is Uzbek leader Islam Karimov, who exploited the Russian fear of Islamic radicalism to justify Uzbek intervention in the Tajik civil war. Karimov has also used the fear of Islamic radicalism to justify his dictatorship in Uzbekistan. Outside leaders who have used the fear of Islamic radicalism to enhance their positions *vis-à-vis* the United States, which also fears the growth of Islamic radicalism in Central Asia, have been the late president of Turkey, Turgut Özal, and the late prime minister of Israel, Yitzhak Rabin. Özal sought to promote the secular Muslim model of Turkey in order to obtain assistance from the US in promoting Turkish influence in Central Asia. As the initial fear of a radical Islamic takeover of the region held by both American and Russian leaders diminished from 1992 to 1995, Turkey not only got less aid from the United States than it had wanted, but also found itself confronted in the region not by Iranian-style Islamic radicalism, but by the reassertion of Russian power: Russian leaders had decided that the presence of Turkey in Central Asia was not a desirable antidote to radical Islam, but an undesirable infringement on the Russian sphere of influence. In addition, the resurgence of the Kurdish rebellion, foreign policy problems in Azerbayjan, Cyprus and Bosnia, and a weakening economy limited Turkish effectiveness in Central Asia.

Israel, whose main Middle Eastern opponent is Iran, fared in some ways better than did Turkey in Central Asia. First, unlike Turkey or Iran, Israel is not seen by Moscow as a major competitor for influence in the region. Consequently, if its assistance policies succeed in helping to alleviate the severe economic problems faced by the Central Asian leaders, and hence reduce the attraction of Islamic radicalism, that outcome is seen as very positive by Moscow. Second, the US shares Israel's antipathy to Iran and Islamic radicalism and has been willing to aid Israeli assistance efforts in Central Asia. This, in turn, reinforces the Israeli-American relationship and, at least in part, helps to maintain Israel's image as a 'strategic ally'.

## NOTES

1. There is also a broad spectrum of belief as to what Islam is and what political role it plays (or can play) in society. See for example John Obert Voll, *Islam: Continuity and Change in the Modern World*, 2nd ed. (Syracuse, NY: Syracuse UP 1994); Emmanuel Sivan, *Radical Islam: Medieval Theology and Modern Politics* (New Haven, CT: Yale UP 1990); Shireen T. Hunter (ed.), *The Politics of Islamic Revivalism: Diversity and Unity* (Bloomington: Indiana UP 1988); Barbara Stowasser (ed.), *The Islamic Impulse* (London: Croon Helm 1987); Daniel Pipes, *In the Path of God: Islam and Political Power* (NY: Basic Books 1993); Alan R. Taylor, *The Islamic Question in Middle East Politics* (Boulder, CO: Westview Press 1988); John L. Esposito, *Islam: The Straight Path* (expanded edition) (Oxford: OUP 1991); and idem. (ed.), *Voices of Resurgent Islam* (Oxford: OUP 1983).

2. See Michael Bradshaw, *The Economic Effects of Soviet Dissolution* (London: Royal Institute of International Affairs 1993); and Michael Kaser and Santash Mehrata, *The Central Asian Economies After Independence* (London: RIIA 1992).

3. For a very good study of the water problem in Central Asia, see Philip E. Micklin, *The Water Management Crisis in Soviet Central Asia*, Carl Beck Paper No.905 (Pittsburgh, PA: University of Pittsburgh Center for Russian and East European Studies 1991).

4. The data on population percentages in Kazakhstan and the other Central Asian states is taken from CIA estimates published in *Current History* (April 1994) (issue devoted to Central Asia) pp.165,170,174,179 and 184.

5. The Uzbeks (and the US government) claim 5%; some Tajiks argue that the Uzbeks deliberately have minimized the Tajik proportion of Uzbekistan's population and that the percentage is closer to 10%.

6. See Jacob M. Landau, 'Islamic versus Other Identities in the Greater Middle East: Comments of the Ex-Soviet Muslim Republics', in this volume, pp.189–98, for a detailed discussion of the identity problem.

7. See M.B. Olcott, 'Central Asia's Islamic Awakening', *Current History* (April 1994) pp.150–5. See also Landau (note 6).

8. For views of former Soviet academics as to the state of Islam in Central Asia, see Sergei P. Poliakov, *Everyday Islam: Religion and Tradition in Rural Central Asia* (translated by Anthony Olcott) (London: M.E. Sharpe 1992); V. Naumkin, 'Islam in the States of the Former USSR', *Annals of the American Academy of Political and Social Science* (Nov. 1992) pp.131–42; and A.V. Malashenko, 'Islam Versus Communism: The Experience of Coexistence', in Dale F. Eickelman (ed.), *Russia's Muslim Frontiers* (Bloomington: Indiana UP 1993).
For western views, see Michael Rywkin, *Moscow's Muslim Challenge: Soviet Central Asia*, revised ed. (NY: M.E. Sharpe 1990); Alexander Benningsen and Marie Brozup, *The Islamic Threat to the Soviet State* (NY: St. Martin's Press 1983); James Critchlow, 'The New Moslem Nations of Central Asia', in David H. Goldberg and Paul Marantz (eds.), *The Decline of the Soviet Union and the Transformation of the Middle East* (Boulder, CO: Westview Press 1994) pp.135–51; M. Atkin, 'Islamic Assertiveness and the Waning of the Old Soviet Order', *Nationalities Papers* 200/1 (Spring 1992) pp.55–74; William Fierman (ed.), *Soviet Central Asia: The Failed Transformation* (Boulder, CO: Westview Press 1991); Mohraddin Mesbahi (ed.), *Central Asia and the Caucasus After the Soviet Union* (Gainesville: University Press of Florida 1994); Michael Mandelbaum (ed.), *Central Asia and the World* (NY: Council on Foreign Relations Press 1994); and Anthony Hyman, *Political Change in Post-Soviet Central Asia* (London: RIIA, April 1994).

9. For studies of Islam in Uzbekistan, see A. Abduvakhutov, 'Islamic Revivalism in Uzbekistan', in Eickelman (note 8) pp.79–97 (an appendix to this article has the program of the Islamic Renaissance Party) and R. Hanks, 'The Islamic Factor in Nationalism and Nation-building in Uzbekistan: Causative Agent or Inhibitor?' *Nationalities Papers* 22/2 (Fall 1994) pp.309–23. For Karimov's view, see Islam Karimov, *Building the Future: Uzbekistan – Its Own Model for Transition to a Market Economy* (Tashkent: Uzbekistan Publishers 1993); and idem., *Uzbekistan: The Road of Independence and Progress* (Tashkent: Uzbekistan Publishers 1992).

10. Interview with the author, Tashkent, Uzbekistan, Oct. 1993.
11. See John L. Esposito in Hunter (note 1) pp.189–90. Nonetheless, there are sufficient similarities between the two countries and Uzbekistan that the threat of a radical Islamic takeover, however much exaggerated by Karimov for domestic and foreign policy purposes, cannot be ignored.
12. Oliver Ray, *The Civil War in Tajikistan: Causes and Implications* (Washington DC: United States Institute for Peace, Dec. 1993); and B. Rubin, 'The Fragmentation of Tajikistan ', *Survival* 35/4 (Winter 1993-4) pp.71–91; and idem., 'Tajikistan: From Soviet Republic to Russian-Uzbek Protectorate', in Mandelbaum (note 8) pp.207–24.
13. Interfax, 6 July 1992 – *Foreign Broadcast Information Service: Former Soviet Union* (FBIS:FSU) 6 Aug. 1992, pp.70–1.
14. Interfax, 19 Nov. – *FBIS:FSU*, 22 Nov. 1993, p.8.
15. *Kommersant*, 4 Nov. – *FBIS:FSU*, 5 Nov. 1993, p.10.
16. Interview, Russian Embassy, Tashkent, Uzbekistan, 29 Sept. 1993. Other reasons for Russian interest in Tajikistan include a desire to prevent Tajik uranium facilities from falling into the hands of Russia's enemies and, on the part of some Russian officers, to re-fight the Afghan war, this time winning it.
17. *Pravda*, 19 Feb. – *FBIS:FSU*, 20 Feb. 1992, p.42.
18. V. Kulistikov, 'Turks from the Adriatic to the Great Chinese Wall are a threat to Russia', *New Times* (Moscow) 20 (1992) p.3. Russia's deputy prime minister, Alexander Shokhin, on 12 June 1993, went so far as to state 'Our friends from the CIS who, looking for better fortunes, are turning to the south should choose between closer economic integration with Russia and with their southern neighbors'. See *Moscow Times*, 14 July 1993, p.1.
19. Cited in Stephen J. Blank, 'Turkey's Strategic Engagement in the Former USSR and U.S. Interests', in Stephen J. Blank *et al.* (eds.), *Turkey's Strategic Position at the Crossroads of World Affairs* (Carlisle, PA: US Army War College, 3 Dec. 1993) p.56. For a Turkish view of relations between the Turks and Central Asia, see M. Saray, 'Political, Economic, and Cultural Relations Between Turkey and (the) Central Asian Republics', *Eurasian Studies* (Ankara) 2 (Summer 1994) pp.47–52. See also Graham E. Fuller and Ian O. Lesser, *Turkey's New Geopolitics* (Boulder CO: Westview Press 1993).
20. See M. Yusin, 'Tehran Declares "Great Battle" for Influence in Central Asia – Russia, the US and Turkey Seek to Prevent Iran From Winning that Battle', *Izvestia*, 7 Feb. 1992; translated in *Current Digest of the Soviet Press* (CDSP) 44/6 (1992) p.18.
21. For a discussion of these techniques and their success, see M.B. Olcott, 'Sovereignty and the "New Abroad"', *Orbis* 39/3 (Summer 1995) pp.353–67.
22. Interview, Uzbek Foreign Ministry, Tashkent, 30 Sept. 1993.
23. *Turkish Daily News* correspondent Semih Idiz called 1993 a year that 'forced Turkish diplomats into a "crisis management mode"'. (*Turkish Times*, 1 Feb. 1994, p.1.)
24. For a Russian view of the threat that the Turkish pipeline system would pose to Russia, see Vladimir Yuratev and Anatoly Sheshtakov of the Russian Ministry of Foreign Economic Relations, 'Asian gas will flow East: New alliance infringes on Russian interests', *Nezavisimaya Gazeta*, 13 May 1993 (*CDSP* 45/14 1993, pp. 16–18). For a western view arguing that Moscow is practicing economic warfare over the pipeline issue, see Stephen J. Blank, *Energy and Security in Transcaucasia* (Carlisle, PA: US Army War College, 7 Sept. 1994). Ironically, the Russian government appeared split on the issue, with the Russian government oil company Lukoil favoring Russia's participation in the oil consortium while the Russian Foreign Ministry opposed it.
25. Cited in a report by Baha Gugnor, 'Russian Fear of Pan-Turkism Grows', *Deutsche Press Agentur*, *Washington Times*, 5 Nov. 1994.
26. Istanbul declaration, *Turkish Times*, 3 Nov. 1994.
27. See Denis Volkov, 'Whom and How Does Islamic Fundamentalism Threaten?', *New Times* (Moscow) 4 (1994) p.25. See also Demitry Volsky, 'Iran-Central Asia: Export of Commodities, and Not of Ideological Merchandise', *New Times* 44 (1993) p.24.
28. *Islamic Affairs Analyst*, Nov. 1992, p.3.
29. See Aleksei Bausin, 'A Submarine Isn't a Needle. You Can't Hide One in the Persian Gulf – Why the West Doesn't Want Russia to Sell Arms to Iran', *Rossiskaya Gazeta*, 19 Jan. 1993

(*CDSP* 45/3 1993, pp.15–16). For a study of Russian arms sales to the Middle East, see Andrei Volpin, *Russian Arms Sales Policy Toward the Middle East* (Washington, DC: Washington Institute for Near East Policy, Research Memorandum No.23, Oct. 1993). See also Yitzhak Klein, 'Russia and a Conventional Arms Non-Proliferation Regime in a New World Order', in Efraim Inbar and Shmuel Sandler (eds.), *Middle East Security: Prospects for an Arms Control Regime* (London: Frank Cass 1995).

30. Itar/Tass, 1 Sept. – *FBIS:FSU*, 2 Sept. 1993, p.8; and, *Moscow Radio*, in Persian, to Iran, 8 Sept. – *FBIS:FSU*, 10 Sept. 1993, p.13. In late May 1992, Moscow gave a similar warning to Turkey when marshal Yevgeny Shaposhnikov, military chief of the CIS, warned Turkey that intervention in Nakhichevan (part of Azerbaizjhan) could escalate the Armenian-Azerbaizjhan conflict into a third world war (*Turkish Times*, 1 June 1992, p.1).

31. Itar/Tass, 29 March – *FBIS:FSU*, 30 March 1993, p.10.

32. Interfax, 31 March – *FBIS:FSU*, 31 March 1993, p.8.

33. *Izvestia*, 1 April 1993. For studies of Tajik-Iranian relations, see Muriel Atkin, 'Tajiks and the Persian World', in Beatrice F. Manz (ed.), *Central Asia in Historical Perspective* (Boulder, CO: Westview Press 1994) pp.127–43; and John Calabrese, 'Iran and Her Northern Neighbors at the Crossroads', *Central Asia Monitor* 5 (1994) pp.21–7. In June 1994, Iran offered to send peacekeeping troops to Tajikistan (*Washington Times*, 22 June 1994).

34. Volsky (note 27).

35. Cited in *Izvestia*, 2 Dec. – *FBIS:FSU*, 6 Dec. 1993, p.16.

36. *Radio Moscow* (Persian), 15 Dec. – *FBIS:FSU*, 16 Dec. 1993, p.48.

37. *Financial Times*, 27 June 1995.

38. *Almaty Kazakh Radio*, 25 Oct. – *FBIS:FSU*, 26 Oct. 1993, p.64; italics are my emphasis.

39. Interview, Russian Embassy, Washington, DC, 1 July 1994.

40. Cited in report by Judy Siegel, *Jerusalem Post*, 13 Jan. 1992.

41. *Alma Ata Kazakh Radio*, 2 April – *FBIS:FSU*, 9 April 1992, p.52.

42. Moscow Interfax, 10 April – *FBIS:FSU*, 14 April 1992, p.56.

43. Itar/Tass, 13 April – *FBIS:FSU*, 14 April 1992, p.56.

44. *Yediot Aharonot*, 13 April – *FBIS:FSU*, 14 April 1992, p.56. Still, there were rumored sales of beryllium and uranium pellets to Iran (*Jerusalem Post*, 9 March 1993), and the subsequent transfer of poorly guarded nuclear materials to the United States also raised Israeli concerns. (See the report by R. Jeffrey Smith, 'U.S. Takes Nuclear Fuel: Officials Feared Terrorism in Kazakhstan', *Washington Post*, 23 Nov. 1994.)

45. Cited in report by Asher Wallfish, *Jerusalem Post*, 8 Sept. 1992.

46. Ibid. The companies he mentioned belong to Shaul Eisenberg, who has spearheaded the Israeli business presence in Kazakhstan, and Yossi Maimon.

47. Cited in report by Asher Wallfish, *Jerusalem Post*, 9 Sept. 1992.

48. Cited in report by Evelyn Gordon, *Jerusalem Post*, 30 June 1993.

49. Cited in *FBIS:FSU*, 2 April 1993, p.60.

50. Cited in report by Evelyn Gordon, *Jerusalem Post*, 30 June 1993.

51. Cited in report by Abraham Rabinovich, *Jerusalem Post*, 11 Sept. 1992.

52. Cited in report by Colin Barraclough, *Christian Science Monitor*, 23 Sept. 1992.

53. Cited in report by Abraham Rabinovich, *Jerusalem Post*, 21 Aug. 1992.

54. Interview with Israeli ambassador to Uzbekistan, Tashkent, Uzbekistan, 28 Sept. 1993.

55. Cited in Abraham Rabinovich, 'Kyrgyzstan's President Wants Midwife for Economic Rebirth', *Jerusalem Post*, 22 Jan. 1993.

56. Ibid.

57. Cf. Kyrgyz statement distributed to members of the UN General Assembly, 48th session, 10 Feb. 1993.

58. Cited in Batsheva Tsur, 'Kirgyzian President Calls for Independence for Palestinians', *Jerusalem Post*, 20 Jan. 1993.

59. *Itar/Tass*, 21 Jan. 1993 – *FBIS:FSU*, 25 Jan. 1993, p.58.

60. Cited in report by Abraham Rabinovich, *Jerusalem Post*, 22 Jan. 1993.

61. Interview, Israeli Embassy, Tashkent, 28 Sept. 1993.

62. Cited in report by David Makovsky, *Jerusalem Post*, 29 July 1992.

63. Cited in *Update on Jews in the CIS and the Baltic Republics*, Consulate General of Israel, New York, 7 Nov. 1993, p.12.
64. Interview, Israeli Foreign Ministry, Jerusalem, 23 Oct. 1994.
65. Interview, Russian Embassy, Tel Aviv, 26 Oct. 1994.
66. Interview, Israeli Foreign Ministry, 23 Oct. 1994.

# The Uniqueness of Islamic Fundamentalism

GABRIEL BEN-DOR

This article explores the notion of fundamentalism, and anchors it in the concepts of extremism, radicalism and scripturalism. It argues that it is possible to study the phenomenon of fundamentalism within the paradigms of rationalism that prevail in modern social science. Furthermore, while all fundamentalist movements share certain characteristics, Islamic fundamentalism differs from other fundamentalist movements in many substantial ways, including political space, the ability to penetrate inter-state boundaries, Islam as a protest movement, the total adherence of believers to a set of behavioral tenets, the difficulty of separating state from religion, a strong orientation to things collective, Islamic legitimacy of states, the commandment of *jihad* and the immediacy of faith in the life of believers. In the light of all this, Islamic countries tend to be rather vulnerable to waves of fundamentalism, which, however, ebb and flow in response to concrete social, political and economic conditions in the relevant countries.

The study of complex social and political phenomena always raises a dilemma of duality. On the one hand, we would like our research to be as universal as possible, not only in order to have as high a value as possible in purely scientific terms (i.e., in terms of the ability to generalize), but also because we instinctively feel that the more cases our explanation includes, the more satisfactory the explanation.[1] In other words, the fewer the exceptions, the greater the sense of having done an adequate job of explanation. The more numerous the exceptions, the greater the sense of doubt that our explanation is only partial, and perhaps even unsatisfactory.

This tendency leads us to the endless attempt to find holistic models that will explain everything that is included in a given system. Yet such attempts, by and large, have not been very successful in contemporary social and political analysis.[2] The universe of cases is too complicated, the variance too great, the variables involved too numerous to explain things once and for all. So while there is no argument that the ultimate model is a deductive one that will include every and all cases, there are many reasons to assume that this is not a realistic goal in the vast majority of the cases.

Indeed, there has been a long tradition of warnings in favor of middle range theories, as Robert Merton used to put it in the 1950s, or partial systemic explanations, a term Joseph LaPalombara used to express a similar idea in the late 1960s and early 1970s.[3] Such warnings were often heeded with good results and there is no reason to ignore them even today. The development of our tools in social science research has not been so rapid or dramatic as to make it possible to do away with the limitations that made it almost impossible to use holistic models two or three decades ago.[4]

The study of fundamentalism is a good case in point. Of course, it would be most desirable and satisfactory to explain all cases of fundamentalism in a single theoretical framework, thereby also eliminating all the messy details involved in comparing different types of fundamentalism. Yet the huge literature on fundamentalism that has come into being in the wake of political events and trends illuminating the topicality of this phenomenon has, by and large, failed to deliver the goods.[5] It has not even been able to come up with good, universally acceptable definitions of what the whole thing is about in the first place, and all attempts to define it in a way that would allow a single theory to cut across regional and cultural differences have come to nought.[6]

This need not be considered a deficiency of the given scholar. In many cases, the difficulty has been the lack of a real theoretical orientation on the part of the authors who were more interested in arguing a point, studying a case or analyzing a theological dispute than in generating general theory. On the other hand, in some other cases, there was the fact of life that the material was just too big and diverse to fit a single theory, so that it is not the fault of the analysis that universality was not to be accomplished.

It makes more sense to treat fundamentalism as a phenomenon that, while to some extent universal, should be understood in terms of the concrete society, theology and culture in which it was born and plays an active role.[7] The will to impose our universal perspective may not suffice to put the phenomenon in a straight jacket, which is too narrow for it. So fundamentalism may be defined as a movement that is radical in terms of its goals, extremist in terms of its methods and literalist in terms of sticking to scripture. Beyond that, we must acknowledge that there are many different forms of fundamentalism and that their comparison may yield important insights into such questions as to why a particular form appears in one place and not another, why the intensity of one is that much greater than the other, and why one dissipates at the same time as the other first makes its appearance on the scene.[8] Such questions can be formulated, and perhaps eventually answered, more easily when we keep in mind the importance of a comparative perspective, and do *not* yield to the temptation to generalize prematurely, before the insights of the comparative effort have been articulated and integrated into our theoretical frameworks.

Hence, we need to reduce the level of analysis.[9] It does not make sense to study fundamentalism as one all the time, and indeed even Islamic fundamentalism is too big a unit of analysis, in the light of huge differences between say, Morocco and Indonesia, in society, history, culture and geography. It makes more sense to speak of fundamentalism in Middle Eastern Islam, as this is a unit that has far more cultural and political coherence.[10] The present chapter takes this perspective as its point of departure.[11]

There is a danger that people will say that Islamic fundamentalism is just like any other. In other words, that they will feel that one fundamentalism is very much like another, and that once one confronts a certain degree of extremism, one can no longer learn anything from other forms of extremism. This seems to me somewhat dangerous, as social phenomena differ greatly from one another, and just as I do not like when people refuse to make comparisons, I also do not like when they refuse to look at differences. As Raymond Aron, the great French-Jewish political sociologist used to say, the essence of social science is to look for similarities in that which appears different, but also to look for differences in that which appears similar. And this is excellent advice indeed.[12]

Also, there are historical examples of cases in which, once confronted with really radical phenomena, people would say, 'oh well, so we all have our radicals, and why should this case be different than any other?'. This type of thinking makes us all blind to the great fluctuations of degree and quality in phenomena that may resemble each other on the surface.

Now, extremism and radicalism normally refer to degrees of intensity in commitment to ideologies and the willingness to make sacrifices and stick consistently to that which appears to be worth believing in. Some have even argued that extremism, as Barry Goldwater put it in 1964, in the service of liberty is no vice, while moderation in the defense of liberty is no merit. Maybe this position is logical and defensible, but I feel that we need not argue about this right now. More to the point, there is merit in the argument that one needs to take a very profound look at what is being fought for so extremely or radically, and to what extent, the type of cause that is the objective of extremism is indeed different than other causes. Failure to do so, in reality, leads to a very superficial assessment of the case in question.

For the moment, I leave aside some difficulties with definitions, such as extremism, radicalism or fundamentalism. As we know, the Muslims themselves dislike all these terms.[13] They refer to the people in question as 'Islamists', or *Islamiyun*, namely those who are committed to the Islamization of the social and political system of their countries, and of other countries as well, for that matter, because Islamic radicalism, in the final analysis, does not really recognize the boundaries of the secular national states, and clearly not those between the various Islamic countries, even if one has to live with them for a while, for pragmatic reasons.

I myself feel that terms and definitions are important.[14] By radicalism, Marx meant those who would change society by the root, or from the root.

By extremism, I think that we mean the commitment and the willingness to use a calculus that gives tremendous value to the achievement of the goals and objectives in question, at the expense of other values. Hence this is a rational movement,[15] but one that works with values that are entirely different in scale from those of others. And fundamentalism refers to scripturalism, and sticking to written commandments and interpretations, as well as the tendency to return to the fundamentals of religion. In this sense, I think that the point has to be made that from the theological point of view, there is no value judgment here when one uses the term 'fundamentalism'.[16]

On the other hand, there are political problems associated with fundamentalism by the very definition of the term. There can be, and probably are, many different attitudes with respect to the existence of extreme and fundamentalist ideologies in democratic regimes, indeed in any kind of regime, but obviously a strong fundamentalist component must be a problem for any kind of regime.[17] There are many reasons for this, but clearly the main problem is that fundamentalists reject any legitimacy not anchored in scripture, and such legitimacy is at times all but impossible to achieve for any kind of regime which is not in itself a fundamentalist one.[18] This is as true with the very existence of the regime as it is true with the specific decision or pieces of legislation undertaken by the regime.

In the case of Islam,[19] we are speaking of a large number of regimes. About 40 countries in the world have an Islamic majority and are classified as Islamic states, at least in the sense that they are formally affiliated with some organization of Islamic states, above all the bloc of Islamic states holding periodic meetings and summit sessions. Of course, quite a few leaders of these states find this a great problem rather than an asset, but they have little choice but to act out their Islamic belonging, or else they will merely make things that much worse for themselves in the domestic political arena.[20]

And here, right away, is one of the first differences between Islamic fundamentalism and other kinds. Islamic fundamentalists are able to penetrate the political systems of other countries, in the name of Islam. This is not to say that the individual Islamic countries are by necessity weak, because some are anything but that. On the other hand, some are just that, and many of them have to contend with strong outside influences, and they find this challenge very troublesome to meet. It is conceivable for Iran to dominate, at least for a while, politics in the Sudan, to have a big impact in Lebanon and so on, at a time when such ideological-religious penetration is very rare in other places in the world.[21]

Of course, there is a Jewish fundamentalism, but it cannot penetrate anything outside Israel.[22] And there is a Christian fundamentalism, and of course, there are many Christians in different places around the world. In particular, there is the Protestant version of fundamentalism in the southern and western parts of the United States, and, of course, there are many millions of Protestants in different countries around the world. And the evangelical activities of people like Billy Graham testify that Protestant fundamentalists indeed have ambitions to work outside their countries.[23] Yet their ability, indeed their ambition, to penetrate the social or political fabric of other countries has been extremely limited in practice, as their theology and political doctrines have not given outside activities a very high priority, so that this is not something that has been carefully thought out, analyzed in theory or acted out in practice.

How about the Catholics, a religion that is organized in a formal global hierarchy? Well, they seem to have a much more universal orientation, and that has been a fact of life since this religion was born. Yet the universalism of the church is in fact the characteristic mode of operation of the established order, and when fundamentalists rebel, in fact when anyone rebels, they often do so in the name of some local particularism, which is interesting.[24] In fact, this presents a contrast to Islam, which tends to get along well with the existence of individual states, which have been able, by and large, to harness Islam and its establishment to their own purposes.[25] But when Islam becomes really radical, it tends to challenge the individual states, and when it becomes very active, either by capturing the machinery of the state, or in opposition to it, it is able to act in several countries, finding support, resources and legitimacy that enable it to do so. On the other hand, Catholic practice is one of a universal hierarchy, which has been immune to fundamentalism, so that if there is strong fundamentalism, it can act only be opposing the universal hierarchy and within specific states. In other words, Islamic fundamentalism has a regional and international space enjoyed by no other religion, and by very few ideologies in this day and age.[26]

Yet the existence of political space is not in and of itself decisively important, if the orientation of the movement in question is not activist and vigorous enough to use it and fill it. In the case of Islam, which is my second major point, it is indeed activist and vigorous enough.[27] This has to do with the fact that Islam is the youngest of the three major monotheistic religions, and the one that is still growing fastest in terms of numbers of believers. Clearly, this is not the case with Jews or the various Christian churches. A Muslim friend argued a while ago that Judaism is the religion of the old, Christianity the religion of the middle-aged and Islam of the young. It is able to proselytize openly, something that Jews have never done and most Christians today find unfashionable and unpalatable. Yet for Islam this has always been a main article of faith, and still is.

Third, Islam is indeed a protest movement,[28] that of the Third World, against what is considered the imperialist and colonial heritage of the Judeo-

Christian traditions of western democracy.[29] Much can be said about this interesting political-psychological phenomenon, but it is a fact of life. Although there are important Christian populations in Africa, mass conversion only exists to Islam, which continues to grow quickly while Christianity on the continent basically stagnates. In the United States, some black ('African-American') athletes are willing to play in leagues dominated by white men, but they register their protest against the modes and identity of the society that the leagues represent by converting to Islam and using Islamic names that differentiate them from white players and from those blacks who lack this kind of consciousness and activism (never mind now the historical accuracy or inaccuracy of what this protest actually represents). The vigor of youth and the vigor of protest complement each other potently.

In addition, we need to take into account the fourth point, which is the total adherence that Islam demands from its believers. In fact, this is not the best way to put it. It is not that Islam demands anything from its believers, but rather that it is not a religion in the usual limited sense of the term. It is a total civilization, encompassing every walk of life of the individual as well as the community.[30] One might argue that this is the case with all religions, that this is what religion is all about, but that is not good enough. Other religions may say 'give Caesar that which is his due' and other formulations like that to indicate that in fact they accept some separation of church from state. But that is not the case with Islam and never has been.[31] One wonders whether it ever will be.

Islam is a religion of commandments, most of them quite practical. These commandments refer to all aspects of life and not only those that are considered properly religious in the technical sense of the term. Islam deals not only with relations between man and God, and not only with ethical relations between human beings and groups. Rather, it deals with everything that the individual believer or groups of believers may encounter in their lifetimes, from commercial relations to marital affairs. In other words, the call of God applies to everything that the believer does, and this call does not recognize any boundaries between different spheres.[32] Hence, separation of religion from state is indeed not a viable option and it does not exist, constitutionally, in any of the Arab countries, though a major experiment has been tried in Turkey (which is an extreme case) with mixed results.

One can argue that much of what I have just said also applies to Judaism, which is also a behavioral religion. It too is based on commandments and its commandments apply to all walks of life. Just as in Islamic jurisprudence we find numerous references to commerce, society and even outright politics, we can find these very elements in the Talmud and *halacha*. Much of this argument is valid on purely theoretical-theological grounds. But in practice, the co-existence of the Jewish religion with strong alien political and military domination led the Jews early in their development to accept the idea of *'dina demalchut dina'*, which is to say, that the law of the Kingdom is the Law, simply because the state has its own domain. This is the key to understanding the difference. Because Judaism was the religion of the few and the weak, it could come to terms with this kind of challenge decisively, and accept the virtual separation of religion from state, since the latter was alien anyhow. But in Islam, the idea of alien domination has never really been accepted, and the basic reference is to the domain of the Muslims themselves.[33] Later, in the case of the Jews, even when they had their own state, the older traditions enabled them to accept some form of the existence of the more or less secular state, even when it is Jewish. But for the Muslims this has not been the case, as one result of their political successes in maintaining their own, more or less independent political entities, which the Jews have not been able to do during most of their long and troubled history.

Since the separation of religion and state is not in practice highly politicized, things Islamic are just more political, almost by definition, than things Christian or Jewish. Hence Islamic fundamentalism has a much more political flavor and many more political implications than other kinds of fundamentalism. We do not like to make generalizations like this, but there it is anyway.[34] And this ties in with the next point, the fifth one. Islam is not just a more political religion, but also one that has a strong orientation towards collective matters and groups. Now, in all religions there is a tension between individual and collective matters, and Islam is no exception. But the balance between the two orientations is different in each of the religions, and that is something that needs to be understood and taken into account.

Of course, all religions demand an adherence from the individual believer in the commandments; this is fundamental to each of the faiths. But in Christianity there are monasteries and monks, implying that individuals have to realize their religious potential more or less on their own, or in small groups that are distinct from the life of the broader community or society around. There are no such things in Islam, which does not even accept the possibility that the realization of Islamic ideals is something that can be accomplished apart from society at large.[35] To the contrary, Islam encourages the overhaul of the entire social system to conform to its ideals; this is in fact the basis for legitimacy in the Islamic state,[36] which is in fact our sixth point.[37]

In few other cases is there such profound belief in the creative potential of the political system. Christians and Jews may be able to accept the existence of a bad state and to go about the business of being good in religious terms, and of course in the case of the Jews this has been the practical result of the divorce between Jews and their state throughout most of their history. But for Muslims things are very different. For them, the existence of the state is acceptable only if it serves the purposes of the Islamic community and its leaders are legitimate only as long as they uphold the principles of Islamic jurisprudence, in which case they are indeed forgiven for other errors and omissions. In other words, the Islamic state has a more moral, ethical and theological character than its Jewish or Christian counterparts, and this creates a different, much higher set of expectations from it.[38] I think that this also ties in with the idea of perfection on the part of leaders, who have to model themselves on the perfection attained by the ideal leader, the Prophet Muhammad. Outsiders sometimes find this puzzling; they perceive Muslims as naive and are simply not able to understand how Muslims can take all this seriously.

However, this is something that is truly Islamic and, one might even argue, something most praiseworthy in terms of making the state accountable to the popular will, or in this case the divine will as deposited with the religion of the people. On the other hand, in practical terms such high expectations also breed a lot of disappointment and frustration, leading to frequent violence in overthrowing unsatisfactory regimes. In no other major religion is there such an intimate interrelationship between religion and state, hence religious extremism in Islam has more and greater political implications and ramifications than in other cases.[39] It is true to say that everything that is Islamic would tend to be more political than in other religions, but certainly in the case of Islamic fundamentalism it is obvious that it is impossible to keep the phenomena far from the political arena, as the lack of separation between religion and state, the strong collectivist orientation and the close connection to political life in general all make the state machinery a close and at times realistic target to Islamic fundamentalist subversion.

The next, and sixth point we need to consider is that of *jihad*,[40] holy war in popular parlance. Fighting for one's faith may be a requirement in most religions, or at least the willingness to fight for the religion and sacrifice oneself may be. But it is only in Islam that there is such an explicit doctrine of fighting for the faith and a doctrine too that is so deeply ingrained in the popular mind.[41] This makes it necessary to comment that in fact the doctrine of *jihad* is an extremely complicated one. *Jihad* is declared only by competent religious authorities and only after taking into account not only the chances of victory, but also the risks to the integrity and the well-being of the Islamic community in general. It follows that *jihad* is declared formally and legally only in few cases, and that it ought not to be considered as an automatic option in every case in which Muslims confront an enemy or an outside force that is able to threaten Islamic lands or resources. On the other hand, this set of qualifications and reservations is not always known and realized on the popular level. While these are intellectually important reservations, they are basically the property of the more educated elites.[42] On the popular level, *jihad* and its implications are invoked much more easily, and *jihad* is in fact one of the most popular concepts among Muslims. I would not go so far as to argue that Islam has a *jihad* mentality[43] or culture, but *jihad* occupies in the mind of most Muslims a much more important and prominent place than in the case of other religions, and of course this has implications to the theology and politics of fundamentalism.[44]

The last point that has to be made is that Islamic commandments and beliefs have a greater sense of immediacy than in other religions. The most extreme case is that of afterlife and martyrdom. In all religions, afterlife is important, and what religious person can be indifferent to the distinctions between heaven and hell? Moreover, what religion can accept the view that the course of the human being comes to termination with the end of the physical existence of the body? For example, in the most important Jewish prayer, the eighteen benedictions, the second of the eighteen ends with blessing the Almighty as the one who raises the dead. In the thirteen principles of the Jewish faith as articulated by the Rambam, the great medieval philosopher-theologian Maimonides, the final principle is again that the Almighty will raise the dead.

Yet in Judaism, in practice, this is not a big thing. Few Jews give this point a really important place in their thinking about life and death, and few would be willing to sacrifice their lives deliberately in order to enjoy a good or better life thereafter. If it is necessary, Jews are willing to die for the sanctification of the Divine Name, but they do so as a necessary evil, when continuing to live in sin or blasphemy would be simply intolerable as an option. However, with many Muslims things are different. Many of them indeed believe that the reward for dying as a martyr for the faith is so immediate and direct that such death is not something to be avoided. In some sects of Islam, notably Shi'is, this is a bigger thing than among others, but of course the very existence of this phenomenon is almost unique. Hence, Israel at times has found it very difficult to deter Shi'i extremists in Lebanon, because deterrence is ultimately making the adversary pay a higher price than justified by any possible gain. Yet the ultimate penalty or price is making the adversary lose his very life. But when such a loss is not considered intolerable, and some are even willing to pay it with joy, the entire calculus of deterrence is undermined to the point of collapse. This is not to say that all or most Muslims are even remotely resembling this particular model of thinking, but the phenomenon does exist in the Islamic community as an important fact of life,[45] and this is not the case in other religions today.[46]

The accumulation of all these points adds up to a fundamentalism that today is more immediate, more violent, more political and more popular than any kind of fundamentalism in any of the other religions. Hence, just saying 'fundamentalism' does not explain the problem. Islam is so different in many relevant aspects that it seems that the practical implications of Islamic fundamentalist activities are also different, in fact more intense, in every way. The result is not a particularly pretty picture, but it cannot be ignored; disregarding it will not make it go away. Nor will beautifying the un-pretty picture in the name of liberal ideals or cultural relativism do any good. It is better to call the spade a spade, calling it a knife or a fork will not make it a useful utensil in any way.[47]

On the other hand, realizing the magnitude of a threatening social or political phenomenon should not make us too pessimistic, discouraged or deterministic.[48] While it is true to say that Islam is both more vulnerable to fundamentalism and is likely to end up with a more violent version of it, there is no need to assume[49] that Muslims will always be fundamentalists or that the majority of them enjoy supporting them. Fundamentalism is the product of failure, humiliation and backwardness[50] and there are many important social and political forces in the Islamic world determined to make progress, so that, among other objectives, they can reduce or perhaps even eradicate fundamentalism. Fundamentalism has come and gone in waves, and while the present wave is serious and dangerous, it is likely that one day, it too will go away, if not forever, then for a long time. In trying to reach that day soon, the forces of moderation and progress in the Islamic countries have many important interests in common with the western democracies and Israel,[51] and the potential of that commonality can and should be explored in depth and with sophistication.

## NOTES

1. See A. Lipjhart, 'Comparative Politics and the Political Method', *American Political Science Review* 65/3 (Sept. 1971) pp.682–93; G. Sartori, 'Concept Misformation in Comparative Politics', *American Political Science Review* 64/4 (Dec. 1970) pp.1033–53.
2. See J. LaPalombara, 'Macrotheories and Microapplications in Comparative Politics: A Widening Chasm', *Comparative Politics* 1/1 (Oct. 1968) pp.52–77.
3. Ibid.
4. T. Skopcol and M. Somers, 'The Uses of Comparative History in Macro-social Theory', *Comparative Studies in Society and History* 22 (1980) pp.174–97.
5. There have been some notable attempts to develop studies of fundamentalism in a comparative perspective. See for instance, H. Lazarus-Yafeh, 'Contemporary Fundamentalism – Judaism, Christianity, Islam', *The Jerusalem Quarterly* 47 (Summer 1988) pp.27–39; Lawrence Kaplan, *Fundamentalisms in Comparative Perspective* (Amherst: The University of Massachusetts Press 1992); Bruce M. Lawrence, *Defenders of God: The Fundamentalist Revolt Against the Modern Age* (San Francisco: Harper and Row 1989); and Martin E. Marty and R. Scott Appleby (eds.), *Accounting for Fundamentalism*

(Chicago: University of Chicago Press 1994). However, these studies tend to be historical discussions of given cases with an attempt to see what is common in them after the analysis, rather than *bona fide* comparative studies in the sense of starting with a common theoretical framework for the simultaneous study of comparable cases. See Lipjhart (note 1).

6. See also the following articles in *The Annals* 524 (Nov. 1992): M.J. Deeb, 'Militant Islam and the Politics of Redemption', pp.53–65, I. Karawan, 'Monarchs, Mullahs and Marshals: Islamic Regimes?' pp.103–19, and I.W. Zartman, 'Democracy and Islam: The Cultural Dialectic', pp.181–91; J. Esposito and J. Piscatori, 'Democratization and Islam', *Middle East Journal* 45/3 (Summer 1991) pp.427–40; Esposito, *Islam and Politics*, 3rd ed. (Syracuse: Syracuse UP 1984); William Montgomery Watt, *Islamic Fundamentalism and Modernity* (London: Routledge 1988); Nazih N. Ayubi, *Political Islam: Religion and Politics in the Arab World* (London: Routledge 1993); James P. Piscatori (ed.), *Islamic Fundamentalisms and the Gulf Crisis* (Chicago: The American Academy of Arts and Sciences 1991); and Mohammad Mohadessin, *Islamic Fundamentalism: The New Global Threat* (Washington, DC: Seven Locks Press 1993). This is just a sample of the vast literature of the last decade, but of course there are many other sources that could be included. For an earlier list, see the bibliography in chapter 2, 'Stateness and the "Return" of Islam', in Gabriel Ben-Dor, *State and Conflict in the Middle East* (NY: Praeger 1983).

7. The large literature quoted previously is quite ambivalent on this point. Some of it treats fundamentalism as a universal phenomenon, but much of it in reality, if not in theory, is really a study of concrete cases that the author happens to be familiar with.

8. One of the best explorations of such questions in the context of Islam is Emmanuel Sivan, *Radical Islam: Medieval Theology and Modern Politics* (New Haven, CT: Yale UP 1985); See also Sivan and Menahem Friedman (eds.), *Religious Radicalism and Politics in the Middle East* (Albany, NY: SUNY Press 1990).

9. See Sartori (note 1).

10. See G. Ben-Dor, 'Political Culture Approach to Middle East Politics', *International Journal of Middle East Studies* 8 (1977) pp.43–63.

11. With all due respect to the large number of publications in the field, the *theoretical* poverty of what we know is such that we are still very much in the beginning. Hence, it may be necessary not only to conduct theoretical studies, but even to think about the conditions for successfully doing so. In other words, this is a matter of *pre-theory*, and not yet theory. See Harry Eckstein, 'On the Etiology of Internal Wars', in Bruce Mazlish *et al.*, (eds.), *Revolution* (NY: Macmillan 1971); and G. Ben-Dor, 'The Politics of Threat: Military Intervention in the Middle East', *Journal of Political and Military Sociology* 1 (Spring 1973).

12. See Harry Eckstein, 'Case Study and Theory in Political Science', in Fred I. Greenstein and Nelson W. Polsby (eds.), *Handbook of Political Science, Strategies of Inquiry* 7 (Reading, MA: Addison-Wesley 1975) pp.80–104.

13. Some of this dislike is part of the general revolt of the people of the Middle East against the domination of their cultural lives by western perceptions and concepts. See Edward Said, *Covering Islam: How the Media and the Experts Determine How We See the Rest of the World* (NY: Pantheon 1981). This piece is not less contentious, controversial and even biased than those that it criticizes, but that does not detract from its great value as documentation of frustration and cultural resistance.

14. 'To speak of "the" fundamentals of fundamentalism would signal arrogance. Yet any effort to describe international fundamentalisms...demands at least some sort of hypothesis. We need heuristic devices to begin a search. "Fundamentals", then, refers to some distinctive, not necessarily unique, features of movements called fundamentalist. They need not be present in some way or measure in all such movements, but they should be characteristic of most of them'. Martin E. Marty, 'Fundamentals of Fundamentalism', in Kaplan (note 5) p.15.

15. Gabriel A. Almond, 'Rational Choice Theory and the Social Sciences', in Gabriel A. Almond (ed.), *A Discipline Divided* (Newberry Park, CA: Sage 1990); G. Ben-Dor, 'Arab Rationality and Deterrence', in Aharon Klieman and Ariel Levite (eds.), *Deterrence in the Middle East: Where Theory and Practice Converge* (Tel Aviv: Jaffee Center for Strategic Studies 1993) p.87–97.

16. In other words, fundamentalism is not a derogatory or pejorative term as it is now often used in everyday political discourse. I feel that this is one of the reasons why the term has become so unpopular in the Middle East. Yet, for the lack of a better term, we may need to stick with it for a while longer.

17. In the Islamic context, as in others, the defining mode of fundamentalist legitimacy is the one anchored in the religious message, not in the procedural aspects of formal democracy. Hence, in the wake of the apparent victory of the fundamentalists in the elections in Algeria in 1991, their 'most outspoken leader affirmed that it is Islam which has been the victor, as always, not democracy. We did not go to the ballot boxes for democracy'. Quoted in M. Kramer, 'Politics and the Prophet', *The New Republic* (1 March 1993) p.39.

18. It seems to me that this is one of the truly universal characterizations attributed to fundamentalism. Indeed, the point appears in the literature trying to compare Islamic and Jewish fundamentalisms most frequently. See Esposito and Piscatori (note 6); and Fatima Mernissi, *Islam and Democracy: Fear of the Modern World* (Reading, MA: Addison-Wesley 1993).

19. The following generalizations about Islam are based, obviously, on my own understanding and interpretation of Islamic theory and practice. They can and will be challenged by others whose understanding and interpretation differ from mine, which is as it should be in legitimate scholarly interchange and controversy. Basically, my views are based on the literature on Islamic fundamentalism that has been cited thus far. For additional early sources that had a great impact on my thinking see the pertinent bibliography in Ben-Dor (note 6). Some of the most important works on Islam which I have found particularly helpful in thinking about the way the practice of Islam reflects theological and ideological underpinnings include: A.J. Arberry (ed), *Religion in the Middle East* (Cambridge: CUP 1969); H.A.R. Gibb, *Mohammedanism* (London: Oxford UP 1949); P.M. Holt, Ann K.S. Lambton and Bernard Lewis (eds.), *Cambridge History Of Islam* (Cambridge: CUP 1970); W. Montgomery Watt, *Islamic Political Thought* (Edinburgh: EUP 1968); Erwin I.J. Rosenthal, *Political Thought in Medieval Islam* (Cambridge: CUP 1958); Reuben Levy, *The Social Structure of Islam* (Cambridge: CUP 1957); Gustave Von Grunebaum, *Medieval Islam* (Chicago: University of Chicago Press 1952); idem., *Modern Islam* (NY: Doubleday 1964); Gibb, *Modern Trends in Islam* (Chicago: University of Chicago Press 1946); W.C. Smith, *Islam in Modern History* (Princeton, NJ: PUP 1957); Joseph Schacht, *An Introduction to Islamic Law* (Oxford: OUP 1964); E.I.J. Rosenthal, *Islam in the Modern National State* (Cambridge: CUP 1965); Elie Kedourie, *Islam in the Modern World* (Washington, DC: New Republic 1980); Clifford Geertz, *Islam Observed* (New Haven, CT: Yale UP 1968), Leonard Binder, *The Ideological Revolution in the Middle East* (NY: Wiley 1964); Richard P. Mitchell, *The Society of the Muslim Brothers* (London: Oxford UP 1969); Bernard Lewis, *The Middle East and the West* (NY: Harper 1964); idem., *The Arabs in History* (NY: Harper 1964).

20. By this, I mean that the political potential of Islam is so strong that it cannot be ignored even by the most secular states, like Turkey, for denying the Islamic element in the state would provoke extremely strong feelings of resentment and opposition to the regime. In light of this, some regimes compromise their convictions in order to keep the potential Islamic opposition reasonably content.

21. For the penetrability of Middle East political systems, see the numerous sources and examples in Ben-Dor (note 5). The earlier 'Arab Cold War', a phrase coined by Malcolm H. Kerr in his book by the same title in 1970 (Oxford: OUP) is increasingly substituted by some form of 'Islamic Cold War', or even hot war, as in the case of the war between Iraq and the Islamic regime in Iran in the 1980s. See Gabriel Ben-Dor and David B. Dewitt (eds.), *Conflict Management in the Middle East* (Lexington, MA: Heath 1987).

22. This is due to the fact that there is only one Jewish state and only one independent Jewish political community. See Sivan and Friedman (note 8); and Lazarus-Yafeh (note 5).

23. See Gilles Keppel, *The Revenge of God: The Resurgence of Islam, Christianity and Judaism in the Modern World* (University Park, PA: Pennsylvania State UP 1994).

24. Indeed, the duality of frequent rebellion against local power structures on the one hand, and basic obedience to the formal central hierarchy is striking, especially in the case of Catholic

activism in Latin America.

25. See Ben-Dor, 'Stateness and Ideology in Contemporary Middle East Politics', *The Jerusalem Journal of International Relations* 9/3 (Sept. 1987) pp.10–35.

26. J.P. Nettl, 'The State as a Conceptual Variable', *World Politics* 20/4 (July 1968) pp.559–92.

27. See the little-known, but extremely interesting, observations in A. Jeffery, 'The Political Importance of Islam', *Journal of Near East Studies* 1 (Oct. 1942) pp.383–95. This piece, which is somewhat polemical due to its birth in the context of the political tensions in India (still including at that time what later became Pakistan and Bangladesh), deserves greater attention.

28. Derek Hopwood, 'A Pattern of Revival Movements in Islam', *Islamic Quarterly* 15/3-4 (July-Dec.) pp.149–58. See also Gabriel R. Warburg and Uri M. Kupferschmidt (eds.), *Islam, Nationalism, and Radicalism in Egypt and the Sudan* (NY: Praeger 1983); and G.R. Warburg and Gad G. Gilbar (eds.), *Studies in Islamic Society* (Haifa: HUP 1984).

29. Rudolph Peters, *Islam and Colonialism* (The Hague: Mouton 1979).

30. This is true to the point with respect to Islamic fundamentalism. By definition, it seems to be so self-contained as to isolate Islam from the rest of the world. See W. Montgomery Watt, *What is Islam* (London: Longmans 1968).

31. See John J. Donohue and John L. Esposito (eds.), *Islam in Transition: Muslim Perspectives* (NY: Oxford UP 1982).

32. Watt (note 30).

33. See also the article by the Ayatollah Khomeini, 'Islamic Government', in Donohue and Esposito (note 31).

34. This generalization seems to be one of the few sustainable ones, although because of its high level it is not so easy to prove, if for no other reason than for the difficulty of including and controlling the many elements of such a complex phenomenon as the high level of politics in a huge civilization of many millions. Yet there is no point in escaping the need to generalize where generalization seems to be appropriate, which is not very often.

35. See C.A.O. Van Nieuwenhuijze, *Social Stratification in the Middle East* (Leiden: E.J. Brill 1965).

36. Levy (note 19).

37. For a thorough review of the literature on the Islamic state, see Ben-Dor (note 6).

38. Rosenthal (note 19).

39. Kedourie (note 19).

40. See Peters (note 29). The subtitle of this useful work is *The Doctrine of Jihad in Modern History*. See also Hannah R. Rahman, 'The Concept of Jihad in Egypt', in Warburg and Kupferschmidt (note 28).

41. Peters (note 29).

42. It is indeed a great pity that there are so many misunderstandings of the complexities of *jihad* not only on the popular level, but even among educated non-Muslims and also Muslims. Perhaps more knowledge about this phenomenon would do away with some of the popular notions of ideological zeal that are currently so strongly associated with the term.

43. Indeed, I do not acknowledge the existence of such a thing as 'mentality' which seems to be unscientific and dangerous. See Ben-Dor (note 10).

44. See Watt (note 30).

45. Indeed, this has become one of the greatest problems facing Israel in the peace process. See for instance, G. Usher, 'The Islamist Movement and the Palestinian Authority', *Middle East Report* (July-Aug. 1994).

46. One can find comparable examples, as in the case of some Tamils in the Sri-Lanka conflict.

47. In this day and age, none of us would like to become involved in a religious war or even accuse other religions and civilizations of extremism or aggression. In the 'new world order', ideology and extremism should decline, not intensify; see Lawrence Freedman, 'The Gulf War and the New World Order', *Survival* 33/3 (May-June 1991) pp.195–210. Yet, there is no way to escape the fact that precisely in this day and age, there is a rekindling of extremism and fanaticism which does threaten Muslims and non-Muslims alike. Belittling or underestimating the danger smacks of paternalism that is bitterly resented by leading Muslim intellectuals, e.g., Mernissi (note 18).

48. Nor should this make us unduly optimistic, as seems to be the case, for example, in 'Islam and the West', *The Economist*, 6 Aug. 1994.

49. As Reinhard Bendix argues, we are genuinely uncertain about future trends in macro-social and political developments and we need, therefore, to be on guard against deterministic fallacies; Bendix, *Nation-Building and Citizenship* (NY: Wiley 1964).

50. R. Wright, 'The Islamic Resurgence: A New Phase?', *Current History* (Feb. 1988) pp.53–6, 85.

51. A.K. Aboulmagd, 'Islam in the Post-Communist World', *Problems of Communism* (Jan.-April 1992) pp.38–43.

# About the Contributors

**Muhammad Hasan Amara** is Lecturer at the Department of Political Studies at Bar-Ilan University. His academic interests are the political behavior of Israeli Arabs (mainly Arab parties, movements and Arab-Jewish relations), politics and language, language and society (or socio-linguistics) and the Palestinian communities in Israel and the West Bank. His publications include a recently completed book, co-written with Sufian Kabaha, entitled *Split Identity: Political Division and Social Reflections in a Divided Village* (Givat Haviva: The Institute for Peace 1996).

**Gabriel Ben-Dor** is a past Rector of the University of Haifa and past President of the Israeli Political Association. He is the author and editor of six books, including *Confidence Building Measures in the Middle East* (Boulder, CO: Westview Press 1994) [co-editor] and *State and Conflict in the Middle East* (NY: Praeger 1983), as well as over one hundred articles in scholarly journals on Middle East politics, comparative political theory, inter-Arab relations, political change and the Arab-Israeli conflict.

**Robert O. Freedman** is Peggy Meyerhoff Pearlstone Professor and Acting President of Baltimore Hebrew University. Among his publications are *Moscow and the Middle East* (Cambridge: CUP 1991), *Soviet Policy Toward Israel Under Gorbachev* (NY: Praeger 1991) and *Israel Under Rabin* (Boulder, CO: Westview Press 1995) [editor].

**Efraim Inbar** is Associate Professor of Political Studies at Bar-Ilan University and Director of the Begin-Sadat Center for Strategic Studies. His books include *War and Peace in Israeli Politics: Labor Party Positions on National Security* (Boulder, CO: Lynne Rienner 1991), *Mideast Security: Prospects for Arms Control* (London: Frank Cass 1995) [co-edited with Shmuel Sandler] and *Regional Security Regimes, Israel and Its Neighbors* (Albany, NY: SUNY Press 1995) [editor]. He has served as Goldman Visiting Professor at Georgetown University and Guest Scholar at the Woodrow Wilson International Center for Scholars.

**Joseph Kostiner** is Senior Lecturer in the Department of Middle Eastern and African History at Tel Aviv University and Senior Research Fellow at the Moshe Dayan Center for Middle Eastern and African Studies. He specialized in the modern political and social history of the states of the

Arabian Peninsula. His recent publications include *Yemen: The Tortuous Way of Unity* (London: The Royal Institute of International Affairs, Chatham House series, 1996) and *The Making of Saudi Arabia, From Chieftancy to Monarchical State, 1916–1936* (Oxford: OUP 1993).

**Menachem Klein** is Lecturer in the Department of Political Studies at Bar-Ilan University and Research Associate at the Begin-Sadat Center for Strategic Studies. Among his publications in the field of Palestinian politics are *The Jerusalem Question in the Arab-Israeli Peace Negotiations* (Jerusalem: Jerusalem Institute for Israeli Studies, forthcoming) and 'Quo-Vadis: Palestinian Dilemmas of Ruling Authority Building Since 1993', *Middle Eastern Studies* (forthcoming).

**Jacob M. Landau** is Professor of Political Science (Emeritus) at the Hebrew University of Jerusalem. Among his many works on the modern Middle East are *Pan-Turkism: From Irredentism to Cooperation* (Bloomington: Indiana UP 1995), *The Arab Minority in Israel, 1967–1991* (Oxford: Clarendon Press 1993), *Jews, Arabs, Turks* (Jerusalem: Magnes Press 1993) and *The Politics of Pan Islam* (Oxford: Clarendon Press 1990).

**Anat Lapidot** teaches at the Department of Middle Eastern History at the University of Haifa, is Lecturer at the Department of History at Bar-Ilan University and Research Associate at the Begin-Sadat Center for Strategic Studies. Her publications include 'The Turkish-Islamic Synthesis: Ideology in the Service of the State', *The New Orient* (1996) as well as 'The Republic of Yemen', in *Middle East Contemporary Survey*, 1993 (Boulder, CO: Westview Press 1995).

**Bruce Maddy-Weitzman** is Senior Research Associate at the Moshe Dayan Center for Middle Eastern and African Studies, Tel Aviv University. He is a specialist in modern history and politics of the Arab world and the Maghrib. His publications include *The Crystallization of the Arab State System* (Syracuse: SUP 1993) and *Middle East Contemporary Survey* (Boulder, CO: Westview Press, annual) [editor].

**Elie Podeh** is Lecturer in the Department of Islam and Middle Eastern Studies at the Hebrew University of Jerusalem and Research Fellow at the Truman Institute for the Advancement of Peace. Among his publications is his recent book *The Quest for Hegemony in the Arab World: The Struggle over the Baghdad Pact* (Leiden: E.J. Brill 1995).

**Haggay Ram** is Lecturer in the Department of Middle Eastern History, Ben-Gurion University of the Negev. He has published several scholarly articles on the cultural history of Iran and Shi'ite Islam, and is the author of *Myth and Mobilization in Revolutionary Iran* (Washington, DC: American UP 1994).

**Shmuel Sandler** is Lainer Professor for Democracy and Civility at Bar-Ilan University, Director of the Bar-Ilan Center for International Communications and Policy and Senior Research Associate at the Begin-Sadat Center for Strategic Studies. Among his books are *The State of Israel, The Land of Israel: Statist and Ethnonational Dimensions* (Westport, CT: Greenwood Press 1993) and *Israel at the Polls: 1992* (Lanham: Rowman & Littlefield 1995) [co-editor].

**Gabriel R. Warburg** is Professor Emeritus of Modern Middle Eastern History at the University of Haifa. His books include *Historical Discord in the Nile Valley* (London: C. Hurst & Evanston 1993) and *Egypt and the Sudan, Studies in History and Politics* (London: Frank Cass 1985). In the past, he has served as Fulbright Scholar-in-Residence at the University of California, Berkeley (1990) as well as Research Fellow at St Antony's College, Oxford (1991) and Wissenschaftskolleg zu Berlin.

**Eyal Zisser** is Lecturer in the Department of Middle Eastern and African History at Tel Aviv University and Research Fellow at the Moshe Dayan Center for Middle Eastern and African Studies. His writings on Syria and Lebanon include, 'Syria and Israel: Toward a Change?', in Efraim Inbar (ed.) *Regional Security Regimes: Israel and Its Neighbors* (Albany, NY: SUNY Press 1995) as well as articles in *Middle East Quarterly*, *Orient* and other academic journals.

# Index